The Seattle Mama's Handbook

Julianne Rowley

Thank You

I started writing this book just two weeks after we found out we were expecting our fourth child. Filled with excitement for the new adventures coming our way, we embarked on this task, hoping morning sickness would bypass this time. Unfortunately, morning sickness reigned supreme, and so it was. My husband took over as chef, chauffeur, and caregiver while I did research during bouts of energy. It is to my husband, who never complained about his relentless schedule, and was always concerned for my well being, that I give my ultimate gratitude. I could not have written this book without you!

My mother, Jean Ely, joined us in July to help with research and caring for my boys. We usually tag-teamed throughout the day. Mark my words...this book would not have been completed on time if it wasn't for you. Thank you, Mom!

Now, for those who joined my team off and on during the writing process with research, editing, & moral support. I am so thankful to you, my friends and fellow mothers, who somehow found time during their busy schedules to help.

Dixie Alley (& her daughter Amanda...my awesome babysitter)

Lisa Ashby
Kayrena Betts
Tiffany Bui
Kollette Chambers
Teresa Dassler
David Ely
Greg & Su Ely
Shannon Grey
Gerrit Huston
Lynnette Malley
Heidi Meany
Donelle Petty
Jacque Santos
Crystal Stevenson
Joy Yates

And...Stephanie Peterson & especially Rachel Herrscher. This book would not be without the two of you. Thank you!

A big THANK YOU to our Seattle Mama's Awesome Advertisers!

Table of Contents

Become a Seattle Mama Today!

Do you live in the Seattle area? Are you a mother? Then why not make it official and become a member of the Seattle Mamas by registering online at www.seattlemamas.com to receive our monthly newletter! You will be notified with the latest local events and activities, receive thought provoking parenting tips, and hear from other Seattle Mama's tried and true ideas on specific topics directed towards your worthy endeavor of being a mother.

Seattle Mamas will not disseminate or sell your contact information. We respect your privacy, and you may remove your name from the list at anytime.

Thank you!

Julianne Rowley

Seattle Mama's LLC

Cover Illustration by Alison Jay

Although a great deal of effort has gone into making this book as up-to- date and accurate as possible, changes constantly occur. Seattle Mama's, LLC, nor the authors of this book, their agents and/or assigns warrants the accuracy of the information in this book, which includes but is not limited to price changes, addresses, names, hours of operation, or management conditions of the attractions and services described. Before visiting a destination, please call to confirm the information provided here. The authors and publisher accept no responsibility for loss, injury, or inconvience sustained by any person using this book.

Chapter 1

Fun Places To Go!

Chapter 1

Fun Places To Go!

There is so much to do along the Puget Sound. This chapter lists general activities for families, stored by topic and county. Remember to check out all of the other chapters in this book for specific activities under topics like outdoor hikes and music. Every chapter has ideas on activities for children and their families.

Family Activities

Boehm's Chocolate Candy Factory

425-392-6652

Tour Hours: Monday-Friday 10:00am-3:00pm

Price: Free

Come visit one of only three hand-dipping chocolate factories in the country. Julius Boehm, a Vienna native, first opened his candy kitchen, with friend George Tedlock, in 1943, shortly after arriving to the United States after fleeing from Hitler's forces. In 1956, Julius Boehm moved the company from Seattle to the foothills of the Issaquah "Alps", where he built the Swiss/Alpine style "Edelweiss Chalet". Self-guided tours are available to view the making of 150 types of chocolate and candy.

A lovely store awaits chocolate lovers. For those who would like to continue the tour, you may visit the second story of the chalet, where Mr. Boehm once resided in wood-lined, Swiss style decor. A replica of a twelfth century Switzerland chapel is also available for tours, which Mr. Boehm built in honor of fallen mountaineer's. The chapel contains beautiful, original murals.

Boeing And Eames IMAX Theaters

Pacific Science Center
206-443-IMAX
www.pacsci.org
Hours: IMAX movie times vary, according to current features. Each movie runs approximately 45 minutes.
Prices: $10 Adults, $8 children
Groups Discounts: $7 per ticket for 15 or more.

Country Village

23718 7th Ave SE, Bothell
425-483-2250
www.countryvillagebothell.com
Hours: Monday-Saturday 10:00am-6:00pm, Sunday 11:00am-5:00pm
45 specialty shops including antiques, a day spa, glass blowing studio, restaurants, bakery, and train rides located in a "country" setting. Enjoy a picnic by the pond, and feed the families of ducks and geese. Country Village also hosts annual festivals, shows, classes, activities, and summer farmer's markets.

Geocaching

www.geocaching.com
You must have a GPS to begin this adventure. Begin by visiting the website for location coordinates to find the caches and an entertaining adventure awaits. The basic idea is for individuals and organizations set up caches all over the world, then share these locations on the internet. Locals can focus on Northwest caches. Once found, a cache may offer a wide variety of rewards. All that is asked is for guests to try to leave something for the cache for those who will follow.

Hiram Chittenden Locks

3015 NW 54th St, Ballard
206-783-7059
Hours: Daily 7:00am-9:00pm
Visitor's Center Hours: 10:00am-6:00pm
Public Guided Tours: Daily at 1:00pm, 3:00pm., plus weekend tours at 11:00am.
Friday-Sunday tends to be the busiest and therefore the most entertaining time to visit the Locks. Watch as small boats to large ships make their way to and from the salt water of the Puget Sound and the fresh water of Lake Washington. Located adjacent to the Locks is the infamous Fish Ladder which displays views from both above and beneath the water the live action of leaping Salmon making their way up the 21 step ladder. Mid to late summer offers the most plentiful Salmon. Accompanying the visitor's center are the beautiful botanical gardens, filled with over 2,000 varieties of trees and flowering plants. This is the perfect spot for a family picnic.

Olympic Game Farm
1423 Ward Rd, Sequim
360-683-4285
www.olygamefarm.com
Hours: Open daily at 9:00am
Prices: Walking Tour: Adults $10, Students (6-12) $9, 5 and under Free
Driving Tour: Adults: $9, Students (6-12) $8, 5 and under Free
Combination Tour: Adults $15, Students (6-12) $13, 5 and under Free
"Get face to face with wild life"! The walking tour includes wolves, tigers, African lion, puma, panther, llamas, coyote, grizzly bears. The driving tour includes elk, wapiti, Kodiak bears, zebra, yaks, rhinoceros, ostrich, bison, deer.

Pacific Science Center
200 2 Avenue North, Seattle Center
206-443-2001
www.pacsci.com
Hours: 10:00am-6:00pm
Prices: $10 Adults, $7 Children
Groups Discounts: 15 or more
Annual Family Pass: $75 includes 3 IMAX tickets per family member, 5 free guest passes. Annual Family Pass: $100: unlimited use, plus 3 IMAX tickets per family member, 5 free guest passes per visit.

The Pacific Science center houses 5 buildings of endless unique interactive and entertaining science-filled activities and exhibits. This includes the Butterfly Atrium, Insect Gallery, Dinosaur Exhibit, 2 IMAX Theaters, Laser Show , Planetarium, a toddler play area complete with a huge tub of water play, a shadow picture room, and one of a kind traveling exhibits.

Pike Place Fish Market
86 Pike Place, Seattle
206-682-7181
800-542-7732
www.pikeplacefish.com
Hours: Monday through Saturday 6:30 am to 6:00pm, Sunday 7:00am to 5:00pm
Home of the famous "flying fish"! The market is a seafood lover's delight filled with the freshest and most entertaining seafood around. You'll find more than just fish... the market is also filled with seasonal flowers, fresh fruits and vegetables from the farm, arts and crafts booths, and a pallet's haven for international food. Overnight fish shipping is available to anywhere in the U.S.

Seattle Aquarium

1482 Alaskan Way-Pier 59, Seattle
206-386-4320
206-386-4300 (Special Needs)
www.seattleaquarium.org
Hours: Summer: 10:00am-7:00pm, September-May 10:00am-5:00pm
Prices: 0-2 Free, 3-5 $5, 6-12 $8, 13+ $12
Seattle Aquarium & IMAX: 0-2 Free, 3-5 $5, 6-12 $12.75, 13+ $17.50
Seattle Aquarium & Odyssey Maritime Discovery Center: 0-2 Free. 3-5 $7, 6-12 $11.50, 13+ $16.50
Group Rates: 20 or more. Call 206-386-4353
Annual Membership: $60 Family Membership plus 5 free guest admissions.
$85 Family Membership plus 1 free admission per visit.
Combination Aquarium and Woodland Park Zoo Annual Membership: $135, plus 2 free zoo admissions.
See, touch, and explore the water world. Marine life exhibits include sharks, river otters, rock fish, ratfish, tide pool, octopus, jellies, Wolf eels, tropical fish, Harbor seals, sea otters, salmon ladder, and touch pools filled with sea stars, sea urchins, sea cucumbers, crabs, barnacles, muscles, fish, and sand dollars. Family First Sundays is a program the first Sunday of each month, where families enjoy special activities and kid craft projects (11am-3pm) based on different monthly themes.

Daily Talks, Feeding Times & Demonstrations:

- Birds that fly Underwater: 10:45
- Harbor Seal Training:11:15
- Sea Otter Training: 11:30
- Octopus Feeding: Noon
- Seahorses: 12:30
- Searching for Sixgills (sharks): 1:00pm
- Underwater Dome Divers: 1:15pm
- Harbor Seal Training: 1:45
- Sea Otter Training: 2:00pm
- Fur Seal Training: 2:15pm
- Octopus Feeding: 3:00pm
- Searching for Sixgills: 3:30pm
- Sea Otters and Seals: 5:00pm

See ad in back

Seattle Space Needle

Seattle Center
400 Broad St, Seattle
206-905-2100
Hours: Monday – Sunday 9:00am-Midnight
Prices: Space Needle Observation Deck: Adults (14-64) $13, 65+ $11, Children (4-13) $6, 3 and under Free
Take the 605' zippy trip up the elevator to the awe-inspiring view of the 360 degree observation deck. With the help of descriptive and detailed maps locate landmarks and city lines, the ever present snow capped Mt. Rainier, the distant Cascades mountain, and the harbor's cargo ships traveling through Elliott Bay.

For those who like to dine while spinning 360 degrees per hour, enjoy an elegant lunch or dinner at the SkyView restaurant.

Snoqualmie Falls

6500 Railroad Ave NE, Snoqualmie
425-985-6906
www.snoqualmiefalls.com
See the breathtaking 268 foot avalanche of water, which is 100 feet higher than Niagra Falls. Picnic in the 2 acre park, hike the trail to the bottom of the gorge, get a close up view on the observation deck, and be sure to stop at the quaint gift shop. Both elegant and casual dining are located atop the falls. Please note that pets are not allowed.

Southbridge Seattle Symphony Music Discovery Center

Benaroya Hall
200 University, Seattle: entrance on 2nd & Union
206-336-6600
www.soundbridge.org
Hours: Tuesday-Sunday 10:00am-4:00pm
Daily Concerts: Monday-Saturday 10:15, Sunday 12:15
Price: $7 Adults, Children 5-12 $5, Under 5 Free.
Annual Family Membership: $50
Soundbridge is a wonderful place for children to learn, explore, and indulge in music splendor. With daily musical storytelling, instrument exploration, classes, student recitals, lectures, workshops, and the following exhibits: "Meet the Musicians, Conductors and Composers" past and present, Listening Posts, musical skills computer games, Virtual Conducting, and "Science of Sound–Music as a Science".

The Boeing Factory

Paine Field
3003 W Casino Rd, Everett
800-464-1476
www.boeing.com/companyoffices/aboutus/tours/index.html
Tour Hours: Monday-Friday 9:00am, 10:00am, 11:00am, 1:00pm, 2:00pm, 3:00pm.
Children must be 8 years old or older to go on the tour.
Price: Free
The Boeing Factory, at 472,000,000 cubic feet or 98.3 acres, is the largest building in the world. It houses the 747, 767, and 777 planes being manufactured inside. In 1968, the year of the 747, Boeing began tours, and continues to accommodate over 100,000 visitors annually. Visit the new 73,068 square foot facility titled, "The Future of Flight Aviation Center".

The Waterfront on Elliott Bay

Alaskan Way, Seattle
Ride the nostalgic trolley, eat fish and chips, visit the Seattle Aquarium, parasail ride, cruise to the Tillicum Village on Blake Island, or catch the Washington State Ferry on the historic Elliott Bay Waterfront. Be sure to stop at shops with Native arts, and jewelry. Nearby is the Myrtle Edwards Park, where you will find a glorious view of Elliott Bay.

Tillicum Village on Blake Island

Pier 55, Alaskan Way, Seattle
206-933-8660
www.tillicumvillage.com
Hours: October: Saturday and Sunday 11:30am, 6th & 7th 4:30pm. November 11:30am, March Saturday 11:30am, April Saturday and Sunday at 11:30am.
Summer Hours (May 1st-September 30th): Sunday and Wednesday 11:30am and 4:30pm, Thursday-Saturday 11:30am, 4:30pm, and 6:30pm
Price: Adults $69, Seniors (60+) $62, Children (5-12) $25, Children 5 and under Free.
Group Discounts: 15+: Call 206-933-8600
Hop aboard the Argosy ferry boat at Pier 55 in Seattle for a 4 hour roundtrip treat. You must arrive 30 minutes prior to departure. Upon arriving on Blake Island, feast for 2 hours on the Salmon buffet. This menu includes salmon prepared in the Native American method, as it has for a thousand years, over cedar stakes in an open fire, a salad bar, Tillicum bread, wild steamed rice, and new red potatoes, with a chocolate dessert shake shaped like a salmon. After dinner, enjoy the Dance of the Wind Show, a combination of the Pacific Northwest Coast Tribal dances. Before you leave the island, guests are provided with 30 minutes to explore and stroll along the scenic shore.

Northwest Trek Wildlife Park

11610 Truck Dr E, Eatonville
360-832-6117
www.nwtrek.org
Hours: Open year-round at 9:30am. Closing time is seasonal 4:00pm-6:00pm.
Prices: Adults $9.50, Students (5-17) $7, Children (3-4) $5
Come explore wildlife at its best...in nature. Hop aboard the tram and get up close to over 200 wild animals including black and grizzly bears, bison, birds, wolves, cougars, moose, reptiles, otters, beavers, and more. The 715 acre park is filled with lakes, 5 miles of trails, and offers something special each season. A hands-on discovery center awaits little ones.

Amusement Places

King County

Arena Sports

www.arenasports.net

Arena Sports Magnuson
7400 Sandpoint Way NE, Seattle
206-985-8990
Hours: Monday-Wednesday 9:00am-10:00pm, Thursday 9:00am-9:30pm, Friday 9:00am-4:00pm, Saturday 9:00am-3:00pm.
Activities: In-line Hockey, Soccer, Inflatable play area (Drop-in)

Arena Sports Redmond
9040 Willows Rd, Redmond
425-885-4881
Inflatable Play Area Hours: Monday-Thursday 10:00am-4:00pm, Friday 10:00am-9:00pm, Saturday 9:00am-8:00pm, Sunday 2:00pm-8:00pm
Activities: Lacrosse, Soccer, Inflatable play area (Drop-in)
See ad in back

Big League Connection

15015 NE 90th St, Redmond
425-885-2862
www.bigleagueconnection.com
Hours: Monday-Friday 12:00pm-7:00pm, Saturday & Sunday 11:00am-5:00pm
Prices: Adults and Children: walk-in cages $7.50 10 minutes, $20 30 minutes, $32.50 1 hour.
Group Discounts: Buy a team membership of 6 or more. Prices vary according to the number of teammates.
Activities: features 20,000 square feet of indoor Baseball and Softball, 6,800 sq. ft. infield (available for rental), baseball hitting cages with automatic, timed pitches, hitting cages with individually fed pitches, portable mounds for indoor field, L-Screens, batting tees, and hitting socks in each cage.

Family Fun Center

7300 Fun Center Way, Tukwila
425-228-6000
www.fun-center.com
Hours: 10:00am-10:00pm (June-August), 10:00am-9:00pm (September-May)
Prices: $2.50 for general admission. Point card system: $.25=1 point. Activities range from $2.50 to $6.50.
Discounts: $25=110 points, $50=230 points, $100=480 points. Each point card can be shared is good for 1 year.
Activities: Arcade, Batting Cages, Bumper Boats, Frog Hopper Ride, Go Karts (must be 4'10"), Laser Tag, Miniature Golf, Rock Wall, Sling Shot, and a Virtual Roller Coaster.

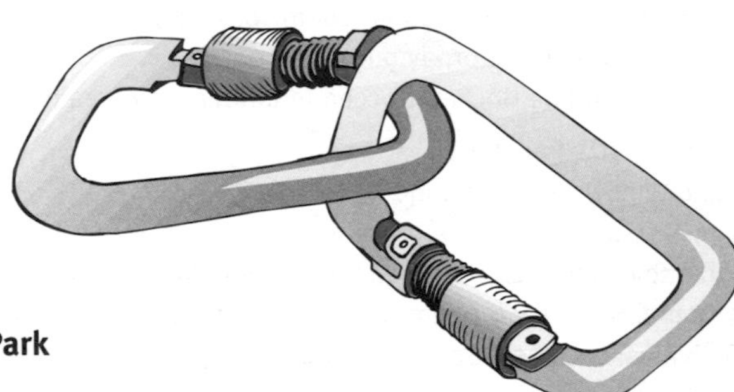

Fun Forest Amusement Park

Seattle Center
203 6th Ave N, Seattle
206-728-1585
www.funforest.com
Hours: 11:00am-9:00pm (June-August), 11:00am-6:00pm (September-May)
Prices: No entrance fee. Prices are based on activities at 2 or more tickets each. Tickets cost $1 each. On weekdays, purchase a bracelet for $20 for unlimited rides from 12:00pm-9:00pm.

Groups Discounts: For groups of 20-49 people, unlimited passes may be purchased for: $18 per person for 9 hours, $15 for 4 hours, $12 for 2 hours.
Activities: Bumper cars (adult and child sizes), Merry-Go-Round, Ferris wheel, miniature golf, large roller coaster, laser tag, miniature golf, climbing wall, video arcades, and prize games.

Gametown Family Fun Center

14822 International Blvd, Tukwila
206-241-9108
Hours: Daily 2:00pm-Midnight
Prices: Games are run by tokens, at $.25 per token. All games: 1 or 2 tokens each. You receive an extra $6 in tokens when you buy $20 worth of tokens.
Activities: Video games, paintball, and online computer

Gameworks

1511 7th Ave, Seattle
206-521-0952
www.gameworks.com
Hours: Monday-Thursday 11:00am-Midnight, Friday 11:00am-1:00am, Saturday 10:00am-1:00am, Sunday 10:00am-Midnight.
Prices: Game card system: $5, $10, $15, $20, $25. $20=2 hour unlimited play, $25=3 hour unlimited play
Activities: Over 250 video games in 25,000 square feet. Special feature games include an 8 car race game, Indy 500, Sky Pirates, Dance, Dance Revolution, prize games for younger children, and several new game additions.

Grand Prix Raceway

3133 S Cedar St, Tacoma
253-272-9000
www.grandprixraceway.com
Hours: Daily 11:00am-10:00pm, Sunday 12:00pm-8:00pm, Closed on Tuesday.
Prices: $14.15 for 15 minutes of riding. Ladies Night: Thursdays: $10.42 for 15 minutes.
Groups Discounts: 15 or more, $11.60 each.
Every Sunday at 5pm, everyone is welcome to compete in a three 15 lap race. The top 8 points earners advance to the top three positions and earn trophies, and extra lap sessions.
Activities: Indoor Go Kart center.

Illusionz Magical Entertainment Center
1025 NW Gilman Blvd, Issaquah
425-427-2444
www.illusionz.com
Hours: Monday-Thursday 12:00pm-10:00pm, Friday 12:00pm-12:00am, Saturday 10:00am-12:00am, Sunday12:00pm-8:00pm
Prices: No Admission Fee: All games and attractions work on a card reader system. Rechargable Gamecard $1, or purchase a $10+ card and $1 card fee is waived.
$10: 1100 Points (100 Free Points)
$20: 2250 Points (250 Free Points)
$50: 5750 Points (750 Free Points)
$100: 12000 Points (2000 Free Points)
Group Discounts: 20 or more.
Summer Special M-F $20 All Day Pass-Unlimited Pass on Miniature Golf, Laser Tag, Ride
Activities: Indoor Roller Coaster Simulator Ride, Batting Cages, Climbing Wall, Play Area w/ slides & ball pits, and indoor restaurant.

Kent Valley Ice Centre
6015 240th St, Kent
253-850-2400
www.familynightout.com
Hours: Seasonal
Prices: $7.25 Adults, $6.25 Children ages 4-12, 3 and under Free
Skate Rental: $2.75
Groups: Call253-850-2400 x10
Activities: Racing games, skill games, sports games, arcades and video games. Batting cages and a huge NHL regulation ice sheet for ice hockey and ice skating.

Laser Quest
2210 S. 320th, Federal Way
253-946-4500
www.laserquest.com
Hours: Monday-Thursday 5:00pm-9:00pm, Friday & Saturday 5:00pm-Midnight, Sunday 5:00pm-8:00pm.
Summer Hours: Monday-Thursday 2:00pm-9:00pm, Friday 2:00pm-Midnight, Saturday 11:00am-Midnight, Sunday 12:00pm-8:00pm
Prices: $7 per game, or $16 games for 3
Activities: Laser Tag, multi-level maze. This center is recommended for children ages 7 and older.

Pump It Up
11605 NE 116th St, Kirkland
425-820-2297
www.pumpitupparty.com
Drop-in Hours (ages 2-5): Tuesday and Wednesday 9:00am-10:15am, 10:30am-11:45am; ages
Prices: $6 for 1st child, $4 for siblings. Parents are always Free.
Group Discounts: "Play Groups": $99 up to 15. Includes 1 hour of play time. Available Monday-Friday before 3:00pm.
Activities: Experience one of a kind indoor inflatables, including bouncers, 20' slides, climbing walls, a basketball bounce house, and a rock 'em sock 'em colliseum. Be sure to bring your SOCKS!

Remlinger Farms
32610 NE 32nd St, Carnation
425-333-4135
www.remlingerfarms.com
Hours: May-October 11:00am-5:00pm, Weekends only in September/October
Prices: Adults & Children: $9, Children under 1 Free
Located inside Remlinger Farms is the Country Fair Family Fun Park, especially designed for children ages 10 and under. Activities include a 4-H animal barnyard, pony trail ride, Tolt River steam train ride, hay maze, hay jump, climbing wall, canoe ride, antique car ride, farm theater, swing carousel, mini rollercoaster, mini Ferris wheel, play area, and a real vintage fire truck and school bus that children can play in. Remlinger Farms is wheelchair and stroller accessible. Also located on the farm's grounds is a full-service bakery, restaurant, ice cream parlor, and picnic areas.

Seattle Water Front Arcade
1301 Alaskan Way, Seattle
206-903-1081
Hours: Monday-Friday 11:00am-9:00pm, Saturday & Sunday 11:00am-10:00pm, Summer Hours: Sunday-Thursday 11:00am-10:00pm, Friday & Saturday 11:00am-11:00pm.
Prices: No entrance fee. Prices based on games: $.25-$1.00 per game
Activities: Video games, ticket redemption games with prizes.

Southgate Roller Rink
9646 17th SW, Seattle
206-762-4030
Hours: Open daily 7:00-10:00
Prices: $7- skates included.

Tilt

2115 S, SeaTac Mall, Federal Way

253-941-3877

Hours: Monday-Saturday 10:00am-9:00pm, Sunday 11:00am-7:00pm

Prices: Bring a lot of quarters.

Activities: Video/Arcade games, win tokens and prizes. Rides for small children. No food allowed.

Wild Waves & Enchanted Village: Six Flags

36201 Enchanted Pkwy S, Federal Way

253-661-8000

www.sixflags.com

Hours: 10:00am-8:00pm

Prices: $31.99 for everyone 48 inches or taller, and $25.99 children under 48 inches, and children age 3 and under are free. Go to their website for advertising specials!

Groups Discounts: 12 or more people. Must reserve 2 weeks in advance.

Season Pass. $79.99 (Best Value!) This includes unlimited visits year-round, free passes on select days, unlimited visits to other Six Flags Theme Parks, and coupon book.

Activities: Waterslides, Wade Pool, River Rides, Hooks Lagoon: family water adventure activities special for little ones, 2005's newest attraction "Zooma Falls" , Roller Coasters, kiddie coasters, Ferris wheel, car ride, antique carousel, and a Pirate Ship. The park offers several varieties of food, shows and performances, and lodging is available nearby if needed.

Snohomish County

Birch Bay Waterslides

4874 Birch Bay Lynden Rd, Blaine
360-371-7500
www.birchbaywaterslides.net
Summer Hours: Daily 10:30-6:30pm
Prices: Cash only Ages 3-5 $9, 6 and older $14. Children age 2 and under are free. After 3pm, 3-5 year olds pay $7, and 6 and older pay $10.
Groups Discounts: Call 360-371-7901
Activities: Waterslides, including the 60' Hydrocliff Drip Slide. Picnic tables, and barbeques provided.

Funtasia Family Fun Park

7212 220th St SW, Edmonds
425-774-4263
Hours: Friday 10:00am-11:30pm, Saturday 10:00am-Midnight,
Prices: No admission fee. Prices based on activities. Family Fun Passes available
Group Discount: 10 or more, 10% discount, 20 or more 20% discount.
Activities: Families can enjoy 7-acres of fun. Activities include a children's playground, miniature golf, video games and tokens with prize redemptions, go karts, bumper cars, laser tag, bumper boats, and batting cages Restaurant inside.

Traxx Indoor Raceway

4329 Chennault Beach Rd, Mukilteo
425-493-8729
www.traxxracing.com
Hours: Sunday-Tuesday 11:00am-11:00pm, Wednesday and Thursday 11:00am-Midnight, Friday and Saturday 10: 00am-1:00am.
Prices: Adults 14 and older: $15 for ten minutes, Children ages 11-13 pay $25. This includes a thrilling mandatory ? hour training course (must pre-schedule).
Kids Track: Ages 10 and under: $7.50 for 6 minutes.
Groups Discounts: Sunday Family Night, after 5pm, 20% off.
Activities: Go Kart racing for all ages, indoor, groups and parties, climbing wall, and a bungee tramp.

Whirly Ball Inc
23401 Hwy 99, Edmonds
425-672-3332
www.whirlyball.net
Hours: Monday-Saturday 12:00-Midnight, Sunday 12:00pm-10:00pm.
Prices: A minimum of 10 players, ages 8 and older, must be available in order to play. They suggest making reservations. The cost is based on how long you play the game, with a minimum of 1 hour per game. Prices are approximately $15 per hour, per person.
Activities: Whirly Ball is a unique game that is described as "the worlds only totally mechanized team sport". It is a combination of basketball, hockey, and Jai-Alai played while riding in a Whirlybug, a bumper-like car. If you've never played the game before, it takes a good 20-30 minutes to learn how to play. So, you'll want to schedule about 1 ? hours for your first game.

Balloon Rides

Go Lightly Inc
17218 SE Covington-Sawyer Rd, Kent
253-638-9696
www.golightlyinc.com
Hours: Saturday and Sunday around Sunrise.1-1/2 hour rides, with up to five people per balloon.
Prices: $200 per person. Children must be 48 inches tall to ride.
Departure Site: Auburn Supermall, depending upon weather.
Includes: Traditional toast, commemorative flight certificate with photo.

Over The Rainbow Balloon Flights
14471 Woodinville-Redmond Rd, Woodinville
206-364-0995
www.letsgoballooning.com
Hours: Make Reservations June-September for sunrise flights, or sunset flights.
Prices: Sunrise: $155 per person, Sunset $185 per person. 1 hour flight. 1-25 people
Ages: 6 and older
Departure Site: Woodinville
Includes:

Soaring Adventures of America Inc

206-241-0098
800-762-7464
www.800soaring.com
Office Hours: 10:00am-6:00pm for reservations.
Prices: $199. Look for website specials for discounted prices.
Departure Site: Determined by weather.
Includes: A 3 hour trip covering 5-10 miles in the hot air balloon. Conclude the balloon ride with a French style celebration toast with champagne or fruit juice. This company has a 100% safety record. All pilots are certified.

The Balloon Depot

877-881-9699
www.balloondepot.com
Hours: 6:15am and 7:00pm
Prices: Am Departure: $165 includes snack and drinks. Pm Departure $185, includes a catered dinner. Price includes photos.
Ages: 5 and older
Departure Site: Carnation and Snohomish

Batting Cages

Big League Connection

15015 NE 90th St, Redmond
425-885-2862
www.bigleagueconnection.com
Hours: Monday-Friday 12:00pm-7:00pm, Saturday & Sunday 11:00am-5:00pm
Prices: $7.50 for 10 minutes, $12 for 15 minutes, $20 for 30 minutes, $32.50 for 1 hour.
Features 20,000 square feet of indoor Baseball and Softball, 6,800 sq. ft. infield (available for rental), baseball hitting cages with automatic, timed pitches, hitting cages with individually fed pitches, portable mounds for indoor field, L-Screens, batting tees, and hitting socks in each cage.

Funtasia Family Fun Park

7212 220th St SW, Edmonds
425-774-4263
Hours: Friday 10:00am-11:30pm, Saturday 10:00am-Midnight.
Prices: No admission fee. Batting Cages: $1/token=18 pitches, $20=1/2 hour, $30= 1hour..
Group Discount: 10 or more, 10% discount, 20 or more 20% discount.

Kent Valley Ice Centre
6015 240th St, Kent
253-850-2400
www.familynightout.com
Hours: 8:00am - 11:00pm
Prices: $2=20 pitches, $10=120 pitches
5 Outdoor Batting Cages with Baseball & Softball slow and fast pitch. Private lessons: $30 per cage for 30 minutes, $50 per cage for 60 minutes.

Northshore Sports Complex
19460 144th Ave NE, Woodinville
425-485-3238
Hours: By reservation 1 hour prior.
Prices: $15/Half Hour, $25/1 Hour

Stod's Baseball Inc
5629 119th SE, Bellevue
425-643-8384
Batting Cages
Hours: Monday-Friday 2:00pm-9:00pm, Saturday and Sunday 10:00am-6:00pm.
Prices: $.50 per minute for all ages.

Stod's North Baseball & Fastpitch
3616 Sound Rd Suite A-3, Mukilteo
888-786-3766
425-355-4000
www.stods.com
Activities: 8 batting cages
Hours: Monday-Friday 3:00pm-9:00pm, Saturday and Sunday 10:00am-6:00pm
Prices: $8 15 minutes, $15 30 minutes, $30 1 hour
Group Rates (Teams): $25 per cage

Strike Zone
270 15th NW, Auburn
206-624-7826
www.strike-zone.us
Hours: 12:00pm-10:00pm, Saturday & Sunday 10:00am-6:00pm
Prices: $12.50 –15 Minutes, $25 –30 Minutes, $35 –1 Hour. Bulk batting sessions available for up to 47% off regular prices: $120 –16 sessions, $220 –32 sessions, $320 –48 sessions.

10,000 square-foot indoor hitting, pitching & fielding cages fit for baseball and softball batting cages and real clay regulation mounds. Batting cages are adjusted per individual.

instruction, training, and recreation. Teams are welcome. Equipment available to borrow, including L-screens, buckets, baseballs, bats, and helmets.

Bowling

King County

AMF Imperial Lanes
2101 22nd S, Seattle
206-325-2525
www.imperiallanes.amfcenters.com
Hours: Monday-Friday 7:00am-11:00pm, Saturday 9:00am-Midnight, Sunday 9:00am-11:00pm.
Prices: Games: Non-peak hours: $2.25, Peak Hours: 6pm–9pm $3.50
Shoe Rental: $3, before 6:00pm $2.50 for children.
Group Rates: $29 group of 4, includes 2 hour play, shoes, snack and soft drink.

AMF Roxbury Lanes
2823 SW Roxbury, Seattle
206-935-7400
www.magiclanesbowl.com
Hours: Sunday-Thursday 11:00am-Midnight, Friday & Saturday 11:00am-2:00am
Prices: Games: $1.75 for children and seniors and $2.50 adults before 5:00pm. After 5:00pm, $3.50 for everyone. Shoes rental is $2.25.
Group Rates: Rent 1 lane for up to 6 people for $29.90 for 2 hours.

AMF Sun Villa Lanes
3080 148th SE, Bellevue
425-455-8155
Hours: Monday-Thursday 11:00am-11:00pm, Friday-Sunday 11:00am-Midnight
Prices: Games: $4.50 before 6pm, $5 between 6-9, $2 after 9pm Monday-Thursday.
Shoe Rental: $4, $3.50 for kids
Group Rates: Fun Pack: 2 hours of bowling for up to 4 people. Cost is $49 weekdays, and $52 Saturdays, Sundays and evenings. Includes shoes, soda, and popcorn.

Hi-Line Lanes
15733 Ambaum Blvd SW, Burien
206-244-2272
www.hilinelanes.com
Hours: Sunday-Friday 12:00pm-2:00am, Saturday 10:00am-2:00am
Prices: Games: Monday-Friday before 4:00pm $2.75, after $3.75. Weekends $3.75, $4.25.
Shoes: $2.25, Children: $2
Summer Special: $8 per 3 games, including shoe rental.
Check the website for information on Junior Bowling Competitions.

Hillcrest Family Bowling Center
2809 NE Sunset Blvd, Renton
425-226-1600
www.bowlhillcrest.com
24 lanes of smoke-free bowling.
Hours: Monday-Thursday 12:00pm-Midnight, Friday 12:00pm-2:00am, Saturday 10:00am-2:00am, Sunday 10:00am-Midnight.
Prices: Monday-Thursday $2.95 per game, $7 9:00pm-Midnight
Shoes:
Wednesday special: 10:00am-9:00pm cost $2 per game.
Group Rates: Family Rate on Sundays, up to 6 people $41 including pitcher of soda.

Kent Bowl
1234 N Central, Kent
253-852-3550
Hours: Monday-Thursday 12:00pm-Midnight, Friday and Saturday 12:00pm-2:00am, Sunday 11:00am-11:00pm.
Prices: Games: $3.85
Shoes Rental: $3
Group Rates: 15 people, 3 games for $12, including shoe rental.

Leilani Lanes

10201 Greenwood N, Seattle
206-783-8010
www.leilanilanes.com
Hours: Sunday-Thursday 9:00am-Midnight, Friday & Saturday 9:00am-2:00am
Prices: Games: Monday-Saturday $3.95
Shoe Rental: $3.95
Group Discounts: $20 (up to 5) per lane, per hour, plus $3 for shoe rental. $21.95 per person includes 3 hours of bowling, the burger bar, and shoe rental. $20.95 per person includes 3 hours of bowling and pizza, and shoe rental. $16.95 per person includes 2 hours of bowling, veggie platter, chips and dip, and shoe rental,

Magic Lanes

10612 15th SW, Seattle
206-244-5060
www.magiclanesbowl.com
Hours: Open daily 24 hours
Prices: Monday-Thursday 8:00am-6:00pm is $1.75 per game, after 6pm-Midnight $3.50 per game, Friday 8:00am-5:00pm $1.75 per game, Saturday 8:00am-5:00pm $2.50 per game, 5:00pm-Midnight, $3.50 per game. After Midnight $1.49 per game
Shoe Rental: $2.50 per pair.
Group Discounts: Rent a lane for 2 hours for 27.20, up to 6 people

TechCity Bowl

13033 NE 70th Place, Kirkland
425-827-0785
www.techcitybowl.com
Hours: Monday-Friday 10:00am-Midnight, Saturday 10:00am-1:00am, Sunday 9:00-1:00am.
Prices: $28 per hour, per lane, Monday-Thursday 9:00am-12:00pm $17 per hour, per lane

West Seattle Bowl

4505 39th SW, Seattle
206-932-3731
www.wsbowl.com
Hours: Monday-Thursday 11:00am-Midnight, and Friday & Saturday 11:00am-1:00am, Sunday 10:00am-11:00pm.
Prices: Before 6:00pm, $2.75, after 6:00pm , $4. Shoe rental is $2.50
Groups Discounts: 15 or more (5 per lane), before 6:00pm $13.50 per lane, per hour, after 6:00pm, $20 per lane, per hour plus $1.50 shoe rental.

Snohomish County

Brunswick Majestic Lanes

1222 164th SW, Lynnwood
425-743-4422
www.brunswickbowl.com
Hours: Monday-Thursday 9:00am-12:00pm, Friday-Saturday 9:00am-2:30pm, Sunday 8:00am-12:00pm.
Prices: Monday-Friday 9:00am-5:00pm, all games are $.99 each, plus shoe rental at $2.75 for kids, and $3.49 for adults. After 5:00pm on weekdays, holidays, and Saturday and Sunday games are $4.25 each. Sunday from 8:00am-12:00pm, games are $.99.
Cosmic Bowling Friday-Sunday from5:00pm-8:00pm. This includes laser lights, black lights and music priced at $4.80 per person.
Groups Discounts: Family Value Pack-up to six people: Monday-Thursday $29.99 for 2 hours of bowling, shoe rental included, and a pitcher of soda, Fri-Sun $39.99.

Evergreen Lanes

5111 Claremont Way, Everett
425-259-7206
www.evergreenlanes.com
Hours: Monday-Thursday 7:00am-Midnight, Friday-Sunday 7:00am-2:00pm.
Prices: Adults: $2.50 per game, Children $1.75. Shoe rental is $2 for adults, $1.50 for children. Sunday mornings from 7:00am-9:00am $1.50 per game, and Monday-Sunday after 9:00pm, games are $1 each.
Groups Discounts: $1.50 per game and free shoe rental. Global Party package: Saturday and Sunday 2:00pm-4:00pm $8.50 for 2 hours of bowling and shoe rental, or $12 per person includes french fries, drinks, shoes and 2 hours of bowling.

Glacier Bowling Lanes

9630 Evergreen Way, Everett
425-353-8292
www.glacierlanes.com
Hours: Monday-Friday 7:00am-11:30pm, Saturday & Sunday 6:00am-Midnight.
Prices: Games: Monday-Friday 7:00am-9:00am $1.50, 9:00am-6:00pm $2.75. Evenings and weekends $3.25 per game. Children pay $2 before 6:00pm, and $2.25 after 6:00pm. Shoe rental is $1.75 for children, $2.25 for adults.
**Free bowling game coupon on website.*
Groups Discounts: Available with reservations, according to group size.

Melady Lanes
420 N Olympic Ave, Arlington
360-435-2466
Hours: Tuesday-Thursday 11:00am-9:00pm, Friday 11:00am-10:00pm, Saturday 11:00am-Midnight, Sunday 12:00pm-6:00pm.
Prices: $15 per lane, per hour, includes shoe rental. Up to 5 people per lane. Tuesday-Friday 1:00pm-5:00pm $3 per person, per hour, plus $1 for shoe rental.
Groups Discounts: Pizza party package-$30: This includes 1 hour of bowling for up to 5 people, 1 large pizza, and 2 pitchers of soda pop.

Robin Hood Lanes
9801 Edmonds Way, Edmonds
425-776-2101
www.robinhoodlanes.com
Fall & Winter Hours: Open daily from 9:00am-Midnight.
Spring & Summer Hours: Open daily from 11:00am-Midnight.
Fall & Winter Prices: $3 before 5:00pm, $4 after 5:00pm. Shoe rental is $2.50 per pair.
Spring & Summer Prices: $1.50 before 5:00pm, $2 after 5:00pm. Shoe rental is $2.50 per pair.

Strawberry Lanes
1067 Columbia Ave, Marysville
360-659-7641
Hours: Monday 10:00am-10:00pm, Tuesday 9:00am-11:00pm, Wednesday 9:00am-Midnight, Thursday 11:00am-11:00pm, Friday & Saturday 9:00am-2:00am, Sunday 9:00am-11:00pm.
Prices: Games: Children are $2.25 before 6:00pm, $2.50 after 6:00pm, Adults are $2.75 before 3:00pm, $3 after 3:00pm. Shoe rental is $2 per pair.
Groups Discounts: 20 or more.

Twin City Lanes
27120 92nd Ave NW, Stanwood
360-629-3001
Hours: Monday-Friday 9:00am-Midnight, Saturday 11:00am-1:00am, Sunday 10:00am-10:00pm.
Summer Hours: Monday 11:00am-5:00pm, Wednesday 11:00am-11:00pm, Thursday 12:00pm-9:00pm, Friday 11:00am-1:00am, Saturday 12:00pm-1:00am, Sunday 12:00pm-9:00pm
Prices: Adults: $3 per game, children 15 and under $2.50. Shoe rental is $1.50.
Special Discounts: Thursdays: $1.50 for everyone.
Group Discounts: 25 or more.

Sound & light show May-August on Friday and Saturday nights.

Miniature Golf

King County

Fun Forest Amusement Park
Seattle Center
203 6th Ave N, Seattle
206-728-1585
www.funforest.com
Hours: 11:00am-9:00pm (June-August), 11:00am-6:00pm (September-May)
Prices: No entrance fee.
Miniatures golf... plus bumper cars (adult and child sizes), Merry-Go-Round, Ferris wheel, large roller coaster, laser tag, miniature golf, climbing wall, video arcades, and prize games.

InterBay Family Golf Center
2501 15th W, Seattle
206-285-2200
Hours: 6:00am-10:00pm
Prices: Adults $7, Children (12 and under) $5

Snohomish County

Family Fun Center
7300 Fun Center Way, Tukwila
425-228-6000
www.fun-center.com
Hours: 10:00am-10:00pm (June-August), 10:00am-9:00pm (September-May)
Prices: $2.50 for general admission. Miniature Golf $6.50 per game.
Discounts: $25=110 points, $50=230 points, $100=480 points. Each point card can be shared is good for 1 year.

Funtasia Family Fun Park
7212 220th St SW, Edmonds
425-774-4263
Hours: Friday 10:00am-11:30pm, Saturday 10:00am-Midnight.
Prices: No admission fee. Miniature golf: $6 per game.
Group Discount: 10 or more, 10% discount, 20 or more 20% discount.

Jazwiek's Golf

7828 Broadway, Everett

425-355-5646

Hours: Monday-Thursday, and Sunday 12:00pm-8:00pm, Friday and Saturday 12:00pm-9:00pm.

Prices: Games: $7 with credit card, or $6 with cash, includes the price of shoe rental. Groups Discounts: 10 or more, $1 off.

Ferry Rides

Alaska Marine Highway System

800-642-0066

www.alaska.gov/ferry

www.ferryalaska.com

Drive your car aboard the ferry, and travel from Bellingham to the Gulf of Alaska for a 3 1/2 day tour. Prices: $341–Adults, $172–12 and under.

Travel from Bellingham to Whittier or Anchorage on a six-day tour: $529 Adults, $269

Cruise to the Aleutian Island chain: 4 days each way Prices: $284–Adults, $145–12 & under. After September 31st, discounted rates Cabins are available with 1 month advance reservation. Prices vary. A cafeteria and a dining room is available on the ferry.

BC Ferries

888-223-3779 or 250-386-3431 (outside of BC)

www.bcferries.com

Call for reservations and prices from 7:00am to 10:00pm.

Year round ferry service throughout coastal British Columbia include:

- Mainland-Vancouver Island
- Sunshine Coast
- Southern and Northern Gulf Islands
- Inside Passage, Queen Charlotte Islands

Seattle Ferry Service

801 N Northlake, Seattle
206-713-8446
www.SeattleFerryService.com
Fall/Winter Hours: 11:00am-3:00pm
Spring/Summer Hours: 11:00am-5:00pm
Departing from Fremont, under the Aurora Bridge, take this cozy ferry on a cruise through the Lake Washington Ship Canal, Lake Union, Portage Bay, and by the Sleepless in Seattle houseboat. The ferry's entertaining skipper will give a narration of the lake's history, and passengers will enjoy chocolate root beer floats in the main saloon. Children under 5 ride free.

Victoria Clipper

Pier 69, Seattle
206-448-5000
www.victoriaclipper.com
Summer schedule: May to September – leaves three times daily: 7:00am, 8:45am, & 3:15pm
Year round schedule: September to May –leaves one time daily at 8:00am.
Price: Round trip: $140.00 (w/30 day advance reservations) or $98:00 per person.
Hotel overnight packages available.
Whale and Sea Life Search - $70.00 per person.
This is a high speed passenger only ferry to Victoria, BC. It leaves from Seattle, Pier 69. You must have the following to enter Canada: Birth certificate and photo ID or passport, Permanent Resident Card (Green Card), Naturalization certificate, or citizen certificate.

Victoria/San Juan Cruises

Bellingham Cruise Terminal
355 Harris Ave, Bellingham
800-443-4552
www.whales.com
Travel to Victoria or the San Juan Islands – May Through October. All cruises depart from Bellingham.

To Victoria

Departure: 9:00am. Arrive in Victoria: 12 noon
Depart Victoria: 5:00pm – Arrive Bellingham: 8:00pm
Price: Adults: $89, Children 6-17 $44.50, Children under 6: Free

To San Juan –summer schedule:
Departure: 9:30am. Arrive in Friday Harbor: 11:00am
Depart Friday Harbor: 4:30pm. Arrive in Bellingham: 6:30pm
Price: Adults: $49, Children $24.50, Children under 6: Free

Visit their website or call for information about Whale Watching.

Washington State Ferries
888-808-7977
206-464-6400

www.wsdot.wa.gov/ferries
Ferry service for Washington State and British Columbia.

Prices: Based on Ferry Routes and Peak vs. Non-Peak Dates
For Current Fares, Visit **www.wsdot.wa.gov/ferries/info_desk/fares**

- Anacortes to Victoria
- Anacortes to San Juan Islands
- Port Townsend to Keystone
- Mukilteo to Clinton
- Edmonds to Kingston
- Seattle to Bainbridge Island
- Seattle To Bremerton
- Seattle to Vashon
- Fauntleroy (W Seattle) to Vashon
- Fauntleroy (W Seattle) to Southworth
- Southworth to Vashon
- Point Defiance to Tahlequah

Historical Sites

King County

The International District

409 Maynard Ave S, Seattle

www.internationaldistrict.org

www.seattlechinatown.org

Pick up the "Pathways to Pride" tour map at the Wing Luke Asian Museum (or print online) and get ready for an international Asian culture delight. Sites to see include the Hing Hay Park, dramatic pagoda and children's park, Nippon Kan Theatre, a national historic landmark built in 1909. Enjoy international cuisine, including Chinese, Japanese, Korean, Thai, Vietnamese, and other Southeast Asian restaurants. Buy fresh ingredients at the local grocery stores and specialty food shops, stop in at the cafes and tea house, and local bakeries.

Skagit County

Skagit County Historical Museum

501 S 4th St, La Conner

360-466-3365

www.skagitcounty.net/museum

Hours: 11:00am to 5:00pm – Tues through Sunday

Price: Adults: $4.00, Seniors (65+) and Children 6-12: $3.00, under 5 is Free.

Groups: Families of 2 adults + children: $8.00

Explore Skagit County's rugged heritage by touring the museums display of the artifacts used by folks who pioneered the valley. Seen are Native American tools, baskets, canoes, etc., also plows, mining and logging equipment used by Europeans who greatly influenced the area. Included is a wonderful display of the past, a hundred years ago. The children will enjoy the Teddy Bear, and doll exhibit, but these items are not "hands on".

Snohomish County

Blackman Home Museum

118 Ave B, Snohomish

360-568-5235

www.snohomishhistoricalsociety.com

Hours: Open April to December on Saturdays and Sundays from 11:00am to 3:00pm.

Cost: By Donation

Parlor Tour is: $12.00 – adults, $10.00 seniors & children.

Tours: 2005: Home Tour: Sunday, September 18th noon to 5:00pm

Holiday Tour: Sunday, December 11th noon to 4:00pm

Tours: 2006: Home Tour: Sunday, September 17th

Holiday Tour: Sunday, December 10th

The Home Tours are self-guided walking tours of six homes. The Parlor Tours are with a guide and take you inside the homes. The museum focus is on the historical homes of the turn of the century, including the Blackman Home built in 1878, and was the home of the first mayor, which it is named after. One can stroll down the area of the Old Snohomish Village, seeing it as it was years ago.

Bothell Historical Museum Foundation

9919 NE 180th, Bothell (Bothell Landing)

425-486-1889

www.bothellmuseum.homestead.com/home.html

Hours: Open on Sunday 1-4pm- May-September, and December

Re-opens on the 4th & 11th for special Christmas tree top displays.

Price: Free Admission

Group tours: Call 425-488-8408, or 425-486-0541.

Wheelchair accessible.

Black Diamond Museum

32627 Railroad, Black Diamond

360-886-2142

www.blackdiamondmuseum.org

Hours: Open year round on Thursdays 9:00am-4:00pm

Summer Hours: Saturday, Sunday, and Thursday 12:00pm-4:00pm.

Winter Hours: Saturday, Sunday 12:00pm-3:00pm.

Prices: Free Admission.

Play on an old caboose, and working model coal-mining town, an authentic jail, and coal mining memorabilia. Tours available. For reservations, call: 253-852-6763

Burke Museum of Natural History & Culture

University of Washington –North Entrance
2102 Bellevue Way, Bellevue
206-543-5590
www.burkemuseum.org
Hours: Open daily from 10:00am-8:00pm
Prices:$6.50 for Adults, $5 $4 for students and youth ages 5-
Free the 1st Thursday each month.
Located at the University of Washington, this museum has a large selection of ongoing and changing cultural and natural exhibits pertaining to the Pacific Northwest. Explore the life and times of Washington State. Observe up close the evolution and geology of our state with dinosaur skeletons of the Stegosaurus, a 140 million year old Allosaurus, 10,000 year old fossil crabs, a 20,000 year old saber-toothed cat, a Mastodon, and a 12,000 year old Giant Sloth skeleton. Take a stroll through the interactive exhibit of the Chinese, Filipino, Hawaiian, Japanese, Maori, Korean, Lao, Native American and Samoan cultures.

Eastside Heritage Center

2102 Bellevue Way, Bellevue
425-450-1046
www.eastsideheritagecenter.org
Hours: Thursday-Saturday 10:00am-2:00pm – Closed Sunday
Prices: Free. Monetary donations accepted.
The tour consists of visiting the Winter Home Built in 1926 by Cecelia and Frank Winter who ran a bulb farm. Their specialty was daffodils and iris bulbs. The home was designed after Cecelia's brother's home in Oregon, and built in the Spanish Eclectic style. The tile inside the home is beautiful, and the outside of the home built in the Spanish-style stucco. Some of the original furniture is on display at the home.

Visit the largest selection of textiles, along with hats and clothing items from the late 1800s to the 1960s. Also on display is a collection of over 70 quilts, domestic goods, hand-made and store-bought games and toys, over 100 dolls of various ages, types, and sizes, records, victrolas, and vintage musical instruments. Also available for viewing are agricultural and industrial items, and several hand-tool collections.

The Winter home can be booked by calling the City of Bellevue Parks and Community Service Department at: 425-452-2752 or call the McDowell House Offices at: 425-450-1049.

Edmonds Museum

118 5th Ave N, Edmonds
425-774-0900
www.historicedmonds.org
Hours: Wednesday-Sunday 1:00pm-4:00pm.
Prices: Free. Monetary donations accepted.
Explore the history of the military from the last century, including an exhibit entitled, "Dressed In Honor", a military collection of Veteran Hank R. Schmoe, along with memorabilia from 1910, a history of early Edmonds memorabilia. "Trunk Tales" is available on-line for teachers and parents to download information to enhance Social Studies education.

Foothills Historical Society

130 N River Ave, Buckley
360-829-1291
306-829-0231 (Tour Reservations)
Hours: Wednesday-Thursday 12:00pm-4:00pm, Sunday 1:00pm-4:00pm. Closed in December.
Prices: Free. Monetary donations accepted.
Group Tours: Limit to 30 can tour the facility for $15, adults free.
See logging, mineral, farming and saw mills artifacts, a small library for research, and main street diorama, including a barber shop, blacksmith, general store, barn, etc. Also on display are Military and vintage clothing. Children can play in the log cabin, lookout, saw shop and a bunk house. Learn about the Buckley Fire Department. Ask for guides and brochures for teachers and parents.

History House

790 N 34th, Fremont
206-675-8875
Hours: Wednesday-Sunday 12:00pm-4:00pm, and Sunday 12:00pm-5:00pm.
Price: Free. Monetary donations accepted.
Take a stroll through the beautiful Sculpture Garden, where you can also enjoy the free summer music concert Series – Sundays at 2:00pm.

Klondike Gold Rush Museum & Historical Park
117 S Main St, Seattle
206-553-7220
Hours: Monday-Sunday 9:00am-5:00pm
Price: Free
This museum marks the gold rush settlers who struck in rich at the Klondike in Canada and brought their riches to Seattle. Seattle was also a stopping point for those seeking for riches on their journey to the Klondike.

Nordic Heritage Museum
3014 NW 67th St, Seattle
206-789-5707
www.nordicmuseum.org
Hours: Tuesday-Friday 10:00am-4:00pm, Saturday and Sunday 12:00pm-5:00pm.
Prices: Adults $6.00, Grades K-12 $4, under 5 free.
This museum offers historical artifacts from the countries of Norway, Iceland, Denmark, Sweden & Finland. Visit the 3 permanent exhibitions, along with temporary exhibits and programs. The "The Dream of America" exhibit tells of the Scandinavian immigration movement between 1840 and 1914, as families left their homes because of scarce land and crop failure, in hopes of a better life. The Iceland exhibit displays the precious possessions they brought with them on their journey to America and how they adjusted to new life in America. The Norway exhibit shows the history, and culture, and history, including a display of two vintage musical stringed instruments called "The Hardanger Fiddle" and the Psalmodikon".

Northwest Railway Museum
38625 SE King St, Snoqualmie
425-888-3030
www.trainmuseum.org
Hours: open 7 days a week 10am to 5pm
Prices: Free Admission to the Museum
Train Ride Prices: Adults $6, Children $4, Seniors $5, 5 and under Free.
Group Discounts: Groups of 5 or more people - $2 for children, $3 for adults.
Train Ride Schedule: Runs April through October. Departs at 11:00am
May to September: Departs at 12:00pm
You need to be at the station 20 minutes before departure to use the restroom (no bathroom aboard the train), park & obtain tickets. The ride is 1 hour 10 minutes round trip – 9 miles through Snohomish Valley. Call ahead for reservations.

Naval Undersea Museum

#1 Garnett Way-Keyport
360-396-4148
www.naval.undersea.museum
Hours: Open 10:00am-4:00pm daily. Closed on Tuesdays October through May.
Price: Free
This is a technology museum appropriate for children ages 8 and older. The exhibit tells of the day-to-day life of the Trident Family. Their mission is to "preserve and collect naval undersea history for the benefit of the US Navy as well as the people of the United States". Kids will love the hands-on activities as they learn about the ocean. View sea creatures on slides. Be sure to take advantage of the educational programs for people of all ages. Enjoy concerts by the Navy Band Seattle and a speaker series.

Northwest Seaport-Maritime Heritage Center

860 Terry Ave N, Seattle
206-447-9800
www.nwseaport.org/index.html

Hours: By reservation
Prices: $10 General Admission, $7 Seniors and Students.
Group Discounts: 30 or less, $3 per person, $45 minimum
This museum aims to restore and preserve some of the oldest and most prestigious boats historic to the Puget Sound and the Northwest Coast. Tour the woodshop filled with vintage tools. Take advantage of their educational programs and musical concerts. Climb aboard an 1889 Tugboat, one of the oldest Lightships in the world, a Salmon Troller, Halibut Schooner, and a Pacific Schooner. The museum recommends wearing warm, waterproof, rugged clothing and non-slick shoes.

Pioneer Square

202 Yessler Way, Seattle
206-667-8687
Seattle's oldest neighborhood houses several historic sites, including The Klondike Gold Rush National Historic Park, King Street's Union Station, The Smith Tower, built in 1914, which overlooks Pioneer Square and upon completion was the tallest building west of the Mississippi, and Seattle's infamous Underground Tour. Take a rest in the heart of Pioneer Square at Occidental Park, or the serene Waterfall Garden, so you can conserve some energy for shopping at the Grand Central Arcade (a former gold rush era hotel). Be sure to visit the Firefighers Memorial. You can spend an entire afternoon at Pioneer Square, so be sure to save room for feasting upon one of the dozens of local restaurants

Seattle Metropolitan Police Museum

317 3rd Ave S, Seattle (Pioneer Square)

206-748-9991

www.seametropolicemuseum.org

Hours: Tuesday-Saturday 11:00am-4:00pm

Prices: $3.00 Adults, $1.50 Ages 11 and under.

Group Tour Rates: Additional $1.50 per person

This museum offers children the opportunity to discover the history behind the Seattle Police Department. Try on the old police and fire fighter uniforms from the early days of the police and fire departments, and practice dialing 9-1-1 in the interactive area of the museum. Tours of the museum are self-explanatory. Visiting this museum is a requirement for some history classes.

The Center For Wooden Boats

1010 Valley, Seattle

206-382-2628

www.cwb.org

Hours: Open daily from 7:00am-10:00pm.

Winter Hours: 10:00am-5:00pm.

Price: Free

Located south of Lake Union, this hands-on maritime history museum offers programs for children and families on Wednesdays. Explore the historic wooden boats, complete with a free daily public sail on a classic boat around Lake Union, at 2:00pm.

The Underground Tour

608 1st Ave, Seattle

206-682-4646

www.undergroundtour.com

Hours: Daily 10:00am-6:00pm (Check website for seasonal changes)

Price: Adults $11, Seniors (60+) $9, Students (13-17) $9, Children (7-12) $5, Children (^ and under) Free.

Take a 1 1/2 hour tour of how Seattle looked in 1890 before it became a sunken city, caused by serious flooding and years of sewage problems. See storefronts, and hear the stories of it's colorful past told by guides. The Seattle we know today, was built 30 feet above the sunken city, hoping to escape further flooding problems. Because of uneven flooring, strollers and wheelchairs are not allowed. Portable stools are available for those who need to rest along the way. There is also a working underground café. Be aware that the guide may discuss a bit of the "shady past" of the underground, plan accordingly.

White River Valley Museum

918 H Southeast, Auburn
253-288-7433
www.wrvmuseum.org
Hours: Wednesday-Sunday 12:00pm-4:00pm,by appointment group tours & research
Prices: $2 Adults, $1 Children and Seniors.
Wednesdays are free for everyone.
Enjoy local stories of the Native Americans, railroading, pioneers, and Japanese immigration. Take a walking/driving tour of the historic mid 1920's downtown Auburn. Enjoy visiting the historical and architectural sites of Auburn. Maps are available at the museum. Watch for Special Exhibits during the year.

Washington State History Museum

1911 Pacific Ave, Tacoma
253-272-3500
www.wshs.org
Hours: Monday-Saturday 10:00am-5:00pm, Sunday 12:00pm-5:00pm
Prices: Adults $8, Seniors $7, Students 6-18 $6, Children 5 & under Free
Family Pass: $25 (up to 4 children)
**Free on Thursdays 5:00pm-8:00pm*
Located just south of King County, this museum Is Included because of the rich state history it has to offer. "Discover the soul and spirit of Washington" as your tour 106,000 square feet of architectural splendor. Filled with theatrical storytelling, interactive exhibits, state of the art displays, and historic artifacts.

Snohomish County

Air Station Aviation History Center

18008 59th Dr NE, Arlington
360-403-9352
Hours: Tuesday and Wednesday 8:00am-4:00pm, Saturday 10:00am-4:00pm.
Cost:

Bothell Historical Museum Foundation

9919 NE 180th St, Bothell
425-486-1889
www.bothellmuseum.homestead.com/homehtml
Hours: 1:00pm to 4:00pm May 2nd to September 26th. Open in December for special Christmas exhibits. See website for time and dates.
Price: Free on Sundays.
Group tours and membership call: 425-488-8408 or 425-456-0541.

Lake Stevens Historical Museum

1802 124th Ave NE, Lake Stevens

425-334-3944

www.lakestevens.org/service/history.html

Hours: Friday and Saturday 1:00pm-4:00pm

Price: By Donation

Family Memberships: $15, $10 Individual, $5 Seniors

This museum is known as one of the finest small town museums in the state. It first opened in September 1989, the 100th anniversary of Washington becoming a state. It entails a history of Native American roots, and the rugged pioneer history. There are 9 permanent displays, featuring a 150 year old quilt, the first pharmacy, history of life and recreation on Lake Stevens including their once famous water skiing athletics, an old school room, information on the old shingle mills, a display of logging tools, equipment, gear, a big copper pot brought by the areas first pioneers, native birds including different species of ducks. A favorite part of the museum is a collection of over 900 historic pictures. Retire to the Reading Room to view old annuals from Lake Stevens high school, scrapbooks, and newspapers. Watch videos of "Old Timers" give their oral history of the Lake Stevens area, or listen to the oral histories on audio tape with a slide presentation.

Visit The Grimm house, built in the 1920's, and restored for public display. The indoors were recreated to represent how a typical home looked in those days.

Museum Of Snohomish County History

1913 Hewitt Ave, Everett

425-259-2022

www.SnoCoMuseum.org

Hours: Wednesday-Saturday 1:00pm-4:00pm.

Price: Free. Monetary donations accepted.

View historic artifacts, images of Snohomish County, and revolving exhibits. These include Seven Snohomish County Communities and Their Industrial Roots, Everett: One Hundred Years of Working for a Living, Bragging, Boasting and Boosting Business: Pomp, Pride and Promotions from Everett's Past, and Tracing Snohomish County's Immigrant Roots. Recent traveling exhibits include The Way We Cooked, Votes For Women, Experiences At The Tulalip Indian Boarding School, and The Asian Pacific American Experience. Books and films are available for sale.

Norwesco Telephone Pioneer Museum
1709 Grove St, Marysville
360-653-0171(By Appointment)
www.home1.gte.net/Norwesco
Hours: Tuesday 10:00am-2:00pm
Price: Free
This museum houses historical archived material acquired through GTE Northwest, and includes the past 75 years of telephones, telephone operator equipment, including old telephone books and a reference library.

Stillaguamish Valley Pioneers Museum
20722 NE 67th Ave NE, Arlington
360-435-7289
www.stillymuseum.org
Hours: Saturday, Sunday, and Wednesday 1:00pm-4:00pm. Closed November, December, and January.
Price: Adults $2, Children 12 and under $1.
Come view the artifacts of the North and South Forks of the Stillaguamish River Valley. Items include logging, dairy, railroad, and military displays. Listen to transportation music as you view thousands of black and white photos. Special tours available.

Museums

King County

Bellevue Art Museum
510 Bellevue Way NE, Bellevue
425-519-0770
www.bellevuearts.org
Hours: Tuesday-Thursday 10:00am-5:30pm, Friday 10:00am-9:00pm, Saturday 10:00am-5:30pm, and Sunday 11:00am-5:30pm.
Prices: $7 per person, ages 6 and under are free. Seniors and students $5.
Group Discount: 10-19 $100, 20-30 people is $140, over 30 people is $210. Students Groups: $3 per student groups of 10 or more, $100 for groups of 20-40, $150 for groups of 50 or more.
This museum focuses on design and crafts. View ceramics, glass, textiles, and iron sculptures.

Children's Museum Center

305 Harrison St, Seattle

206-441-1768

www.thechildrensmuseum.org

Hours: Monday-Friday 10:00am-5:00pm, Saturday and Sunday 10:00am-6:00pm.

Prices: Adults and Children $7.50, Grandparents and 55+ $6.50.

A kid-sized, hands-on museum housing exhibits celebrating the lifestyles of families throughout the globe. Exhibits include the Bijou Theatre complete with light effects and costumes, Cog City where children explore the concept of cause and effect with pulleys, pipes, mazes and levers, Discovery Bay, Global Village, Imagination Studio, Mindscape with a recording studio and interactive computer technology, Mountain Forest, and Neighborhood. Wheelchair friendly.

Coast Guard Museum of The Northwest

Pier 36, Seattle

206-217-6993

Hours: Monday, Wednesday, Friday 9:00am-3:00pm.

Prices: Free

Children can view a movie educating them on what it's like to be in heavy flowing, rapid filled waters. The entrance into the Pacific Ocean from the Columbia River is one of the most hazardous waterways in the world. Enjoy artifacts, pictures, and 20 models of different types of ships.

Experience Music Project-EMP

325 Fifth Ave North (Seattle Center) Seattle

206-367-5483

877-367-5483

www.emplive.com

Hours: Memorial Day to Labor Day: Open 10:00am to 8:00pm daily.

Labor Day to Memorial Day: Open Tuesday to Thursday 10:00am to 6:00pm, Friday & Saturday 10:00am to 8:00pm, and Sunday 10:00am to 6:00pm.

Prices: Adults: 18+: $19.95, Youth: 7 to 17: $14.95, 6 and under Free.

Explore all types of music through interactive exhibits, over 80,000 artifacts that shaped the history of music, and live performances. Celebrate the past, present and future of music with special display items such as Bob Dylan's and Bo Diddley's electric guitars, archives of film, photographs, stage costumes, and original hand written lyrics by noted musicians. Children can become musicians as the play a guitar, pound on the drums, and sing .This museum also has a restaurant.

Frye Art Museum
704 Terry, Seattle
206-622-9250
www.fryeart.org
Hours: Tuesday-Saturday 10:00am-5:00pm, Thursday 10:00am-8:00pm, and Sunday 12:00pm-5:00pm.
Prices: Free
Enjoy permanent and temporary art exhibits, including the Education Gallery. Student exhibitions include the National Youth Art Month Student Exhibition, and Poetry of Art. Ask for a guided learning experience, which helps children relate to and understand art. Choose from 4 different tours: I and The Frye, Learning My Way, The DaVinci Mode, and Becoming ARTiculate.

Snohomish County

Blackman House Museum
118 Ave B, Snohomish
360-568-5235
360-568-5235 (Group Reservations)
www.snohomishhistoricalsociety.com
Hours: Saturday and Sunday 11:00am to 3:00pm – April to December
Guided Tours: Reserved for groups, schools, and organizations.
Price: By donation

Special Events:

2005:
Home tour: September:18th 12:00pm to 5:00pm
Holiday Parlor Tour: December 11th 12:00pm to 4:00pm

2006:
Home Tour: September 17th 12:00pm to 5:00 pm
Holiday Parlor Tour: December 10th 12:00pm to 4:00pm

The tour consists of visiting the Blackman House built in 1878, in the old Snohomish Village. Blackman house is named after the first mayor of Snohomish. You can see artifacts and photographs pertaining to the history of the old Snohomish Village, and Blackman House. In the home there are handmade clothes and other clothing of the era See how they cooked on wood stoves. There is a museum shop where photos and more are for sale.

Imagine Children's Museum

3013 Colby Ave, Everett

425-258-1006

www.ImagineCM.org

Hours: Tuesday and Wednesday 10:00am-4:00pm, Thursday and Friday 10:00am-5:30pm, Saturday 10:00am-4:00pm, and Sunday 12:00pm-4:00pm.

Prices: $5 for all people ages 1 and older.

This newly remodeled museum is filled with adventure and fun for hours of hands-on activities and role-playing. Climb aboard the Ferry exhibit, scale a mountain, care for animals in the Wildlife Clinic, view the entire museum from the Treehouse, ride a tractor or milk a cow on the Farm, imagine you're a pilot on the Plane exhibit, create art masterpieces in the Art Studio, build in the Construction Studio, pretend you're a star on the Theatre stage, and much more. Check the website for details about field trips and portable Family Nights for schools and business.

Kids Quest Children's Museum

155 108th NE, Bellevue

425-637-8100

www.kidsquestmuseum.com

Hours: Tuesday-Saturday 10:00am-5:00pm, Friday extended hours open until 8:00pm, Sunday 12:00pm-5:00pm.

Prices: $6 for everyone.

Group Discount: 10 or more, $3 each.

This is a new interactive museum, opening in December 2005, tailored for children birth to 12 years. There are 3 primary exhibits.

The Backyard (birth-4 years) is a training area for motor skills, includes parental education for first time parents, and pre-reading skills.

The Garage holds an 8 wheeler truck in a classroom for study and learning. There is also an inventor's studio, an artist studio, and more.

The Waterway is a 2,500 square feet waterway. Learn how to water paint, enjoy water with music displays, and learn about anything to do with water.

Museum of Flight

9404 E Marginal Way, South Seattle

206-764-5720

www.museumofflight.org

Hours: Daily 10:00am-5:00pm

Prices: $14 Adults, $7.50 5-17 years old, Free ages 5 and under.

Free the first Thursday of every month from 5:00pm-9:00pm.

Group Discounts: 10 or more, $13 Adults, $6.50 children.
Climb aboard the Air Force One jet used by Presidents Eisenhower, Kennedy, Johnson, and Nixon. View restored World War I and World War II planes in the new McCaw Personal Courage Wing, and prepare to be inspired with the courageous stories of the heroic American Fighter Aces of World War I and II. Tour the Red Barn which houses collections from the first 100 years of aviation, including hands-on activities and the Wright Brother's story, and a view of the birth certificate of the aviation industry. Recently donated to the museum is the world's fastest jet, the Concorde Supersonic Airliner. This is a treat, considering there were only 20 ever built. Enjoy movies about the history of aviation, starting with birds, and visit their library. Bring your kids to participate in weekly Family Fun Workshops, and educational programs. Be sure to visit during SeaFair, as the U.S. Navy squadron, the infamous Blue Angels, take off and land at the museum's airfield. You just might have the opportunity to meet the pilots.

Museum of History And Industry-MOHAI

2700 24th E, Seattle
206-324-1126
Hours: Open Daily 10:00am-5:00pm, 1st Thursday of every month 10:00am-8:00pm.
Prices: Adults 18-61: $7, Children 5-17 and Seniors 62+: $5, Children 0-4: Free.
First Thursdays are FREE
The MOHAI first opened it's doors on February 15, 1952, and stands today as one of Washington's largest private heritage museum. Over 60,000 visitors attend the museum annually. With a vast collection of the Northwest's diverse culture, economic, and social history, children can explore the life of the early inhabitants of the great Northwest. This includes the following interactive exhibits Boom Town a recreation of Seattle during 1880's, The Great Seattle Fire exhibit, the Salmon exhibit which explains the importance of Salmon, the Hall of Washington State's Icons, including an actual Boeing B-1 on display, the Evergreen playground on vintage sporting goods, a fishing boat where kids can climb in and cast nets into the "sea", and brushes with history-a painting exhibit, and much more. Also available are expert lectures, and traveling museum collections available for classrooms.

Odyssey Maritime Discovery Center

2201 Alaskan Way Pier 66, Seattle
206-374-4000
www.ody.org
Hours: Tuesday-Saturday 10:00am to 5:00pm, Sunday 12:00pm-5:00pm
Prices: Adults $7.00, Military/Seniors $5, Children $5 (5-18), and $2 (2-4 yrs).Under 2 is free.
Group Rates Available

This is a hands-on maritime museum, complete with virtual computer films simulating boat, kayak, and other maritime rides. Learn how to operate a crane loading and unloading container ships. Explore a plethora of exhibits, including Harbor Watch, Sharing the Sound Gallery about our region's diverse natural habitat, Sustaining the Sea Gallery about the fishing industry and how fish are caught, processed and sold, and the Ocean Trade Gallery. Summer workshops are available.

Pacific Science Center
200 2nd Ave N, Seattle
206-443-2001
206-443-IMAX
www.pacsci.org
Hours: 10:00am-6:00pm
Prices: $10 Adults, $7 Children
Groups Discounts: 15 or more
Activities: 5 buildings including the Butterfly Atrium, Robots, Insect Gallery, Dinosaur Exhibit, 2 IMAX Theaters, Laser Show, Planetarium, and 200 Hands-on Exhibits.

Rosalie Whyel Museum of Doll Art
116 108th NE, Bellevue
425-455-1116
www.dollart.com
Hours: Saturday 10:00am-5:00pm, Sunday 1:00pm to 5:00pm.
Prices: $7.00 Adult $6.00 Senior (65 & older), $5.00 Children (5 to 17 yrs.), 4 & under Free.
Awarded the Juneau Trophy for the Best Private Doll Museum in the world in 1994. There are over 3,000 dolls on display, ranging from antique to modern dolls, along with teddy bears, toys, dollhouses, and miniatures. Take time to smell the flowers as you meander through the English garden.

Seattle Art Museum
100 University Street, Seattle
206-654-3100
www.seattleartmuseum.org
Hours: Tuesday-Sunday: 10:00am-5:00pm, Thursday: 10:00am-9:00pm
Prices: 13+ $7, plus $2 for special exhibits

Note: The first Thursday of every month is Free!
The Seattle Art Museum features 23,000 objects specializing in African, Asian, Northwest Coast Native American, Modern, and European art. Additional exhibits include 3,000 objects of African sculpture, masks, textiles, basketry, and decorative arts, and a Japanese display of exotic robes and kimonos. The Seattle Art Museum contains one of the finest collections of Northwest Coast Native American collections of art. A unique aspect to this museum is the "Please Touch" room. Children can enjoy dressing up in historic costumes, make straw hats, construct paper baskets, and play with puppets.

Seattle Asian Art Museum
1400 East Prospect St-Volunteer Park, Seattle
206-654-3100
www.seattleartmuseum.org
Winter Hours: (Labor Day to Memorial Day) Wednesday-Sunday 10:00am-5:00pm, Thursday 10:00am-9:00pm.
Summer Hours: Tuesday-Sunday 10:00am-5:00pm, Thursday 10:00am-9:00pm.
Prices: $3 Adults, $2 students and seniors 6 and under are free
Free the first Thursday & Saturday of every month
The first Saturday is family day. Enjoy demonstrations, hands-on art activities, and performances based on current exhibits. The Seattle Asian Art Museum is closed for Renovation: Reopens January 14th, 2006. At the reopening, a special exhibit entitled, "Orchid Pavilion", will welcome all visitors. Permanent art galleries include Korean art, Japanese art, Chinese art, and Southeast Asian art. A "Please Touch" room is also available for children to explore the Asian culture room.

Wing Luke Asian Museum
407 7th S, Seattle
206-623-5124
www.wingluke.org
Hours: Tuesday-Friday 11:00am-4:30pm, Saturday & Sunday 12:00pm-4:00pm
Price: $4 Adults, $3 Students and Seniors, $2 Children ages 5-12, under five Free.
Visit this one of a kind exhibit of the Asian and Pacific Islander settlers of Washington State. 10 Asian Pacific American groups are featured, including, Cambodians, Chinese, Filipinos, Japanese, Koreans, Laotians, Pacific Islanders, South Asians, Southeast Asian hill tribes and Vietnamese. Learn about their stories of determination, great courage, and success. "One Song, Many Voices" exhibit includes photographs and artifacts from the early Asian American business and community groups, including restaurants, social clubs, a barber shop, an herbal shop and hand laundry. Enjoy a rich cultural experience as you view musical instruments, festival clothing, and food practices. Chinese lanterns suspend from 16-foot high rafters, alongside a 35-foot traditional Chinese dragon and a 50-foot dragon boat.

Planetariums

Pacific Science Center

200 2 Avenue North, Seattle

206-443-2850

www.seattlelaserdome.com

Cost: Matinees: $1 per person, Thursday Shows "Cheap Date Night": $5 per person, Friday-Sunday Shows: $7.50 per person.

Show Times: Daily Matinees: 1:00pm, 2:00pm, 3:00pm.

Evening Shows: Thursday "Cheap Date Night": $5 8:00pm, 9:15pm, Friday and Saturday 8:00pm, 9:15pm, 10:30pm, and Midnight, Sunday 8:00pm, 9:15pm.

This is noted as the largest laser theater in the world, featuring 15,000 watts of digital sound. Come to the North entrance of Pacific Science Center located in The Seattle Center.

Sightseeing Tours

City Pass Booklet

Price: $42 Adults, $25 Children (ages 4-13)

The City Pass includes a ticket voucher to Seattle's top attractions: Argosy Cruise Harbor Tour, Museum of Flight, Pacific Science Center, Seattle Aquarium, Space Needle, and the Woodland Park Zoo. You have 9 days, beginning with the date of first use, to visit all six attractions. You save approximately 50% off regular admission price for all six attractions. You may purchase the City Pass at any of the listed attractions.

Argosy Cruises

Pier 55, Seattle

206-623-1445

www.argosycruises.com

Prices: Seniors receive $2-$3 dollars off, Children under 5 Free.

1 hour Harbor Cruise: $18.75, Children $8.50

2 1/2 hour Lock Cruise: $35, Children $11

2 hour Lake Union & Lake Washington Cruise: $28, Children $10

1 1/2 hour Cruise (leaves from Kirkland): $26.25, Children $9

Groups: 6 or more receive 15% off.

Seattle Harbor Cruises, Lake Cruises, Locks Cruises, Royal Argosy Lunch & Dinner Cruises

See ad in back

Chinatown Discovery

Redmond
425-885-3085
www.seattlechinatour.com
Ages: Children 5-11, Adults 12+
Prices: Tours include the following:
Touch of Chinatown: 1 1/2 hour tour. Adults: $14.95, Children: $9.95
Chinatown by Day: 3 hour tour. Adults: $31.95, Children: $16.95
Nibble Your Way Through Chinatown: 2 hour tour. Adults: $21.95, Children: $12.95
Chinatown By Night: 3 ? hour tour. Adults: $39.93, Children $22.95
Group Rates: 10 or more.
Enjoy the fragrance of incense, Chinese herbs, hom bows, and roast duck as you travel through Chinatown. See an Asian museum, market, and historical sites.

Gray Line of Seattle Sightseeing

206-624-5077
800-544-0739
www.graylineofseattle.com
Prices: Prices vary according to your site tour and destination.
Group Rates Available
Tours of Seattle, Boeing, Mt. Rainier, cruises to Victoria or the San Juan Islands, 1 hour loop of downtown Seattle on a double decker, and much more.

Island Mariner Whale Watching

5 Harbor Loop, Bellingham
360-734-8866
877-734-8866
www.orcawatch.com
Prices: $75 per person
Time: Departs at 10:00am, Returns at 5:00pm
"The oldest and best". Take the Island Caper, a large boat, on a 7 hour whale watching tour to the San Juan Islands. This 70-90 mile cruise is narrated by 2 naturalists, who tell the history and geology of the islands, and point out landmarks (lighthouses, etc.). There are several birds and wild life native to the islands, so keep a watch for porpoises, sea lions, Harbor seals, the Tufted Puffin, Peregrine Falcons, Bald Eagles, and more. On the rare event that Orcas are not spotted, you will be given a free tour at another time. Visit their website to print a $10 off coupon.

Also available is the Bellingham Bay History Cruise. This 2 ? hour sunset tour is great for all ages. Get close up and personal with the historical sites, go down waterways, past shipyards, and view the environment of Belligham. Tour is $20 per person.

Mt. Rainier Tours-Seattle Tours

206-768-1234

www.seattlecitytours.com

Hours: 7:00am-10:00pm year round.

Prices: 3 Hour Tour: Adults $40.10, Children $27. All day tour: Adults $73, Children $49.

Enjoy 3 hour city tours, or 10 hour all day tours, which includes a city tour, Mt. Rainier's basin viewing waterfalls, and scenic views. After a full day of sight-seeing, you'll enjoy a hearty cookout on the mountain. The evening ends as the tour proceeds to the Paradise Inn.

Ride The Ducks

Seattle Space Needle

206-441-3825

www.ridetheducksofseattle.com

Hours: Daily at 10:00am-6:00pm. A new tour begins every 30 minutes.

Prices: Adults are $23, Children 12 and younger $13, Children 0-2 years are free.

Info: Tour Seattle by Land and Sea in WWII Amphibious Landing Craft. This tour takes you around downtown Seattle, including Pike Place Market, and the historic Pioneer Square. Drive over the bridge as you continue the tour on Lake Union. Great for children.

Seattle Seaplanes

1325 Fairview Ave E, Seattle

206-329-9638

www.seattleseaplanes.com

Prices: $67 per person for a 20 minutes scenic flight of Seattle, or $410 per hour for up to 4 passengers.

See all of Seattle, Mt. Rainier, and San Juan Islands. It is safe, affordable, and fun. The seaplanes leave Lake Union every hour, every day.

Spirit of Washington Dinner Train

625 4th, Renton

800-876-7245

www.spiritofwashingtondinnertrain.com

Group Discounts: 25+ groups $58.34 per person, includes tax and gratuity.

Dates: 7 days a week Monday-Friday 6:30pm, Saturday 12:00pm, 6:30pm, and Sunday 11:00am, 5:30pm

Prices: Adults: $59.95 per person. $74.99 per person for upper glass dome dining area. Includes a 360 degree panoramic view.

Children $20 each for ages 12 and under.

Dinner menu includes your choice of 6 main menu items including, prime rib, smoked roasted salmon, marinated pork, stuffed chicken breast, stuffed Portobello mushrooms, and vegetarian lasagna. Begin your journey from downtown Renton to the Columbia Winery in Woodinville while feasting upon a delicious gourmet meal. Once you arrive in Woodinville, spend 45 minutes touring the winery, wine tasting, or simply strolling through the beautiful garden and gift shop. A delectable dessert awaits guests as they travel back to where their journey began. Plan on a total of 3 hours and 45 minutes.

Zoos

King County

Woodland Park Zoo
5500 Phinney Ave N (West Gate)
750 N 50th St (South Gate)
206-684-4800
206-615-0076 (Zoo Tunes Summer Concert Series)
www.zoo.org
Hours: Open 365 days a year.
May 1-September 14: 9:30am-6:00pm
October 15-March 14: 9:30am-4:00pm
September 15-October 14, March 15- April 30: 9:30am-5:00pm
Cost: $10 (13-64), $7 (3-12), Free (0-2), $2 discount for seniors & persons w/disabilities
Group Discount: 20+ receive 10% discount
Annual Membership:
Lion's Lair: $65 Family Membership plus ? price for up to 5 visitors each visit, free admission to more than 120 zoo's and aquariums in U.S. and Canada, quarterly magazine subscription, free winter parking.
Gorilla Troop: $65 = 1 adult plus his or her children, or grandchildren.
Wolf Pack: $85 = 2 adults with children, plus 2 one time guest passes.

Elephant Herd Plus: $135 one free guest per visit, 4 one time guest passes.
Parking $3.50

- African Savanna Safari 1:30 Wednesday-Sunday
- African Village Exploration 3:00pm Wednesday-Sunday
- African Village Theater 11:30 Wednesday-Sunday
- Animal Contact Experience 10:30am-4:00pm Daily
- Attracting Butterflies to Your Garden 1:30pm Tuesday
- Brown Bears 12:00pm Tuesday
- Croc Talk 1:30pm Mondays
- Discovery Barn 11:00pm-4:00pm Daily
- Elephant Talk 2:00pm Daily
- Gorillas 11:30am Tuesday
- Hippos 10:30am Saturday
- Hornbills 1:30pm Wednesday
- Jaguars 10:30am Sunday, 2:30pm Friday
- Jaguar Quest 12:00pm-3:00pm Wednesday-Saturday
- Jive on Jaguars 1:00pm Wednesday-Saturday
- Malayan Tapirs 11:30am Sunday
- Orangutans 11:30am Sunday
- Penguin Feeding 11:00pm Friday
- Piranha Feeding 11:15am Friday
- Pony Rides 11:00am-4:00pm Saturday and Sunday: $2
- Raptors 12:30pm and 3:30pm Friday, Saturday, and Sunday
- Snow Leopards 11:00am Monday-Wednesday
- Tigers 1:00pm Wednesday
- Wolves/Elk 1:00pm Tuesday and Thursday

Cougar Mountain Zoo

19525 SE 54th St, Issaquah
425-391-5508
www.cougarmountainzoo.org
Hours: January-November 9:00am-5:00pm
Prices: Seniors 62+: $7, Adults 13-61: $8.50, Children 2-12: $6, and 2 & under: Free
First established in 1972 for the purpose of educating and preserving endangered animals, the zoo has influenced a greater appreciation and awareness, and educated the public about the earth's wildlife community. Visitors receive rare close encounters with Reindeer, Antelope, Lemurs, Birds, Macaws, and other wildlife. Be sure to pay close attention to the zoo's rules.

The daily lecture schedule is as follows:

- 10:30am Reindeer mini-lecture
- 11:00am Crane mini-lecture
- 11:30am Lemur mini-lecture
- 12:00pm Antelope mini-lecture
- 12:30pm Mammal walk
- 1:30pm Bird walk
- 2:00pm Cougar mini-lecture
- 3:00pm Ratite mini-lecture
- 3:30pm Macaw mini-lecture

Guided tours, outreach programs, lectures and special events are also available.

Snohomish County

Hands-On Farm

15308 52nd Ave W, Edmonds

425-743-3694

Hours: Open in April, tour groups only, and weekends in October.

Prices: $2.50 per person/weekends

A tour guide will lead you through the tactile farm, where children can feed and pet friendly animals, including pygmy goats, pigs, cows, roosters, a turkey, and much more. This is a great spot for little one's first exposure to animals up close and personal.

Marysville City Zoo-Petting Zoo

6915 Armar Rd, Jennings Memorial Park

360-651-5088

360-363-8400 (Group Reservations)

Hours: Weekends in May, and June-August Tuesday-Sunday 10:00am-6:00pm.

Price: Free. Donations encouraged.

The petting zoo draws 40,000 visitors each year between May and August. Children can meet friendly farm animals, including calves, pigs, Billy goats, burros, ducks, rabbits and much more. The Petting Zoo is supported by the Marysville School District Future Farmers of America and operated by the City's Parks and Recreation staff.

Reptile Zoo

22715 SR 2, Monroe

360-805-5300

www.reptileman.com

Hours: 10:00am-6:00pm, 365 days a year.

Prices: $4 per person 3+ years of age.

Come see the newest addition...the 2-headed turtle, and the only albino alligator in the Pacific Northwest. The Serpentarium is home to the world's 10 deadliest snakes, with several devenomized so children can handle them. View the largest spiders and centipedes, and hold lizards, iguanas, and frogs. Plan on a 45 minute to 1 hour tour.

If you're looking for fun and inexpensive cultural entertainment for your kids, a few local museums offer free admission on certain days of each month.

Free First Thursday of Every Month:

Seattle Art Museum:

206-654-3100

10:00am-9:00pm

Burke Museum of Natural History and Culture

206-543-5590

10:00am-8:00pm

Museum of History and Industry (MOHAI)

206-324-1125

10:00am-8:00pm

Wing Luke Asian Museum

206-623-5124

11:00am-4:30pm

Museum of Flight
206-764-5720
5:00pm-9:00pm

Seattle Asian Art Museum
206-654-3100
10:00am-9:00pm
*Also free first Saturday

By Donation the Last Hour

Children's Museum @ Seattle Center House –Lower Level
206-441-1768

Always Free

Issaquah Depot Museum

Frye Art Museum

Klondike Gold Rush National Park Museum

Discount Movies

Crossroads Cinemas
1200 156th NE, Bellevue
425-562-7230
1/2 price movies before 6pm, 3 & under free

Olympic Theatre
107 N Olympic Ave, Arlington
360-435-3939
Prices: Tuesday Night Bargain Night: 2 for 1 Admission
www.Olympictheatre.net

Grand Cinemas Alderwood
18421 Alderwood Mall Blvd,
Lynnwood
425-774-3536
Prices: All Movies, All Showings
$4.50

Puget Park Drive-Inn
13020 Meridian Ave S, Everett
425-338-5957
Prices: Ages 6-11 $3, 5 & Under Free, Adults $7.50
Listen on 107.3FM
www.sterlingrealty.com

Edmonds Theatre
425 Main St, Edmonds
425-778-4554
Prices: Adults $7, Children $5 w/ free bag of popcorn

Chapter 2

The Great Outdoors

Chapter 2

The Great Outdoors

Call me biased, but Western Washington is one of the most breathtakingly beautiful areas in the world. Natural features abound at our doorstep with doted islands, jagged snow capped mountains, towering forests and gentle valleys. Approximately 5,000 miles of trails cover the state of Washington. The question is...Which trails are appropriate for children and youth? This chapter focuses on the more prominent places best suited for children and families.

Did you know that American families spend more than 90% of their time inside? Sometimes, being in an outdoor natural setting can be more health advantageous than being indoors. The wide-ranging health benefits of outdoor activities for both adults and children have been well noted. From reducing tension and stress, stimulating the mind to improving overall muscle tone and flexibility, outdoor activities increase both your physical and mental health-all while appreciating the beauty of nature. So...Seek out nature. It's right here waiting for you!

Resources

Websites

Dude Ranches In Washington

www.duderanches.com/Washington

Find all of the different Dude Ranches in the state of Washington on one site. Check out the different outdoor experiences available to your family. Saddle up partner!

National Parks Service

www.nps.gov

The National Parks Service has a great website filled with detailed maps and information about the National Parks in the state of Washington. Begin your search by selecting the Parks and Recreation section to find the perfect location for your next outdoor family trip.

National Wildlife Federation - Kids

www.nwf.org/kids

This is the link for the "Just for Kids Ranger Rick" website for children ages 1-18. You can find all sorts of great activities to do in your own backyard that are very educational and fun. There is an area just for parents and one for educators about the Wildlife information and current activities.

National Recreation Reservation Service (NRRS)

877-444-6777

www.reserveusa.com

The NRRS is a one-stop reservation service for the USDA Forest Service, Army Corps of Engineers, National Park Service, Bureau of Land Management and Bureau of Reclamation outdoor recreation facilities and activities. With over 45,000 reservable facilities at over 1,700 locations, the NRRS is the largest outdoor recreation reservation service in the country.

Northwest Hiker

www.nwhiker.com/washNF.html

Northwest hiker is a great resource for finding trails by region. What I like most about this site are the details including current weather conditions by region, and the web cams covering the weather conditions at various locations in the mountains. Before going out with your children in the mountains, check out the weather to avoid bad weather is an important safety precaution. They also list ranger stations and phone numbers.

NWSource

www.nwsource.com/outdoors
The NW Source-Outdoors section is a must see website if you're looking for great outdoor opportunities with your children. This website is full of pictures and descriptions with the option to search by activity, i.e. Biking, Camping, Paddling, Hiking and more. In addition, you will find the 'Best of the Northwest'. Register with NW Source and receive free newsletters with up coming events and more.

Recreation.gov

www.recreation.gov
This government site makes it easy to search for government managed recreation sites through out the United States. Search by state, then click on one of the following main topics: Auto Touring, Boating, Camping, Climbing, Historical / Cultural Sites, Education Programs, Fishing, Fish Hatcheries, Hiking, Horseback riding, Hunting, Lodging, Off road Vehicle Access, Water Sports, Wildlife Viewing, and Winter sports.

Washington Department of Fish and Wildlife (WDWF) – Go Play Outside

www.wdfw.wa.gov/gpo/kids_corner.htm
WDFW organization is dedicated to providing resources and educational opportunities for children to learn about the outdoors and enjoy the wonderful diversity of wildlife and the outdoors that so richly exist in Washington. The "Go Play Outside" initiative offers hands-on experiences through mentoring, provided by established outdoor users. The new Youth Fishing Initiative is a high profile element of the "Go Play Outside" campaign.

WDFW is seeking and recognizing partnerships with local, state, and national organizations, nonprofit groups, license dealers, outdoor sports businesses, and outdoor recreation groups to help sponsor and provide "Go Play Outside" events.

Washington State Parks

www.parks.wa.gov
This is the homepage for Washington State Parks and lists all the information you need to find a great camping location in one of our state's many beautiful campgrounds.

Books

Best Hikes with Children Western Washington & the Cascades

Vol 1&2
With the focus on children, this book gives an overview of the basics for preparedness, including the 10 essentials taught to Boy Scouts. Learn about how to watch the weather conditions, have the right gear and stay in appropriate difficulty levels.

Beyond Mount Si

The best hikes within 85 miles of Seattle. This is a book filled with great description about specific hikes and includes a difficulty rating system to help determine if the hike is age appropriate for your child(ren).

Mountain Biking the Puget Sound Area

This book is a must for mountain bikers both novice and expert alike. The book contains detail descriptions of the trail conditions, helpful tips and easy to read detailed trail maps. The index sorts trails into various helpful categories that make it easy to identify trails appropriate for children.

The Mountaineers Books

www.mountaineersbooks.org

The Mountaineers Books has published over 500 titles. Located right here in the Seattle, you can find their titles in all major book stores. You can also request a catalog on the website or search the catalog and purchase title on the website. This is a must see website for information on mountaineering printed materials.

Parks & Recreation

King County

King County Parks and Recreation Division

www.metrokc.gov/parks/trails/trails1.htm

Seattle Parks and Recreation

www.ci.seattle.wa.us/parks/parkspaces/parkmap.htm (park finder website)

Alki Beach Park

1702 Alki Ave SW, West Seattle

(206) 684-4075

Hours: 4:00am-11:30pm

Alki Beach Park is one of Seattle's most well known hot spots, especially during the summer. It hosts a paved 2.5 mile trail that stretches between Alki Point and Elliott Bay's shore. The wide trail makes it perfect for strollers and family biking. Soft sand attracts many sand castle builders and beach volley players. Ferries and ships pass by under the back drop of the Seattle skyline and Cascade mountains.

Discovery Park
3801 W Government Way, Seattle
206-386-4236
www.cityofseattle.net/parks
Hours: Daily, 4:30am-11:00pm
Discovery Park is the largest park in Seattle with 534 acres. Majestic views overlook the Puget Sound. The Park is full of biking, and running trails. Monthly calendars list classes for young naturalists of all ages and their families, including birding, nature walks, and conservation classes. Youth ages 12-16 with an interest in the natural world can become Junior Naturalists and undergo fun training at the park, learn tips on working with children, and volunteer at the Nature Day Camp during the summer.

Nature Day Camp: Each weeklong session in this tremendously popular day camp gives your child the chance to explore the park and learn about its plants and animals.

Green Lake Park
7201 E Greenlake Dr N, Seattle
206-684-4075
www.cityofseattle.net/parks
Hours: Daily, 24 hours
One of Seattle's most notable parks, Green lake is circled with a 2.8 mile path, divided into two lanes, one for walking and strollers and the other for wheels. A large sand pit with digging toys and a playground awaits children of all ages. Green lake hosts three swimming areas, a wading pool on the north end of the lake, beach access with lifeguards on watch during the summer, and an indoor swimming pool at the community center. Boat rentals are available, or take the family to the pitch and putt golf course.

Marymoor Park
6046 W Lake Sammamish Pkwy NE, Redmond
www.metrokc.gov/parks
Hours: Daily, 8am-dusk
One of Eastside's best parks. Marymoor park (or "MaryMoo" park as my son calls it) has numerous features great for families, including several playgrounds, plenty of open space, a model airplane airport, a climbing wall, an off leash area for dogs, and a wetland boardwalk. The park also hosts many musical festivals and community events. A unique notable feature at Marymoor is wireless internet access for free so you can work and play at the same time! Racing classes are available on the Velodrome for kids of all ages. There is so much to do, one can spend the entire day here if you wish, or come back again and again and never get bored.

Seward Park

5898 Lake Washington Blvd S, Seattle
206-684-4396
www.cityofseattle.net/parks/parkspaces/sewardpark.htm
Hours: Daily, 4:00am-11:30pm
This park contains 300 acres of forest along the Lake Washington shore. Features include an art studio, picnic sites, tennis courts, trails & paths, beaches, and swimming in the raft/play area with a life guard on duty during specific hours. A paved 2.5 mile trail loops around the park. School programs are available.

*Dogs are not allowed.

Tolt MacDonald

31020 NE 40th St, off State Route 203 near Carnation
www.metrokc.gov/parks/rentals/pommay99.htm
Hours: Daily, 8:00am - dusk
Located at the confluence of the Snoqualmie and Tolt Rivers in the beautiful Snoqualmie Valley, this park covers more than 574 acres on both sides of the Snoqualmie River. Features include RV and Tent Camping, a playground for children, hiking, mountain biking trails, baseball and soccer fields.

Saint Edwards State Park

14500 Juanita Dr NE, Kenmore
425-823-2992
www.parks.wa.gov/parkpage.asp?selectedpark=Saint%20Edward&pageno=1
Hours: Daily, 8am-dusk
Price: $5 parking fee
This is a wooded park with access to the shoreline, beautiful trails and picnic areas. Some of the trails are easy enough for kids and families but will not work well with strollers. The highlight of the park is the playground completed in 2003, which includes the Owl Forest for tots with and tons open space for running, an awesome climbing structure and multiple levels and openings and hiding places perfect for hide and seek.

Snohomish County

Snohomish County Park Directory

www1.co.snohomish.wa.us/Departments/Parks/Information/Park_Directory

McCollum Pioneer Park
600 128th St SE, Everett
Exit off I-5
McCollum Park is a 78 acre family-oriented park, providing ball fields, jogging / walking nature trails, a junior Olympic-sized, heated outdoor swimming pool, shaded and open space lawn areas with picnic tables and shelters, a BMX bicycle racing track, and a baseball field. An Adopt-A-Stream's Northwest Stream Center, a stream and wetland ecology learning facility, is also located on 20 acres of forested wetlands next to North Creek.

Meadowdale Park
6026 156th SW, Edmonds
This is a short mile long trail that descends down through thick forest to the park boarding the Puget Sound. The Park features a sand volley ball court, pavilion and open grass space. The Park has a nice beach front with great views over the sound. The hike is short enough for most kids to enjoy. Access to the park requires the hike down the trail. There is road access but is only available for those with limited mobility. The trail down to the park is fairly steep during the first quarter mile before it becomes almost entirely level. Small kids will need to be carried.

Wyatt Park
10508 Chapel Hill Road, Lake Stevens
Wyatt Park overlooks the beautiful waters of Lake Stevens and the picturesque snow-capped Cascade Mountains. Swim in the secured swimming area, picnic or sunbathe on the lawn, fish from the dock, or launch your boat for water-skiing and boating from the modern boat launch

Gardens

Bellevue Botanical Gardens

12001 Main St, Bellevue
425-451-3755
www.bellevuebotanical.org
Hours: 7:00am-Dusk
Price: Free. Donations are accepted.
Enjoy year-round beauty in the garden and trails.
Spring: Pulmonia, Rhododendrons, Tulips, and Camellias.
Summer: Blue Angel, Chrysanthemum, Hydrangea, Amber Waves, Night Raven, Neon Flash, and Hansa.
Fall: Bright red, yellow, orange, copper, coral leaves mixed with the evergreens.
Winter: Sparkleberry, Beautyberry, Chinese Witch Hazel, Crabapple, Oregon Grape, Rose Hips, Midwinter Fire, and Fuchsia.
Stroll along the tranquil trail of The Lost Meadow with the Western Red Cedar, Douglas Fir, Big Leaf and Vine Maple trees as your guide. Refresh your senses along the Yao Japanese Garden path, the Waterwise Garden, Serene Woodlands, Alpine Rock Garden, and the Botanical Reserve. Please note that dogs are not allowed in the gardens.

Bradner Garden Park

29th Ave S and S Grand, South Seattle
206-684-4075
www.cityofseattle.net/parks/parkspaces/gardens.htm
Hours: Daily from 4:30am to 11:30pm
Price: free
This new park was built with gardening education in mind. The 1.6-acres is one of the first pesticide free gardens and thus provides a great habitat for butterflies and other animals that would otherwise be driven away.

Kubota Garden

Renton Ave S and 55th Ave S, Seattle
205-684-4584
www.kubota.org
Hours: Daylight
Price: free
The serene Kubota Garden is a 4.5 acre Japanese style garden hidden in the city offering a welcome escape to busy city life. Designed by Fujitaro Kabuta beginning in the late 1920's, the gardens were continually manicured for six decades becoming the beautiful landscaped which envelopes the garden today. The Seattle Landmarks Preservation Board declared Kubota Garden a National Historic Landmark over 30 years ago, and it is now kept by the Seattle Parks & Recreation. The one mile trail is filled with a wide variety of birds and other wildlife, stone gardens, overlooks, waterfalls, stone mountain side with a mini walk into the mountains, springs, ponds, the Fera Fera forest, and 12, 000 year old stones left by the last glacier.

Washington Park Arboretum

2300 Arboretum Drive E, Seattle
206-543-8800
depts.washington.edu/wpa
Hours: 10:00am-4:00pm (Visitors Center)
Exit off Hwy 520 (Buses 11, 43, and 48 run near the Arboretum)
The Washington Park Arboretum hosts 230 acres of spectacular urban green space on the shores of Lake Washington adjacent to The University of Washington. Its 230 acres comprise a dynamic, living museum with collections of oaks, conifers, camellias, Japanese maples and hollies that are known internationally as the largest in the country, an extensive network of trails, a Japanese garden, Woodland garden, and Rhododendron glen.. The University of Washington, in association with the Center for Urban Horticulture, manages the Arboretum.

Bird & Wildlife (Watching)

King County

Camp Long
5200 35th Ave SW, Seattle
206-684-7434
www.camplong.org
Hours: 10:00am-6:00pm (rock climbing hours)
This park stretches 68 acres and is the only place in town with a campsite. Bring your climbing gear, register at the kiosk, and go rock climbing for free on Schurman Rock 6 days a week. Keep your eyes wide open for foxes and flying squirrels, ducks, owls, frogs, and salamanders. Tables are available for a nice picnic in the park, and nature classes are offered throughout the year.

Carkeek Park
950 NW Carkeek Park Rd, Seattle
206-684-0877
www.cityofseattle.net/parks
Hours: Daily 6:00am-10:00pm.
Monday-Friday 10:00am-4:00pm (Environmental Learning Center)
This is a great place for children to view nature along the wetlands which offers a short boardwalk through still, dark water full of ducks, other birds, and places to pause, and a trail that passes through native plantings to the creek. During the salmon run in late fall, Piper's Creek is alive with salmon returning to their spawning grounds. Watch for American Dippers feasting on salmon eggs.

Cedar River Watershed Education Center

19901 Cedar Falls Road Southeast, North Bend
206-233-1515
cityofseattle.net/util/cedarwatershed/
Summer Hours: Tuesday-Sunday 10:00am-6:00pm
Winter Hours: Tuesday-Friday 10:00am-4:00pm
Price: Free

The Cedar River Watershed, managed by the Seattle Public Utilities, provides most of Seattle's drinking water. To keep this area pristine, its 90,000 acres is off-limits to unaccompanied visitors. The Education Center however provides a way for the public to access and appreciate an area that is both magically and beautiful. A stream bordered by stone steps runs under the building and through the front courtyard, and in late summer, tadpoles, salamanders, and water bugs can be seen in its clear waters. Decks invite visitors to glimpse turquoise blue Rattlesnake Lake, accessible via a 1.5 mile gravel trail loop that starts near the entry courtyard.

Bird-watchers can be on the lookout for Osprey, Pileated Woodpeckers, Western Tanagers, and other species. Check the blackboard near the Center's front door for an update of what's been spotted recently. Summer Naturalist lead tours are available.

Mercer Slough Natural Park

1625 118th Avenue SE, Bellevue
425-452-2752 (Winters House Visitor Center)
425-450-0207 (Environmental Center)
Hours: Daily 8:30am-5pm
www.ci.bellevue.wa.us

The 320 acre Mercer Slough Natural Park is a world away from the buzz of the I-90 corridor, and features the largest remaining wetlands in the metro area. Home to the great Blue Heron Rookery, otters, beavers and a wide variety of birds and animals this is a great spot for birding. On Saturdays from May to October, Rangers provide guided canoe trips from Enatai Beach Park across Lake Washington to the Slough, children are welcome. Pre-registration is required through the Winters House Visitor Center. Nature-oriented classes and camps are available including classes for hiking and canoeing to explore nature

West Hylebos Wetlands State Park
South 348th St and Fourth Ave S, Federal Way
Hours: Daily, dawn to dusk
Cost: Free

www.hylebos.org/statepark/index.htm
This 69 acre bog features a mile long boardwalk easily accessible by strollers. Children will be able to touch and feel the carpets of moss and huge old growth trees. Keep your eyes out for woodpeckers, flying squirrels, and if you are lucky you might see a weasel, mink beavers, and snakes.

Snohomish County

Bob Heirman Wildlife Preserve At Thomas' Eddy
14913 Connelly, Snohomish
Park Features: River Access, Fishing, Nature Trails, Picnic Tables, Portable Restrooms, 2 Pristine Lakes, Fragile Wetlands.
*Dogs Not Permitted

North Creek
1011 183rd St Se, Mill Creek
Park Features: Interpretive Board Walk, Interpretive Signs, Viewpoint, Picnic Tables, Portable Restrooms.

North Creek Park & Water Detention Facility
1011 183rd Street SE, Mill Creek

Spencer Island
4th St SE, Everett
(425) 388-6616
Park Features: Interpretive Signs and Boardwalk, Slough Access, Freshwater Wetland, Saltwater Wetland, Trails, Picnic Tables, Portable Restrooms
Wildlife: Deer, Coyote, River Otter, Small Mammals, Amphibians Waterfowl, Shorebirds
Dogs Not Permitted

Boating, Canoeing, Rafting, & Kayaking

Boating Safety Information
360-586-6592
www.parks.wa.gov/boating/asp

Rentals

Agua Verde
Lake Union & Lake Washington
1303 NE Boat St. Seattle
206-545-8570
www.aguaverde.com/kayak.htm
Sea kayak rental on the lower level.

Aquasports Paddle Center
7907 159th Pl NE, Redmond
425-869-7067
www.aqua-sports.com
Full Service: Classes, Sales, Rentals

Cascade Canoe & Kayak Centers Inc at Entai Beach Park
425-430-0111
www.canoe-kayak.com
Sales, Classes, Rental, Tours, Races
Classes in Bellevue-Enatai Beach Park-Bellevue

Green Lake Boat Rental
206-527-0171
Canoe, paddle boat, and row boat rental.
Price: $10/hour

Mariner Sea Touring Kayaks
2134 Westlake N, Seattle
206-284-8404
www.marinerkayaks.com

Mercer Slough Nature Park

1625 118th Ave SE, Bellevue
425-452-2752
425-450-0207
www.ci.bellevue.wa.us
Hours: Daily 8:30am-5pm
Price: Free
For muddy fun, explore the forests, marshes, swamps, and bogs of the 320-acre Mercer Slough Nature Park, the largest remaining wetland in the metro area. Set close to the rush and bustle of the I-90 corridor

Ranger-guided canoe trips leave every Saturday from May-Oct from Enatai Beach Park. Canoers paddle across Lake Washington to the Slough. Kids are welcome, and no experience is necessary, but pre-registration is required as classes fill quickly. Non-Bellevue residents pay $7.20/person or $18/canoe; Bellevue residents' fees are slightly lower. Register through the Winters House Visitor Center. [425.452.2752/dpettersson@ci.bellevue.wa.us]

Moss Bay Rowing & Kayaking Center

1001 Fariview N, Seattle
206-682-2031
www.mossbay.net
Classes: Kayak, Rowing, Sailing
Kids Camp: Age 6 and older, offered all summer

Northwest Outdoor Center On Lake Union

2100 Westlake N Suite#1, Seattle
206-281-9694
www.nwoc.com
Classes & hourly rentals.

University of Washington Waterfront Activities Center

Southwest corner of Husky Stadium parking lot
206-543-9433
Canoes and rowboat rentals. This is a great location because you can take a canoe through the waterways channels boarding the Washington Park Arboretum.

Tours, plus...

Aqua Trek Sea kayaking Adventures
5822-157th Pl SW, Edmonds
425-743-3446

Gig Harbor Kayak Center
8809 North Harborview Drive , Gig Harbor
888-42-YAKIT
253-851-7987
Classes, Sales, Tours
Equipment, instruction & guide provided.

Island Outfitters
2403 Commercial Ave, Anacortes
(866) 445-7506
www.seakayakshop.com

Kayak Port Townsend
(877) 578-2252

Outdoor Odysseys San Juan Kayak Tours
82 Cedar St, Friday Harbor
800-647-4621
www.outdoorodysseys.com

River Recreation
Bothell
(425) 741-5901
www.riverrecreation.com
River rafting, Kayaking, Lessons, Training, Kid camps and Guided trips including riverside B-B-Q, They take care of everything.

Vashon Island Kayak Company
8900 SW Harbor Dr, Vashon Island
206-463-9257
www.pugetsoundkayak.com

Western Canoeing & Kayaking Inc
1717 Salton Rd
Abbotsford, B.C.
1-866-644-8111
www.westerncanoekayak.com

Charters

Argosy Cruises
Pier 55, Seattle
(206) 623-1445
See ad in back

Bearfoot Charters
(206) 281-9791

Emerald City Charters
Pier 54, Seattle
(206) 624-3931

Fishing Lakes & Ponds

Cascade Kamloops Trout Farm
1240 Darrington St, Darrington
360-436-1003

Gold Creek Trout Farm
15844 148th Ave NE, Woodinville
425-483-1415

Springbrook Trout Farm
19225 Talbot Rd S, Renton
253-852-0360
You catch, they clean. Picnic rentals available.

Troutlodge U-Fish
17612 219th Ave E, Orting
360-893-7786

Climbing Instruction

REI Alderwood
3000 184th St SW Suite 952, Lynnwood
425-640-6200

REI - Redmond Town Center
7500 166th Ave NE, Redmond
425-882-1158

REI – Seattle Flagship
222 Yale Ave N, Seattle
206-223-1944
888-873-1938

REI - Southcenter/Tukwila
240 Andover Park W
206-248-1938
Snohomish County

Stone Gardens Gym
2839 NW Market St, Seattle
206-781-9828
Ages: 5-16
Price: 1 1/2 Hours-$20, plus $4 Shoe Rental, $2 Harness Rental
Classes: 2 Hour Class/Week for 4 Weeks: $80 (includes equipment)

Vertical World
www.verticalworld.com

3 Locations

East Bremerton
5934 St Hwy 303 NE
360-373-6676

Redmond
15036B NE 95
425-881-8826

Seattle
2123 W Elmore St
206-283-4497

Trails

King County

King County Trails
www.metrokc.gov/parks/trails/trails1.htm

Download a City Map

ftp://extranet.metrokc.gov/gis/Web/VMC/recreation/rtmap.pdf

Beaver Lake

This is an excellent challenging trail for youth ages 10+ riders. Choose from 3 - 6 mile circuits of rolling trails that entail are narrow (single track) packed dirt.

Directions: Take 2nd Issaquah Exit off 1-90, and turn left onto E Lake Sammamish Pkwy, then right at SE Forty-third. The road turns into Southeast 228th. Turn Right at SE Twenty-fourth. Continue on this road for 1.4 miles, where the road takes a sharp left and changes into Beaver Lake Road. Continue for another 2.4 miles to a small parking area along the side of the road. The trail begins on the other side of the road.

Burke-Gilman / Sammamish River Trail

www.metrokc.gov/parks/trails/trails/burke.htm

Starting in Fremont in down town Seattle it winds along lake union around along and around Lake Washington through Bothell. At Blythe Park in Bothell the trail becomes the Sammamish river trail ultimately ending up at Marymoor Park. The trail adjoins to many parks along the way, and is paved for a comfortable riding which makes it a good choice for children. It can become quite busy on weekends and evenings, so its a good idea to keep little ones in jogging strollers, unless they are old enough to stay on the right side of the trail moving with the flow.

Length: 27 miles

Access Points: Gasworks Park, Matthews Beach Park, Tracy Owen Station Park, Woodinville's Jerry Wilmot Park, Blythe Park, 60 Acre Park, and Marymoor Park.

Cedar River Trail

www.metrokc.gov/parks/trails/trails/cedar.htm

The Cedar River Trail follows an old railroad right-of-way from downtown Renton to King County's Landsburg Park, alongside the scenic Cedar River. A branch of the trail connects with King County's Lake Wilderness Park and continues to Four Corners.

Part of the trail is paved (Renton to 196th Ave SE), and the rest is crushed gravel.

Interurban and Green River Trails

www.metrokc.gov/parks/trails/trails/intergr.htm
Length: 14 miles (Interurban)
Length: 12 miles (Green River)
The Interurban and Green River Trails comprise a system of 46 miles. The Interurban Trail currently covers 14 miles from I-405 in Tukwila to 3rd Ave SW. The Green River Trail spans 30 miles from Seattle's Alki Point to King County's Auburn Narrows Park. The trail in not quite completed...its completed sections traverse the industrial heart of the valley from South Seattle through Kent, connecting to a number of neighborhoods and community trails.

Access Points: King County's Fort Dent Park, Seattle's Alki Point Park, Kent's Brisco Meander Park, Russell Road Park, Foster Park, Auburn's Brannon Park.

Lake Wilderness

This is a great place for family walks, jogger strollers and family biking. The path is wide, paved and almost completely flat.

Directions: Take the Maple Valley Enumclaw exit off I-405. Drive through Maple Valley and turn right onto White Rd SE. Pass the Lake Wilderness Elementary, and on the left you'll find the Lake Wilderness Park.

Pioneer Park

Located on Mercer Island, this park is one of the most well groomed parks in the city. The park's trail is ideal for new mountain bikers, with 5 miles of mostly level trails filled with crushed rock or hard packed dirt.

Directions: Take the Island Crest Way exit off I-90, turn right at SE Sixty-Eighth Street, and park in the Park and Ride at the shopping center.

Redmond Watershed

This is an excellent trail for novice mountain bikers because of the smooth, well maintained trails. Ride along the Redmond watershed's 800 acres full of wildlife including deer, rabbits, woodpeckers, beavers, red-tail hawks, blue herons, chipmunks and squirrels.

Directions: Cross SR202 and bear right onto Avondale Rd. Drive for 1.5 miles and stay to the right on Novelty Road. Continue East for 2.5 miles. Park at the Redmond watershed preserve parking lot on the left.

Snoqualmie Valley Trail

www.metrokc.gov/parks/trails/trails/snoqv.htm

The Snoqualmie Valley Trail offers the opportunity to get out and explore one of the most beautiful agricultural valleys in the region. The trail meanders past working farms and well preserved open space areas, and connects to the cross-state John Wayne Pioneer Trail in Iron Horse State Park. Points of interest include the Told-MacDonald Park, Meadowbrook Farm, Three Forks Natural Area and the Tokul Trestle.

Length: 36 miles

Access Points: McCormick Park; Nick Loutsis Park, 356th PL SE, Rattlesnake Lake Recreation Area, NE 4th & Ballarat Ave in North Bend.

Soos Creek Trail

www.metrokc.gov/parks/trails/trails/soos.htm

The Soos Creek Trail features a gentle grade in a natural setting suitable for leisurely strolls, bicycle rides and horse rides. A connection to the Lake Youngs Trail (9 miles, unpaved) can be made along SE 216th St corridor. The trail is 4 miles and paved with soft shoulders.

Access Points: Gary Grant Park at SE 208th and 137th Ave SE, Soos Creek Trailhead at 145th Ave SE between SE 240th St and SE 256th St Meridian, Soos Creek South Trailhead at 152nd Way SE.

Wilburton Hill Park

These trails are ideal for new mountain bikers. The trails are smooth packed dirt or crushed gravel making them ideal for younger mountain bikers. The trails also drain well making them a good choice during the rainy season.

Directions: Take the NE 8th St exit off I-405. Head east and turn right on 124th NE, and continue to the south corner of Main St. Wilburton Park is be on the left.

Snohomish County

Snohomish County Trails

www1.co.snohomish.wa.us/Departments/Parks/default.htm

Centennial Trail

Enormously popular, this 6' wide paved trail is great for walking, bicycling, hiking, and horseback riding. The trail connects Snohomish, Lake Stevens, and Arlington and will eventually will extend to Skagit County. Visit the trailhead and rest stop in the town of Machias which hosts a replica of a railroad depot built in the late 1890s. The depot once served a rail line which today is the Centennial Trail.

Access Points: Snohomish – Intersection of Pine and Maple Street.

Pilchuck, Machias, 20th Street, Lake Stevens, Hwy 92 overpass

Interurban Trail

Bike riders, walkers, joggers, and others enjoy travelling the 11.8 miles of paved surface. Most of the trail is separated from motorized vehicles but there are portions where the trail runs the road shoulder. For this reason sections of the trail is not suitable for kids.

Meadowdale Park

6026 156th SW, Edmonds

This is a short mile long trail that descends down through thick forest to the park boarding the Puget Sound. The Park features a sand volley ball court, pavilion and open grass space. The Park has a nice beach front with great views over the sound. The hike is short enough for most kids to enjoy. Access to the park requires the hike down the trail. There is road access but is only available for those with limited mobility. The trail down to the park is fairly steep during the first quarter mile before it becomes almost entirely level. Small kids will need to be carried.

Lord Hill Regional Park

www1.co.snohomish.wa.us/Departments/Parks/Information/Park_Directory/Regional_Parks/Lord_Hill.htm

Ride Horseback, hike or mountain bike across 6 miles trials and 1,300 acres of evergreen forest. Since the trails are not paved, they are as suitable for younger children on bikes. Bring a picnic and explore a beautiful nature preserve. If you are lucky you may spot beavers building a dam.

Directions: Take the Snohomish-Wenatchee exit off of I-5 onto US2 in Everett. Take the second (east) Snohomish exit off US2, and turn right onto 2nd Ave. Turn left onto Lincoln Ave S which becomes the Old Snohomish-Monroe Hwy, and turn right onto 127th Ave SE. Drive South approximately 2-1/4 miles, then turn left onto 150th St SE and proceed to the park entrance on the left.

Snohomish River Estuary

Everett

The Estuary is located where the Snohomish river meets the Puget Sound. Fresh water mixes with the saltwater and the area is teaming with wildlife. The Estuary features walking and running trails. If you own a Kayak or small boat this is a great place to go for a paddle.

Southwest County Olympic View Park
Olympic View Dr, Edmonds
www1.co.snohomish.wa.us/Departments/Parks/Information/Park_Directory/Combination_Parks/Olympic_View.htm
The Southwest County Park is covers120acres of open space, and encompasses a series of forested ravines, and the Perrinville Creek which flows through the eastern portion of the Park to Brown's Bay on Puget Sound traveling through Lynnwood and Edmonds.

Hiking

Hiking with children can be a rich and rewarding experience for both the parents and especially for the kids. Hiking with children does take extra precautions. Taking a closer look at the weather forcast and making sure you all have the basic in place first is important. Young children have a tendancy to run and play with out looking carefully at the terrain around them. For this reason it is important to pick hiking trail appropriate for you children's age and ability. That being said Washington has so many hikes that are and can be very safe for children that are easy enough for even small kids to manage.

I suggest that if you are not familiar with the hikes mentioned in this book, that you purchase one of the books in the Resources section in this chapter. There you will find more details on these hikes as well as many more hikes suitable for kids.

Ape Cave

Distance: up to 1/2 mile one way
Elevation Gain: 100ft
Difficulty: Easy
Description: These caves are actually the longest intact lava tubs in the United States. Lava flowed through these tubs forming a hard outer shell. When the laval flowed out, the empty cavity remained.

Directions: Located within the Mount Saint Helens National Monument from Randle, drive South on Road No. 25. Turn West on Road No. 90, and drive to Road No. 83 at the South end of the Swift Reservoir. Turn left on Road No. 8303, and continue another 2 miles where you will see the visitor center.

Bridal Veil Falls

Distance: 2 miles one way
Elevation gain: 1000
Difficulty: Better suited for children ages 8+

Directions: Take Hwy 2 towards Steven's Pass until you reach the first Skykomish River bridge. At mile post 35, just before crossing the river the second time, turn right on Mt Index Road and drive .3 miles. Turn into the large parking lot and look for the abandoned logging road. This is where the trail begins.

Boulder River Waterfall

Distance: 1 1/2 miles each way
Elevation gain: 250 feet
Difficulty: Easy
Description: Hike through one of the last low elevation old growth forests. The crest of the hike is only at an elevation of 1,200 feet, so expect warmer temperatures and less snow fall in the winter. This trail hosts some camping spots available at the end of the trail.

Directions: Drive East on Hwy 530 until you've almost reached milepost 41. Turn right on Road No. 2010, pass French Creek Campground, and at 3.6 miles from the highway. At a major switchback, find the Boulder Creek trial elevation 960 feet. The trail begins at the end of an old logging railroad.

Deception Falls Nature Trail

Distance: 1 mile round trip
Elevation gain: 100 feet
Difficulty: Easy
Description: This is an easy walk through old growth lush forest, and moss covered trees. A beautiful waterfall awaits hikes with a mist and spray of water. The trail and observation of the falls are manageable for those in wheel chairs. The parking lot has picnic tables just inside the forest.

Directions: Take Hwy 2 past Skykomish, drive an additional 8 miles, and follow the signs. It's hard to miss.

Iron Goat Trail

Distance: Up to 6 miles
Elevation gain: None
Difficulty: Easy
Description: Take a walk along a part of history as the trail runs down the old steam engine train route of The Great Northern Railroad. Children will love the tunnels and exploring opportunities.

Directions: From Hwy 2, drive East to milepost 55, then turn left onto Road No. 67. Continue 2.1 miles, turn left on Road No. 6710, and drive 1.4 miles to the trailhead.

Lake Elizabeth

360-677-2414 (Skykomish Ranger)

Distance: 1 mile round trip
Elevation gain: None
Difficulty: Easy
Description: You can just spend the day or even camp, fish or swim along this trail perfect for children of all ages. The distance is short enough that you can carry their gear and yours if you decide to back pack and camp.

Directions: From Hwy 2, head East toward Steven's Pass. Turn right between mile-posts 45 and 46 and the Money Creek Campground. Cross the river and drive 1 mile on the Old Cascade Highway, then turn right onto Money Creek Road No. 6420. Drive 7 miles to Lake Elizabeth.

Snoqualmie Tunnel

Distance: Up to 5 miles
Elevation Gain: 100 feet
Difficulty: Easy
Description: Hike through an adventurous old trail tunnel. Be sure to bring plenty of flashlights and sweaters since it does get dark inside and even cold in the summer.

Direction: Head East on I-90 to exit 54, just over the pass. Turn right off the ramp, then immediately turn left. Follow the signs for Iron Horse State Park. Once at Iron Horse, drive ? mile and take a right to reach the trailhead.

Twin Falls

Distance: 1.75 miles one way
Elevation Gain: 300 feet
Difficulty: Easy
Description: Walk through magnificent old growth forest along side the South Fork Snoqualmie River. The walk is worth every bit of the effort once you reach the falls. There is a viewing platform that helps give the best vantage point at the falls.

Directions: Drive East on I-90 to Exit 34 (the Edgewick Rd) and turn right on 468th Avenue SE. Continue 0.6 mile at the road's end.

Camping

Washington is full of wonderful campgrounds more than can be attempted to cover in this book. It seems that every family has their favorites and it is great to talk to neighbors and friends to get new ideas to try. I will attempt to list some resources that will help you find new and wonderful campgrounds in Washington.

National Parks

National Parks Service Website

www.nps.gov

reservations.nps.gov (Camp Reservations)
The National Parks Service has a great website that takes you to wonderful maps and detailed information about the National Parks in the state of Washington. Start by searching through the Parks and Recreation area and you will be able to compare different locations for great outdoor family trips.

Mount Rainer National Park

www.nps.gov/mora/recreation/camping.htm
Mount Rainier National Park encompasses 235,625 acres, ranging in elevation from 1,610' to 14,410' above sea level. The "mountain" is an active volcano encased with over 35 square miles of snow and ice, and surrounded by old growth forest and stunning wildflower meadows. Whether you're looking for scenic drives or challenging hikes, or to enjoy historic architecture or mountain climbing, Mount Rainier has something for you.

Olympic National Park
360-565-3130

www.nps.gov/olym/pphtml/camping.html
Glacier capped mountains, the wild Pacific coast, the temperate rain forest, and magnificent stands of old-growth forests cover the Olympic National Park. About 95% of the park is designated wilderness, which further protects these diverse and spectacular ecosystems.

North Cascades National Park
360-856-5700 x 515 (Camping Information)

www.nps.gov/noca/pphtml/camping.html
The North Cascades have long been known as the North American Alps. Characterized by rugged beauty, this steep mountain range is filled with jagged peaks, deep valleys, cascading waterfalls and glaciers. North Cascades National Park Service Complex contains the heart of this mountainous region in three park units which are all managed as one and include North Cascades National Park, Ross Lake and Lake Chelan National Recreation Areas.

US Forest Service

www.fs.fed.us/recreation/map/state_list.shtml#WashingtonState
www.reserveusa.com (Camp Reservations)
From this site you will be able to search for various campgrounds.

Other Camping Locations

Washington State Parks

www.parks.wa.gov/parks

This is a great site to help find the best park and make reservations.

www.camis.com/WA/camping/maps.asp?map=1

Camp Ki RV Resort

2904 Lakewood Rd, Arlington

360-652-0619

Flowing Lake County Park

17900 48th SE, Snohomish

360-568-2274

Flowing Lake offers a multitude of recreation activities. The campground contains over 30 campsites, most include water and electrical hookups. The ranger staff present interpretive programs in the rustic amphitheater and guided nature walks throughout the summer season. Many picnic tables and picnic shelters are available.

Gold Bar Nature Trails

Maycreek Rd, Gold Bar

(360) 793-1888

Kayak Point Regional Park

15610 Marine Dr, Stanwood

360-652-7992

425-388-6600 (Reservations)

425-388-6601 (Yurt Village)

Features bay and beach access, fishing, a boat launch, forested trails, bayside trails, picnic tables (holds up to 75 people), and public restrooms. Guests can choose between the campsite, YURT Village, or the Kayak Kottage. This is a great site for families, clubs, scouts, churches, and schools.

Lake Connor Park

14320 28th St NE, Lake Stevens

425-334-5055

425-334-5044 (Sales Office)

Tolt MacDonald

31020 NE 40th St, off State Route 203 near Carnation

www.metrokc.gov/parks/rentals/pommay99.htm

Located at the confluence of the Snoqualmie and Tolt Rivers in the beautiful Snoqualmie Valley, this park covers more than 574 acres on both sides of the Snoqualmie River. Features include RV and Tent Camping, a playground for children, hiking, mountain biking trails, and baseball and soccer fields. Tent and RV camping available.

Horseback Riding

Gold Creek Equestrian Center

16528 148th Ave NE, Woodinville

425-806-4653

www.gold-creek.com

Lang's Horse & Pony Farm

21463 Little Mountain Rd, Mt Vernon

360-424-7630

www.comeride.com

Guided trail rides up to 2 hours

Tiger Mountain Outfitters

24508 SE 133rd, Issaquah

425-392-5090

3 Hour Trail Rides in the Tiger Mountain State Forest

Camps

Camp Kiloqua

15207 Goodwin Rd, Stanwood

360-652-9912

Camp Volasuca

617 1st , Sultan

360-793-0646

Cedar Springs Camp

4820 SR 92, Lake Stevens

425-334-6215

Evergreen Academy
16017-118th Pl NE, Bothell
425-488-8000

Evergreen Academy
18670 Woodinville-Duvall Rd Tolt Woodinville
425-788-7575

Hidden Valley Camp Boys & Girls
24314 Hidden Valley Rd, Granite Falls
425-334-1040

Run To Win Outreach
7907 SW 212th St SW, Edmonds
425-776-2946

Warm Beach Christian Camps & Conference Center
20800 Marine Dr, Stanwood
(425) 743-5471

Wolf Camp
28819 Se 82nd ,Monroe
(360) 799-1997

Chapter 3

Community Recreation

Chapter 3

Community Recreation

Throughout the Puget Sound, there are many opportunities for children of all ages to participate in youth, sports, and recreation. Most of the sports programs offered through these community recreation programs are recreational and non-competitive, although some recreation programs do offer competitive leagues.

Community Recreation

Kind County runs a large recreation program with several recreation facilities which offer a range of recreation programs, along with some cities within the county which offer their own recreation programs. It Snohomish County recreation is offered through participating cities. This section was created as a quick reference to compare each center with what each has to offer. I tried to include as many recreation programs in this section as possible, but many centers offer more programs than are listed. If you are interested in every thing each center has to offer, contact them, and they will provide you with seasonal information. Please note that programs and activities change continually, and most programs are seasonal or could be terminated at any time due to the lack of participants.

Program Fees

Fees differ throughout each recreation facility. Many recreation departments offer reduced rates for those with reduced income. Some centers also offer early registration discounts. Others also offer discounts for those who are willing to volunteer, or coach for their programs. Each center can provide the specific fee information for everything they offer.

Parent Involvement/Coaching

Getting involved in your child's sports and activities is crucial to helping them succeed. Recreation departments are always in need of parents to volunteer to coach many of the sports they offer. Two or three hours each week for practice, and games (which you would already be attending), and contacting team members weekly (via e-mail is best) is usually all it takes. You can also team up with friends to help coach a team so you can share the responsibility.

Traditional vs. Non-Traditional Sports & Recreation

The traditional sports such as basketball, baseball, soccer, and football are the most popular sports that most recreation departments offer. However, non-traditional sports are also becoming more popular such as rock climbing, bowling, horseback riding, ski/snow boarding, chess, and lacrosse. It's great to get your child involved in different programs and activities to give them an opportunity to try new things.

Outdoor Activities/Summer Camps

Different centers offer a variety of outdoor activities and summer day camps for children. Their was such a variety, that all these activities were simply listed under outdoor activities. Some centers offer summer day camps which offer multiple weekly field trips to different parks. Others offer outdoor classes like mountain biking, hiking, fishing, and outdoor adventure outings. Contact the centers which offer summer camps/outdoor activities to find more details.

Community Centers

King County

Alki Community Center
5817 SW Stevens St
206-684-7430
www.cityofseattle.net/parks/centers/alkicc.htm
Hours: Monday, Tuesday, Thursday 1:00pm-9:00pm, Wednesday & Friday 10:00am-9:00pm.
Youth Sports: Flag football, indoor soccer, tennis and basketball.
Classes/Activities: Ballet, art, pottery classes, Friday night skate program, before and after school program, Pre-school program

Ballard Community Center

6020 28th Ave NW
206-684-4093
www.cityofseattle.net/parks/centers/ballard.htm
Hours: Monday, Wednesday, Friday 11:00am-9:00pm, Tuesday and Thursday 1:00pm-9:00pm
Youth Sports: T-Ball, Youth Sports Program for ages 5-19 (which sports?)
Classes/Activities: Before and afterschool programs, Pre-school, day camps (K-6th), ballet, pre-ballet, jazz, and dance workshops, piano, pottery, language and nature classes, day camps for children and teens.
Swimming Pool: 1471 NW 67th St, 206-684-4094
Plus: Indoor play area for infants to 5 year olds. $2/day. Closed during the summer. Each year the Center hosts special events, including the Annual Daddy-Daughter Dinner, Spring Egg Hunt, Neighborhood Flea Market, and Friday Family Nights.

Bainbridge Island Park & Recreation

206-842-2306
www.biparks.org
Hours: Monday-Friday 8:30 am -5pm
Youth Sports: Baseball, basketball, volleyball, tennis, track and field soccer, martial arts
Classes/Activities: Youth music and arts classes, science lab, culinary classes, creative writing, pottery, and gymnastics.
Swimming Pool: Indoor Aquatic Center: 206-842-2302

Bitter Lake Community Center

13035 Linden Ave N
206-684-7524
Hours: Monday-Tuesday 1:00pm-9:00pm, Wednesday, Thursday, Friday 11:00am-9:00pm.Open Saturdays during the school year.
Youth Sports: Basketball, football, Nerf soccer, girl's volleyball, roller skating, and tennis lessons.
Classes/Activities: Piano lessons, dance, science, drama, tap, Karate-Butokukan, gymnastics, cooking classes, before and after school programs, Pre-school, grade school, and teen programs, volunteer opportunities, day camps, and family events.
Plus: Outdoor wading pool.

Burien Community Center
425 SW 144th St
206-988-3700
www.ci.burien.wa.us
Hours: Monday-Thursday 9:30am-8:30pm, Friday 9:30am-5:00pm.
Activities: Ballet, Mom & Me dance, gymnastics, karate, a variety of art classes, and after school activities, teen activities, a skate park, yoga, and shows in their auditorium.
Swimming Pool: Indoor: King County Evergreen Pool

Delridge Community Center
4501 Delridge Way SW
206-684-7423
www.cityofseattle.net/parks/centers/delridge.htm
Hours: Monday 1:00pm-9:00pm, Tuesday/Thursday 11:00pm-9:00pm, Friday 1:00-9:00 pm
Classes/Activities: Piano lessons, computer classes, dance classes, teen programs, preschool programs, before and after school programs, and computer literacy.

Des Moines Park & Recreation
1000 S 220th St
206-870-6527
www.cityofseattle.net/parks/centers/
Hours: Monday-Friday 8:00am-4:00pm
Youth Sports: Basketball, baseball, soccer, martial arts, tennis, Li'l Champ sports camp.
Classes/Activities: Ballet, dance, before and after school programs, summer camps, gymnastics, art classes, acrobat.
Swimming Pool: Mount Rainer Pool **206-824-4722**

Garfield Community Center
2323 East Cherry St
206-684-4788
www.cityofseattle.net/parks/centers/garfieldcc.htm
Hours: Monday, Wednesday, Friday 1:00pm-9:00pm, Tuesday/Thursday 10:00am-9:00pm, Saturday 10:00am -5:00pm
Youth Sports: Basketball, Flag football, track and field, t-ball
Classes/Activities: Piano lessons, dance classes
Swimming Pool: Indoor- Medgar Evers pool 500 23rd Ave: 206-684-4766

Garfield Teen Life Center
428 23rd Ave
206-684-4550
www.cityofseattle.net/parks/centers/teenlifecenter.htm
Hours: Monday-Thursday 2:00pm-9:00pm, Friday 2:00pm-11:00pm, Saturday 8:00pm-12:00am
Youth Sports: Basketball, martial arts, circuit training, track and field, flag football
Classes/Activities: Dances, Bar-b-que's
Swimming Pool: Indoor- Medgar Evers Pool 206-684-4766

Green Lake Community Center
7201 E Green Lake Dr N
206-684-0780
www.cityofseattle.net/parks/centers/grnlakcc.htm
Hours: Monday -Friday 10:00am-9:00pm, Saturday 9:00am-5:00pm, Sunday 12:00pm-5:00pm
Youth Sports: Basketball soccer, tennis, volleyball, baseball
Classes/Activities: Chess, dance, music, piano, swim lessons
Swimming Pool: Indoor- Evans pool 206-684-4961

Evans Community Center
206-684-4961
www.cityofseattle.net/parks/centers/
Hours: vary by season
Classes/Activities: Swim Lessons
Swimming Pool: Indoor

Hiawatha Community Center

2700 California Ave SW
206-684-7441
www.cityofseattle.net/parks/centers/hiawatha.htm
Hours: Monday/Tuesday 1:00pm-9:00pm, Wednesday-Friday 11:00am-9:00pm, Saturday 10:00am-5:00pm, Sunday 12:00pm-5:00pm
Youth Sports: N/A
Classes/Activities: Pre-school, before and after school programs
Swimming Pool: Outdoor wading pool

High Point Community Center

6920 34th Ave SW
206-684-7422
www.cityofseattle.net/parks/centers/highpt.htm
Hours: Monday 1:00pm-9:00pm, Tuesday-Friday 11:00am-9:00pm
Youth Sports: Basketball, t-ball, volleyball, indoor soccer, tennis Flag football, track
Classes/Activities: Ballet, creative dance, hip-hop, Before and after school program
Swimming Pool: Use Southwest Community Center Pool, and Coleman Pool during the summer

International District/Chinatown Community Center'

719 8th Ave S
206-233-0042
www.cityofseattle.net/parks/centers/IDChinatown.htm
Hours: Monday, Wednesday, Friday 11:00am-9:00pm Tuesday/Thursday 1:00pm-9:00pm
Youth Sports: Basketball, Volleyball, martial arts
Classes/Activities: Cultural events and classes, open gym

Jefferson Community Center-Seattle

3801 Beacon Ave S
206-684-7481
www.cityofseattle.net/parks/centers/jeffercc.htm
Hours: Monday/Friday 1:00pm-10:00pm, Wednesday1:00pm-9:00pm Tuesday/Thursday 10:00am-9:00pm
Youth Sports: T-ball, Tennis, Soccer, Basketball
Classes/Activities: Dance, pottery, teen programs

Langston Hughes Performing Arts Center
104 17th Ave S
206-684-4757
www.cityofseattle.net/parks/centers/langston.htm
Hours: Monday-Friday 10:30am-8:30pm, Saturday 9:30am -1:30pm
Classes/Activities: Dance, theatre, music and art classes

Laurelhurst Community Center
4554 NE 41st St
206-684-7529
www.cityofseattle.net/parks/centers/laurelcc.htm
Hours: Monday, Wednesday, Friday 11:00am-9:00pm, Tuesday/Thursday 1:00pm-9:00pm
Youth Sports: T-ball, Tennis, soccer Basketball
Classes/Activities: Toddler play area, music, art and dance

Magnolia Community Center
2550 34th Ave W
206-386-4235
www.cityofseattle.net/parks/centers/magnoliacc.htm
Hours: Monday, Tuesday, Friday 1:00pm-9:00pm, Wednesday/Thursday 10:00am-9:00pm
Youth Sports: Gymnastics, Tennis
Classes/Activities: Before and after school programs, Dance, music and pottery

Magnuson Community Center
7110 62nd Avenue NE
206-684-7026
www.cityofseattle.net/parks/centers/magnuson.htm
Hours: Monday-Wednesday 10:00am-6:00pm, Thursday/Friday 10:00am-9:00pm
Youth Sports: Fencing, volleyball, basketball
Classes/Activities: Dance, outdoor nature camps and day and summer camps

Meadowbrook Community Center
10517 35th Ave NE
206-684-7522
www.cityofseattle.net/parks/centers/meadowbrookcc.htm
Hours: Monday, Wednesday, Friday 1:00pm-9:00pm, Tuesday/Thursday 10:00am-9:00pm
Youth Sports: T-ball, baseball, karate, tennis, Nerf soccer flag football, volleyball
Classes/Activities: Swim lessons, art, creative dance, pre-school, culinary classes, sign language
Swimming Pool: Indoor

Loyal Heights Community Center
2101 77th St
206-684-4052
www.cityofseattle.net/parks/centers/loyalhtd.htm
Hours: Monday, Wednesday, Friday 1:00pm-9:00pm Tuesday/Thursday 10:00am-9:00pm
Youth Sports: Basketball
Classes/Activities: Preschool, summer day camps, and teen programs

Miller Community Center
330 19th Ave E
206-684-4753
www.cityofseattle.net/parks/centers/miller.htm
Hours: Monday, Wednesday, Friday, 1:00pm-9:00pm, Tuesday/Thursday 10:00am-9:00pm, Saturday 10:00am-5:00pm
Youth Sports: T-ball, Karate, basketball, tennis
Classes/Activities: Help tutoring, computer lab, before and after school programs

Montlake Community Center
1618 Calhoun St
206-684-4736
www.cityofseattle.net/parks/centers/montlakecc.htm
Hours: Monday, Wednesday, Friday 11:00am-9:00pm, Tuesday/Thursday 1:00pm-9:00pm
Youth Sports: Nerf soccer, basketball, t-ball, baseball
Classes/Activities: Pottery, sports camps, before and after school programs

Phinney Neighborhood Association
6532 Phinney Ave N, Seattle
206-783-2244
www.Phinneycenter.org
Hours: Monday-Friday 9:00am-10:00pm, Saturday 9:00am-2:00pm
Youth Sports: Martial arts, kick boxing, karate
Classes/Activities: Kindermusik, dance, sign-language, pre-school (co-op) Before and after school programs, all-day camps during school breaks.
Plus: Annual Halloween Carnival, Fall Concert Series, Winter Festival, Crafts Fair.

Queen Anne Community Center
1901 First Ave W
206-386-4240/284-5180?
www.cityofseattle.net/parks/centers/queenannecc.htm
Hours: Monday-Friday 9:00am -9:00pm
Youth Sports: Basketball
Classes/Activities: Ballet, pre-school, before and after school program play gym, baby toddler room
Swimming Pool: Queen Anne Pool 206-386-4282

Ranier Beach Community Center
8825 Ranier Ave S
206-386-1925
www.cityofseattle.net/parks/centers/ranierbeach.htm
Hours: Monday-Wednesday 1:00pm-9:00pm, Thursday/Friday 11:30am-9:00pm, Saturday 10:00am-5:00pm, Sunday 12:00pm-5:00pm
Youth Sports: Flag Football, basketball, track, girl's softball, girl's volleyball, martial arts
Classes/Activities: Dance, before and after school programs, daycare program, community tech center
Swimming Pool: Indoor - 206-386-1944

Ranier Community Center
4600 38th Ave S
206-386-1925
www.cityofseattle.net/parks/centers/raniercc.htm
Hours: Monday/Friday 1:00-9:00pm, Tuesday/Thursday 11:00am-9:0pm, Saturday 10:00am-5:00pm
Late night hours Friday/Saturday 7:00pm-11:00pm
Youth Sports: Basketball, martial arts
Classes/Activities: Rhythmic gymnastics, before and after school programs, indoor play ground

Ravenna-Eckstein Community Center
6535 Ravenna Ave NE
206-684-7534
www.cityofseattle.net/parks/centers/ravennaecksteincc.htm
Hours: Monday &Wednesday 10:00am-9:00pm, Tuesday, Thursday, Friday 1:00pm-9:00pm
Youth Sports: T-ball, coach pitch baseball, flag football, track, volleyball
Classes/Activities: Indoor toddler play area, day camps, art, ballet, piano lessons

Southpark Community Center
8319 Eighth Ave S
206-684-7451
www.cityofseattle.net/parks/centers/southpakr.htm
Hours: Monday-Thursday 12:00pm -9:00pm, Friday 11:00am-11:00pm, Saturday 1:00pm-9:00pm
Youth Sports: Tennis, soccer, volleyball, flag football, basketball, soccer, track, football
Classes/Activities: Before and after school programs, technology center
Swimming Pool: Outdoor- Summer wading pool 206-684-7796
Indoor- Rainer Beach Pool 206-386-1944, Southwest Pool

Southwest Community Center

2801 SW Thistle St
206-684-7438
www.cityofseattle.net/parks/centers/swcc.htm
Hours: Monday & Wednesday 10:00am-9:00pm, Tuesday, Thursday, Friday 1:00pm-9:00pm
Youth Sports: basketball, martial arts
Classes/Activities: Before and after school programs, summer day camps, swim lessons
Swimming Pool: Indoor – 206-684-7440

SeaTac Recreation Department

206-973-4630
www.cityofseattle.net/parks/centers/
Hours: Monday-Thursday 8:00am-10:00pm, Friday 8:00am-7:00pm, Saturday 10:00am-4:00pm (Oct-March)
Youth Sports: Karate, basketball, soccer, baseball, softball
Classes/Activities: Preschool, dance classes, special

Tukwila Community Center

12424 42nd Ave S
206-768-2822
www.cityofseattle.net/parks/centers/
Hours: Monday-Friday 6:15am – 9:00pm, Saturday 8:00am-4:00pm
Youth Sports: Martial arts, tumbling, trampoline, gymnastics, basketball, tennis, soccer, skate park
Classes/Activities: Before and after school programs, preschool, dance, art pottery, golf clinics and swim lessons
Swimming Pool: Indoor 4414 S 144th: **206-267-2350**

Van Asselt Community Center

2829 S Myrtle St
206-386-1921
www.cityofseattle.net/parks/centers/vanasseltcc.htm
Hours: Monday, Wednesday, Friday 11:00am-9:00pm, Tuesday/Thursday 1:00pm-9:00pm
Classes/Activities: Play fields, tennis courts, youth and teen programs, after school programs
Swimming Pool: Outdoor- wading pool **206-684-7796**

Yesler Community Center
917 E Yessler Way
206-386-1245
www.cityofseattle.net/parks/centers/yeslercc.htm
Hours: Monday, Wednesday, Friday 1:00pm-9:00pm, Tuesday/Thursday 10:00am-9:00pm
Youth Sports: Flag football, volleyball, basketball
Classes/Activities: Teen programs, after school program, Summer day camps, culinary classes

Snohomish County

Mountlake Terrace Community Center
425-776-9173
www.ci.mountlake-terrace.wa.us/departments/parks/index.html
Youth Sports: triathlon training, volleyball, wallyball, basketball, sports leagues
Classes/Activities: dance, indoor playground for preschoolers, before and after school programs, day camps, lifeguard training (ages 15+), lifeguard skills (11-14), CPR & First Aid (11-14), babysitting basics
Swimming Pool: Indoor at Mountlake Terrace Recreation Pavilion

Rosehill Community Center
4480 Chennault Beach Rd, Mukilteo
425-355-1514
Hours:
Youth Sports:
Classes/Activities:
Swimming Pool: Indoor or Outdoor

Recreation Centers

Snohomish County

Edmonds Parks & Recreation & Cultural Services Department
425-771-0230
Youth Sports: gymnastics, basketball, volleyball, yoga, soccer
Classes/Activities: babysitting basics, dance, pottery, painting, drawing, piano, art, etiquette, baby signing, Spanish, scrapbooking, sewing, knitting, outdoor recreation.

Everett Parks & Recreation

signmeup.everettwa.org
Youth Sports: gymnastics, tennis, karate, rock climbing, rowing
Classes/Activities: dance, outdoor recreation, orienteering, guitar, gun safety, musical theatre, piano, Taiko drumming, babysitting basics, ballet, preschool, day camps.
Classes/Activities:

Lynnwood Recreation Center

18900 44th Ave W, Lynnwood
425-771-4030
Youth Sports: gymnastics, cheerleading, soccer, multi-sport camps, Taekwondo, self-defense
Classes/Activities: music, cooking, ballet, art, puppet making, sculpture, painting, cartooning, sewing, beading, wood carving, babysitting basics.
Swimming Pool: Indoor/Winter, Outdoor/Summer

Marysville Parks & Recreation

360-363-8400
Youth Sports: tennis, soccer, basketball, junior golf
Classes/Activities: summer camps

Mill Creek Parks & Recreation

425-745-1891
425-921-5737
www.cityofmillcreek.com/parksrec
Youth Sports: martial arts, skyhawks sports camps, gymnastics
Classes/Activities: cooking, arts & crafts, gardening, music, theatre

Swimming Pools

King County- Indoor pools- Ballard Pool **206-684-4094**

Evans Pool- **206-684-4961**

Forest Park Swim Center- **425-257-8309**

Lynnwood Recreation Pool- **425-775-1971**

Medgar Evers Pool- **206-684-4766**

Madison Pool- **206-684-4979**

Meadow Brook Pool-
206-684-4989

Queen Anne Pool-
206-386-4282

Rainer Beach Pool-
206-386-1944

Southwest Pool-
206-684-7440

Outdoor Pools: Coleman Pool- **206-684-7494**

Mounger Pool **206-684-4708**

Mountlake Terrace Recreation **Pavilion-425-776-9173**

Snohomish County- McCollum County Park Pool **425-357-6036**

Youth Organizations & Centers

King County

Girls Club of Puget Sound
708 Martin Luther King Jr Way, Seattle
206-720-6428

Snohomish County

Alderwood Boys & Girls Club
19719-24th Ave W, Lynnwood
425-774-3022
www.abgcsnoco.org
Hours: Mon-Fri 6:15 am- 6:15 pm Sat 10am- 2pm
Youth Sports: Soccer, Basketball, Volleyball
Classes/Activities: Before and after school program, drop-in program, teen center, computer lab, Martial arts, culinary classes, art, photography, summer day camps.

Boy Scouts Of America- Mt. Baker Council
1715 100th Pl SE, Everett
425-338-0380
Classes: Full Scouting Program and supply store.

Boys & Girls Clubs-King County
www.positiveplace.org/locations.htm
Federal Way: 253-941-2722
IWASIL (Seattle): 206-325-3942
Kirkland: 425-827-0132
Mercer Island: 206-232-4548
North Seattle: 206-784-5396
Rainier Vista (Seattle): 206-725-4197
Redmond/Sammamish: 425-936-9295
Skyway: 206-957-2754
Southwest (Seattle): 206-762-3221
Wallingford: 206-547-7261
Youth Sports: Baseball, basketball, football, Martial arts, Soccer, t-ball, and volleyball.
Classes/Activities: Before and after school programs, computer lab, culinary classes, drop-in programs, fine arts, photography, summer day camps, teen centers, and more.

Boys & Girls Clubs: Snohomish County

www.bgcsnoco.org
Alderwood: 425-774-3022
Arlington: 360-435-4442
Edmonds: 425-774-0630
Everett: 425-259-5147
Granite Falls: 360-691-1300
Lake Stevens: 425-377-0250
Monroe: 360-794-4775
Mukilteo: 425-355-2773
South Everett/Mukilteo: 425-355-6899
Snohomish: 360-568-7760
Sultan: 360-793-2515
Tulalip: 360-651-3400

Youth Sports: Baseball, basketball, football, Martial arts, Soccer, t-ball, and volleyball.

Classes/Activities: Before and after school programs, computer lab, culinary classes, drop-in programs, fine arts, photography, summer day camps, teen centers, and more.

Camp Fire USA- Snohomish County Council

4312 Rucker Ave, Everett
425-258-5437
Classes: Year-round clubs and camps.

Girls Scout-Totem Council

7100 Evergreen way Suite C, Everett
425-348-6244
877-377-0171
800-767-6845 (Main Office)
www.girlscoutstotem.org
Classes/Activities: Girl scouting club and camps

Granite Falls Community Coalition

204 W Stanley, Granite Falls
360-691-1121
www.gfallscoalition.org
Classes/Activities: Community resource center to prevent and treat addiction, Adolescent / family counseling

Sno-King Youth Club
700 Main, Edmonds
425-775-2633
www.skyc.net
Activities: Soccer, Basketball, Baseball, Softball

YMCA of Snohomish County
Everett Family Branch
2720 Rockefeller Ave
425-258-9211
www.ymca-snoco.org
Hours: Mon-Fri 5am -9pm Sat 8am-6pm Sun 12pm-5pm
Youth Sports: Basketball T-ball, Soccer, floor hockey, volleyball, cheerleading
Classes/Activities: Before and after school programs, swim lessons, pre-school
Swimming Pool: 2 indoor pools

YMCA Mukilteo Family Branch
10601 47th Pl W
425-353-9622
Hours: Mon-Fri 5am -9pm Sat 8am-6pm Sun 12pm-5pm
Youth Sports: Basketball, t-ball, Indoor and Outdoor soccer
Classes/Activities: swim lessons, skate park, before and after school programs
Swimming Pool: Outdoor pool during summer.

YMCA Monroe Family Branch
110 S Lewis St
360-805-1879
Hours: Mon, Wed, Fri 8am -5pm Tues/Thurs 8am-2pm
Youth Sports: T-ball, soccer, and Skyhawks programs
Classes/Activities: Before and after school programs, fitness classes

YMCA Marysville Family Branch
6420-60th Dr NE
360-653-9622
Hours: Mon-Fri 5am-10pm Sat 8am-6pm Sun 12-5pm
Youth Sports: Basketball, T-ball, Outdoor soccer, floor hockey, tumbling
Classes/Activities: Before and after school programs, fitness classes, swim lessons, scrap booking, book clubs
Swimming Pool: Indoor

YMCA Southeast Family Brach
13723 Puget Park Dr SE, Everett
425-629-4067
Hours: Mon-Fri 5:30 am- 9:30 pm Sat 8am-6pm
Youth Sports: Basketball, Floor hockey, t-ball, outdoor soccer, kickball
Classes/Activities: Gymnastics, parent/toddler creative dance, before and after school programs, teen programs
Swimming Pool: Outdoor- summer use only

Chapter 4

Sports

Chapter 4

Sports

Remember The Golden Rule…Do unto others as you would have others do to you! Whether you are the athlete or spectator, sports are the perfect venue to put into practice this timeless rule. When it comes to good sportsmanship, it's up to the parents to set the example and lay the foundation. The JR.NBA/JR.WNBA states "make it clear that every game has a winner and a loser (and sometimes, events transpire that may seem unfair). There is a right way and a wrong way to behave prior to, during, and after the game, regardless of the outcome". Remember to refrain from criticizing the coach, opponents, and referees.

A good idea, recommended in an article entitled, "Teaching Good Sportsmanship" by Carleton Kendrick found on **www.familyeducation.com** , is for either the coach, or parents, to have each child sign a Good Sportsmanship contract. This contract could entail "no cheating, no losing one's temper, no negative criticism of teammates, coaches, referees, or opposing players, no blaming teammates for mistakes or poor team performance, no taunting, and to congratulate opposing team".

I love this comment, also made by the JR.NBA/JR.WNBA league, "The real test of character is always more apparent in times of difficulty. Help your child through your own responsible leadership. They will benefit over the long-term the lessons they learn, both in (sports) and in life.

Always remember to:

- Praise their accomplishments.
- Teach the kids how to learn from their mistakes without embarrassing them.
- Turn everything into a positive experience: "If you hadn't thrown the ball in so quickly after you missed it, they would have scored a run."
- Win or lose, sit all the kids down on the bench and point out at least one specific thing worthy of praise that each child did during the game.

(www.familyeducation.com)

Safety Tips

- Warm Up
- Wear appropriate head gear, gloves, and pads
- Helmets should have a fit snug and not tilt forward or backward. Foam fittings may be needed
- Drink plenty of fluids

Team Sports

Baseball-King County

Baseball

Big League Connection
15015 NE 90th Street, Bldg. 3, Redmond
425-885-2862 (Reservations for: group/team event, lesson, party, or batting cages.)

20,000 square feet of Baseball and Softball "Training Heaven". This includes 6,800 square feet practice field with a portable mound for all levels, sliding pad, and safety screens.

Summer Camps: Ages 8-13. Indoor and outdoor baseball. Monday-Thursday 9:30am-3:00pm. Lunch is provided. Summer camps also available at the Woodinville Baseball Field.

Specialties: 1 on 1 training year round. Learn to throw new pitches and improve mechanics.

Eastlake Little League
Redmond
425-868-1004

Highline E Little League
14649 16th S, SeaTac
206-243-9229

Issaquah Little League
Issaquah
425-391-9747

Kenmore Little League
Bothell
425-485-6421

Kent Little League
Kent
253-872-3848

Maple Valley Pony Baseball
Renton
425-226-9108

Northwest Christian Sports League (NCSL)
www.ncsl.cc

North Kenmore Little League
Bothell
425-481-1618

Northshore Little League
Bothell
425-486-7333

Northwest Baseball Academy
425-482-6922

Seattle Mariners Baseball Club
Seattle
206-346-4001

Tahoma Little League
Maple Valley
425-433-1333

Washington State Baseball Academy
Auburn
253-333-2158

Woodinville West Little League
425-481-2846

Baseball-Snohomish County

Everett Aqua Sox Baseball Club
3802 Broadway, Everett
425-258-3673

Kenmore Little League
425-485-6421

Mountlake Terrace Youth Athletic Association (MTYAA)
www.mtyaa.org

Northwest Christian Sports League (NCSL)
www.ncsl.cc

North Everett Little League
2434 State St, Everett
425-258-3149

North Kenmore Little League
425-481-1618

Northshore Little League
14400 NE 145th St, Bothell
425-486-7333

Northwest Baseball Academy
425-482-6922

Sno-Valley North Little League
425-844-1991

South Everett Little League
6515 Morgan Rd, Everett
425-335-0112

South Snohomish Little League
425-337-6207

Woodinville West Little League
425-481-2846

Basketball

JR.NBA & JR.WNBA Leagues:

Bellevue Parks & Community Services
425-452-5294

Northshore YMCA-Bothell
425-485-9797

Covington Community Center
253-639-1775

Fairchild Air Foce Base
509-247-5601

B&GC of Snohomish County-Lynnwood
425-258-2436 x2

JCC of Mercer Island
206-232-7115

Redmond/Sammamish B&GC
425-836-9295

Ballard B&GC
206-783-5775

Northwest Christian Sports League (NCSL)
www.ncsl.cc

Seattle Parks & Recreation
206-684-7091

Rainier Vista Boys &Girls Club
206-725-4197

Arlington Junior Football Association
www.eteamz.com/eagleyouthfootball

Auburn Junior Football Association
www.eteamz.com/ajf

Cascade Junior Football League-Bellevue
www.eteamz.com/cjfl

Edmonds Cyclones Jr. Football
www.eteamz.com/edmondscyclones

Interbay Football Club- Seattle
www.eteamz.com/InterbayFootballClub

Lake City Junior Football
www.eteamz.com/lcjrfootball

Lakewood Youth Football Association
www.eteamz.com/lyfa2000

Maple Valley Junior Football
425-432-2428

Mountlake Terrace Youth Athletic Association (MTYAA)
www.mtyaa.org

Mukilteo Junior Football
www.eteamz.com/mukilteojrfootball

Puget Sound Junior Football League
www.psjfl.org/welcome.htm

Richmond Jr. Football Bantams Blue-Mountlake Terrace
www.eteamz.com/richmondbantamblue

Sliver Lake Football Association-Everett
www.eteamz.com/silverlakefootball

Woodinville Junior Football-Snohomish
www.eteamz.com/wjfa

Washington Youth Sports Association

Youth Football Association
www.eteamz.com

Hockey

Arena Sports Magnusen
7400 Sandpoint Way NE, Seattle
206-985-8990
www.arenasports.net

See ad in back

Everett Youth Hockey
www.everetteventscenter.com/IceRink/Hockey/youthhockeyleagues.ashx?p=59
Ages: 5-16

Seattle Junior Hockey
22202-70th Ave W, Mountlake Terrace
425-672-7744

Seattle Junior Hockey Association
7012-220th SW, Mountlake Terrace
425-771-2006

Sno-King Amateur Hockey Association
425-821-7133
www.snokinghockey.com

Western Washington Female Hockey Association (WWFHA)
15600 NE 8th St Suite B1, Bellevue
(425) 641-3265
www.wwfha.com
Ages: 8 and older

Highland Ice Arena
18005 Aurora Ave N, Shoreline
206-546-2431

Lynnwood Ice Center
19803 68th Ave W, Lynnwood
425-775-7512

Olympic View Arena
22202 70th Ave W, Mountlake Terrace
425-672-9012

Kingsgate Arena
14326 124th Ave NE, Kirkland
425-823-1242

Castle Ice Arena
12620 164th Ave SE, Renton
425-254-8750
See ad in back

Kent Arena
6015 S 240th St, Kent
253-850-2400

Lacrosse

Washington Boys Youth Leagues
www.walax.com

Olympic Conference-Western Division

Lynnwood Lacrosse Club
mathomas@wellfargo.com

Lynnwood
teddg@seanet.com

Mukilteo
mukilteo_laxx@hotmail.com

North Seattle
rshiplett@remax.net

Northshore
wattwiz@comcast.net

Overlake
johnwiley@overlake.org

Snohomish Lacrosse Club
ethanj@msn.com

Stanwood Lacrosse
stanwoodlacrosse@hotmail.com

Cascade Conference-Central Division

Bellevue Lacrosse Club
bellevuelacrosse@yahoo.com

Mercer Island 5/6
bcreswell@nwcap.com

Mercer Island 7/8
caseyellis@comcast.net

Lakeside
Harry.Ostrander@usbank.com

Queen Anne
matt@lakeview-mortgage.com

Casacde Conference - Eastern Division

Eastlake
DavidF@jensenfey.com

Eastlake
jaanderson@lwsd.org

Issaquah
scott-wiley@comcast.net

Maple Valley
macornelison@netzero.net

Warrior Lacrosse Camps for Boys
800-944-7112

University of Washington
www.laxcamps.com
Grades 3-12, includes 15 minutes private sessions during the week. Choose between overnight and extended day camps.

Seattle Rugby Club
www.seattlerfc.org/youthcamp.aspx
The Seattle Rugby Club offers camps for children and youth ages 4-14, on Sunday afternoons March-May.

South Youth Rugby
11405 NE 111th Place
Kirkland, Was 98033
www.natashap@microsoft.com

Volleyball

Puget Sound Volleyball Assoc
6902 220th St SW, Mountlake Terrace
425-673-4103

Soccer

Arlington Soccer Club
360-435-4703

Boomer's Arlington Indoor Soccer Dome
19805 74th Ave NE, Arlington
360-435-7086

Everett Soccer Dome
2201 California St, Everett
425-339-2622

Li'l Kickers
Silver Lake Columbia Athletic Club, Mill Creek
505 129th St SE, Everett
206-985-8990
Ages: 18 months - 9 years

Marysville Youth Soccer Club
360-653-5119

Mukilteo Youth Soccer Club
425-745-4499

Northwest Christian Sports League (NCSL)
www.ncsl.cc

Northshore Youth Soccer Association
23718 Bothell-Everett Hwy, Bothell
425-486-5106

Northwest Nationals Select Soccer Club
425-357-1687

Premier Development Club
425-513-5591

Silver Lake Soccer Club
425-481-2665

Snohomish County Soccer (12 different Associations in Snohomish County)
2418 California St, Everett
425-252-2099
425-775-2633
www.ncyouthsoccer.com
www.fkyc.net

Snohomish Soccer Dome
511 Maple Ave, Snohomish
360-568-6812

Snohomish Youth Soccer
25 Pine Ave, Snohomish
360-568-2577

Strictly Soccer
360-863-9487
www.strictlysoccer.com
Indoor coed soccer classes for children ages 2 -10. Customized year-round instruction is also available for home schools, team training, and adult clinics.

Washington State Soccer Association
7802 NE Bothell Way, Bothell
425-485-7855

Woodinville Indoor Soccer
12728 178th St, Woodinville
425-481-5099

Sports Leagues

Alderwood Little League
19711 24th Ave. W, Lynnwood
425-775-5437

Northwest Christian Sports League
PMB 673 13300 Bothell-Everett Hwy, Lynnwood
425-743-3067
www.ncsl/cc

Washington Cultural Exchange
15401-63rd Ave NE, Kenmore
425-488-0456
www.littleleague.org

Solo Sports

Aircraft Schools

Northwest Aviation College
Auburn
259-939-4960
800-246-4960
www.afsnac.com/af1.html
FAA Approved

Regal Air
Paine Field, Everett
800-337-0345
www.regalair.com/flightschool/our_fleet.asp
FAA Approved

Blue Bound
www.bluebound.com/states/Washington/flying.htm
List of local flight schools in Washington State.

Boating Instruction

ProCAPTAINS
3010 77th Ave SE, Mercer Island
206-236-0099
www.procaptains.com

Seattle Parks & Recreation-Green Lake Small Craft Center
5900 W Green Lake Way N, Seattle
206-684-4074

Mount Baker Rowing & Sailing Center
3800 Lake Washington Blvd, Seattle
206-386-1913

Seattle Sailing Club
7001 Seaview Ave NW, Seattle
206-782-5100

Chess

Chessmates Foundation
2208 NW Market, Seattle
206-789-9614

Seattle Chess Foundation
206-852-8738
www.seattlechessfoundation.com

The Seattle Chess Club
www.seattlechessclub.org

U.S. Chess Federation
www.nwchess.com

Cycling

Cascade Bicycle Club Education Foundation
P.O. Box 15165, Seattle
206-523-1952
www.cascade.org/Education/kidsrides.cfm
This club has a special youth section dedicated to bicycle safety and skill building. Activities include bicycling camps, basic skills class, Sprocket Hero Assembly Program (for schools), and bike safe rodeos. They also have resources for low cost and donated helmets. Youth can sign up for the Kid's Ride Series. For this, parents must accompany their child(ren) on the 5-10 mile bike ride. Helmets must be worn!

Fencing

Rain City Fencing Center
12368 Northup Way, Bellevue
425-497-8897

Golf

King County

Auburn Golf Course
29630 Green River Rd SE, Auburn
253-833-2350
Summer Junior Golf Camp: Ages 10-17
Private Lessons: Ages 5-17

Bellevue Municipal Golf Course
5500 140th Ave NE, Bellevue
425-452-7250
www.cityofbellevue.org
Junior Camps: Ages 10-17
Private lessons: Ages 13-17

Carnation Golf Course
1810 W Snoqualmie River Rd NE, Carnation
425-333-4151
www.pnjga.com
Basic Golf Lessons: Ages 4 - 18.

Cascade Golf Course
14303 436th Ave SE, North Bend
425-888-0227
www.cascadegolfcourse.com
Junior golf program: Ages 7-17

Druids Glen
29925 207th Ave SE, Kent
253-638-1200
www.druidsglengolf.com
Summer Junior Clinic: Ages 6 - 17

Enumclaw Golf Course
45220 288th Ave SE, Enumclaw
360-825-2827
Summer Junior Camp: Ages 10-14, Private Lessons: Any age
Private lessons: Any age.

Golf Club at Newcastle – Coal Creek Course
15500 Six Penny Lane, Newcastle
425-793-5566
www.newcastlegolf.com
Junior Camp: Ages 6-14
Private lessons: Any age

InterBay Family Golf Course
2501 15th Ave W, Seattle
206-285-2200
www.premiergc.com
Golf Lessons: Ages 6 & up,
Junior Golf Camp (summer only): Ages: 6-9
Ages: 10-17
Competition Group: Ages10-17

Jackson Park Golf Course
1000 NE 135th, Seattle
206-363-4747
www.premiergc.com
Beginners class "Little Linkers": Ages 8-11
Summer Golf Camp for Juniors: Ages 6-16
Beginners Class: Ages 9-13
Advanced Class: Ages 9-17

Jade Green Golf Club
18330 SE Lake Holm Road, Auburn
253-931-8562
Private Lessons: Ages 6-9
Private Lessons: Ages10+ 6 lessons
Summer Golf Camps: Age 6-16 yrs

Mt. Si Golf Course
Boalch Ave SE, Snoqualmie
425-391-4926
www.mtsigolf.com
Lessons: Ages 5-17
Special Junior Program: Ages 5-17 Available year round.
Summer Camps: Ages 6-17
*Free Spring Golfing: "Clubs for Kids" provides clubs for 3 hours of free golfing.

Riverbend Golf Complex
2020 W Meeker Ave, Kent
253-854-3673
www.cityofkent.com
Free Saturday Clinics: Ages 6-17
Year-Round Golf Camps: Ages 6-14

Twin River Golf Course
4446 Preston Fall City Rd SE, Fall City
425-222-7575
Private Lessons: All ages
Group lessons: All ages
Junior Summer Golf Camp: Ages 7 to 17

Willows Run Golf Club
10402 Willows Road NE, Redmond
425-883-1200
Private Lessons:
Junior Summer Golf Camp: Ages 6-17

Snohomish County

Battle Creek Public Golf Course
6006 Meridian Ave N, Marysville
360-659-7931
www.battlecreeklinks.com
Group Golf Lessons: Ages 8-17
Includes putting, chipping, full swing, etiquette, & rules.
Private Golf Lessons: Ages 8-17y

Blue Boy West Golf Course
27927 Florence Acres Rd, Monroe
360-793-2378
Junior Summer Golf Clinic: Ages 7-17

Cedarcrest Golf Course
6810 84th St NE, Marysville
360-659-4566
www.ci.marysville.wa.us
18 Hole Championship Golf Course
Private Lessons: 10+
Junior Camps: 8+

Echo Falls Country Club
20414 121st Ave SE, Snohomish
206-362-3000
www.echofalls.com
Private Lessons: Ages 6-18
Summer Junior Camp: Ages 6-18

Everett Municipal Golf Courses
144 Marine View Dr, Everett
425-259-4653
www.legionmemorialgolf.com
Junior Players Club: Instruction for children of all ages.

Greens at Lobo Ridge
12015 84th St SE, Snohomish
360-568-1638
www.grassrootsjrgolf.org
This unique 9-hole golf course is dedicated specifically to Junior Golf! 5-18 years.
Group Instruction:. (7-13 yrs).
Focus: Life skills such as: etiquette, also golf putting, chipping, full swing, and fun.

Harbor Pointe Golf Club
11817 Harbour Pt. Blvd., Mukilteo
425-355-6060
www.harbourpointegolf.com
Golf Lessons: Ages 8-17

Kayak Point Golf Course
15711 Marine Dr, Stanwood
360-652-9676
www.kayakpoint.com
Summer Junior Golf Camps: Ages 7-11, & 12-17
Private Lessons: Ages 7-17

Lynnwood City Golf Course
20200 68th Ave W, Lynnwood
425-672-4653
www.lynnwoodgolf.com
Junior "Learn to Play" Program: Ages 11-17
Junior Camp: Ages 8-17

Nile Shrine Golf Course
6601 244th St SE, Mountlake Terrace
425-776-5154
www.nilegolf.com
Private Lesson: Ages 7-17
Golf Camp: 7-17

Golf Driving Ranges

King County

InterBay Golf Center
2501 15th Ave W, Seattle
206-285-2200
www.premiergc.com
Lessons: Ages 6+
Junior Camps: Ages 6-9
Competition Group: Ages 10-17 yrs

Jade Greens Public Golf Course
18330 SE Lake Holm Rd, Auburn
253-931-8562
Private Lessons: Ages 6-9
Private Lessons: Ages 10+
Summer Golf Camps: Ages 6-16

Jefferson Park Golf Club
4101 Beacon S, Seattle
206-762-4513
www.premiergc.com
Private Lessons: Ages 5+
Also available: Kid's Camps, and Junior Clinics.

Maplewood Golf Course
4050 Maple Valley Hwy, Renton
425-430-6800
www.ci.renton.wa.us.
Private Lessons: Ages 7+
Group Lessons: 7+
Camps: Ages 7-17

Mt. Si Golf Course & Driving Range
9010 Boalch Ave SE, Issaquah
425-391-4926
www.mtsigolf.com

Redwood Golf Center Inc
13029 Woodinville-Redmond Rd NE, Redmond
425-869-8814
Private Lessons: Ages 7 to 17
Group lessons: Ages 7-17
Golf Camp for Children: 7-17

Southcenter Golf
18791 Southcenter Pkwy, Tukwila
206-575-7797
www.southcentergolf.com
Junior Golfers: Ages 6-17
Summer Junior Golf Camps:
Free Golfing: Saturdays at 10:00am and 11:00pm

University of Washington Golf Range
206-543-8759
depts.washington.edu/ima/
Private Lessons: Call for information
Group Lessons: 7-16

Willows Run Golf Course
10402 Willows Rd, Redmond
425-883-1200
www.willowsrun.com
Private Lessons: Ages 6-17
Junior Summer Golf Camps: Ages 6-17

Snohomish County

Columbia Super Range
511-128th SE, Everett
425-338-2424
www.columbiathletic.com
Private Lessons: Ages 8+
Junior Golf Camp: Ages 8-12

Golf Zone
6804 188th St Ne, Arlington
360-403-9660
Private lessons: Ages 7+
Junior Summer Golf Camp: Ages 7-11, 12-16

Kaddyshack Golf Center Inc
4003 204th St SW, Lynnwood
425-775-8911
"Little Caddies" Group Lessons: Ages 4-8
Price: Varies: Only offered January - March
Private lessons: 7+

Longshots Driving Range
1215 80th St SW, Everett
425-355-2133
Private Lessons: Ages 7+

Gymnastics/Cheerleading

King County

Auburn Gymnastics Center

1221 29th NW, Auburn

253-876-9991

www.auburngymnastics.com

Classes: Provide fun, successful, happy, healthy, & confident children.

Age: 2+

Hours: 1 hour to 1-1/2 hour classes.

Emerald City Gymnastics Academy

17969 NE 65th, Redmond

425-861-8772

www.emeraldcitygymnastics.com

Class Focus: Gymnastics, motor fitness, agility, balance, coordination. vault, bars, beam and floor gymnastics.

Ages: 3+

Gymnastics East

13425 SE 30th, Bellevue

425-644-8117

www.gymeast.com

Classes: Dance, cheer, tramp, gymnastics, tumbling, and Tiny Tots.

Ages: 18 months to 18

Prices: $44.50 per 40 minute class, $49.50 per 50 minute class, $62.75 per 1 hour 25 minute class, and $72 per 1 ? hour class

Gymnastics East

19510 144th Ave NE, Woodinville

425-486-8836

www.gymnasticseast.org

Classes: Dance, cheer, tramp, gymnastics, tumbling, Parent/Tot, and Tiny Tots

Age: Walking to 18

Open Gym: Summer months 5:00pm-7:00pm.

Metropolitan Gymnastics Inc
6822 S 190th, Kent
206-575-4138
www.metropolitangym.com
Classes: Recreational & Competitive Gymnastics, rhythmic dance, tumbling
Toddlers: Obstacle course & balance training.
Age: 3 months to 20

Northwest Aerials School of Gymnastics
12440 128th Ln NE, Kirkland
425-823-2665
www.nwaerials.com
Classes: Gymnastics, dance, focus on fitness, coordination, confidence, & creativity.
Age: walking to teen

School of Acrobatics and New Circus Arts
674 S Orcas St, Seattle
206-652-4433
www.sancaseattle.org
Classes: Trapeze, Tight Rope, Juggling, Tumbling, Balance, Trampoline, gymnastics, And acrobatics.
Ages: 2 1/2 to 14+

Seattle Gymnastics Academy Inc
12535 26th NE, Seattle
206-362-4433
www.seattlegymnastics.com
Classes: Little ones: building baby movements, sitting, crawling, etc. Older children: Tumbling, gymnastics.
Ages: 6 months to toddlers, and 5+
Time: Girls: Ages 6 to 8 months/ 35 minute lessons, Ages 18 months to 5 /45 minute lessons, Ages 5+ /1 hour lessons. Boys: Ages: 5 to 8/1 hour lessons, Ages 8 + /1 hr to 1 1/2 hours.

The Little Gym
Seattle
7777 15th Ave NE
206-524-2623
www.thelittlegym.com
Classes: Motor skills for tiny tots, gymnastic skills for older children.
Age: Parent/child: Ages: Infant -3, Ages 3-6 pre-school, Ages 6-12 grade school.
Time: 45 min (3 & under) to 1 hour (3 to 12 yrs).

See ad in back

Kent
18437 E Valley Hwy
425-656-0737
www.thelittlegym.com
Classes: Motor skills for tiny tots, gymnastic skills for older children.
Age: Parent/child: Ages: Infant -3, Ages 3-6 pre-school, Ages 6-12 grade school.

Tumble Town Gymnastics
19102 Des Moines Memorial Dr, SeaTac
206-439-8234
Classes: Competition gymnastics. Birthday party packages available
Ages: Tots to Teens

Snohomish County

Cascade Elite Gymnastics Inc
23101 56th Ave W, Mountlake Terrace
425-672-6887
Classes: Tuddle Time (18 mo. & toddlers), and older children gymnastic classes.
Age: 18 months and up

Gymagine Gymnastics
3616 South Rd 83, Mukilteo
425-513-8700
Classes: Toddlers: cartwheels, tumbling, summersaults, & jumps. Older children regular gymnastics.
Age: 18 months to 18 years.

Gymnastics Connection
14213 NE 193rd Pl, Woodinville
425-486-6887
Classes: All competitive gymnastics. Gymnastic training in a loving, encouraging environment.
Age: 18 months to 18 years
Time: 50 min (18 mo-6 yrs), 1 hour (7-10 yrs), 2-1/2 hours (10 yrs & up)

Leading Edge Gymnastics Academy Inc
711 100th St SE, Everett
425-353-9137
Classes: Gymnastics, tumbling, trampoline, cheerleading classes, boys & girl teams.
Age: 18 months and up

The Little Gym of Everett
7207 Evergreen Way, Everett
425-348-4848
Classes: Motor skills for tiny tots, gymnastic skills for older children.
Age: Parent/child: Ages: Infant -3, Ages 3-6 pre-school, Ages 6-12 grade school.
Price: 20 classes with price varying from $245 to $295.
Time: 45 min (3 & under) to 1 hour (3 to 12 yrs).
See ad in back

The Little Gym of Kenmore
6748 NE 181st St., Kenmore
425-481-5889
Classes: Motor skills for tiny tots, gymnastic skills for older children.
Age: Parent/child: Ages: Infant -3, Ages 3-6 pre-school, Ages 6-12 grade school.
Time: 45 min (3 & under) to 1 hour (3 to 12 yrs).

Northshore Gymnastics Center
19460 144th Ave NE, Woodinville
425-402-6602

Rising Stars Gymnastics
3707 NE 124th St NE, Marysville
360-653-7827

Sky Valley Gymnastics & Cheer
17631 147th St SE, Monroe
360-805-9844

Martial Arts Instruction

King County

Aikido of West Seattle
4421 Fauntleroy Way SW, Seattle
206-938-5222
www.aikidos.com
Programs: Children 4-9 yrs.
Focus: non-competition, non violence

Aikido-Seattle School
3422 NE 55th, Seattle
206-525-1955
www.seattleschoolofaikido.org
Programs: For children 5 & up
Focus: Non-aggressive, non-violent, non-competitive, self discipline.

AMC Kickboxing & Pankration
427 6th S, Kirkland
425-822-9656
www.pankration.com
Programs: Children 6-11yrs., 12& up
Focus: Good sportsmanship, fitness, self-confidence, good attitude.

ATA Black Belt Academy
128 SW 153rd St., Burien
206-242-6032
www.seattleata.com
Programs: Pre-school 3-7 yrs. & children 7-12 yrs., teens 13+.
Focus: Creating Tomorrows Leaders

Body & Mind Enso Center
8410 165th Ave NE, Redmond
425-869-0276
www.enso-center.org
Programs: Children 5-18 yrs.
Focus: Inner strength, harmony, personal growth, of body & mind, inner peace.

Kim's Taekwondo Martial Arts
24030 132nd SE, Kent
253-638-3001
Programs: For children 5 yrs.& older

Kung-Fu Club of Seattle
656-1/2 S King, Seattle
206-624-9898
www.seattlekungfuclub.com
Programs: Children 5 & up, teach Kung-Fu & Tai Chi

Minakami Karate Dojo
3000 NE 125th, Seattle
206-363-7717
www.minakamikarate.com
Program: Classes for children 4+

Oom Yung Doe School
14310 NE 20th, Bellevue
425-641-1323
www.oomyungdoenw.com
Programs: For children 4-9 yrs, jrs. 10-18 yrs.
Focus: Personal development. Teach Kung Fu, Bagwa, Ai-Ki-Do, & Ship-Pal-Gae.

Seattle Martial Arts
8005 Greenwood Ave.N, Seattle
206-783-7240
www.seattlemartialarts.com
Programs: Children's classes for 4 to12 yrs
Focus: self-confidence, fitness, self-defense & lots of fun.

USA Karate
1535 NE 177th St, Shoreline
206-440-5533
www.usakaratedojo.com
Programs: "Little Dragons" Children's classes 5-8 yrs, also 12 & under..
Focus: Self-confidence, discipline, courtesy, awareness, respect.

Washington Karate Association
8618 3rd Ave NW, Seattle
206-784-3171
www.washingtonkarate.com
Programs: For children 4 yrs. & up.
Focus: Self-control, discipline, technique, respect for self and others.

World Martial Arts & Health
2002 NW Market, Seattle
206-782-7000
www.yunsmaratialarts.com
Programs: Children 4-7 "Little Ninja", also Juniors 8-14 yrs.
Focus: Hand to eye coordination. Wingchun base, & modern Kung-Fu.

Snohomish County

Aau Karate
1535 NE 177th St, Shoreline
206-440-5533
www.usakaratedojo.com
Programs: For children age 5 & up.
Focus: Shito-Ryu, Judo. Teach self-defense, discipline, confidence, balance, & fitness

Aikido Heiwa-Martial Arts For Peace
6812 196th St SW Suite C, Lynnwood
425-774-0915
www.AikidoHeiwa.com
Programs: Children classes 7-12 yrs.
Focus: The way of harmony & energy, situational awareness, discipline.

ATA Black Belt Academy
7207 Evergreen way, Everett
425-347-6591
www.atakick.com
Programs: Karate for Tiny Tigers 3-6 year olds, also 7 year & up.
Focus: Respect, honor, courtesy, perseverance.

ATA Taekwondo/Karate For Kids
15620 Hwy 99
425-742-4282
www.masterchos-ata.com
Programs: Children 4 yrs & up, "Tiny Tigers" Program.
Focus: Core values: character building, self- respect, courtesy, perseverance.

Bailey's Traditional Tae Kwon Do College
700 Main St
425-778-4006
www.traditionaltaekwon-do.com
Programs: Children 7yrs & up
Focus: Courtesy, self-control, integrity, perseverance, & indomitable spirit.

Champion Tae Kwon Do and Fitness
10100 Mukilteo Speedway, Mukilteo
425-493-2840
Programs: Children 4 yrs & up
Focus: Activity that improves self-confidence, discipline, concentration & health.

Creekside Karate
1103 Gohr Rd, Sultan
360-793-4377
Programs: Children's "Little Dragon" classes, 6-9 yrs. Also classes for 9+
Focus: Teach Shorin-Ryu Jujitsu, Aikido, Judo & Kempo. Confidence building & "Stranger Danger".

Combative Tactics Exploration Training (C.T.E.T)
509 Main Number 1, Sultan
360-793-2801
www.trainctet.com
Programs: Children's classes in Kickboxing, 5 to 12 yrs.
Focus: Teaching danger awareness.

Dragon's Lair Martial Arts Studio LLC
10121 Main, Bothell
425-481-6970
www.dragonslair-mgf.com
Programs: "Little Ninja" class 4-7yrs, & 4+ classes
Focus: Hand to eye coordination. Wingchun base & modern Kung-Fu.

Evergreen Karate
10116 NE 185th St, Bothell
425-486-4105
www.evergreenkarate.com
Programs: Little Dragons Program, 4-6 yrs, & classes for 7 yrs & up.
Focus: Children's self-awareness, stranger safety & life skills.

Family Karate Center
909 SE Everett Mall Way Suite A-175, Everett
425-355-4030
www.fkceverett.com
Programs: Traditional Karate, Children's "Kinderate" 5-7 yrs, also 8-13 yrs, & 14.+.
Focus: , Respect, self-confidence, self-discipline, manners & courtesy.

Family Karate Ronin Dojo
3505 1/2 136th St NE, Marysville
360-657-2222
www.ronindojo.com
Programs: Children "Kinderate" 4-7 yrs, Jrs. 7-12
Focus: Teach self-development & self-esteem

Fiedler's Kung Fu Academy
612 112th St SE, Everett
425-355-5367
www.fiedlerskungfuacademy.com
Programs: Classical Kung Fu for children 5-18 yrs
Focus: Gymnastics, kicks & punches, self-defense.

Jones' Taekwondo
2629 N Machias Rd, Lake Stevens
425-397-0484
Programs: Children 6 yrs & up
Focus: Showing respect, self-control

Jungyae Moosul Academy of Woodinville
14039 NE Woodinville-Duvall Rd, Woodinville
425-481-3921
www.jungyae-ma.com
Programs: Children 8-12 yrs, Korean-style martial arts.

Kyuki-Do Martial Arts
17624 15th Ave SE, Suite 102A, Bothell
425-481-3921
Programs: Children 6 & up
Focus: Humility, patience, & respect.

Master Lee's Black Belt Academy
16000 Mill Creek Blvd, Mill Creek
425-338-3035
Programs: Children 5-12 yrs. Teaches: Tae Kwon Do, & Karate
Focus: Discipline & respect

Master Lee's Black Belt Academy
723 Ave D, Snohomish
360-568-4098
Focus: Children 5-12, teach Tae Kwon Do & Karate, discipline & respect.

Master Pierce's Taekwondo Center
19505 44th Ave W, Lynnwood
425-744-7893
www.masterpierce.com
Programs: 4yrs & older,
Focus: Mental development, self-confidence, & self-control

Monroe Ko's Martial Arts
120 W Main St, Monroe
360-805-1898
www.hwangs.com
Programs: Children ages 4-7 & 8 yrs. & up
Focus: Self-defense, self-control, courtesy, & respect.

Nia's Black Belt Academy
14815 Chain Lake Rd, Monroe
360-794-3481
www.masterna.com
Programs: Taekwondo, Self-defense children's classes 4 yrs & up.
Focus: Courtesy, self-control, perseverance, indomitable spirit.

Olympic Tae Kwon Do
17311 135th Ave NE, Bldg #C-500, Woodinville
425-402-6693
Programs: Tae Kwon Do & Kickboxing children's classes, 5-11 yrs, also 12+

Pearson's Black Belt Academy
2801 Wetmore Ave, Everett
425-252-5222
www.pearsonsma.com
Programs:"Charlies Kid's Club" Children's Classes 6-11 yrs
Focus: Kickboxing, w/emphasis on discipline..

Samurai Karate Academy
23104 55th Ave W, Mountlake Terrace
425-697-3300
www.samurai-karate.com
Programs: For children 5 yrs & up
Focus: Formal Japanese Karate, discipline for body & spirit, & respect.

Seibukan Karate-Do
7213 267th St NW
360-629-6614 or 360-639-LIFE
www.stanwoodsportsclub.com
Programs: Children's classes for 6yrs & up.
Focus: Self-confidence, self-discipline, respect for elders, & focus.

Shin's Taekwondo Academy
6524 NE 181st, Kenmore
425-402-8900
www.tkd.com
Programs: 4 yrs & up
Focus: Courtesy, integrity, perseverance, self-control, & indomitable spirit.

Temple Kung Fu
7705 230th Ave, Edmonds
425-775-7370
www.kungfutemple.com
Programs: Children's classes 5 yrs & up.
Focus: Awareness, avoiding danger, discipline & focus.

Tiger Kids Martial Arts
15728 Main St, Mill Creek
425-337-1116 or 425-745-1891
www.cityofmillcreek.com/parksrec/tiger_kids.htm
Programs: For children 5 yrs. on up
Focus: Kung-Fu, Kenpo, Karate, also develop motor skills, coordination, self-confidence, respect, stranger awareness & safety skills.

Traditional Taekwon Do College at Duvall
14701 Main St NE, Duvall
425-844-8962
www.duvalltkd.com
Programs: Kids 1st grade up to 15 yrs.
Focus: Classes in Taekwon Do, self-control, ability to work, & perseverance.

Tsubaki Kanagara Shrine
17720 Crooked Mile Rd, Granite Falls
360-691-6389
www.tsubakishrine.com
Programs: Children 5 yrs. & up.
Focus: Mind & body coordination, self-discipline, self-esteem, self-control.

US Tae Kwondo
1206 State Ave, Marysville
360-651-1171
www.ustkdonline.com
Programs: Children 4 yrs. & up
Focus: Five Step Program

World Martial Arts
1120 164th St SW, Lynnwood
425-742-1313
www.mydojang.com
Programs: "Little Grasshoppers" 3 yrs to 4-1/2 yrs, also 5-11 yrs, and 12+
Focus: Tae Kwon Do, Judo, Hap Ki Do, self-control & respect.

Y S Lee Martial Arts
6501 196th St SW, Lynnwood
425-744-0100
Programs: Children 5 yrs & up in Taekwondo.
Focus: Patience, self-confidence, skills in public speaking.

Motocross

Northwest Motocross Forums
16904 3rd Ave SE #B, Bothell
425-741-3278
eric@ewmxschools.com

South Snohomish Motocross Instruction
425-337-2801

Gary Semic's Motocross Schools & Videos
www.gsmxs.com

Motocross Training Center
www.motocrosstrainingcenter.com

Racquetball Courts-Public

Kent Commons
525 4th Ave N, Kent
253-856-5010

YMCA of Snohomish County
425-252-1196

Rock and Mountain Climbing Instruction

Stone Gardens
2839 NW Market St, Seattle
206-781-9828
Cost: Bouldering: $12.00 a day for adults, $10.00 a day for 17 and under. Includes climbing shoes, or you can wear your own sneakers.
One on one rope climbing: $24.00 an hour
Hours: Monday-Saturday: 10:00am-10:00pm, Tuesday-Thursday 6:00am-11:00pm, Sunday 10:00am-7:00pm.
Age limit: 6 and up
Special Programs for Children:
Hours: 5:00pm to 7:00pm, M-F 10:00am-12:00pm
Price: children 6-16 $25.00
Families can spend a whole day "bouldering" or free climbing around a huge indoor gravel pit. Textured walls slope and angle at varying degrees of difficulty. They have areas for beginners to advanced climbers, and places for toddlers to climb. There is also a rope section many find fun and challenging. Assistance is available to help young children get strapped into harnesses with ropes attached to the ceiling to prevent falling.

R.E.I.

Alderwood Mall/Lynnwood
3000 184th St SW Suite 952
425-640-6200

Seattle
222 Yale Ave N
206-223-1944

Southcenter/Tukwila
240 Andover Park W
206-248-1938

Redmond Towne Center
7500 166th Ave NE
425-882-1158

Cascade Crags
2820 Rucker Ave, Everett
425-258-3431

Sailing

1010 Valley, Seattle
206-382-2628
www.cwb.org
Hours: Open daily from 7:00am-10:00pm.
Winter Hours: 10:00am-5:00pm.
Learn to sail by CWB volunteers. Beginner course: SailNOW $270/$300. This 6 week course class begins with a Saturday classroom session from 11:00-3:30pm, ending with a sail on Lake Union. Also included is a 1 year membership, and 2 hours on the water each class. Students receive a logbook, the textbook The Complete Sailor, and a practice line for knot tying.

Scuba Diving

Bubble Diving-Open Water

Woodinville
425-424-3483
206-241-0779
www.bubblesbelow.com
Classes Available: Monday-Wednesday, Saturday
Open Water Classes: $180 for group class; up to $500 for one-on-one private class.
Age: 10+

Deep Fathom Supply

2645 Harbor SW, Seattle
206-938-7784
www.deepfathom.com
Open Water Class: 1 day in the pool plus 2 days in the open water.
Age: 12+

Discount Divers Supply
206-298-6998
www.discountdivers.com
Open Water Classes include beginning, advanced, rescue, and deep diving.
Ages: 10-11 with restrictions, 12+ to certify.

Lighthouse Diving Centers:
www.lighthousediving.com
Lynnwwod
425-771-2679
Seattle
206-524-1633
Classes: Weekends, evenings, private, advanced.
Ages 12+

Northwest Sports Divers
425-487-0624
www.nwsd.biz
Classes: $230-$450 for private lessons.
Age: 12+

Silent World Diving Systems
425-747-8842
800-841-DIVE
www.silent-world.com
Classes: Beginning, Specialty, and Advanced.
Ages:12+

Starfish Diving Inc.
206-286-6896
www.starfishdivinginc.com
Classes:
Ages: 12-14 Junior Scuba, 15+ Open Water Scuba

TLSea Diving
888-448-5732
www.tlseadiving.com
Classes: $179 Open Water certification/beginning class, plus $40 for book or $60 CD Rom. You must bring your own equipment: mask, snorkel, fins.
Ages 10+: Classes includes 2 days in pool, 2 days in the water.

Under Water Sports
www.underwatersports.com
Classes: $179 include Open Water, and Advanced.
Equipment Extra: $200-$250.
Ages: 12+

Skate Parks & Arenas

Alki Community Center
5817 SW Stevens St, Seattle
206-684-7430
www.cityofseattle.net/parks
Roller skating in the gym every Friday evening during the school year.

Auburn Skate Connection
1825 Howard Rd, Auburn
253-833-4040/4990
Roller skating. Family Night is on Saturday and Sunday nights, Tots Skate is held on Tuesday and Saturday mornings from 10:30-11:30-Parents skate free.

Ballard Skate Park
NW 57th St
206-684-4093

Bellevue Skate King
2301 140th Ave NE, Bellevue
425-458-4707
www.bellevueskateking.com

Castle Ice
12620 164th Ave SE, Renton
425-254-8750
See ad in back

Roller skating

Bellevue Skate Park
14224 Bellevue-Redmond Rd, Bellevue
425-452-2722
www.cityofbellevue.org

Skateboarding and inline skating.

The Bloc Indoor Skate Park
7806 NE Bothell Way, Kenmore
425-765-2488
www.cityof Kenmore.com
18,000 square feet of indoor skating. Includes a beginner's section.

Bothell Skate Park
9815 NE 188th Ave, Bothell
425-486-7430
www.ci.bothell.wa.us
Skateboards and inline skaters.

Comcast Community Ice Rink
2000 Hewitt Ave- Everett Events Center
425-322-2650
www.everetteventscenter.com
NHL regulated ice rink available for public skating, classes, and hockey leagues.

The Edge Skate Park
Redmond
425-556-2370
www.ci.redmond.wa.us
Skateboard and inline skating.

First Lions Skate Park
Kiwanis Park, Lakewood
253-589-2489
www.ci.lake-wood.wa.us
12,000 square feet.
Web cam.

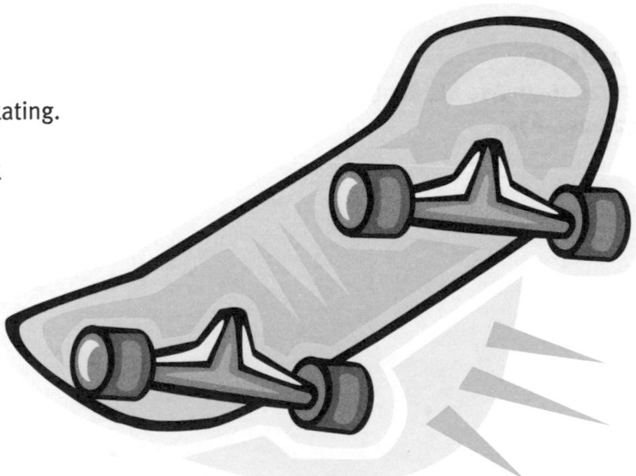

Highland Ice Arena
18005 Aurora Ave N, Shoreline
206-546-2431
www.highlandice.com
Ice hockey, ice skating, lessons

Issaquah Skate Park
301 Rainier Blvd, Issaquah Community Center
425-837-3300
www.ci.issaquah.wa.us
Skateboarding and inline skating.

Kent Valley Ice Centre
6015 240th St, Kent
253-850-2400
www.familynightout.com

Kirkland Skate Court
202 Third St, Peter Kirk Park
425-828-1211
www.ci.kirkland.wa.us
Skateboarding and inline skating.

Liberty Park Skate Park
Houser Way S, Renton
425-430-6600
www.ci.renton.wa.us
Skateboarding and inline skating.
8,400 square feet with beginner to expert courses.

Lynnwood Ice Center
19803 68th Ave W, Lynnwood
425-640-9999
Ice hockey, ice skating, lessons

Lynnwood Roll-A-Way
6210 200th St SW, Lynnwood
425-778-4446
www.bowlandskate.com
Roller rink includes a glow-in-the-dark floor.

Mercer Island Skate Park
Mercerdale Park
206-236-3545
www.ci.mercer-island.wa.us
Skateboarding and inline skating.

North Bend Skate Park
750 E North Bend Way-Torguson Park
425-888-0486
www.ci.north-bend.wa.us
Skateboarding, inline skating, and a BMX track

Olympic View Arena
22202-70th Ave W, Mountlake Terrace
425-672-9012
www.olyview.com
Ice hockey leagues

Redmond Arena Sports
9040 Willows Rd, Redmond
425-885-4881
www.arenasports.net

Seattle Center Skate Park
Seattle Center
206-684-7200
www.seattlecenter.com
8,900 square foot outdoor park designed for skateboarding and inline skating.

Seattle Skating Club
22202-70th Ave W, Mountlake Terrace
425-672-6885/7744

Skate Barn West
2900 Lind Ave SW, Renton
425-656-2863
www.skatebarn.com
Indoor skate park for bikes, skateboarding, inline skating. Skate camp and skate team.

Skate Deck
9700 19th Ave SE, Everett
425-337-0202
www.everettskatedeck.com

Roller skating

Skate King
2301 140th NE, Bellevue
425-458-4707
425-641-2047 (Reservations)
www.bellevueskateking.com
Roller skating

Skate Inn Marysville
7313 44th Ave NE, Marysville
360-659-3900
Roller skating

Southgate Roller Rink
9646 17th Ave SW, Seattle
206-762-4030
www.southgaterollerrink.com
Roller skating and inline skating. Rentals available.

Walter E Hall Skate Park
1226 SW Casino Rd, Everett
425-257-8300
www.ci.everett.wa.us

TLC Family Skating Center
10210 SE 260th, Kent
253-852-9379
Roller skating

Swimming Instruction

King County

Aqua Dive Swim & Fitness Club
12706 33rd NE, Seattle
206-364-2535

Aqua Skool
9441 Dr NE, Clyde Hill
425-637-7233

Kidswim
14540 Bothell Way, NE, Lake Forrest Park
206-364-7946

Kinder Swimmer
Maple Valley, Renton
425-432-7946
www.kinderswimmer.com
Private swim instruction with small class sizes for infants on up.

Mercerwood Shore Club
4150 E Mercer Way, Mercer Island
206-232-1622

Safe N Sound Swimming
2040 Westlake Ave N, Seattle
206-285-9279
www.snsswim.com
Private 1 on 1 Instruction

Suzie Erwin's Swim Lessons
11804 SE 87th, Newcastle
425-235-8992

Swim Seattle
206-575-0808

Waterbabies Aquatic Program
425-643-3533

Wedgewood Swim Pool Inc
7727 28th NE, Seattle
206-523-8211

Snohomish County

Mill Creek Swim Club
15622 Country Club Dr, Mill Creek
425-745-3474

South Snohomish County Dolphins
425-774-4744

Aqua Club Inc
18512-58th Ave NE, Kenmore
425-486-5758

Swimming Pools-Public

Bellevue Aquatic Center
601 143rd Avenue NE, Bellevue
425-452-4444
Olympic Size & Ward Water Therapy Pools
Hanicap Facilities

Kenneth Jones Pools
30421 16th S, Federal Way
253-839-1000

Mt Rainier Pool
22722 19th S, Des Moines
206-824-4722

Lynnwood City
18900 44th Ave W, Lynnwood
425-744-6440

Mountlake Terrace Recreation Pavillion
5303 228th St SW, Mountlake Terrace
425-776-9173

Seattle City Parks & Recreation Swimming Pools

Ballard Pool
1471 NW 67th
206-684-4094

Colman Pool (Summer Only)
8603 Fautleroy Way SW
206-684-7494

Evans Pool
7201 E Green Lake Dr N
206-684-4961

Helene Madison Pool
13401 Meridian N
206-684-4979

Mounger Pool (Summer Only)
2535 32nd Ave W
206-684-4708

Meadowbrook Pool
10515 35th NE
206-684-4989

Medger Evers Pool
500 23rd Ave
206-684-4766

Queen Anne pool
1920 1st W
206-386-4282

Rainier Beach Pool
8825 Rainier S
206-684-1944

Southwest pool
2801 SW Thistle
206-684-7440

YMCA of Greater Seattle

Downtown YMCA
206-382-5010

Meredith Mathews East Madison YMCA
1700 23rd
206-322-6969

West Seattle YMCA
4515 36th SW
206-935-6000

Auburn Valley YMCA
1005 12th SE, Auburn
253-833-2770

Skiing

Bonney's Pro Am Water Skiing
3656 Ave NE, Redmond
425-885-5634

Cascade Ski School Inc
PO Box 64035, Tacoma
253-564-1245

Chief Kitsap Ski School
206-248-3463

Clancy Ski School
11111 SR 2, Skykomish
360-973-2634
425-348-3622

Chief Kitsap Ski School
Stevens Pass
206-248-4363

Powderpigs Ski School
PO Box 1302, Issaquah
425-392-7277

Seattle Community Ski School
303 N 55th, Seattle
206-782-5641

Ski Klasses Inc
425-774-3259
www.skiklasses.com

Ski-Masters Watersports Ski & Wakeboard School
6820 NE 175th St, Kenmore
425-481-2754

Team Alpental-Snoqualmie
Bellevue
425-644-1781

Tennis Courts-Private

Columbia Athletic Clubs
505 128th St SE, Everett
425-745-1617

Columbia Tennis Club-Pine Lake
2930 228th Ave SE, Sammamish
425-313-0123
www.columbiaathletic.com

Columbia Tennis Club-Silver Lake
425-337-7477

Forest Crest Tennis Club
4901 238th SW, Mountlake Terrace
425-774-0014

Gold Creek Tennis & Sports Club
15327 140th Pl NE, Woodinville
425-487-1090

Mercerwood Shore Club
4150 E Mercer Way, Mercer Island
206-232-1622

Sammamish Club
2115 NW Poplar Way, Issaquah
425-313-3131

Seattle Tennis Club
922 McGilvra Blvd E
206-324-3200
www.seattletennisclub.org

Tennis Courts-Public

Amy Yee Tennis Court
2000 Martin Luther Kind Jr Way S
206-684-4764

Robinswood Tennis Center
2400 151st Pl SE, Bellevue
425-452-7690
www.cityofbellevue.org

Triathlons

The American Triathlon & Duathlon Calendar
www.trifind.net
Information on the world's triathlons and multi-sport events. Click on your state, and you will find the list of all the triathlons in the state, including those for children.

Issaquah's Kids Triathlon
Lake Sammamish State Park (near swim beach)
425-392-0579
Date: June, August
Ages: 6-12
Distance:
6-9: 75 yard Swim, 2 mile Bike, ? mile Run
10-12: 100 yard Swim, 3 mile Bike, 3 mile Run

Heart of the Sound Triathlon - Vashon Island
Seattle
Date: June, August, September, October
Ages: 7-19
7-9: 100 yard Swim, 1.8 mile Bike, 1/2 mile Run
10-12: 200 yard Swim, 3.6 mile Bike, 1 mile Run
13-15: 600 meter Swim, 11 K Bike, 29 K Run
16-19: 100 meter Swim, 32 K Bike, 58 K Run

SeaFair Kids Triathlon
Seward Park
www.SeaFair.com
Date: July
Ages 6-12
Distance: 1/2 mile Swim, 12 mile Bike, 3.1 mile Run

Youth Triathlon @ Juanita Beach Park
Kirkland
www.signmeup.com/reg/register.aspx?fid=RB2VNK7
Date: August
Ages: 6-12

Track (& Field)

Eastside Runners
www.eastsiderunners.com
"The running club for every type of runner." From races for mom's and their babies to races for senior citizens, you will find information on races fit for your needs, and those closest to your home.

Jingle Bell Run
www.jinglebellrun.org
Date: December
Distance:
Ages: Kids of all ages, including little ones in strollers with their parents!

This annual race, held in December in downtown Seattle, is a kid-friendly and fun race.

Seattle Kids Marathon

www.seattlemarathon.org
Date: November
Distance: 1.2 Miles
Ages: Grades K-8th

To equal the "26.2" mile marathon, children read 13 books, and do 13 good deeds (13 books + 13 good deeds = 26 miles). The last leg of the marathon is the 1.2 mile run. Finishers receive a certificate, space blanket, and a Seattle Marathon t-shirt presented at the finish line on race day.

Wakeboarding/Waterskiing

Ski-Masters Watersports

3307 Lake Washington Blvd N, Renton
888-481-2754
425-481-2SKI (Instruction Reservations)
www.seattlewatersports.com
Price: $40.00 per lesson. All equipment supplied for $10.00 a day.
Ages: All ages and abilities.

Wakeboarding lessons are taught by certified AWSA instructors who give personalized instruction.

Lake Sammamish Water Ski Club

www.lswsc.org
Formed in 1959, this water ski club is youth and family oriented. They are the oldest and largest water-ski club west of the Mississippi. They are a terrific resource for water-ski/wakeboard lessons, and events related to waterskiing/wakeboarding.

Canoes & Kayaks-Sales, Trips, & Classes

Aqua Trek Sea Kayaking Adventures

5822-157th Pl SW, Edmonds
425-743-3446

Cascade Canoe & Kayak Centers Inc

www.canoe-kayak.com
3519 108th Ave SE
Enatai Beach Park, Bellevue
425-430-0111

Paddle Sports Shop & Sporthouse

1060 Nishiwaki Ln, Renton

425-430-0111

Prices: Canoe, Kayak-single: $15/hr + $6/add hr., Kayak-double: $22, + $10/add hr., Kayak-sit on top: $10 + $5/add hr. Rental includes boat, life jacket, and paddle.

Cascade offers classes, rentals, conditioning, and races. They suggest making reservations 1 day in advance.

Green Lake Small Craft Center

5590 W Green Lake Way N, Seattle

206-684-4074

206-527-0171: Green Lake Boat Rental

Juanita Beach Rental

Lake Washington

425-587-3331

Hours: Saturdays & Sundays 10:00am-6:00pm

Ages: 6+

Kayaks and canoes available for rent.

Mt. Baker Rowing & Sailing Center

3800 Lake Washington Blvd S, Seattle-Stan Sayres Park

206-386-1913

www.pan.ci.seattle.wa.us/parks/boats/mtbaker.htm

Junior Crew: competitions for up 160 youth, ages 13-18.

Classes: Youth beginning canoe & kayak

Northwest Outdoor Center on Lake Union

2100 Westlake N Suite #1, Seattle

206-281-9694

www.nwoc.com

Western Canoeing & Kayaking Inc

171 Salton Rd, Abbotsford BC

866-644-8111

www.westerncanoekayak.com

Park & Recreation Sports:

Washington Parks & Recreation

Youth sports information call: 206-684-7091

Flag Football - ages 6-17
September to November

Girls Volleyball - ages 10-17
September to November

Cross Country - ages 7-17
206-684-7093
Run twice a week and Saturdays at Woodland Park. PNW Youth Cross-country Meets: October and November. :

Tennis Lessons - ages 8-17
Tiny Tot Tennis- ages 4-7

Swimming

City of Redmond Parks & Recreation Department

425-556-2300 x3
E-mail: recreationoffice@redmond.gov
Fall/winter Boys & Girls Youth Basketball:
For grades 1-6

Sports Camps

Skyhawks

www.skyhawks.com
Sport Camps: Baseball, Basketball, Cheerleading, Flag Football, Golf, Hockey, Lacrosse, Multi-Sport, Soccer, Tennis, and Volleyball

Sport Camps are held in the following cities: Arlington, Auburn, Bellevue, Bothell, Burien, Covington, Duvall, Edmonds, Everett, Fall City, Federal Way, Issaquah, Kenmore, Kent, Kirkland, Lynnwood, Maple Valley, Mercer Island, Mill Creek, Mukilteo, North Bend, Redmond, Renton, Sammamish, Seattle, Shoreline, Snohomish, Snoqualmie, Vashon, Woodinville, and Woodland.

Spectator Sports

Seattle Tixx
425-778-5522
www.SeattleTixx.com

Seattle SuperSonics: Basketball
League: NBA
Key Arena @ Seattle Center
www.supersonics.com

Seattle Storm: Basketball
League: WNBA
Key Arena
www.storm.wnba.com

Seattle Mariner's: Baseball
League: MLB (Major)
Safeco Field
www.seattle.mariners.mlb.com
Family Nights: Select Mondays during the summer months.

Everett Aquasocks: Baseball
League: MLB (Minor)
www.aquasocks.com
425-258-3673

Seattle Seahawks: Football
League: NFL
206-827-9777
www.seahawks.com

Everett Hawks: Indoor Football
League: NIFL
Everett Events Center
www.everetthawks.com

Seattle Sounders: Soccer
League:
Seahawk Stadium
800-796-KICK
www.seattlesounders.net

Seattle Thunderbirds: Hockey
League: WHL
Key Arena
206-448-PUCK
www.seattle-thunderbirds.com

Everett Silvertips: Hockey
League:
Everett Events Center
425-252-5100
www.everettsilvertips.com

University of Washington Huskies
League: College Sports
206-543-2200
www.gohuskies.collegesports.com

Men's Spectator Sports:
Baseball, Basketball, Crew, Cross Country, Football, Golf, Soccer, Swimming, Tennis, and Track

Women's Spectator Sports:
Basketball, Crew, Cross Country, Golf, Gymnastics, Soccer, Softball, Swimming, Tennis, Track, and Volleyball.

Sports Radio Stations

The Seattle Times has a great website that lists all the sports broadcasting in the area. It lists the time of the broadcast, and the station. Listings include local, national, and international sports, i.e. The Tour de France, NASCAR, the NFL, the World Cup, and Wimbledon.

Visit www.seattletimes.nwsource.com/sports/tvradio

950 KJR AM

710 KIRO AM

850 KHHO AM

1000 KOMO AM

1380 KRKO AM

Chapter 5

Music

Chapter 5

Music

The Magic of Music

The Secret Great Parents Know About Raising Their Kids

Few things can be more valuable to a child than the opportunity of studying music during their youth. Besides giving them a love and appreciation for this great art form, it increases their quality of life, and prepares them in ways that cannot be done with any other activity. The research has been stunning and clearly indicates that music gives young people the skills they need to enjoy super-success in life. A short list of these skills includes:

- Creative Thinking
- Concentration
- Self-Esteem
- Performing Under Pressure
- Motor Skill Development
- Imagination
- Analytical Thinking
- Discipline
- Self-Expression
- Increased Intelligence
- Problem Solving
- Coordination

Music Study and Intelligence

A research team exploring the link between music and intelligence reported that music training is far superior to computer instruction in dramatically enhancing children's abstract reasoning skills, the skills necessary for learning math and science. – *Neurological Research, Vol. 19, February 1977*

A child's intelligence is increased by playing a musical instrument because 80-90% of the brain's motor-control capabilities are devoted to the hands, mouth, and throat. BY developing highly refined control in those areas, a child is stimulating almost the entire brain, thereby increasing its total capabilities. – *Frank R. Wilson, MD, Clinical Professor of Neurology, University of California, San Francisco School of Medicine*

The musician is constantly adjusting decisions on tempo, tone, style, rhythm, phrasing, and feeling-training the brain to become incredibly good at organizing and conducting many activities at once. Dedicated practice of this orchestration can hae a great payoff for lifelong attention skills, intelligence, and an ability for self-knowledge and expression. – *John J. Ratey, MD, "A User's Guide to the Brain"*

Music Study and Academics

High School music students have been shown to hold higher grade point averages (GPA) than non-musicians at the same school. In a study in California, music students had an average GPA of 3.57; non-musicians averaged 2.91. Further, 16% of the music students held a 4.0 GPA while only 5% of the non-music students did.

Students involved in the arts score up to 125 points higher on the SAT than the national average.

A Rockefeller foundation study found that college music majors have the highest admittance rate into medical school (66%). By contrast, only 44% of biochemistry majors were admitted.

In a study by the Norwegian Research Council for Science and the Humanities, a connection was found between students having musical competence and high motivation to achieve success in school.

Hungary is one of the poorest nations in the world, yet they rank highest in academic excellence. In that country, there is a mandatory music requirement for grades one through nine. The first four hours of each day are set aside for music, orchestra and choir. In fact, each of the top three nations in the world have mandatory music requirements for their students in the lower grade levels. By contrast, America spends 29 times more money than any other nation on education, yet does not share this commitment to music and ranks 14th out of 17 countries in academic excellence.

Music Study and Success In Society

Secondary students who participated in band and orchestra reported the lowest lifetime use of all substances (alcohol, tobacco, illicit drugs). –Texas Commission on Drug and Alcohol Abuse Report

The very best engineers and technical designers in the Silicon Valley industry are, nearly without exception, all practicing musicians. *–Grant Venerable, "The Paradox of the Silicon Savior"*

Music Study and Life

Learning to play a musical instrument enhances coordination, concentration and memory, improves eyesight and hearing, teaches discipline, fosters self-esteem, stimulates imagination and self-expression and develops the motor systems of the brain in a way that cannot be done by any other activity.

Students who participated in arts programs in selected elementary and middle schools in New York City showed significant increases in self-esteem and thinking skills. *–National Arts Education Research Center*

Studying music encourages self-discipline and diligence, traits that carry over into intellectual pursuits and lead to effective study and work habits. Creating and performing music promotes self-expression and provides self-gratification while providing pleasure to others. *–Michael E. Blakely, MD*

Music is about communication, creativity, and cooperation. By studying music in schools, students have the opportunity to build on these skills, enrich their lives, and experience the world from a new perspective. – *Bill Clinton, former President of the United States of America*

Personal expression is encouraged through the arts. This develops flexible and fluent thinking abilities as well as skills of close scrutiny and careful evaluation. – *Oklahoma State Department of Education*

Music study gives young people an edge that they can't get anywhere else. Congratulations on your desire to provide this vital opportunity for your children. It will be one of the most important things you ever do as a parent. Good luck in the magical journey of music study and life.

This information has been provided by The Art City Music Academy.

Find A Teacher

The Music Teacher's National Association (MTNA) and the WSMTA, Washington State Music Teacher's Association (WSMTA) is an excellent non-profit organization for parents looking for local music teachers to fit their child's needs and style.

How it works: Leave a message on the line, and a WSMTA teacher from your area will call you back within 1 week, talk a bit about what kind of teacher you're looking for, then give you 3-4 names of qualified teachers in your area who have openings.

Regional MTNA chapters' referral lines:

Eastside Chapter	**425-378-0464**
Edmonds Chapter	**206-364-1336**
Seattle Chapter	**206-583-0849**
Snohomish Chapter	**425-252-3339**
South King County	**425-228-8721**
Lake Washington Chapter	**425-885-7011**

Kevin Paustien, the band director at Mt. Baker Middle School and the Bank Curriculum Officer for WMEA, offers this advice. "There isn't a directory for private teachers - the population shifts so quickly, it is impossible to track. Your best resource and guideline to contact private teachers is to contact your local band directors, at middle school and high school levels, for recommendations. Also, music stores usually have teachers who teach lessons at their stores - for woodwind teachers concentrate on music stores that do a large volume of band instrument business. These 2 resources will help parents find qualified teachers who work in their area.

Here are some things to watch for once a teacher has been located:

- Ask about the length and frequency of the lessons; they usually range from 30 minutes to one hour and should occur once each week. Regularly scheduled times are optimum so families can plan their other activities.
- Private teacher rates are set by each teacher, so parents should ask BEFORE choosing a teacher to make sure their budget can accommodate - some teachers are as low as $15.00 per half hour up to $50.00 per half hour.
- Make sure the outcome of the lessons is best suited to the teacher's background - a classical teacher is not always well-versed in jazz styles and improvisation, and vice versa.

- Some private teachers have VERY strong requirements of students to practice certain amounts of time each week - parents should ask BEFORE selecting the teacher. It can be tough if a student wants a "fun, relaxed" experience gets with a private teacher who only wants to teach the next start of the Seattle Symphony; equally disappointing for the highly motivated student to match up with the casual teacher. Again, local band directors can help make better fits.
- Some instruments are much more difficult to find teachers for than others - oboe and bassoon teachers are not as available as flute and saxophone teachers.
- Parents might also ask if the student will receive some instruction in music theory; will there be additional costs like method books, accompanists for recitals, specialty equipment (like mouthpieces, reeds, etc)."

Music Instruction-Suzuki

Suzuki Method

Shinichi Suzuki was a violinist, educator, philosopher and humanitarian. Born in 1898, he studied violin in Japan for some years before going to Germany in the 1920's for further study. After the end of World War II, Dr. Suzuki devoted his life to the development of the method he calls Talent Education.

Suzuki based his approach on the belief that "Musical ability is not an inborn talent but an ability which can be developed. Any child who is properly trained can develop musical ability, just as all children develop the ability to speak their mother tongue. the potential of every child is unlimited."

Thoughtful teachers have often used some of the elements listed here, but Suzuki has formulated them in a cohesive approach. Some basic differences are:

- Suzuki teachers believe that musical ability can be developed in all children.
- Students begin at young ages.
- Parents play an active role in the learning process
- Children become comfortable with the instrument before learning to read music.
- Technique is taught in the context of pieces rather than through dry technical exercises.
- Pieces are refined through constant review
- Every Child Can Learn

Suzuki students are normal children whose parents may have little or no musical experience. Their parents have simply chosen to introduce them to music through the Suzuki approach, a unique philosophy of music education developed over forty years ago by Japanese violinist Shinichi Suzuki

More than forty years ago, Suzuki realized the implications of the fact that children the world over learn to speak their native language with ease. He began to apply the basic principles of language acquisition to the learning of music, and called his method the mother-tongue approach. The ideas of parent responsibility, loving encouragement, constant repetition, etc., are some of the special features of the Suzuki approach.

Parent Involvement

As when a child learns to talk, parents are involved in the musical learning of their child. They attend lessons with the child and serve as "home teachers" during the week. One parent often learns to play before the child, so that s/he understands what the child is expected to do. Parents work with the teacher to create an enjoyable learning environment

Suzuki Music Instructors

Jal Feldman
Instrument: Piano
Lynwood, Seattle
425-778-1859
Email: JALFELDMAN@AOL.COM
Registered Suzuki Book Units: Piano 1-3

Richard Cox
Instrument: Guitar
Silverdale
360-613-5700
Email: rick@fretsandstrings.net
Registered Suzuki Book Units: Guitar 1

Robert Vierschilling
Instrument: Guitar
Seattle
206-372-5637
Email: robertvier@earthlink.net
Ages 3+

Christine Dunaway
Instrument: Violin
Seattle
206-329-0486
206-550-0551
Email: cdunaway@u.washington.edu

Heather Marie Rehwald
Bellevue
425-818-3077
www.heathermarie.net
Instrument: Violin, Viola

Music Instruction

A Piano Studio
425-259-2884
Everett
Instrument: Piano
Age: 7+

Academy Of Music Northwest
425-778-7711
www.amnw.org
info@amnw.org
Bellevue
Classes: Music Theory, Music & Movement, Children's Choir
Age: 3-18
A not-profit organization that will teach regardless of means.

Columbia Boys Choir & Columbia Girls Choir
Lynnwood
425-486-1987
866-486-1987
www.columbiachoirs.com
Programs: Train singers from 15 school districts. Auditions are required.
Age: 3 to Adult

Drummer's Evolution
425-260-9144
www.DrummersEvolution.com
Seattle, Kirkland, Snohomish, Mill Creek, Canyon Park, Lake Stevens
Instrument: Drums
Age: 5+
His goal is "to teach students to reach for their goals, while having fun doing it."

Evolutions A Voice Studio
Duvall
425-869-4274
Instrument: Voice
Age: 15+

4/4 School Of Music
425-485-8310
www.44School.com
Bothell, Lynnwood, Everett, Edmonds
Instrument: Guitar, Drums, Voice, Bass, Saxophone, Flute, Clarinet, Trumpet, Trombone, Garage Band
Age: 5+

Greg's Pickin Parlor
123 N Blakely St
360-794-0547
Monroe
Instrument: Guitar

InstaLearn
425-355-9830
Mukilteo

Joy Of Music Co
425-353-2835
Instrument: Piano/Keyboard
Age: 6-11

Kenneth L Moses Piano Instruction
20505 Highway 99, Lynnwood
425-774-6299
Instrument: Piano
Age: 3+

Lindenmuth Scott Guitar Instruction
425-776-6362
Instrument: Guitar

Northwest Conservatory Of Music
360-794-6256
Instrument: Piano
Age: 3+

Piano-Keyboard & Theory Lessons
23106 67th Pl W, Mountlake Terrace
425-776-3512
Instrument: Piano, Organ
Age: 4+

Sonja Sarr
Marysville
360-658-4945
swingingsarr@yahoo.com
Beginning Piano, Jazz Piano

Suzuki Violin School
425-745-0477
Instrument: Violin
Age: 3+

The Guitar Guy
425-776-6362
Edmonds
Instrument: Jazz, Blues, and Classical Guitar

The Piano Studio
3625 Lombard Ave, Everett
425-257-2884
Instrument: Private Piano Lessons

The Voice Teacher
425-488-1297
Kenmore
Instrument: Voice: classical, musical theater, pop
Age: 12+

Mini Music

Kindermusik

www.kindermusik.com

Kindermusik incorporates naturally evolving music classes in a nurturing, energetic, imaginative environment filled with music, dancing, story time, and play classes. Through these classes, children learn language skills, literacy, listening, problem solving, social skills, self-esteem, and musicality. Each class includes materials for children to continue their learning with thematic CD's, activities, instruments, and children's books.

The following is a list of Kindermusik classes:

- Village: Newborn-1 1/2 years
- Our Time: 1 1/2 -3 years
- Imagine That: 3-5 years
- Young Child: 5-7 years
- Sign & Singing: 6 months-3 years

Kindermusik Instructors

Tanya Witruk

www.makingmusik.com/jingleandjamstudios

425-379-5907

Millcreek, Snohomish, Lynnwood
Village, Our Time, Imagine That, Young Child

Darlene Maxwell-Arts & Music Center

www.kindermusiknorthwest.com

425-337-5328

Everett/Mill Creek, Arlington, Granite Falls
Village, Our Time, Imagine That, Young Child
Other: Group Piano

Jessica Lee Bodge

www.bodgemusicacademy.com

425-347-8818

Lynnwood, Mukilteo, Seattle
Village, Our Time, Young Child

Lizzie Yarnold
pmea@comcast.net
206-306-1700
Shoreline
Our Time

Analiisa Reichlin
analiisa@studio3music.com
www.studio3music.com
425-385-3636
Village, Our Time, Imagine That, Young Child
See ad in back

Carolyn Fridenmaker
carolyn@heartsoulmusik.com
www.heartsoulmusik.com
425-787-8446
Edmonds, Seattle

Market Street Music
nancy@marketstmusic.com
www.kindermusikwithnancy.com; www.marketstmusic.com
206-417-5236
Kirkland

Chloe Wilcox
chloe.wilcox@juno.com
425-359-9661
Snohomish
Our Time, Imagine That

Nicole Muhlestein
Pro Club-Youth Department
nikihm@hotmail.com
425-861-6247
Redmond/Bellevue
Village, Our Time, Imagine That

The Musik Place
MISSCYNTHIA@THEMUSIKPLACE.COM
425-885-5303
Redmond
Village

Christine Floyd
thefloyds49@hotmail.com
360-659-1810
Marysville
Village, Our Time, Imagine That, Young Child

Judy Lawrence
lawrence@telebyte.com
360-297-7355
Kingston/Poulsbo
Village, Our Time, Young Child

Linda Slater
lcslater1@juno.com
206-842-0126
Bainbridge Island
Birth-7 years
Village, Our Time, Imagine That, Young Child

Louis Magor
Kindermusik@Kenyon
www.kenyonhall.org
kenyonhall@earthlink.net
206-937-3613
Seattle, West Seattle
Village, Our Time, Imagine That, Young Child

Tamara Frei
musicalbeginnings@comcast.net
www.beginningmusic.com
360-479-1268
Bremerton
Village, Our Time, Imagine That, Young Child

Cheryl Bouck
castaker@wmconnect.com
360-674-7035
Port Orchard
Our Time

Gabrielle Burgess
BeallComp@aol.com
members.aol.com/busybmusik/index.htm
206-463-9916
Vashon
Young Child

Lauren's Kids & Music
kinderlauren@mindspring.com
www.gokidsandmusic.com
253-709-7916
Maple Valley, Renton
Village, Our Time, Imagine That, Young Child
Other: Small Groups Piano, Small Groups Violin, Music for Little Mozart, B-day Parties

Michelle Cary
MissAndiCR@aol.com
425-888-5605
North Bend
Village, Our Time, Imagine That, Young Child

Luanne Kauppila
luanne@luannesmusicstudio.com
www.luannesmusicstudio.com
360-825-8870
Enumclaw
Village, Our Time, Imagine That, Young Child
Other: Sign & Singing (new class)

The Musik Nest
www.themusiknest.com
425-427-0984
Issaquah, Bellevue
Village, Our Time, Imagine That, Young Child

Sharon Chang
206-726-3677
Village, Our Time
Other: Piano and Dance lessons

Do-Re-Me & You
Shelley
425-290-9705
Kindermusik Products
Find fun, whimsical, and educational musical products perfect for a child's world.

Local Children's Choir

Pacifica Children's Chorus
4742 42nd Ave SW, Seattle
206-927-9095
206-527-9095 (auditions appointments)
www.pacificachoirs.org
Cost: Scholarships Available
Ages: 6 and Up
Preparatory Class (ages 3-6)

The Pacific Children's Chorus is divided into four groups:

- Children's Chorus (beginner, grades 1-2)
- Treble Junior Choir (intermediate grades 3-6)
- Treble Ensemble (main performing choir, grades 4-10, audition required)
- Chamber Singers (non-trebled voice choir, grades 7-10, audition required)

Students acquire musical skills through singing, ear training, games, and written theory. The choir's repertoire includes folk, world, classical, jazz, contemporary, and sacred music. Grades 4-12 can also study folk dancing and performance.

Sonja Sarr: swingingsarr@yahoo.com
Frank DeMiero: frank@smpjazz.com

Local Opera House

Seattle Opera House
225 Mercer St, Seattle
206-389-7602

Local Symphonies

Seattle Symphony/Benaroya Hall
200 University St, Seattle
206-215-4747
www.seattlesymphony.org/benaroya/

Programs for children:

Tiny Tots: birth – 5 years
Time: Tuesdays and Saturdays: 40 minutes concerts, 5-6 daily session
Price: 6 Sessions
Illsley Ball Nordstrom Recreation Hall
Pre-concert lobby activities start 1/2 hour prior.

Discover Music: 5-12 years
Time: Saturday at 10:00am
Price:
S. Mark Taper Foundation Auditorium

Discover Music Enhancement Class: 5-12 years
Time: 1st Sunday each month, October-May
Price:
Concerts for Teens & Adults
Popular Classics
Time: Fridays at 7:00pm
Community Concerts: Free
Check the website for upcoming local concerts.

Southbridge Seattle Symphony Music Discovery Center
Benaroya Hall
200 University, Seattle: entrance on 2nd & Union
206-336-6600
www.soundbridge.org
Hours: Tuesday-Sunday 10:00am-4:00pm
Daily Musical Storytelling: Tuesday-Saturday 10:15, Sunday 12:15
Price: Free for Members: $50 family annual membership, or $7 Adults, $5 Children 5-12, Under 5 Free. This includes admission to the Music Discovery Center.
Soundbridge is a wonderful place for children to learn, explore, and indulge in music splendor. Enjoy daily musical storytelling, instrument exploration, classes, student recitals, lectures, workshops, and the following exhibits: "Meet the Musicians, Conductors and Composers" past and present, Listening Posts, musical skills computer games, Virtual Conducting, and "Science of Sound–Music as a Science".

Everett Youth Symphony
www.eyso.info
Mukilteo
425-258-2028
Find information on concerts, conductors, auditions dates, community events, volunteering, the photo gallery, and their newsletter.

Music Stores

King County

A# Music
204 SW 43rd St, Renton
425-251-5929

Capital Music Center
718 Virginia St, Seattle
206-622-0171

Donn Bennett Drums Shop & Music Studio
13212 NE 16th, Bellevue
425-747-6145

Easthill Music Center
25680 104th SE, Kent
253-852-3025

Enumclaw Music
1515 Colet St, Enumclaw
360-825-1191

Gordon Sound
9476 Silverdale Way,
Silverdale
360-692-2957

Green River Music
108 S Division, Auburn
253-833-2240

Guitar Center
12608 120th Ave NE, Kirkland
425-814-9640

Guitar Center
230 Andover Park W, Tukwila
206-243-9077

Hammond Ashley Violins
19825 Des Moines Memorial Dr, Des Moines
206-878-3456

Helmer's Music
1640 S 318th Pl, Federal Way
253-839-2124

John's Music Center
4501 Interlake N, Seattle
206-548-0916

Kennelly Keys Music Inc
19720 5th NE, Seattle (Northgate)
206-440-8299

Kennelly Keys Music Inc
3830 Stone Way N, Seattle
206-547-2737

Lakewood Music Center
6111 Lakewood Towne Center Blvd SW, Lakewood
253-581-2926

Mills Music
13500 1 Bellevue-Redmond Rd, Bellevue
425-643-3100

Mills Music
10120 Main, Bothell
425-486-5000

Pacific Music
16729 Cleveland St, Redmond
425-885-9703

Plateau Music
4532 Klahanie Dr SE, Issaquah
425-369-9333

The Trading Musician
5908 Roosevelt Way NE, Seattle
206-522-6707

Washburn Piano Co
Bellevue, Seattle
800-753-7015

West Campus Music Center
32042 23rd S, Federal Way
253-927-0434

Snohomish County

Bentley's String Instruments
2937 Broadway Ave, Everett
425-303-9248

Bigfoot Music
3405 172nd NE Suite 21, Arlington
360-651-1199

Cascade Music
3rd & State, Marysville
360-659-8555

Cascade Music
7009 265th St NW #108, Stanwood
360-629-7300

Guitar Center
19509 Hwy 99, Lynnwood
425-672-8807

Heritage Music Center
8622 271st NW, Stanwood
360-639-9044

Kennelly Keys Music Inc
4918 196th St SW, Lynnwood
425-771-7020

Mills Music
Hwy 99, Lynnwood
425-775-6500

Pedigo Piano
4707 Evergreen Way Suite B, Everett
425-259-0887

Websites

5 Ways to Get the Most Out of Music Lessons
www.44school.com/5ways.htm

Classical Composers Homepage
www.music.indiana.edu/music_resources/composer.html
A collection of 165 classical music composers, links to their biographies, links to websites dedicated to each composer, and classical music education links.

Operabase
www.operabase.com
An international website listing information about opera artists, performances, festivals, and related links.

Musicals 101
www.musicals101.com
Read about the history of musical theater, and find information about current musicals.

Chapter 6

Theatre, Dance and Creative Arts

Chapter 6

Theatre, Dance and Creative Arts

The arts are much more than just fun "extra" activities for kids. Participation in the arts opens up children's worlds and mind, and offers them the skills they need for a bright future.

Did you know that...

- The arts teach kids to be more tolerant and open.
- The arts allow kids to express themselves creatively.
- The arts promote individuality, bolster self-confidence, and improve overall academic performance.
- The arts can help troubled youth, providing an alternative to delinquent behavior and truancy while providing an improved attitude towards school.

Young artists, as compared with their peers, are likely to:

- Attend music, art, and dance classes nearly as three times as frequently.
- Participate in youth groups nearly four times as frequently.
- Read for pleasure nearly twice as often.
- Perform community service more than four times as often.

(Living the Arts Through Language + Learning: A Report on Community-Based Youth Organizations, Shirley Brice Health, Stanford University and Carnegie Foundation for the Advancement of the Teaching, Americans for the Arts Monograph, November 1998).

Kids involved in the arts are more likely to be class officers, participate in math and science, and excel in academic involvement.

Encourage your child to try new things and explore new interests continually. You may stumble upon a passion for acting, dance, art, and even broadens their horizons.

Theatre

King County

Clay Martin's Puppet Theater

425-831-2109
800-300-5196

www.leapfrog-entertainment.com

Clay Martin's theater has been is business for over ten years. His programs include the 300 year old story of Punch & Judy, King Arthur, and Robin Hood, Moby Dick, Frankenstein, and The Hounds of Baskerville. His Victorian Toy Theater is quite unique, where last year he performed the production of Mozart's Opera, Bastien & Bastienne with professional opera singers accompanied by a live string quartet. He also includes a short lecture on history and construction of puppets and marionette's.

Seattle Children's Theatre

201 Thomas St
206-441-3322

www.sct.org

Rated by Time Magazine as "one of the outstanding theaters of it's kind". Families will enjoy a variety of performances including musicals, classic adaptations, and plays. They also offer classes through their Drama School. Visit their website for information on seasonal productions.

The Playhouse

200 Madison Ave N, Bainbridge Island
206-842-8569

www.theplayhouse.org

Hours: Tuesday-Saturday 10:00am-3:00pm.

Performances at the Bainbridge Performing Arts include theatre productions for school-aged children, Robin Hood, and The Adventures of Stewart Little. "BPA" offers school-aged children theatre school. Visit their website for a current list of classes and children's productions.

Broadway Bound Children's Theatre

717 N 36th St, Seattle
206-679-3561
206-526-KIDS (Summer Camps)
www.broadwaybound.org
Enjoy 3 full-length musical productions annually.
Summer camps and individual classes are available. Your child will learn how to develop their theatrical skills and potential through fun and hard work.

Book-It Repertory Theatre

305 Harrison St, Seattle
206-216-0833
www.book-it.org
Show Times: Wednesday, Thursday, Friday, and Saturday 7:30pm, Saturday and Sunday 2:00pm. 2 Locations: Seattle Center and Seattle Children's Museum
Student Matinee's Available. Show times vary. Check their website for updated information.
Book-It All Over: Cost is $550. Touring stories with a performance, book, study guide, and a workshop for 30 students. For grades Kindergarten through 8th.

Snohomish County

The Marysville Opera House

1225 3rd St, Marysville
360-657-5532

Acting:

Kids Stage at Francis J. Gaudette Theatre

303 Front St N, Issaquah
425-392-3303
www.villagetheatre.org
Pre-k through 12th Grade

Kids Stage at Everett Performing Arts Center

2710 Wetmore Ave, Everett
425-257-6341
www.piedpier@villagetheatre.org

Kidstage Class Registration:
Issaquah: 425-392-1942 x 148
Everett & Stanwood: 425-257-6371
Season Tickets Available
Camps: Creative Critters (Pre-K, K); Fairy Tale Players (Pre-k, K); Princesses, Wizards, and Knights (K-2); Theatresports (Grades 3-5); Broadway Jr. (Grades 2-4); Clowning Around (Grades 3-5); Wizards, Villains, and Magical Characters (Grades 3-5) ; Putting on a Show! – Big River (Grades 5-9); Hip Hop (Grades 6 & up); Playwriting (Grades 6 & up); Rockin' on Broadway (Grades 5-9); Golden Age of Broadway (Grades 4-8); European Invasion! (Grades 6 & up); Broadway Bound (Grades 4-8) ; Broadway Today (Grades 8 & up). All camps have final demonstration on Fridays

Seattle Children's Theatre
201 Thomas St, Seattle
206-441-3322 (Ticket Office)
206-443-0807 (Drama Classes)
www.sct.org
Ages: 3 1/2 to 19
Classes:
Summer: 1-2 hour classes/per day for 1-2 week sessions: $145-$185
Fall/Winter: 1-2 hour classes for 11 weeks: $145-$185

Kirkland Performance Center
350 Kirkland Ave, Kirkland
425-893-9900
www.kpcenter.org
Their state of the art stage is available for school group performances. They also perform several children's plays throughout the school year.

Northwest Puppet Center
9123 15th NE, Seattle
206-523-2579
www.nwpuppet.org
An internationally renowned puppet center presents performances by Carter Family Marionettes and esteemed guest artists. It features an exhibit museum, archive and library focused on the puppetry arts. Programs are also brought to communities near and far with touring performances and educational outreach.

Stone Soup Theatre
4035 Stone Way N, Seattle
206-633-1883
www.stonesouptheatre.com
Summer Classes: 2 Locations:
Stone Soup Theatre, and Heritage Park in Lynnwood
Creative Dramatics: Ages 6-10, Improvisation: Ages 10-13
Auditions for plays held in the Spring
Ages 14-18, Improvisation: Ages 14-18 (experienced)

Dance Instruction

King County

All That Dance
8507 35th Avenue Northeast, Seattle
206-524-8944
www.all-that-dance.com
Classes: Ballet, Ballroom, Creative Dance, Hip-Hop, Jazz, Swing Dancing, Tap
Ages: 3 and Older
Special Events: Spring Performance at Shorecrest Performing Arts Center in Shoreline
Summer Dance Camps: Monday-Friday, 2 ? hours. Dates Vary.

Allegro Dance Academy
1311 S Central, Kent
253-813-9630
www.allegrodance.com
Classes: Ballet, Drama, Hip Hop, Jazz, Lyrical, Musical Theater, Pointe, and Pre-Dance.
Plus: Voice, and Dance Company
Ages: 3 to Adult
Special Events: Summer Dance Classes in July

American Dance Institute
8001 Greenwood Ave N, Seattle
206-783-0755
www.americandanceinstitue.com
Classes: Parent Toddler Class, Creative Dance, Pre-Ballet, Ballet, Musical Theatre, Improvisation and Choreography, Tap, Hip-Hop, Jazz, Flamenco, and Irish Step Dancing
Ages: 18 months (with Parent) to Adult

ARC Dance Productions
9250 14th Ave NW, Seattle
206-352-0798
www.arcdance.org
Classes: Classical and Contemporary Ballet, Modern, and Jazz.
Programs: Children's (ages 3-6), Student (ages 6-20), Mentor/Apprentice (ages 16-21), and Progressive Open (teen through adult).
Ages: 3 to Adult
Special Events: Summer classes: Ballet, Character, Men's Technique, Modern, Jazz, Pas de Deux, Pointe/Variations, and Theater Dance.

Backstage Dance Studio
13420 SE 32nd, Bellevue
425-747-5070
www.backstagedance.org
Classes: Terrific Two, Creative Movement, Pre-Ballet, Ballet-Tap Combo, Ballet, Tap, Jazz, Lyrical & Hip Hop combined, Modern, Musical Theatre (ages 8+).
Ages: 2 to 18
Special Events: Competition Dance for Teens

Ballard Community Center
6020 28th Ave NW, Ballard
206-684-4093
www.cityofseattle.net/parks/centers/Ballard.htm
Classes: Creative Ballet, Pre-Ballet, Jazz, Dance Workshops
Ages: 3+

Ballet Bellevue
204th 100th Ave NE, Bellevue
425-455-1345
www.balletbellevue.org/contact.htm
Classes: Pre-Ballet through Ballet V
Ages: Children to Adult

Creative Dance Center
12577 Densmore Ave N, Seattle
206-363-7281
www.creativedance.org
Classes: Infant, Parent/Toddler, Parent/Child (ages 2-4), Creative Dance , Dance and Art, Creative Modern, Modern, Jazz Hip Hop, Ballet, Yoga, and Family Folk Dance.
Ages: Infant to 15
Special Events: Creative Arts Preschool: Ages 4-6. Includes Art, Creative Dance, Music, Free Play Time, Storytelling, and Snack Time. 2 days/week.

Dance Academy of Bellevue
775 112th NE, Bellevue
425-454-6008
www.danceacademyofbellevue.com
Classes: Pre-Ballet, Ballet, Creative Movement, Hip Hop, Jazz, Tap
Ages: 3 to Adult
Special Events: Birthday Parties: $170 for Dance Academy Students, up to 15 children.

Dance Fremont
900 N 34th Suite 102, Seattle
206-633-0812
www.dancefremont.com
Classes: Ballet, Point, Modern, and Jazz: Offered September-June
Nurturing Pathways (2 Months-Walking), Waddlers (Walking-age 2), Toddlers (ages 2-3), Creative Dance (ages 3-5), Preporatory 1 (ages 5-6) Preporatory II (age 7), Classical Modern (ages 8+), Classical Ballet (ages 8+, Open Jazz (ages 11+), Performance Jazz (ages 8+) must be enrolled in Ballet & Modern V Classes.
Ages: 2 Months with Parent, and Walking to Adult
Special Events: Summer Camps July-August

Dance Time
11961 124th Ave NE, Kirkland
425-820-6003
Classes: Pre-Ballet, Ballet, Flamingo, Hip Hop, Jazz, Lyrical, and Modern.
Ages: 3 and Older

Dance Arts
31040 E Lake Morten Dr SE, Kent
253-630-0951
www.dancearts.net
Classes: Ballet, Creative Movement, Hip Hop, Jazz, Lyrical, and Tap.
Ages: Preschool to Adult

Discovery Dance
16600 NE 80th St, Redmond
425-882-4780
425-556-2300 (Registration)
www.julie@discoverydance.com
Classes: Playful exploration of dance through movement, rhythm and song. Develops body awareness, motor skills, and creativity in a fun, friendly environment.
Ages: Two Classes offered Friday Afternoon and Saturday Morning: Ages 1-3 w/ Parent, Ages 1-4 w/ Parent.
Special Events: Ten-week classes offered quarterly for kids walking to age three.

Elizabeth's Dance Dimensions
12121 Northup Way, Bellevue
425-883-2206
www.dancedm.com
Classes: Creative Tiny Tots (3-5), Kinderchild (3-5), Pre Pro Kids (5-6) Pro Kids (7-8), Acro, Ballet, Hip Hop, Jazz, Lyrical, Tap, Turns Leaps & Progression.
Ages: 3 to Adult

Ewajo Centre Inc
2719 E Madison, Seattle
206-322-0155
www.ewajocentre.com
Classes: Afro, Ballet, Jazz, Latin, and Modern.
Ages: 3 and Up
Special Events: Summer Classes

Evergreen City Ballet
10 E Main, Auburn
253-833-9039
www.evergreencityballet.org
Classes: Ballet, and Creative Movements.
Ages: 3 to Adult

International School of Classical Ballet
507 6th St S, Kirkland
425-822-7694
www.interballetschool.com
Classes: Classical Dance, Point, Variations, Pas De Deux, Character, Jazz, Tap and Modern Dance, Mat-Stretch Class. Based on the Russia Ballet traditions.
Ages: 3 to Adult
Hours: Monday-Friday 1:00pm-9:00pm, Sat 9:00am-1:00pm
Special Events: Summer Classes: Monday-Friday: 10:00am-3:00pm

Johnson & Peters Tap Dance Studio
6600 1st Ave NE, Green Lake
206-935-7620
www.tapdanceseattle.com
Classes: Specialize in Tap.
Ages: 7 on Up

Kirkland Dance Center
835 7th Ave, Kirkland
425-828-6362
www.Kirklanddance.org
Classes: Hip Hop, Jazz, Tap, Ballet, Irish, Salsa, Tango, Swing, Hustle, and Funk.
Ages: 3 to Adult

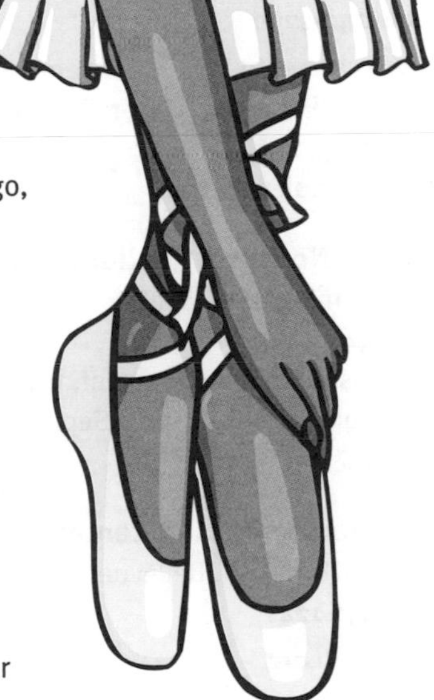

Langston Hughes Performing Arts Center
104 17th Ave S, Seattle
206-684-4757
www.cityofseattle.net/parks/centers/langston-htm
Classes: Acting, Art, Dance, Music, Writing for Children and Teens.
Ages: 7-18
Special Events: National Historical Landmark former Jewish Synagogue of Chevra Bikur Cholim.

Madrona Dance Studio
800 Lake Washington Blvd, Seattle
206-325-3056
www.spectrumdance.org
Classes: Movement for Toddlers, Ballet, Creative Dance, Jazz, and Hip Hop.
Ages: 2 and Older

Maple Valley School of Ballet
P.O. Box 1408, Maple Valley
425-432-3196
www.maplevalleyballet.com
Classes: Creative Ballet, Ballet, and Modern Dance.
Ages: 4 and Older
Special Events: Performances at Local High School

Mercerart
7513 SE 27th St, Mercer Island
206-232-6237
www.mercerartdance.com
Classes: Ballet, Hip Hop, Jazz, and Musical Theater.
Ages: 3 and Older

Momentum Dance Academy
15823 1st S, Burien
206-242-1230
www.momentumdanceacademy.com
Classes: Pre Ballet, Ballet, Ballroom, Hip Hop, Jazz, Mom and Me, Modern, Tap, and Tumbling.
Ages: Toddler and Up

Pacific Northwest Ballet School
301 Mercer Street, Seattle
206-441-2435
Classes: Creative Movement, Pre-Ballet, Student-Level Classes (ages 8+).
Auditions held in August, September, and January
Ages: 6 and Older

The Francia Russell Center
13440 NE 16th St, Bellevue
425-451-1241
www.pnb.org
www.pnb.org/pnbschool/workshops.html
Classes: Creative Movement, Pre-Ballet, Student-Level Classes (ages 8+).
Auditions held in August, September, and January
Ages: 6 and Older
Special Events: Summer Workshops for ages 4 to 7. Each one-week session focuses on a different theme (Sleeping Beauty, Nutcracker, Swan Lake, etc,)

Premier Dance Center
2623 151st Pl NE, Redmond
425-867-2300
www.premieredancecenter.com
Classes: Ballet, Hip Hop, Jazz, Lyrical, and Tap.
Ages: Toddlers on Up
Special Events: Summer Dance Classes

Seattle Children's Dance and Movement
915 E Pine St, Seattle
206-240-6313
Classes: Technique, Improvisation, Choreography, Tumbling, Partnering and Self Expression.
Ages: 1 to 12

Snohomish County

Applause Studio
Mill Creek
www.applausestudio.org
Classes: Ballet, tap, jazz, hip hop, ballroom, swing, break dancing, musical theater
Other: Group & private voice, private piano & guitar, art & drama.
Ages: 2+
See ad in back

Alderwood Dance Spectrum
19231-33rd Ace W, Lynnwood
425-771-2994
www.alderwooddancespectrum.com
Classes: Ballet, Jazz, Tap, Lyrical, Hip Hop, and Hula.
Ages: 2 1/2 and Older
Special Events: Christmas Show, and Dance Recital at Everett Special Events Center.

Allegro Dance Studios
304 Lincoln Ave, Mukilteo
425-513-2919
www.allegrodance.com
Classes: Ballet, Drama, Hip Hop, Jazz, Lyrical, Musical Theater, Pointe, and Pre-Dance.
Plus: Voice, and Dance Company
Ages: 3 to Adult
Special Events: Summer Dance Classes in July

Ballet Academy of Performing Arts
22811-100th Ave W, Edmonds
425-771-4525
www.ballet-academy.net
Classes: Ballet, point, Jazz, Hip Hop, Tap, and Lyrical Dance.
Ages: Ages 3 to Adult

Barclay-Shelton Dance Centre
413 Bell Street, Edmonds
425-776-8111
Classes: Ballet, Modern, Jazz, Tap
Ages: Children to Adult/Beginning to Advanced

Cameo/Carrabba Dance Inc
18104 102nd NE Suite 104, Bothell
425-483-4272
www.cameodance.com
Classes: Ballet, Tap, Jazz, Hip Hop, Modern, and Break Dance.
Ages: Children to Adult
Special Events: Dance Camps

Camille's Dance Edge
7526 Olympic View Dr, Edmonds
425-672-1225
www.danceedgeonline.com
Classes: Acro, Ballet, Hip Hop, Jazz, Lyrical, and Tap.
Ages: Pre-School to Adult
Special Events: Competitions

Clan Heather Dancers
Everett
1-877-467-8648
www.nas.com/clanheather
Classes: Scottish & Irish Dance
Ages: Preschool to Adult
Special Events: Competitions and St. Patrick Day Events.

Dansation Dance Center
3616 South Rd, Mukilteo
425-353-2623
Classes: Professional Dance Instruction, Musical Theater Group
Ages: Children to Adult

Everett Dance Theatre
7207 Evergreen Way, Everett
425-348-5955
Classes: Professional Dance
Ages: 3 to Adult

Express Yourself Studios
17624 15th Ave SE Suite 109a, Mill Creek
425-482-2075
Classes: Ballet, Jazz, Tap, Hip Hop, Break Dancing.
Ages: 2 to Adult

Hip Kidz Dance Academy
16823 Larch Way, Lynnwood
425-745-8511
www.hipkidz.org
Classes: Ballet, Lyrical, Jazz, Tap, Hip Hop, Tumbling
Ages: 3 and Up

LeValley Martha School of Dance
360-568-2448
Classes: Ballet
Ages: 3 to Adult

Marysville Performing Art Centre
4101 78th Pl NE, Marysville
360-651-9000
Classes: Professional
Dance Instruction
Ages: Children to Adult

Mountlake Terrace Recreation & Pavilion
www.cityofmlt.com
Classes: Ballet, Pointe, Baby Dance, Tap, Jazz, Lyrical Jazz, Hip Hop, Modern, Belly, and Yoga.
Ages: Preschool to Adult

Naneanani Hula Studio
425-259-3144
Classes: Hula
Ages: Children to Adult

No Limit Dance Studios
403 State Ave, Marysville
360-658-9464
Classes: Hip Hop, Jazz, Ballet, and Lyrical
Ages: 3+

Olympic Ballet
700 Main St, Edmonds
425-774-7570
www.olympicballet.com
Classes: Classic Ballet School
Ages: 3 to Adult

Pacific Chamber Ballet
6925-216th SW Suite F, Lynnwood
425-778-1600
Classes: Ballet
Ages: Children to Adult

Pacific West Performing Arts
204 Ave C, Snohomish
360-563-2793
Classes: Jazz, Tap, Ballet, Modern, Hip Hop, Miracloe, & Acro
Ages: 3+

Pilchuck Dance Academy Inc.
7315 NE 43rd Ave, Marysville
360-659-1099
Classes: Ballet, Jazz, Tap, Lyrical, Pointe, Pas De Deux, Flaminko, Swing.
Plus: Piano, Vocal, Spanish
Ages: 3 through Adult

Reflections School of Dance
13823 Seattle Hill Rd, Snohomish
425-338-9056
www.reflectionsschoolofdance.com
Classes: Ballet, Hip Hop, Jazz, Lyrical Jazz, Pointe, Pre-Dance, and Tap.
Ages: 4+

Sky Valley Dance Center
15186 Woods Creek Rd, Monroe
360-805-0331
www.skyvalleydance.com
Classes: Ballet, Basisc Dance, Creative Movement, For Boys Only (ages 7+), Hip Hop, Jazz, Lyrical, Modern, and Tap,
Ages: 3+
Plus: Kindermusik

Studio I
13300 NE 175th St, Woodinville
425-489-0861
Classes: Professional Dance Instruction
Ages: Children to Adult

Turning Pointe Dance Centre
18001 Bothell-Everett Hwy, Woodinville
425-398-0933
19501 144th Ave NE
425-485-8051
www.TurningPointeDanceCentre.com
Classes: Ballet, Jazz, Tap, Lyrical, Hip Hop, Point, Scottish Highland, Modern, Pilates.
Ages: 3 to Adult

Wendy's School of Dance
1715 228th St SE, Bothell
425-481-7899
www.wendysschoolofdance.com
Classes: Ballet, Creative Movement, Hip Hop, Jazz, Modern, Musical Theater, Pre-Ballet, Pre-Pointe.
Ages: 3 through Adult

Woodinville Dance Academy
18500 156th Ave NE, Woodinville
425-481-5526
www.woodinvilledance.com
Classes: Ballet, Hip Hop, Jazz, Lyrical, Modern, Pointe, and Tap
Ages: 3 to Adult

Art Instruction

Chapter 3 also lists several art classes available through local community centers and recreation centers.

Coyote Center
2719 E Madison #201, Seattle
206-323-7276
They offer weekend and after school courses for youth ages 10-15 years, in visual and performing arts, taught by professionals throughout central Seattle. Courses included Fine Arts, Photography, Welding, Singing, Cooking, Film, Radio, Rocketry, Soapbox Derby Cars, Hot Glass, Fiction, and more.

Creation Station
19511 64th Ave W, Lynnwood
425-775-7959
www.creationstationinc.com
Hours: Monday-Saturday 10:00am-6:00pm, Sunday 10:00pm-5:00pm (Sept-June).
Price: $4.95 per creator.
Children can choose from over 115 objects to build their one of a kind creations. With materials such as recyclable plastic, foam, wood, fabric, tubes, donated by local businesses and manufacturers, children have the freedom and opportunity to become inventors, artists, and crafters. This is such a unique studio, with something for everyone. Children can sign up for summer camps, and art classes. You can also buy materials to for a rainy day at home.

KidsArt
17210 Redmond Way, Redmond
425-498-2425
Fine art drawing and painting classes beginning at age 4.

Little Art School
4714 38th Ave SW, Seattle
206-938-0248

Monart School of the Arts
17 NW Alder Pl Suite 205, Issaquah
206-760-3797
Fine art classes for children, teens, and adults. Summer art camps also available

Monart Drawing School
2 Seattle Locations:

2900 E Madison St, Suite #200
6329 Ravenna NE
206-522-1659
www.drawingschool.com
Instruction is based on the best selling books "Drawing with Children", and "Drawing for Older Children and Teens" by Mona Brookes. Classes encourage creativity and expression.

Neo Art School
4649 Sunnyside N Suite 121, Seattle
206-632-2530
Award winning art classes, camps, after school, and parent-child classes.

Plateau Academy of Fine Art
Sammamish
206-679-0976
Drawing, clay, cartoon and animation, painting, and sculpture art classes.

Roaring Mouse Creative Arts Studio
7526 20th Ave NE, Seattle
206-522-1187
Art classes and day camps for children ages 2 ? to adults.

Spill the Paint Art Studio
416 228th Ave SE, Sammamish
425-837-0026
Art classes for children to adults.

Studio K
10200 NE 1st Place, Bellevue
425-637-8558
Drop in arts and crafts , classes, and summer day camps for ages 3+.

The Little Artist
2545 California SW, Seattle
206-935-4185
www.littleartiststudio.com

The Studio
1075 Bellevue Way NE, Bellevue
425-736-3060
Fine art classes include teaching the techniques for drawing and painting, soft chalk pastel, water color and oil paint.

Youth Advancement Through Music & Art
7400 Sand Point Way NE
206-523-9167

King County

Earth Ware & Fire
13018 SE Kent-Kangley Rd, Kent
253-630-6645
Hours: Tuesday, Wednesday: 11:00am-6:00pm, Thursday-Saturday: 11:00am-8:00pm, Sunday 12:00pm-6:00pm

Mary Kay's Outback Ceramics
701 Langston Rd, Renton
425-235-7445
By Appointment Only

Glazed & Amazed
5405 Ballard, NW, Seattle
206-789-7160
Workshops: $20 with snack Thursdays 1:30-3
Store Hours: Tuesday-Friday: 11:00am-9:00pm, Saturday: 11:00am-7:00pn, Sunday: 12:00pm-5:00pm

Paint Away! Ceramic Painting Studio
Redmond Town Center
7329 164th Ave NE, Redmond
425-861-8388

Paint The Town
2 Locations:
4527 University Village Ct NE, Seattle
206-527-8554
7329 164th Ave NE, Redmond
425-861-8388

The Glaze Cottage
2539 Gateway Center Blvd S, Federal Way
253-946-4502

Snohomish County

Create-A-Day
19849 State Route 2, Monroe
360-794-6864
Hours: Monday, Thursday 11-7, Friday 11-8, Sunday 12-6

Creatively Yours Ceramic Painting
3333 184th St SW, Lynnwood
425-774-3975
www.paintedbykathy.com
Hours: Monday-Saturday 10-9, Sunday 11-6

Michelle's Ceramics
11219 Callow Rd, Lake Stevens
425-334-9202
Hours: by Reservation only

Sewing and Quilting

Northwest Sewing
10722 5th NE, Seattle
206-362-3333
Classes: Kid's Camps. Scheduled by instructors.
Age: 7 and Older

Craft Supply Stores:

Ben Franklin Craft & Frame Shop
18505 Hwy 2, Monroe
425-481-2779
360-794-6745

Craft Mart Super Store
233 Marysville Mall Way, Marysville
360-653-9828

Craft Star
701 Hwy 9, Lake Stevens
425-397-0577

Creating A Good Book
9501 State Ave Suite J, Marysville
360-653-5934

Maries Craft & Gift
18001 Bothell-Everett Hwy, Bothell
425-486-6142

Michaels Arts & Crafts
1325 SE Everett Mall Way, Everett
425-267-9088

Michaels Arts & Crafts
3115 Alderwood Mall Blvd, Lynnwood
425-771-6979
Hours: Monday-Saturday 9-9, Sunday 10-7

Pacific Fabrics & Crafts
10203 Evergreen Way, Everett
425-353-8866

R & M What Knots/Painted Treasures
23406-94th Ave W, Edmonds
206-542-1592

The Scrapbook Barn
305 SE Everett Mall Way, Everett
425-438-3555

Think Ink
7526 Olympic View Dr, Edmonds
425-778-1935

Unicus Creations
6 112th St SW, Everett

Chapter 7

School and Educational Resources

Chapter 7

Schools & Educational Resources

Almost ten years ago, I received my Bachelor of Science Degree in Elementary Education. Knowing I would someday become a mother increased my desire to learn all I could about teaching children. During my short tenure as a teacher, I learned one of the most critical aspects to each child's success...parent involvement. With all the students I have observed both as a teacher and as a mother, I have noticed the consistency of student success in correlation with how involved a parent is with their child's education. Parents are children's first and most important teachers, but all adults have a stake in raising a generation of well-educated children. Environmental, social, and economic factors have a powerful effect on student performance. Parents are their children's best advocates.

Some Helpful Tips

Parents' willingness to contact teachers on a regular basis about their children's progress is perhaps the first step to becoming involved in their children's education. Armed with good information about a child's performance, parents can proceed in both direct and indirect ways to influence the child's progress. Mothers and fathers can become directly involved in children's education by:

- Setting a designated time each day for homework to be done, and checking the child's work for completeness and understanding
- Limiting time spent with friends and watching television
- Providing support for educators, essential leadership for programs, and ideas for improvements in the education system.
- Taking advantage of opportunities to become involved with school administration and policy development. Attend school board meetings and join the PTA.

PTSA

Washington State- Parent Teacher Association (PTA)

www.wastatepta.org

The mission of the PTA:

- To support and speak on behalf of children and youth in the schools, in the community and before governmental bodies and other organizations that make decisions affecting children;
- To assist parents in developing the skills they need to raise and protect their children;
- To encourage parent and public involvement in the public schools of this nation.

The Objects of the PTA

- To promote the welfare of the children and youth in home, school, community, and place of worship.
- To raise the standards of home life.
- To secure adequate laws for the care and protection of children and youth.
- To bring into closer relation the home and the school, that parents and teachers may cooperate intelligently in the education of children and youth.
- To develop between educators and the general public such united efforts as will secure for all children and youth the highest advantages in physical, mental, social, and spiritual education

Be sure to visit **www.wastatepta.org**, to see if your school has a PTA. Click on: Find your local PTA, and type in your city and state. It will list all the PTA associations in your city.

Helpful Tips for Choosing a School

When researching schools, whether it be a private/parochial school, language schools, or public schools, remember the following tips to help you refine your search and choose the school that best fits your child(ren)'s needs.

Interview the principal. Find what makes each school unique. What are the school's goals and priorities? What is the average class size? Is the principal a good listener? Does he or she have a good relationship with the students, teachers, and parents?

Speak with some of the teachers. Be prepared to ask questions important to your family.

Visit several classrooms. Are students engaged?

What is the school environment? Look at the classroom decorations, attitudes of students, teachers, and staff? Ask for some examples of school sponsored student and family activities.

If needed, be sure to find out about childcare-before and after school programs, and reduced lunches.

The National Association for the Education of Young Children (NAEYC) suggests the following guidelines when researching kindergarten classrooms/teachers.

Top 10 Signs of a Good Kindergarten Classroom

Kindergarten is a time for children to expand their love of learning, their general knowledge, their ability to get along with others, and their interest in reaching out to the world. While kindergarten marks an important transition from preschool to the primary grades, it is important that children still get to be children — getting kindergarteners ready for elementary school does not mean substituting academics for play time, forcing children to master first grade "skills," or relying on standardized tests to assess children's success.

Kindergarten "curriculum" actually includes such events as snack time, recess, and individual and group activities in addition to those activities we think of as traditionally educational. Developmentally appropriate kindergarten classrooms encourage the growth of children's self-esteem, their cultural identities, their independence and their individual strengths. Kindergarten children will continue to develop control of their own behavior through the guidance and support of warm, caring adults. At this stage, children are already eager to learn and possess an innate curiosity. Teachers with a strong background in early childhood education and child development can best provide for children what they need to grow physically, emotionally, and intellectually. Here are 10 signs of a good kindergarten classroom:

- Children are playing and working with materials or other children. They are not aimlessly wandering or forced to sit quietly for long periods of time.
- Children have access to various activities throughout the day, such as block building, pretend play, picture books, paints and other art materials, and table toys such as legos, pegboards, and puzzles. Children are not all doing the same things at the same time.
- Teachers work with individual children, small groups, and the whole group at different times during the day. They do not spend time only with the entire group.
- The classroom is decorated with children's original artwork, their own writing with invented spelling, and dictated stories.

- Children learn numbers and the alphabet in the context of their everyday experiences. Exploring the natural world of plants and animals, cooking, taking attendance, and serving snack are all meaningful activities to children.

- Children work on projects and have long periods of time (at least one hour) to play and explore. Filling out worksheets should not be their primary activity.
- Children have an opportunity to play outside every day that weather permits. This play is never sacrificed for more instructional time.
- Teachers read books to children throughout the day, not just at group story time.
- Curriculum is adapted for those who are ahead as well as those who need additional help. Because children differ in experiences and background, they do not learn the same things at the same time in the same way.
- Children and their parents look forward to school. Parents feel safe sending their child to kindergarten. Children are happy; they are not crying or regularly sick.
- Individual kindergarten classrooms will vary, and curriculum will vary according to the interests and backgrounds of the children. But all developmentally appropriate kindergarten classrooms will have one thing in common: the focus will be on the development of the child as a whole.

General Resources

Finding the Right School

206-706-4891

Cost: $80 an hour.

Finding the Right School, was developed by Regan Wensnahan, who wrote her master's thesis about the process Seattle parents take in choosing a kindergarten. You will receive a 2 hour private consultation to discuss the critical questions and answers to help find the best fit for each child.

Preschool Referrals

National Association for the Education of Young Children
800-424-2460
www.naeyc.org
Whether you're looking for a quality child care program, preschool, or school for your child, or you're interested in activities you can do at home to encourage your child's development, NAEYC can help! They are a non-profit organization, and have a great database of accredited schools and programs. Go to the parents and families link on their website to search for specific information to fit your needs.

Edmonds Communtiy College - Parent Coops
Six preschool sites, plus baby and toddler classes

Edmonds, Lynwood, Mountlake Terrace, Mill Creek
Family Life Dept office: 425-640-1665
www.edcc.edu/fled

Mountlake Terrace Coop Preschool
6205 222nd St SW, Mountlake Terrace
425-744-0874
www.edcc.edu/hhs/fled

Pacific Northwest Montessori Association
1-800-550-pnma
www.pnma.org

Shorenorth Preschool Coop
2545 NW 200th, Shoreline
206-440-1411
www.seanet.com/~noreen

West Edmonds Coop Preschool
9521 240th St SW, Edmonds
425-640-1665
www.sled.edcc.edu/west.asp

King County

Auburn Co-Op
St. Mathews Church
123 "L" NE, Auburn
253-833-9111 x 4830

Benson Hill Co-Op
Village Chapel
17418 108th SE, Renton
253-833-9111 x 4829

Burien Co-op Preschool
Burien Community Center
425 SW 144th St, Burien
206-241-6714

Black Diamond Co-Op
Black Diamond Presbyterian Church
P.O. Box 725, Black Diamond
253-833-9111 x 4882

Campus Co-Op
Green River Community College
12401 SE 320th St, Auburn
253-833-9111 x 4820

Children's Center at 70th and Sandpoint
Serving Children's Hospital and Regional Medical Center Families
6901 Sandpoint Way NE, Seattle
206-987-4700

Community School of West Seattle
4843 18th Ave SW, Seattle
206-762-2101
www.communityschoolwestseattle.org

Concordia Lutheran School
7040 36th Ave NE, Seattle
206-525-7407
www.concordialutheranschool.com

Covington Co-Op
Covington Community Church
17455 SE Wax Rd, Covington
253-833-9111 x 4833

Enumclaw Co-Op
Hope Lutheran Church
Garfield & Elmont, Enumclaw

Fauntleroy Children's Center
9131 California Ave SW, Seattle
206-932-9590
NAEYC Accredited

Federal Way Co-op Preschool
Federal Way United Methodist Church
29645 51st Ave, Federal Way
253-568-6904

Globel Kids Language Academy LLC
4426 Carnaby St, Kent
253-520-7572

Kent-Meridian Co-Op
9425 S. 248th, Kent
253-951-1115
www.kmcoop.org

Lake Forest Park Montessori
19935 - 19th Ave NE, Seattle
206-367-4404
www.lfpm.com

Ladybug Montessori
5042 18th Ave E, Seattle
206-524-7839

North City Cooperative Preschool
2545 NE 200th, Seattle
(206) 362-4069
www.northcitycoop.org

The Learning Tree Montessori
1721 15th Ave, Seattle
206-324-4788
www.learningtreemontessori.com

Ninth Avenue Children's House
1800 9th Ave Suite 210, Seattle
(206) 626-6525

Pacific First Montessori
1420 5th Ave Suite 300, Seattle
206-682-6878

Pacific Northwest Montessori Association
1-800-550-pnma
www.pnma.org

Scenic Hill Preschool & Kindergarten
26108 Woodland Way S, Kent
253-854-2874
glenhatch@ad.com

Shoreline Community College Parent Education and Coop Preschool Program
16101 Greenwood Ave N, Seattle
206-546-4593
oscar.ctc.edu/shoreline/parentcoop/html

Shoreline Cooperative Preschool
2545 NE 200th, Seattle
206-362-3257
www.shorelinecooperativepreschool.org

Shorenorth Parent Education Center
2545 NE 200th, Seattle
206-440-1411
www.seanet.com/~noreen/

Sky's the Limit Montessori
624 Meridian E, Milton
253-942-7677
www.skysthelimitmontessori.org

Tahoma Co-Op
Tahoma High School
18200 SE 240th, Maple Valley
253-833-9111 x 4832

The Stroum JCC's Seattle Facility
8606 35th Ave NE, Seattle
206-526-8073
www.sjcc.org

Thomas Academy
20 49th St NE, Auburn
253-852-4437
www.thomasacademy.org

The Villa Academy
5001 NE 50th, Seattle
206-527-9388
www.thevilla.org

U.W. Children's Center at Radford Court
Serving U.W. Families
6311 65th Ave NE, Seattle
206-543-3737

U.W. Children's Center at West Campus
Serving U.W. Families
3904 Cowlitz Rd, Seattle
206-548-9850

U.W. Children's Center at Laurel Village
Serving U.W. Families
4200 Mary Gates Memorial Dr, Seattle
206-525-5122

Veranda Montessori School
526 N 105th St, Seattle
206-782-5250

Eastside

Arbor Schools
1107 228th Ave SE, Sammamish
425-392-3866

Crystal Springs Cooperative Preschool
20012 Filbert Dr, Bothell
425-481-1177
elmo.shore.ctc.edu/shoreline/crystalsprings/index.html

Eton School
2701 Bellevue-Redmond Rd, Bellevue
425-881-4230
www.etonschool.com

Falls Christian Academy
35909 SE Fish Hatchery Rd, Fall City
425-396-7722
(Located between Fall City and Snoqualmie)

Finn Hill Cooperative Preschool
7718 NE 141st S, Bothell
425-485-1577
www.finnhillpreschool.com

Happy Heart Montessori
In Home Toddler-Preschool
Kirkland
425-823-8788

Inglemoor Cooperative Preschool
Carl Sandberg Elementary School
12801 84th Ave NE, Kirkland
425-821-2378
www.inglemoorcooperativepreschool.org

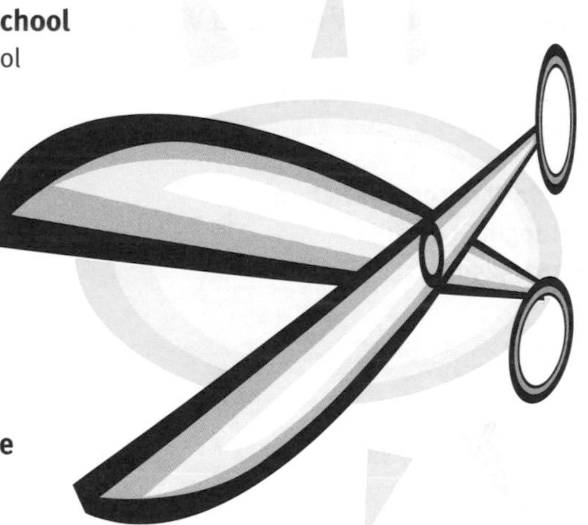

Kirkland Montessori
PO Box 262, Kirkland
425-822-1662
www.kirklandmontessori.com

Lake Forest Park Cooperative Preschool
6124 NE 181st, Kenmore
425-486-3466
preschool.fox-industries.com/

Northshore Community Cooperative Preschool
18315 Bothell Way NE, Bothell
(425) 485-4860
www.northshorecoop.org

Pacific Northwest Montessori Association
1-800-550-pnma
www.pnma.org

Sammamish Learning Center
22629 SE 29th St, Sammamish
425-313-1545
www.slckids.com

Strom Jewish Community Center
3801 E Mercer Way, Mercer Island
206-232-7115
www.sjcc.org

Woodinville Family Preschool
23713 49th Ave SE, Bothell
425-481-9707
success.shore.ctc.edu/shoreline/woodinville/home.html

Woodinville Toddler Group
Lake Washington Technical College (LWTC)
18900 168th Ave NE, Woodinville
425-670-0114
www.woodinvilletoddlergroup.org

Three Tree Montessori
220 SW 160th St, Burien
206- 242-5100
www.threetree.org

University Child Development Center
5062 9th Ave NE, Seattle
206-547-5059
www.ucds.org

Snohomish

Monroe Montessori School
733 Village Way, Monroe
360-794-4622
www.monroemontessori.com

Pacific Northwest Montessori Association
1-800-555-pnma
www.pnma.org

Snohomish County Christian School
17931 64th Ave W, Lynnwood
425-742-9518
www.sccslions.org

Child Resource and Referral Agency

Head Start
Created in 1965, Head start is a preschool designed for low income families, serving 1 million children in the United States. They also offer services of education, health, and provide support to parents, as they strive to prepare children for school.

Edmonds Community College-Snohomish County Head Start
14 East Casino Rd, Bldg. 4, Everett
425-712-9000

Puget Sound Educational Service District Head Start
400 SW 152nd St, Burien
206-439-6910
www.psesd.org/ecfs/default.html

Children's Home Society of Washington EHS
3300 NE 65th St, Seattle
206-695-3200
www.chs-wa.org"

Denise Louie Education Center
801 South Lane St, Seattle
206-621-7880
www.deniselouie.org

First AME Child and Family Center
4436 Rainier Ave. S, Seattle
206-322-0354
www.seafame.com

Neighborhood House Head Start
905 Spruce St. #213, Seattle
206-461-8467
Fax: 206-461-3857
www.nhwa.org/child_development.html

Seattle Public Schools Head Start
PO Box 34165, MS 31-555,
Seattle, WA 98124-1165
206-252-0976
www.seattleschools.org/area/headstart/index.dxml

United Indians of All Tribes Foundation Head Start
P.O. Box 99100
Seattle, WA 98199
206-285-4425
www.unitedindians.com/fondprograms.html

Child Care Resources

Seattle/North King County
1225 South Weller Suite 300, Seattle
206-329-1011
Referral Line
206-329-5544
Provider Line
206-329-5333
Hours: M-F 8:30-5:00

East King County
16315 NE 87th St Building B, Redmond
Referral Line
425-865-9350
Provider Line
425-865-9033
Hours: M, T 9:00-4:30

South King County
841 N Central Ave Suite 126, Kent
253-852-1908
Referral Line
253-852-3080
Provider Line
253-852-2566
Hours: W, TH 8:30-4:30

Public/Private/Parochial

Neighborhood Scout

www.neighborhoodscout.com/washington_school_rankings/seattle.html

"Discover the best schools districts in the Seattle area". This site is a national based, and had good reviews from The Wall Street Journal. You will find information comparing Washington State school districts including teacher ratio, spending, rate of graduation, SAT scores, and more. You are required to subscribe in order to have access to this information.

National Education Association (NEA)

www.nea.org/goodnews/wa01.html

This website lists the testing scores in math, reading, and writing skills within local school districts, and compares them with national scores. It also gives other information relating to issues in the public schools.

Private School Review

www.privateschoolreview.com
Find detailed information on the over 200 private day schools and high schools in Washington State's King and Snohomish Counties.

PSK12 Public School Ranking

www.psk12.com
With limited free use, find access to public school ranking information

Seattle Public Schools

www.seattleschools.org
Chalk full of information about the Seattle Public Schools.

The Seattle Times Website

www.seattleimes.com
Click on School Guide. You will find detailed information on budget spending, school rankings, schools within each school district, and more. You will also find within the districts the names of alternative schools, gifted and talented (challenging) schools, cooperative schools, and homeschooling supportive schools.

Public Schools Districts: King & Snohomish Counties

Office of Superintendent and Education

Old Capital Building
P.O. Box 47200
Olympia, WA 98504
360-753-2858

Auburn School District

253-931-4900
www.auburn.wednet.edu

Bellevue School District

425-456-4000
www.bsd405.org

Edmonds School District

425-670-7000
www.edmonds.wednet.edu

Everett School District

425-385-4000
www.everett.k12.wa.us/everett

Federal Way Public Schools

253-945-2000
www.fwps.org

Issaquah School District

425-837-7000
www.issaquah.wednet.edu

Kent School District

253-373-7000
www.kent.k12.wa.us

Lake Washington School District
425-702-3200
www.lkwash.wednet.edu

Lake Stevens School District
425-335-1500 (or 7500)
www.lkstevens.wednet.edu

Marysville School District
360-653-7058
www.mslv.k12.wa.us

Mercer Island School District
206-236-3310
www.misd.k12.wa.us

Monroe School District
360-794-7777
www.monroe.wednet.edu

Mukilteo School District
425-356-1274
www.mukilteo.wednet.edu

Northshore School District
425-489-6000
www.nsd.org

Seattle Public Schools
206-252-0207
www.seattleschools.org

Snohomish School District
360-563-7300
www.sno.wednet.edu

Snoqualmie Valley School District
425-831-8000
www.snoqualmie.k12.wa.us

Stanwood Camano School District
360-629-1200
www.stanwood.wednet.edu

Schools for Children with Special Needs

Every school district in Washington State is required to have a preschool program for children with special needs, starting at age 3. Refer to your school district to find out the preschool program information specific to your area.

Seattle Public Schools-Special Needs

www.seattleschools.org/area/speced/seaac.htm
This is the Seattle Public School's website for children and adolescents with special needs. You will find information on meetings, classes, the annual resource fair, contact information, monthly newsletters, and much more.

The Little Red School House

775-6070

www.littlered.org
Found in 1963 and licensed by the Washington State Office of the Superintendent of Public Instruction, this school addresses the needs of children age 5 years or younger with developmental delays and disabilities. This includes at risk children, children with Cerebral Palsy, Down Syndrome, Spina Bifida, and vision, hearing impairments, and more. Physical and Occupational Therapists, Family counselors, Speech Pathologist, and Early Childhood Educators are available.
Sites: Lynnwood, Everett, Tulalip Reservation

Gifted & Talented Resources

Council for Exceptional Children

800-328-0272

www.ericec.org/minibibs/eb18.html
Homeschooling resources for gifted students, including contests and competitions, curriculum K-8th grade, National Standards information, and more.

Gifted Children

www.gifted-children.com
Their focus in on "identification, encouragement, and development". You can sign up for membership ($10) to receive newsletters filled with updated news and current information related to the various aspects related to children who are gifted, and an "Ask The Expert" column.

Great Schools.Net

www.greatschools.net/cgi-bin/showarticle/wa/97/parent
Resources for gifted and talented education, related informational links, book referrals, and parent comments.

Hoagies Gifted Education Page

www.hoagiesgifted.org/

Hoagies provides numeorus resources, articles, and links for parents, educators, teens, and kids. Find information on gifted characteristics, testing, a shopping guide, and much more.

National Association for Gifted Children (NAGC)

www.nagc.org

This is a non-profit organization for parents, educators, and community members who desire to support the needs of gifted children. The website lists publications and materials, legislative updates, and more. You have the option to sign up for a membership ($25) to receive a quarterly parent magazine.

Reading List for Gifted Students

depts.washington.edu/cscy/resources/giftreadlst.htm

Great resources for teachers and parents, including links and education information.

Education News.Org

www.educationnews.org

Sign up for the free online newsletter to receive information on national research on the gifted and talented, resources, educational guides, the TAG Family Network, related web links.

The Robinson Center for Young Scholars

depts.washington.edu/~cscy

This organization is especially designed for teens. They focus on how to optimize development, achievement, and contributing to the community. Their services include diagnosis and counseling, early college entrance transitioning, talent searches.

Washington Association of Educators of the Talented and Gifted

HYPERLINK "http://www.waetag.org" www.waetag.org

Although this is specifically designed for educators, parents of gifted and talented children may also be interested in attending the conferences which discuss valuable information related to the gifted education.

Homeschooling Resources

At Home In Seattle (@HIS)

nidip1@comcast.net
A Christian homeschool support group.

Homeschooling

homeschooling.about.com/mbody.htm?once=true&
Free newsletter guide filled with articles and resources related to homeschooling. Topics include setting up a homeschool area, teaching and testing, academics, finding support groups, organizing school supplies, homeschooling education laws, etc. You'll also find curriculum links a buyer's guide, and a local fun days calendar.

K-12 Independence

www.k12.com" www.k12.com
Get complete homeschool curriculum for grades Kindergarten through 12th.

King County Library System

www.kcls.org/pp/homeschoolgen.cfm
Dozens of excellent homeschooling reading resources for families and children.

Washington Homeschool Groups (WHO)

www.washhomeschool.org
Find a homeschool support group in your area.

Washington Home School Organization

www.washhomeschool.org
Homeschooling statistics, support groups, information and resources, the Washington State law, events and news.

Language Schools

American Culture Exchange

206-217-9644

www.cultural.org
The A.C.E. language program consists of after-school classes available to local Seattle schools. Language classes consist of German, Spanish, Russian, Arabic, and Chinese. Request a language not listed, and they will try to accommodate. Call A.C.E. to enlist your child's school for language classes available from Kindergarten age through 5th grade.

Adpro LLC
13256 NE 20th St, Bellevue
425-637-2936
www.adproesl.com
English (ESL) and Japanese language instruction for children ages 3 and older.

Alliance Francaise De Seattle
4649 Sunnyside N, Seattle
206-632-5433
French language classes, cultural classes, and private instruction available.

Asia Pacific Language School
14040 NE 8th St Suite 302, Bellevue
425-641-1703
This school offers both private tutoring and classes, including preschools and after-school programs.

Berlitz Language Centers
520 112th NE, Bellevue
425-451-0162
www.berlitz.us
Berlitz offers several different choices for teaching children another language. From individual tutoring and group courses, to Before- and- After school programs and language camps. CD-Roms, books, tapes, and other materials are also available to increase learning. Over 50 languages are available for tutoring.

Canoe Island French Camp
Orcas Island
360-468-2329
www.canoeisland.org
Ages: 9-15
Date 2 week session
Price: $800+/per week
Learn French is the beautiful setting, along with French cooking, fencing, art, drama, international culture, sailing, photography and more. Camp to Counselor ratio is 3:1.

Dante Alighieri Society of Washington
206-320-9159
www.danteseattle.org

Dan Tranh
viethai24@yahoo.com.
Free Vietnamese lessons are held weekly on Sundays.

Dutch Oranje Language & Culture Schools
4141 81st Ave SE, Mercer Island
425-844-2653
www.oranjeschool.com
Classes: Saturday 9:30am-12:00pm
Ages: 3-12
Cost: 1st year $500 per children 2nd year or 3rd child $400, plus $50 registration fee.

Global Kids Language Academy
4426 Carnaby St, Kent
253-520-7572
www.globalkidslanguage.com
This is a Japanese Language Immersion Preschool, with a Japanese and Culture Program for school aged children. Both programs realize each child excels at their own pace, with their individual learning style. Children learn content through theme related activities including art, crafts, games from different cultures, science, math, social studies, writing, reading, music, and dance.

Seattle Language Academy
126 NW Canal St Suite 101, Seattle
206-325-4109
www.sealang.com
For children and young teens, private lessons are available for the following languages: Arabic, Chinese, French, German, Greek, Italian, Japanese, Portuguese, Russian, Spanish, Turkish, Latin, and Ancient Greek.

The Storybook Center, Inc
8028 132nd Ave NE, Redmond
425-881-1923
Language classes for babies on up.

Military

The Washington State Operation: Military Kids
Office of Superintendent of Public Instruction
360-725-6044
monaj@ospi.wednet.edu

Washington State University Extension Program

253-445-4612

wrightkc@wsu.edu

Their mission is "to create replicable and sustainable support networks for geographically dispersed military youth in schools and communities before, during, and after the deployment of a parent or loved one".

The Washington State Operation: Military Kids project focuses on the following:

- Supporting military kids coping with the stress of knowing their deployed parents or loved ones may be in harms way;
- Delivering recreational, social, and educational programs for military youth living in civilian communities;
- Collaborating with schools to ensure staff are attended and able to support the unique needs of military students;
- Educating the public on the impact of the deployment cycle on soldiers, families, kids and the community as a whole;
- Becoming a part of on-going 4-H Programs in locations where there are military kids and families;
- Creating community support networks for "suddenly military" youth "in their own backyards" where soldier parents are deployed

Providing the following community-based outreach activities geared to raise awareness and provide support for military kids and their families:

Speak Out for Military Kids - A youth speakers' bureau, formed by military and non-military youth that provide presentations to schools and community groups to help educate and raise awareness about military life, deployment, and reunion.

Hero Packs - Civilian youth participate in community service projects to assemble and distribute knapsacks filled with a variety of items to be given to military children and youth as a "thank you" for the sacrifices made while their parents are deployed.

Mobile Technology Labs - To be used to communicate and connect geographically dispersed "suddenly military" children with their deployed parents.

Tutors/Learning Centers

Dartmoor Learning
3 Locations:
Woodinville
17305 139th Ave NE
425-402-6788

Bellevue
13401 Bellevue-Redmond Rd
Suite A10
425-649-8976

Issaquah
4548 Kalahanie Dr SE
425-427-9078

Kumon Learning Centers
888-586-6673
www.kumon.com" www.kumon.com
Kumon believes, "Every child can succeed"! This after-school math, reading, and writing program, founded in Japan in 1958, uses a systematic approach that helps children develop solid command of math, reading, and writing skills. Worldwide, there are 3.6 million students enrolled in 43 countries.

Woodinville
17708 134th Ave NE
425-702-0188

Shoreline
15555 15th Ave NE
206-533-2300

West Shoreline
749 N 175th St
206-353-4179

Totem Lake
12700 NE 124th St #203
425-820-7747

Wedgewood-Seattle
7500 1/2 35th Ave NE
206-522-5345

Redmond
8133 161st Ave NE
425-869-3939

Greenwood
129 N 85th St
206-365-1600

University Village
4530 Union Bay Pl NE #210
206-524-0915

Capital Hill
3209 Eastlake Ave E
206-726-8880

Bellevue
14904 B Bel-Red Rd
425-747-5916

Bellevue Downtown
10623 NE 8th St Suite A
425-646-2907

Mercer Island
9725 SE 36th St
206-236-1815

Pine Lake-Sammamish
21333 SE 20th St
425-277-6106

Beacon Hill-Seattle
2531 16th Ave S
206-795-6216

Bellevue
4401 Somerset Blvd SE
425-746-7592

Seattle Learning Center
8001 Lake City Way NE, Seattle
206-525-0818

Sylvan Learning Centers
888-338-2283
www.educate.com" www.educate.com
At Sylvan, they create confident, independent students by discovering and targeting the causes of academic frustrations. Using the results of a comprehensive Skills Assessment, they create a personalized curriculum that addresses and eliminates underlying issues. Through positive reinforcement and a unique instructional method known as Mastery Learning, they ensure that each student achieves success.

Bellevue
4140 128th Ave SE, Suite 2A
425-641-7609

Federal Way
32717 1st Ave S
253-838-0507

Kent
25720 104th SE
253-854-7111

Kirkland
12233 116th Ave NE Suite 101
425-823-6727

North Seattle/Ballard
2232 NW Market St
206-297-4595

Seattle
8830 25th Ave SW
206-762-5200

Sammamish
3056 Issaquah Pine Lake Rd
425-392-2952

Snohomish County

Kumon Learning Centers
888-586-6673
www.kumon.com" www.kumon.com
Kumon believes, "Every child can succeed"! This after-school math, reading, and writing program, founded in Japan in 1958, uses a systematic approach that helps children develop solid command of math, reading, and writing skills. Worldwide, there are 3.6 million students enrolled in 43 countries.

Bothell/Mill Creek
18001 Bothell-Everett Hwy Suite G
425-806-0095

Lynnwood
2109 196th St SW Suite 3
206-992-0081

Edmonds
22315 Hwy 99 Suite F
425-771-0905

Marysville
7302 44th Ave NE #A
425-290-1660

Mukilteo
304 Lincoln Ave
425-290-1660

Sylvan Learning Centers
888-338-2283
www.educate.com" www.educate.com
At Sylvan, they create confident, independent students by discovering and targeting the causes of academic frustrations. Using the results of a comprehensive Skills Assessment, they create a personalized curriculum that addresses and eliminates underlying issues. Through positive reinforcement and a unique instructional method known as Mastery Learning, they ensure that each student achieves success.

Everett
425-355-1627

Lynnwood
425-774-3922

Silverdale
360-698-0440

Snohomish
360-568-2600

Stanwood
360-629-9989

School & Teaching Supplies-Retail

King County

Academic Aids Inc
14230 NE 20th, Bellevue
425-746-8033
Hours: Monday-Friday 10:00am-6:00pm, Saturday 10:00am-5:00pm, Sunday12:00pm-4:00pm

Artist & Craftsman Supply
4350 8th Ave NE, Seattle
206-545-0091
Hours: Monday-Saturday 9:00am-7:00pm, Sunday 10:00am-6:00pm

Children's Bookshop & Teaching Supplies
Bellevue
14210 NE 20th
425-653-7577

Burien
152 SW 152nd
206-242-9790

Kent
225 W Meeker
253-852-0383

Christian Supply
156 SW 152nd St, Burien
206-243-0600
Hours: Monday-Saturday 9:00am-8:00pm

Homeschool Potpourri Store
12815 NE 124th St, Kirkland
425-820-4626
Hours: Monday10:00am-7:00pm, Tuesday-Friday 10:00am-5:00pm

Lakeshore Learning Store
11027 NE 4th St, Bellevue
425-462-8076
www.lakeshorelearning.com" www.lakeshorelearning.com
Hours: Monday-Friday 9:00am-8:00pm, Saturday 9:00am-6:00pm, Sunday 11:00am-5:00pm
School Supplies, books, crafts, math, science, educational toys, & more.

Math 'N' Stuff
8926 Rossevelt Way NE, Seattle
206-522-8891
www.mathnificent.com" www.mathnificent.com
Hours: Tuesday-Saturday 10:00am-6:00pm
Puzzles, Games, Gizmos, Gadgets, Study Aids, Teacher Resources & Curriculum
Hours: Tuesday-Saturday 10:00am-6:00pm

Northlight Communications/Sign2Me
11395 5th Ave NE Suite B, Seattle
206-364-4676
www.sign2me.com" www.sign2me.com
Hours:
Signing Products for the Hearing World

Science Art & More
6417 Roosevelt Way NE, Seattle
206-524-3795
Hours:
Educations Toys, Materials, & Microscopes

Snohomish County

Alphabet Soup Educational Bookstore
9623 32nd St SE, Everett
425-377-9454
Hours: Monday-Friday10:00am-6:00pm

Children's Bookshop & Teaching Supplies
19720 44th Ave W, Lynnwood
425-673-2416
Hours:

Insta-Learn By Step
11324 Mukilteo Speedway, Mukilteo
425-355-9830
Hours:

Chapter 8

Libraries and Books

Chapter 8

Libraries & Books

Together with the schools, churches and organizations, and hospitals, the library is one of the cornerstones of a healthy community. Libraries give people the opportunity to experience adventure, develop creativity, explore great minds, and experience culture and art while providing a place for gathering.

Libraries reflect diversity, character, and give a greater sense of community to our neighborhoods. They provide enriching activities and resources for school children and preschoolers over summer vacations, evenings, and weekends.

As parents help their children learn to read, the library works as a partner in opening new worlds for our children, thus beginning an endless chain of learning. When you read to your child, they begin to develop a love of stories and poems, and soon will want to read for their own information or pleasure. As they become readers their world is forever expanded and enriched. The benefits to your child are immeasurable, and in the process you will find your world also being enriched. Having access to information though the printed world is an absolute necessity. Knowledge is power, and books are filled with it!

Involve your children in reading programs at your local library. Your kids will love it! The programs are fun, and even better… they're free.

Libraries

The Seattle Public Library System

Special Programs and Events: Each library offers a variety of child, teen, and family programs and events throughout the year. This includes author visits, workshops, storytelling, poetry readings, "Doughnut Drop In" with great book recommendations for teens, Movie Night with Free popcorn for teens, ESL, and more. Check your local library's website for current scheduled events.

Study Zone: Homework tutoring for elementary, middle school, and high school students. Participating libraries are included in this chapter.

Annual Summer Reading Program: The Seattle Public Library offers children the opportunity to earn a free paperback book and certificate. Simply read 10 books during the summer and turn in the form to any library.

King County

Seattle Public Library

800 Pike St

206-386-4636

www.spl.lib.wa.us

The Seattle Public Library offers new services for patrons with disabilities and special needs. The Kurzweil Reading Edge is an adaptive equipment resource available for patrons who are blind or with low-vision, that allows access to the libraries magazines, newspapers, professional journals, brochures, books, and other printing resources. Also available through the Library Equal Access Program (LEAP) is a service called WAVRS (Washington State Video Relay Service) available for the deaf and hard of hearing patrons. This service allows people to visually communicate using ASL via on-line video interpreters.

Washington Talking Book & Braille Library

2021 9th Ave, Seattle

206-615-0400

800-542-0866

www.wtbbl.org

Hours: Monday through Friday 8:30am – 5:00pm

The WTBBL collection includes fiction and non-fiction books on tape, in braille, and in large print for school-aged readers. Books and cassette machines are available for both home and classroom use. The children's librarian can help parents and students find books.

Reading Programs: Summer Reading Program: Read 10 books and receive a certificate and a free paperback book.

Special Programs: Children, their families, and friends are periodcally invited to the Library for performances designed for total inclusion of children with no usable vision. See website for scheduled performances.

The Orrico Children's Room: Visit the children's room for services dedicated for infants and toddlers with vision loss. You'll find a rotating collection of toys and baby books with braille added, and engaging toddler books on tape, also available for check out.

Mobile Services

2025 9th Ave, Seattle
206-684-4713
www.spl.org
Seattle's Children: Bookmobiles visit eligible fulltime, year-round childcare centers and other special daycare institutions throughout the city.

Ballard Branch

5614 22nd Ave NW
206-684-4089
www.spl.org
Hours: Monday and Tuesday 1:00pm - 8:00pm, Wednesday 10:00am - 8:00pm, Thursday-Saturday 10:00am - 6:00pm, and Sunday 1:00pm - 5:00pm.
Story Time: Preschool Story Time (ages 3-5): Thursday 10:30am – 11:00 am
Pajama Story Time (Families): 2nd Tuesday 6:45pm – 7:30pm. A family program of stories, songs and a simple craft activity.

Beacon Hill Branch

2821 Beacon Ave S
206-684-4711
www.spl.org
Hours: Monday and Tuesday 1:00pm - 8:00pm, Wednesday 10:00am - 8:00pm, Thursday-Saturday 10:00am - 6:00pm.
Story Time: Preschool Story Time: Thursday 11:00am – 11:30am

Broadview Branch
12755 Greenwood Ave N, Seattle
206-684-7519
www.spl.org
Hours: Monday and Tuesday 1:00pm - 8:00pm, Wednesday 10:00am - 8:00pm, Thursday-Saturday 10:00am - 6:00pm, and Sunday 1:00pm - 5:00pm.
Story Time: Preschool Story Time: Thursday 10:30am – 11:00am

Capitol Hill Branch
425 Harvard Ave E, Seattle
206-684-4715
www.spl.org
Hours: Monday and Tuesday 1:00pm - 8:00pm, Wednesday 10:00am - 8:00pm, Thursday-Saturday 10:00am - 6:00pm, and Sunday 1:00pm-5:00pm.

Central Library
1000 Fourth, Seattle
206-386-4636
206-684-4209 (Registration)
www.spl.org
Hours: Monday-Wednesday 10:00am - 8:00pm, Thursday-Saturday 10:00am - 6:00pm,
and Sunday 1:00pm - 5:00pm.
Story Time: (Newborn to 12 months): Monday 11:30am – 12:00pm
Spanish Story Time (ages 3-6): Monday 10:30am – 11:00am
Children Story Time (ages 3-8): Tuesday & Friday 10:30am – 11:00am
Toddler Story Time (ages 18 months-3 years): Wednesday 10:30am – 11:00am
Parent-Teen Book Group (Grades 6-8): Sunday 3:00pm – 4:00pm
Pizza and Pages Book Group (Grades 6-12): 3rd Tuesday 6:30pm – 7:30pm Best Books and Quick Picks
Reading Programs: Summer Reading Program: Read 10 books and receive a certificate and a free paperback book. Watch for details about special performances.
Special Programs: Art Corps Workshops for teens.

Columbia Branch
4721 Rainier Ave S, Seattle
206-386-1908
www.spl.org
Hours: Monday and Tuesday 1:00pm - 8:00pm, Wednesday 10:00am - 8:00pm, Thursday-Saturday 10:00am - 6:00pm, and Sunday 1:00pm - 5:00pm.
Story Time: Children Story Time (ages 1-8): Friday 10:30am – 11:00am.

Delridge Branch
5423 Delridge Way SW, Seattle
206-733-9125
www.spl.org
Hours: Monday and Tuesday 1:00pm - 8:00pm, Wednesday 10:00am - 8:00pm, Thursday-Saturday 10:00am - 6:00pm.
Story Time: Children Story Time: Thursday 11:00am – 11:30am

Douglass-Truth Branch
2300 E Yesler Way, Seattle
206-684-4704
www.spl.org
Hours: Closed for expansion. This library is expected to re-open in late summer/early Fall of 2006.
Nearby Libraries include the International District Chinatown Library, Madron-Selly Library, Columbia Library, Beacon Hill Library, Capital Hill Library, and Central library.

Fremont Branch
731 N 35th St, Seattle
206-684-4084
www.spl.org
Hours: Monday and Tuesday 1:00pm - 8:00pm, Wednesday 10:00am - 8:00pm, Thursday-Saturday 10:00am - 6:00pm.
Story Time: Preschool Story Time: 11:00am – 11:30am

Green Lake Branch
7364 E Green Lake Dr N, Seattle
206-684-7547
www.spl.org
Hours: Monday and Tuesday 1:00pm - 8:00pm, Wednesday 10:00am - 8:00pm, Thursday-Saturday 10:00am - 6:00pm.
Story Time: Preschool Story Time: Wednesday 10:30am – 11:00am
Toddler Story Time (ages18 months-3): Thursday 10:30am – 11:00am
Pajama Story Time: 7:00pm – 7:30pm.

Greenwood Branch
8016 Greenwood Ave N, Seattle
206-684-4086
www.spl.org
Hours: Monday and Tuesday 1:00pm - 8:00pm, Wednesday 10:00am - 8:00pm, Thursday-Saturday 10:00am - 6:00pm.
Story Time: Preschool Story Time: Thursday 11:15am – 11:45am
Toddler Story Time (ages 18 months-3): Thursday 10:30am – 11:00am
Pajama Story Time (ages 3-6): 6:30pm – 7:00pm Bring that special bedtime stuffed animal and wear jammies to story time to hear relaxing, friendly stories and quiet music. Date vary.

High Point Branch
3411 SW Raymond St, Seattle
206-684-7454
www.spl.org
Hours: Monday and Tuesday 1:00pm - 8:00pm, Wednesday 10:00am - 8:00pm, Thursday-Saturday 10:00am - 6:00pm.
Story Time: Preschool Story Time: Thursday 10:30am – 11:00am Children 3-5 years old are invited to celebrate stories, songs, finger plays and fun. This group meets Thursday at 10:30 a.m. (as scheduled).

International District / Chinatown Branch
713 Eighth Ave S, Seattle
206-386-1300
www.spl.org
Hours: Monday and Tuesday 1:00pm - 8:00pm, Wednesday 10:00am - 8:00pm, Thursday-Saturday 10:00am - 6:00pm.

Lake City Branch
12501 28th Ave NE, Seattle
206-684-7518
www.spl.org
Hours: Closed for construction. Scheduled to reopen Fall 2005

Madrona-Sally Goldmark Branch
1134 33rd Ave, Seattle
206-684-4705
www.spl.org
Hours: Monday and Tuesday 1:00pm - 8:00pm, Wednesday 10:00am - 8:00pm, Thursday-Saturday 10:00am - 6:00pm.
Story Time: Preschool Story Time (ages 3-5): Wednesday 10:30am – 11:00am

Magnolia Branch
2801 34th Ave W, Seattle
206-386-4225
www.spl.org
Hours: Monday and Tuesday 1:00pm - 8:00pm, Wednesday 10:00am - 8:00pm, Thursday-Saturday 10:00am - 6:00pm.
Story Time: Preschool Story Time n(ages 3-5): Friday 10:30am – 11:00am

Montlake Branch
2300 24th Ave E, Seattle
206-684-4720
www.spl.org
Hours: Monday and Tuesday 1:00pm - 8:00pm, Wednesday 10:00am - 8:00pm, Thursday-Saturday 10:00am - 6:00pm.
Story Time: Preschool Story Time (ages 3-5): Thursday 10:30am – 11:00am

New Holly Branch
7058 32nd Ave S, Seattle
206-386-1905
www.spl.org
Hours: Monday and Tuesday 1:00pm - 8:00pm, Wednesday 10:00am - 8:00pm, Thursday-Saturday 10:00am - 6:00pm.
Story Time: Children Story Time: Thursday 10:30am – 11:00am

North East Branch
6801 35th Ave NE, Seattle
206-684-7539
www.spl.org
Hours: Monday and Tuesday 1:00pm - 8:00pm, Wednesday 10:00am - 8:00pm, Thursday-Saturday 10:00am - 6:00pm, and Sunday 1:00pm - 5:00pm.
Story Time: Evening Preschool Story Time (3-5): Wednesday 7:00pm – 7:30pm
Toddler Story Time (ages 18 months-3): Thursday 10:30am – 11:00am
Preschool Story Time(ages 3-5): Thursday 11:30am – 12:00pm

Northgate Branch
10548 Fifth Ave NE, Seattle
www.spl.org
Closed for construction. Scheduled to reopen in 2006.

Queen Anne Branch
400 W Garfield St, Seattle
206-386-4227
www.spl.org
Hours: Monday and Tuesday 1:00pm - 8:00pm, Wednesday 10:00am - 8:00pm, Thursday-Saturday 10:00am - 6:00pm.
Story Time: Toddler Story Time: Thursday 10:30am – 11:00am

Rainier Beach Branch
9125 Rainier Ave S, Seattle
206-386-1906
www.spl.org
Hours: Monday and Tuesday 1:00pm - 8:00pm, Wednesday 10:00am - 8:00pm, Thursday-Saturday 10:00am - 6:00pm, and Sunday 1:00pm - 5:00pm.
Story Time: Preschool Story Time (3-5): Wednesday 10:30am – 11:00am
Preschool Story Time (3-5): Thursday 10:30am – 11:00am

South Park Branch
8604 Eighth Ave S, Seattle
www.spl.org
This new library location is currently under construction. It is scheduled for completion the second half of 2006.

Southwest Branch
9010 35th Ave SW, Seattle
206-684-7455
www.spl.org
This branch is tentatively scheduled to undergo an expansion/remodel. Check website for details.
Hours: Monday and Tuesday 1:00pm - 8:00pm, Wednesday 10:00am - 8:00pm, Thursday-Saturday 10:00am - 6:00pm.
Story Time: Preschool Story Time: Thursday 10:30am – 11:00am

University Branch
5009 Roosevelt Way NE, Seattle
206-684-4063
www.spl.org
Hours: Monday and Tuesday 1:00pm - 8:00pm, Wednesday 10:00am - 8:00pm, Thursday-Saturday 10:00am - 6:00pm.
Story Time: Toddler Story Time (ages 18 months-3): Friday 10:00am – 10:30am
Preschool Story Time (ages 3-5): Friday 10:30am – 11:00am

Wallingford Branch
1501 N 45th St, Seattle
206-684-4088
www.spl.org
Hours: Monday and Tuesday 1:00pm - 8:00pm, Wednesday 10:00am - 8:00pm, Thursday-Saturday 10:00am - 6:00pm.
Story Time: Evening Preschool Story Time (ages 3-5): Tuesday 7:00pm – 7:30pm

West Seattle Branch
2306 42nd Ave SW, Seattle
206-684-7444
www.spl.org
Hours: Monday and Tuesday 1:00pm - 8:00pm, Wednesday 10:00am - 8:00pm, Thursday-Saturday 10:00am - 6:00pm, and Sunday 1:00pm - 5:00pm.
Story Time: Toddler Story Time (ages 2-3): Wednesday 10:30am - 11:00am

King County Library System
960 NW Newport Way
800-462-9600
www.kcls.org
The King County Library System has implemented reading programs to motivate children and youth to read throughout the year. Each library is participating.

Summer Reading Program: Keep track of the minutes you read, or that someone reads to you. Earn prizes based on how many minutes read.

"Read Three, Get One Free": A book-review-and-reward program available at any KCLS community library. Participating teens ages 12-18 can select a free paperback book for every three books they read and review.

Ready-Set-Read: KCLS's school year reading program.

Special Programs: Watch for special performances and events at your local library throughout the year.

ABC Express Service

425-369-3488
This "library on wheels" offers a wide variety of books, music and movies for children from birth to age 5. Once a month, children and their childcare providers throughout KCLS' service area can climb aboard this colorful, 26-foot van for one-on-one assistance selecting their own library materials!

Algona-Pacific Library
255 Ellingson Rd, Algona
253-833-3554
www.kcls.org/alpac/alpachom.cfm
Hours: Monday-Thursday 10:00am - 9:00pm, Friday 10:00am - 6:00pm, Saturday 10:00am - 5:00pm
Story Time: Wee Ones Story Time (ages 8-24 months): Wednesday 10:15am
Toddler Story Time (ages 2-3): Tuesday 10:15am
Preschool Story Time (ages 3-5): Tuesday 11:00am

Auburn Library
1102 Auburn Way S
253-931-3018
www.kcls.org
Hours: Monday-Thursday 10:00am - 9:00pm, Friday 10:00am - 6:00pm, Saturday 10:00am - 5:00pm, Sunday 1:00pm - 5:00pm.
Story Time: Baby-On-Board Story Time: Wednesday 11:00am, Ages 12 to 24 months, one adult per baby. Bounce your baby on your lap and listen to stories. A short playtime follows Story Time. Toddler Tales Story Time: Monday 10:15am, Ages 2 to 3, siblings welcome. Come to the library for short stories, flannel boards and finger plays.
Preschool Story Time (ages 3-5): Monday 11:00am.
Family Story Time (ages 2 ? -5): Wednesday 10:15am.

Bellevue Regional Library
1111 110th Ave NE
425-450-1765
www.kcls.org
Hours: Monday-Thursday 10:00am - 9:00pm, Friday 10:00am - 6:00pm, Saturday 10:00am - 5:00pm, Sunday 1:00pm - 9:00pm.
Story Time: Lunch Time Story Time (Families): Tuesday 12:00pm & Friday 12:00pm.
Family Story Time: Tuesday 7:00pm World Language/English Bilingual.
Story Time (ages 3+): Wednesday 10:30am.

Black Diamond Library
24301 Roberts Dr
360-886-1105
www.kcls.org
Hours: Monday-Wednesday: 11:00am - 8:30pm, Thursday & Friday 11:00am - 6:00pm, Sunday 1:00pm - 5:00pm.
Story Time: Family Story Time (ages 3-7): Monday 10:30am & Tuesday 10:30am.

Bothell Regional Library
18215 98th Ave NE
425-486-7811
www.kcls.org
Hours: Monday-Thursday 10:00am - 9:00pm, Friday 10:00am - 6:00pm, Saturday 10:00am - 5:00pm, Sunday 1:00pm - 9:00pm.
Story Time: Mother Goose on the Loose (ages birth-2): Tuesday 10:30am.
Once Upon a Wednesday (ages 2+): Wednesday 9:30am.

Boulevard Park Library
12015 Roseberg Ave S
206-242-8662
www.kcls.org
Hours: Monday-Thursday 11:00am - 8:30pm, Friday & Saturday 11:00am - 5:00pm.
Story Time (18 months-3): Monday 11:00am.

Burien Library
14700 Sixth SW
206-243-3490
www.kcls.org
Hours: Monday-Thursday 10:00am - 9:00pm, Friday 10:00am - 6:00pm, Saturday 10:00am - 5:00pm, Sunday 1:00pm - 5:00pm.
Story Time (ages 2-3): Tuesday Toddler Time: Tuesday 10:30am – 11:00am.
Preschool Story Time (ages 3-6): Monday 10:30am – 11:00am.
Spanish Story Time (ages 3-6): Monday 7:00pm - 7:30pm. Introduce children who speak only English to the Spanish language, and those who speak Spanish to the English language.
Mother Goose Early Toddler Time (ages 1-2): Tuesday 10:30am – 11:00am.
Special Programs: Pizza and Pages (ages 12-18 months): Teen Book Group: 2nd Tuesdays. Enjoy pizza and a discussion of what you're reading. Talk about the latest books for teens. Drop-ins welcome.

Carnation Library
4804 Tolt Ave
425-333-4398
www.kcls.org
Hours: Monday, Wednesday, and Saturday: 10:00am - 5:00pm, Tuesday and Thursday: 1:00pm - 8:30pm.
Story Time: Preschool Story Time: Wednesday 10:30am.

Covington Library
27100 164th Ave SE
253-630-8761
www.kcls.org
Hours: Monday-Thursday 10:00am-9:00pm, Friday 10:00am-6:00pm, Saturday 10:00am-5:00pm, Sunday 1:00pm-5:00pm.
Story Time: Wee Ones Story Time (8-24 months): Wednesday 9:30am or 10:30am.
Toddler Story Time (ages 2-3): Monday 10:15am & Tuesday 10:15am.
Preschool Story Time (ages 4-5): Monday 11:00am & Tuesday 11:00am.
Special Programs: Teen Book Group: Talk about books, movies, TV and life in general. And hey, there's food.
Special Programs: Study Zone.

Crossroads: The Library Connection at Crossroads
15600 NE 8th St Suite K-11
425-644-6203
www.kcls.org
Hours: Monday-Saturday 10:00am - 9:00pm, Sunday 11:00am - 6:00pm.

Des Moines Library
21620 11th Ave S
206-824-6066
www.kcls.org
Hours: Monday-Thursday 10:00am - 9:00pm, Friday 10:00am - 6:00pm, Saturday 10:00am - 5:00pm, Sunday 1:00pm - 5:00pm.
Story Time (ages 3-6): Wednesday 11:15am.
Summer Spanish Language Family Story Time (ages 3-8): Thursday 4:30pm - 5:30pm.
Story Time Visits & Tours: For school groups, preschools and daycares.

Duvall Library
15619 NE Main St
425-788-1173
www.kcls.org
Hours: Tuesday and Saturday 10:00am - 5:00pm, Wednesday and Thursday 1:00pm - 8:30pm, Friday 10:00am - 6:00pm.

Fairwood Library
17009 140th SE, Renton
425-226-0522
www.kcls.org
Hours: Monday-Thursday 10:00am - 9:00pm, Friday 10:00am - 6:00pm, Saturday 10:00am - 5:00pm, Sunday 1:00pm - 5:00pm.
Story Time: Toddler Story Time (ages 2-3): Monday & Tuesday 10:00am.
Wee Ones (ages 8-24 months): Monday 10:45am - 11:15am.
Preschool Story Time (ages 3-6): Tuesday 10:45am - 11:15am.
Special Programs: Study Zone.

Fall City Library
33415 SE 42nd Pl
425-222-5951
www.kcls.org
Hours: Monday and Wednesday 1:00pm - 8:30pm, Tuesday, Friday, and Saturday 11:00am - 5:00pm.
Story Time: Preschool Story Time: Tuesday 10:30am.

Federal Way Regional Library
34200 1st Way S
253-838-3668
www.kcls.org
Hours: Monday-Thursday 10:00am - 9:00pm, Friday 10:00am - 6:00pm, Saturday 10:00am - 5:00pm, Sunday 1:00pm - 9:00pm.
Special Programs: Teen Book Group: Fun, food, friends and books the 3rd Tuesday of every month. Talk about a favorite book or one you're reading for school.

Federal Way 320th Library
848 S 320th St
253-839-0257
www.kcls.org
Hours: Monday-Thursday 10:00am - 9:00pm, Friday 11:00am - 6:00pm, Saturday 10:00am - 5:00pm.
Story Time: (ages 1-2): Friday 10:15am - 10:40am.
Toddler Time (ages 2-3): Wednesday 10:30am – 11:00am.
Preschool Time (ages 3-5): Wednesday 1:00pm - 1:30pm.
Spanish/English Story Time: Tuesday 7:00pm - 7:30pm.
Fun Family Fridays (ages 2-5): Friday 11:00am - 11:30am.

Foster Library
4060 S 144th, Tukwila
206-242-1640
www.kcls.org
Hours: Monday-Thursday 11:00am - 9:00pm, Friday 11:00am - 5:00pm, Saturday 11:00am - 5:00pm, Sunday 1:00pm - 5:00pm.
Story Tim (ages 2-6): Monday 6:45pm.
Special Programs: Teen Book Group: Ages 13 to 18. Read and talk about books. Snacks are provided. just bring a book to share with the group.

Issaquah Library
10 W Sunset Way
425-392-5430
www.kcls.org
Hours: Monday-Thursday 10:00am - 9:00pm, Friday 11:00am - 6:00pm, Saturday 10:00am - 5:00pm, Sunday 1:00pm - 5:00pm.
Story Time: Lunch Bunch Story Time (ages 3+): Tuesday 12:00pm.
Mother Goose Story Time (ages 1-2): Wednesday 9:45am.
Toddler Story Time (ages 2-3): Wednesday 10:30am.
Special Programs: Teen Programs: Strategy Games: Last Friday of Every Month 2:30-4:30pm. Teen Book Group: see website for more information.

Kenmore Library
18138 73rd NE
425-486-8747
www.kcls.com
Hours: Monday and Wednesday 11:00pm - 9:00pm, Tuesday, Friday, and Saturday 11:00am - 5:00pm.
Story Time (ages 1-5): Wednesday 10:30am.
Special Programs: Come Check Out the Great Blue Herons in the Library. Great Blue Heron Cam- A- Peek Into Life in the Treetops. View nesting herons via cams set into the treetops behind the library in Kenmore, Washington. The cameras were placed in the birds' nesting area several months before their return to the rookery.

Kent Regional Library
212 2nd Ave N
253-859-3330
www.kcls.org
Hours: Monday-Thursday 10:00am - 9:00pm, Friday 11:00am - 6:00pm, Saturday 10:00am - 5:00pm, Sunday 1:00pm - 5:00pm.
Story Time: Sleepy Story Time: Tuesday 7:00pm. Wear your pajamas and bring your teddy bear for this 30-minute bedtime Story Time.
Tiny Toddlers (walking – 2 years): Thursday 10:15am.
Baby Fun Time (Newborns to 9 months): Thursday 11:00am.
"Royal" Story Time (ages 4-10): Wednesdays 10:30am.
Fun Family Friday: 11:00am.
Stories, catchy tunes, puppets, finger plays and fun.

Kingsgate Library
12315 NE 143rd, Kirkland
425-821-7686
www.kcls.org
Hours: Monday-Thursday 10:00am - 9:00pm, Friday 11:00am - 6:00pm, Saturday 10:00am - 5:00pm, Sunday 1:00pm - 5:00pm.
Story Time: Preschool Story Time (ages 3-6): Wednesday 10:30am.
Mother Goose Story Time (ages 1-2): Thursday 10:30am.

Kirkland Library
308 Kirkland Ave
425-822-2459
www.kcls.org
Hours: Monday-Thursday 10:00am - 9:00pm, Friday 11:00am - 6:00pm, Saturday 10:00am - 5:00pm, Sunday 1:00pm - 5:00pm.
Story Time: Toddler Story Time (ages 2-3): Tuesday 10:00am.
Preschool Story Time (ages 4-6): Tuesday 11:00am.
Mother Goose Story Time (ages 1-2): Wednesday 10:00am.
Youngster Story Time (ages 2-4): Wednesday 11:00am.
Family Story Time (ages 3-6): Wednesday 7:00pm.
Japanese Story Time (ages 3-6): Monday 10:00am.
Japanese Baby Story Time: Monday 3:30pm - 4:00pm.
Special Programs: Teen Book Club: meets in the Teen Section of the Library.

Lake Forest Park Library @ Lake Forest Park Towne Centre
17171 Bothell Way NE, Seattle
206-362-8860
www.kcls.org
Hours: Monday-Thursday 10:30am - 9:00pm, Friday 10:00am - 6:00pm, Saturday 10:00am - 6:00pm.
Story Time: Picnic Story Time(ages 3-6): Tuesdays 12:00pm.
Special Programs (ages 11+): Pizza and Books: Bring your appetite and love of reading to the library. Eat pizza and discuss hot titles for teens.

Lake Hills Library
15228 Lake Hills Blvd, Bellevue
425-747-3350
www.kcls.org
Hours: Monday-Thursday 10:00am - 9:00pm, Friday 11:00am - 6:00pm, Saturday 10:00am - 5:00pm.
Special Programs: Study Zone.

Maple Valley Library
21844 SE 248th St
425-432-4620
www.kcls.org
Hours: Monday-Thursday 10:00am - 9:00pm, Friday 11:00am - 6:00pm, Saturday 10:00am - 5:00pm, Sunday 1:00pm - 5:00pm.
Story Time: Pajama Story Time (ages 3-7): Monday 7:00pm. Wear your PJs, bring a blanket or a favorite stuffed and enjoy wonderful bedtime stories.
Preschool Story Time (ages 3-7): Tuesday 10:30am & Wednesday 10:30am.
Toddler Story Time (ages 18 months-3): Friday 10:30am.
Special Programs: Teen Book Discussion Group Bring a friend and come prepared to talk about books and enjoy some tasty treats.

Mercer Island Library
4408 88th Ave SE
206-236-3527
www.kcls.org
Hours: Monday-Thursday 10:00am - 9:00pm, Friday 11:00am - 6:00pm, Saturday 10:00am - 5:00pm, Sunday 1:00pm - 5:00pm.

Muckleshoot Library
38811 172nd Ave SE, Auburn
253-931-6779
www.kcls.org
Hours: Monday 1:00pm - 5:00pm, Tuesday, Wednesday, and Thursday 10:00am - 5:00pm, Friday 1:00pm - 5:00pm.

Newport Way Library
14250 SE Newport Way, Bellevue
425-747-2390
www.kcls.org
Hours: Monday-Thursday 10:00am - 9:00pm, Friday 11:00am - 6:00pm, Saturday 10:00am - 5:00pm, Sunday 1:00pm - 5:00pm.

North Bend Library
115 E 4th
425-888-0554
www.kcls.org
Hours: Monday-Thursday 10:30am - 8:30pm, Friday 11:00am - 6:00pm, Saturday 10:00am - 5:00pm, Sunday 1:00pm - 5:00pm.
Story Time: Toddler Story Time (ages 18 months-3): Tuesday 9:45am.
Preschool Story Time (ages 3-6): Tuesday 10:45am.
Evening Story Time: Wednesday 6:30pm.

Redmond Regional Library
15990 NE 85th
425-885-1861
www.kcls.org
Hours: Monday-Thursday 10:00am - 9:00pm, Friday 11:00am - 6:00pm, Saturday 10:00am - 5:00pm, Sunday 1:00pm - 9:00pm
Story Time: Japanese Story Time: Thursday 7:00pm. For Japanese speaking children and children interested in the Japanese language.
Family Story Time (ages 3+): Monday 7:00pm.
Toddler Story Time (age 2): Wednesday 10:15am & Friday 10:15am or 10:45am.
Preschool Story Time (ages 3-5):
Spanish Story Time: Thursday 7:00pm. For Spanish speaking children and children learning Spanish as a second language.
Russian Story Time: Monday 11:00am. For Russian speaking children and for children interested in the Russian language.
Mother Goose Story Time (ages 1-2): Thursday 10:30am.

Richmond Beach Library
19601 21st Ave NW, Shoreline
206-546-3522
www.kcls.org/rb/home.cfm
Hours: Monday-Thursday 10:30 - 9:00pm, Friday and Saturday 10:30am - 5:00pm.
Story Time (ages 2-6): Thursday 1:30pm.
Bedtime Stories for Ages 2-6: Wednesday 7:00pm. Children can wear their pajamas!
Special Programs: Study Zone.

Sammamish Library
825 228th Ave NE
425-836-8793
www.kcls.org
Hours: Monday-Thursday 10:00am - 9:00pm, Friday 11:00am - 6:00pm, Saturday 10:00am - 5:00pm, Sunday 1:00pm - 5:00pm.
Story Time: Young Toddler Story Time (ages 1-2): Fridays 10:00am and 10:45am.
Toddler Story Time (ages 2-3): Tuesday 10:00am and Wednesday 10:00am.
Tiny Tales Story Time (ages 6-12 months): Tuesday 11:00am.
Preschool Story Time (ages 3 1/2 -6): Tuesday 2:00pm and Thursday 10:00am.
Pajama Evening Story Time (ages 3-6): Mondays 7:00pm.
Spanish Story Time (ages 3-8): Wednesday 3:00pm. For Spanish speaking children and for those families wanting to learn Spanish as a second language.
Special Programs: Study Zone.

Shoreline Library
345 NE 175th
206-362-7550
www.kcls.org
Hours: Monday-Thursday 10:00am - 9:00pm, Friday 11:00am - 6:00pm, Saturday 10:00am - 5:00pm, Sunday 1:00pm - 5:00pm.
Story Time: Toddler Time (ages 2-3): Monday 10:15am & 11:00am.
Young Toddler Time (ages 1-2): Tuesday 10:15am.
Preschool Story Time (ages 3-6): Wednesday 10:30am.
Korean Story Time (ages 3-6): Wednesday 1:30pm. Speakers of all languages are welcome.

Skykomish Library
100 5th St
306-677-2660
www.kcls.org
Hours: Monday and Thursday 1:00pm - 7:00pm, Friday 1:00pm - 5:00pm, Saturday 10:00am - 2:00pm.

Skyway Library
7614 S 126th
206-772-5541
www.kcls.org
Hours: Monday-Thursday 11:00am - 9:00pm, Friday and Saturday 11:00am - 5:00pm.
Story Time: Toddler Story Time (ages 1-3):
Preschool Story Time (ages 3+): Monday 10:30am.
Special Programs: Teen Books and Snacks: Between the ages of 12 and 16 and love to read? Join the Skyway Book Club! Snacks are provided, just bring yourself and a book to share with the group.
Study Zone.

Snoqualmie Library
38580 SE River St
425-888-1223
www.kcls.org
Hours: Monday and Thursday 1:00pm - 8:30pm, Tuesday and Wednesday 11:00am - 5:00pm, Saturday 11:00am - 5:00pm.
Story Time: Preschool Story Time (ages 2-6): Wednesday 11:00am.

Library Connection @ Southcenter
1115 Southcenter Mall, Tukwila
206-242-6044
www.kcls.org
Hours: Monday-Saturday 10:00am - 9:00pm, Sunday 11:00am - 6:00pm.

Techlab
425-369-3389
www.kcls.org
Trained staff can schedule hands-on on-site sessions at various community agencies and organizations such as senior centers, park districts, community or recreational centers, social service agencies, residential facilities, or other gathering places in the community.

Target audiences include, but are not limited to, seniors, low-income populations, ESL and new immigrant populations, latchkey children, and young adults.

The Traveling Library Center (TLC)
425-369-3456
877-905-2008
www.kcls.org
The Traveling Library Center (TLC) provides services to eligible residents of King County who are not able to visit their community libraries.

Tukwila Library
14475 59th Ave S
206-244-5140
www.kcls.org
Hours: Monday 10:00 - 5:00pm, Tuesday 2:00pm - 8:00pm, Wednesday 10:00am - 5:00pm, Thursday 2:00am - 8:00pm, Saturday 10:00am - 2:00pm.
Story Time (ages 2-6): Wednesday 10:30am.

Valley View Library
17850 Military Rd S, SeaTac
206-242-6044
www.kcls.org
Hours: Monday-Thursday 10:00am - 9:00pm, Friday 10:00am - 6:00pm, Saturday 10:00am - 5:00pm.
Story Time: Mother Goose on the Loose (ages 1-2): Friday 10:00am.
Baby Rhyming Time (Newborn to 12 months): Wednesday 10:00am.
Spanish Story Times at the Valley View Library (ages 2-12): Bimonthly from August-December, 2005. Stories, games and music in Spanish and English for Spanish-speaking children and for children learning Spanish as a second language.
Special Programs: Study Zone.

Vashon Library
17210 Vashon Hwy SW
206-463-2069
www.kcls.org
Hours: Monday-Thursday 11:00am - 8:30pm, Friday 11:00am - 6:00pm, Saturday 10:00am - 5:00pm, Sunday 1:00pm - 5:00pm.
Story Time: Family Story Time: Wednesday 10:30am – 11:00am, Ages 2 to 7, younger children welcome with adult. Please join us for stories, songs and fun.
Brown Bag Story Time: Wednesday 12:30pm - 1:15pm, Ages 5 to 10. Bring a sack lunch to eat while you enjoy great stories read aloud.

White Center Library

11220 16th SW, Seattle
206-243-0233
www.kcls.org
Hours: Monday-Thursday 11:00am - 9:00pm, Friday 11:00am - 5:00pm, Saturday 11:00am - 5:00pm.
Story Time: Preschool Story Time – Raising Readers (ages 3-6): Tuesday 10:45am.

Woodinville Library

17015 Avondale Rd NE
425-788-0733
www.kcls.org
Hours: Monday-Thursday 10:00 - 9:00pm Friday 10:00am - 6:00pm, Saturday 10:00am - 5:00pm, Sunday 1:00pm - 5:00pm
Story Time: Preschool Story Time (ages 3-6): Monday 10:30am.
Evening Family Story Time (ages 3-6): Tuesday 7:00pm.

Woodmont Library

26809 Pacific Highway S, Des Moines
253-839-0121
www.kcls.org
Hours: Monday-Thursday 10:00am - 9:00pm Friday 10:00am - 6:00pm, Saturday 10:00am - 5:00pm.
Story Time: Brown Bag Story Time (ages 2-8): Tuesday 12:00pm.
Pajama Time Story Time (ages 3+): Tuesday 7:00pm. Kids may come in their pajamas and slippers.
Summer Spanish Language Family Story Time (ages 3-6): Monday 7:00pm. Stories, songs and activities all in Spanish.

Sno-Isle Regional Library System
Special Programs and Events: Simply click on your local library, select the calendar of events option, and choose your preferred category (i.e. music, holiday, international, book discussions). A list of upcoming events will be shown.

Live Homework Help: The Sno-Isle Library System offers online homework for children and teens. You will need your library I.D. number to access help. They also provide excellent links to national homework sites.

Summer Reading Programs and Events: Select libraries offer a full list of fun activities and programs for children throughout the summer. Check with your local library each summer for information about earning free books, craft and storytime events, and more.

Arlington City Library

135 N Washington Ave
360-435-3033
www.sno-isle.org
Hours: Monday - Thursday 10:00am - 9:00pm, Friday – Saturday 10:00am - 5:00pm. Sunday (Sept-June) 1:00pm - 5:00pm.
Story Time: Preschool Story Time (ages 3-5): Thursday 10:30am.

Bookmobile-Sno-Isle Libraries

7312 35th Ave NE, Marysville
360-651-7059
877-766-4753 ext. 7059
www.sno-isle.org

Brier Library
23303 Brier Rd
425-483-0888
www.sno-isle.org
Hours: Monday-Wednesday 12:00pm - 8:00pm, Friday-Saturday 12:00pm - 6:00pm.
Story Time: Preschool Story Time (ages 2-5): Friday 11:00am.
Special Programs: Crafty Tales: Wednesday 2:00pm – 4:00pm (summertime), and 6:30pm (September-May). Create imaginative crafts while listening to stories.

Clinton Library
4781 Deer Lake Rd
360-341-4280
www.sno-isle.org
Hours: Tuesday 1:00pm - 8:00pm, Wednesday - Saturday 1:00pm - 5:00pm.
Story Time: Storytimes for Small Folks (ages 18 months-5 years): Tuesday 7:00pm.

Coupeville Library
788 NW Alexander
360-678-4911
www.sno-isle.org
Hours: Monday, Wednesday 10:00am - 8:00pm; Tuesday, Thursday, Friday, Saturday 10:00am - 5:00pm.
Story Time: Thursday 9:30am.

Darrington Library
1005 Cascade St
360-436-1600
www.sno-isle.org
Hours: Monday, Wednesday 11:00am - 8:00pm, Tuesday, Friday, & Saturday 11:00am - 5:00pm
Story Time: Preschool Story Time (ages 3-5): Friday 11:00am.

Edmonds City Library
650 Main St, Edmonds
425-771-1933
www.sno-isle.org
Hours: Monday-Thursday 10:00am - 9:00pm, Friday 10:00am - 6:00pm, Saturday 10:00am - 5:00pm, Sunday 1:00pm - 5:00pm
*Story Time:
Special Programs: Summer Presentations (ages 5-11): Wednesday 2:00pm.

Freeland Library
5495 Harbor Ave
360-331-7323
www.sno-isle.org
Hours: Monday, Tuesday, Thursday 11:00am - 8:00pm, Wednesday 10:00am - 5:00pm, Friday, Saturday 11:00am - 5:00pm, Sunday 1:00pm - 5:00pm.
Story Time: Storytimes for Small Folks (ages 18 months-5 years): Wednesday 10:00am.

Granite Falls Library
815 East Galena
360-691-6087
www.sno-isle.org
Hours: Monday - Thursday 11:00am - 8:00pm, Friday, Saturday 11:00am - 5:00pm
Story Time: Preschool Story Time: Monday 11:00am
Special Programs: Monday, 1:00pm

Lake Stevens Library
1804 Main St
425-334-1900
www.sno-isle.org
Hours: Monday, Tuesday, Wednesday 12:00pm - 9:00pm, Friday, Saturday 10:00am - 5:00pm
Story Time: Preschool (ages 2-5) Tuesday 11:00am
Family Story Time (all ages): Wednesday 7:00pm-9:00pm

Langley Library
104 Second St
360-221-4383
www.sno-isle.org
Hours: Monday-Wednesday 11:00am - 8:00pm, Thursday-Saturday 11:00am - 5:00pm
Story Time: Storytimes for Small Folks (ages 18 months-5 years): Tuesday 11:00am

Lynnwood Library
19200 44th Ave W
425-778-2148
www.sno-isle.org
Hours: Monday-Thursday 10:00am - 9:00pm, Friday 10:00am - 6:00pm, Saturday 10:00am - 5:00pm, Sunday 1:00pm - 5:00pm
Story Time: Toddler Story Time (18 months): Monday 10:00am & 11:00am.
Family Story Time: Tuesday 7:00pm Stories, activities, and crafts for the whole family.
Reading Programs: Reading Quest: Set own goals. Once you've met the goals, bring your reading quest card to the library and receive a free book, and prizes. This is a year round program.

Marysville Library
6120 Grove St
360-658-5000
www.sno-isle.org
Hours: Monday-Thursday 10:00am - 9:00pm, Friday 10:00am - 6:00 pm, Saturday 10:00 am - 5:00pm, Sunday 1:00pm - 5:00pm.
Story Time: Preschool Story Time (ages 3-5): Monday 10:15am.
Evening Family Story Time: Thursday 7:00pm.
Tickly Toddle (ages 1-2): Thursday 10:30am. A story time filled with movement, word-play and rhythm-n-rhyme. A playtime will follow the program, so please bring a few of your child's favorite toys.

Mill Creek City Library
15429 Bothell-Everett Hwy
425-743-5544
425-337-4822
www.sno-isle.org
Hours: Monday-Thursday 10:00am - 9:00pm, Friday, Saturday 10:00am - 6:00pm.
Story Time: Preschool Story Time (ages 3-5): Tuesday 10:30am. Get your child ready to read with stories, songs, finger plays and imaginative play.
Toddler Story Time (ages 2-3): Wednesday 10:30am.
Baby Bee Story Time (up to 18 months): Thursday 9:30am. Bring your baby and enjoy some quality time reading, learning and playing.

Monroe City Library
1070 Village Way
360-794-7851
www.sno-isle.org
Hours: Monday-Thursday 10:00am - 9:00pm, Friday, Saturday 10:00am - 5:00pm, Sunday (Sept - June) 1:00pm - 5:00pm.
Story Time: Preschool Story Time (ages 3-5): Wednesday 10:30am
Family Story Time: Tuesday 7:00pm

Mountlake Terrace City Library
23300 58th Ave W
425-776-8722
www.sno-isle.org
Hours: Monday-Thursday 10:00am - 9:00pm, Friday, Saturday 10:00am - 5:00pm, Sunday (Sept-June) 1:00pm - 5:00pm.
Story Time (ages 18 months-5): Thursday 10:00 am.

Mukilteo Library
4675 Harbour Pt Blvd
425-493-8202
www.sno-isle.org
Hours: Monday-Thursday 10:00am - 9:00pm, Friday 10:00am - 6:00pm
Saturday 10:00am - 5:00pm, Sunday (Sept-June) 1:00pm - 5:00pm
Story Time: Baby and Me Story Time (up to 18 months): Tuesday 10:00am & 11:00am. Rhymes, and stories, plus a 20 minutes playtime. Pre-registration Required.
Family Story Time: Thursday 10:00am & 11:00am.

Oak Harbor Library
1000 SE Regatta Dr
360-675-5115
www.sno-isle.org
Hours: Monday-Thursday 10:00am - 9:00pm, Friday and Saturday 10:00am - 5:00pm, Sunday (Sept.-June) 1:00pm - 5:00pm.
Story Time: Preschool Story Time (ages 3-5): Thursday 9:30am & 10:30am.

Snohomish Library

311 Maple Ave
360-568-2898
www.sno-isle.org
Hours: Monday-Thursday 10:00am - 9:00pm, Friday and Saturday 10:00am - 5:00pm, Sunday (Sept-June) 1:00pm - 5:00pm.
Story Time: Baby and Me Story Time (up to 18 months): Monday 10:30am.
Tiny Tots Story Time (ages 2-4): Thursday 2:00pm.

Stanwood Library

9701 271st St NW
360-629-3132
www.sno-isle.org
Hours: Monday-Thursday 10:00am-9:00pm, Friday and Saturday 10:00am - 5:00pm.
Story Time: Toddler Time: Wednesday 10:30am
Preschool Story Time: Thursday 10:30am.
Reading Programs:

Sultan Library

319 Main St Suite100
360-793-1695
www.sno-isle.org
Hours: Monday-Thursday 11:00am-8:00pm, Friday and Saturday 11:00am - 5:00pm.

Book Stores

King County

All For Kids Books & Music

2900 NE Blakely, Seattle

206-526-2768

www.allforkidsbooks.com

Hours: Monday-Saturday 10:00am-6:00pm, Sunday 12:00pm-5:00pm.

After Labor Day: Tuesdays 10:00am-8:00pm.

Story Time: Tuesdays 10:30am. All Ages.

Reading Programs: 2 Week Summer Reading/Writing Workshop: $300/wk 10:00am-4:00pm. Bring your own lunch.

Alphabet Soup

1406 N 45th, Seattle

206-547-4555

Hours: Monday-Saturday 10:00am-9:00pm.

Barnes & Noble

15600 NE 8th, Bellevue

425-644-1650

Hours: Sunday-Thursday 9:00am-10:00pm, Friday-Saturday 9:00am-11:00pm.

Story Time: Thursday 10:30am, Saturday 1:30pm.

Reading Programs: Summer Reading Program for kids Grades 1-6, Read 8 books and fill out form to get free book, ends September 10th.

Special Programs: Become a Member for $25 and save 10 % on anything at any store and online and for entire household.

Barnes & Noble

626 106th NE, Bellevue

425-451-8463

Hours: Sunday-Thursday 9:00am-10:00pm.

Story Time: Thursday 10:30am.

Reading Programs: Summer Reading Program Grades 1-6, Read 8 books get a free book

Special Programs: Character appearances Peter Rabbit, Clifford etc is ongoing. Lennox Users Group meets 2nd Tuesdays 7pm, Author Readings and Signings Ongoing.

Barnes & Noble
31325 Pacific Hwy S, Federal Way
253-839-2535
Hours: Sunday-Thursday 9:00am-10:00pm, Friday-Saturday 9:00am-11:00pm.
Story Time: Saturday 11:30pm
Special Programs: Corporate Discount Card 15% off, Institutional Discounts 25% off nonprofit organizations.

Barnes & Noble
1530 11th Ave NW, Pickering Place, Issaquah
425-557-8808
Hours: Sunday-Thursday 9:00am-10:00pm, Friday-Saturday 9:00am-11:00pm.
Story Time: Wednesday 7:00pm.
Summer Reading Programs: Read 8 books and fill out sheet and get a free book.
Special Programs: Membership Card $25 for 12 months, 10% off for B Dalton and online and all other Barnes & Noble Stores for everyone in the household.

Barnes & Noble
600 Pine, Seattle
206-264-0156
Hours: Open daily 9:00am-11:00pm
Special Programs: Membership Card $25 for 12month 10% off for household at any store or online, Bestsellers 20-30% off.

Barnes & Noble
2675 NE University Village Mall, Seattle
206-517-4107
Hours: 9:00am-11:00pm
Story Time: Sunday 11:00am, Tuesday 11:00am, Friday 11:00am.
Summer Reading Program: For grades 1-6. Read 8 books, fill out a form, and get a free book.
Special Programs: Children's author readings and signing events throughout the year.

Borders
1501 4th Ave, Seattle
206-622-4599
Hours: Monday-Saturday 8:00am-9:00pm, Sunday 10:00am-8:00pm.
Special Programs: Author book signings and readings, monthly book discussions.

Borders
17501 Southcenter Pkwy, Tukwila
206-575-4506
Hours: Monday-Thursday 10:00am-10:00pm, Friday-Saturday 10:00am-11:00pm, Sunday 10:00am- 9:00pm.
Story Time: Days and times vary each month.
Special Programs: Author Reading and Signings ongoing, Music Performances and signing ongoing, Book Group discussions. Teacher discounts 25%.

Borders
1824 S 320th, Federal Way
253-946-5877
Hours: Sunday-Thursday 10:00am -10:00pm, Friday-Saturday 10:00am -11:00pm.
Special Programs: Author Readings & Signings.

Borders
16549 NE 74th, Redmond
425-869-1907
Hours: Monday-Thursday 9:00am -10:00pm, Friday-Saturday 9:00am-11:00pm.
Story Time: Tuesday & Wednesday 10:15am, 11:00am.
Reading Programs: Reading with Rover every other week in the evening during school year.
Special Programs: Authors reading and signing ongoing.

Borders
2508 S. 38th St, Tacoma
253-473-9111
Hours: Monday-Saturday 9:00am - 11:00pm, Sunday 9:00am - 9:00pm.
Special Programs: Watch for Author signings and Music performances.

Borders
3000 184th St SW, Alderwood Mall, Lynnwood
425-776-7530
Hours: Monday-Thursday 10:00am - 9:30pm, Friday 10:00am-11:00pm, Sunday 10:00am-9:00pm.
Special Programs: Author & Music Artists Signings.

Island Books

3014 78th Ave SE, Mercer Island
206-232-6952
Hours: Monday-Friday 9:30am-7:00pm, Saturday 9:30am - 6:00pm.
Story Time: Thursday or Saturday Evening.
Reading Programs: Reading group meets last Thursday evening every month.
Special Programs: Mostly local authors signings and readings.

Snohomish County

Barnes & Noble

19401 Alderwood Mall Parkway, Lynnwood
425-771-2220
Hours: 9:00am-11:00pm.
Story Time: Wednesday & Saturday 11:00am.
Reading Programs: Summer Reading Program. Read 8 books, fill out a book reading form, and receive a free book.
Harry Potter reading group on Thursday nights in Sept for 8 weeks,
Classic Mystery, Star Trek & American Girl book groups meet evenings once a month.
Special Programs: Various Author signings and readings ongoing, Book release parties.

Barnes & Noble

18025 Garden Way NE, Woodinville
425-398-1990
Hours: Sunday-Thursday 9:00am -10:00pm, Friday & Saturday 9:00am-11:00pm.
Story Time: Saturday 11:00am.
Reading Programs: Science fiction & fiction reading and discussion groups meet monthly, New book release parties.
Special Programs: Open mike poetry nights, Author readings and signings, writers group.

Bookworks
1510 3rd St, Marysville
360-659-4997
www.marysvillebookworks.com
Hours: Monday-Saturday 9:30am-5:30pm.
Special Programs: gallery showing, author signings

Half Price Books
19500 Hwy 99, Lynnwood
425-776-8885
Hours: Daily 10:00am-10:00pm.
Special Programs: Teachers get 10% discount, cash offer on any used books you bring in.

Chapter

Media in the Home

Chapter 9

Media in The Home

Today, more than ever, there is a need for parents to be involved in their children's media choices. Making educated, well-informed decisions is the key for parents and their children.

What is your Family Watching?

Did you know?

- American children, ages 2-17, watch television on average almost 25 hours per week or 3 ? hours a day. Almost one in five watch more than 35 hours of TV each week (Gentile & Walsh, 2002).
- Television is the top after school activity chosen by children ages 6 – 17 (Center for Media Education, 1997).
- 28% of children's television shows contain four or more acts of violence (Woodward, 1999).
- 44% of children and teens report watching different programs when their parents are not around (Strasburger & Donnerstein, 1999).
- Beginning in 2000, all new television sets contain a V-Chip that parents can program to filter out objectionable programs.
- During the 1998/1999 television season the prime time evening hours were the most popular time slot for children ages 2 – 11 (Barron's, 1999).
- Young children who see media violence have a greater chance of exhibiting violent and aggressive behavior later in life than children who have not seen violent media (Congressional Public Health Summit, 2000).
- Violence (homicide, suicide, and trauma) is a leading cause of death for children, adolescents and young adults; more prevalent than disease, cancer or congenital disorders (American Academy of Pediatrics, 2001).

Media's Effect on Body Image

The popular media have increasingly held up a thinner and thinner body image as the ideal for women. The ideal man is also presented as trim, but muscular. These images give our children unfair expectations of what they are supposed to live up to.

In a survey of 9 & 10 year old girls, 40% have tried to lose weight according to an ongoing study funded by the National Heart, Lung and Blood Institute (USA Today, 1996).

One author reports that at age 13, 53% of American girls are "unhappy with their bodies." This grows to 78% by the time girls reach 17 (Brumberg, 1997).

In a study on fifth graders, 10-year-old girls and boys told researchers they were dissatisfied with their own bodies after watching a music video by Britney Spears or a clip from the TV show "Friends" (Mundell, 2002).

You can find more information on these and other topics at **www.mediafamily.org**.

Some Solutions and Suggestions

- To prevent impulse watching, use the TV guide before turning on the set.
- Videotape TV shows for your child so they have a backup when there is nothing appropriate on the television for them to watch.
- Keep television sets out of children's bedrooms.
- Two hours of quality television programming per day is the maximum recommended by the American Academy of Pediatrics.
- Use the V-Chip in your TV to screen objectionable programs.
- Know what your children are watching. Go online and review some of the popular programs.
- Be aware of Kid-Friendly TV ratings and warnings.
- Educate yourself and your family about media choices.
- Make informed decisions regarding the media you will allow in your home.
- Turn off the TV! Pick one of our activities from this book and go have some fun.

Helpful Websites

National Institute on Media and the Family

www.mediafamily.org
The National Institute on Media and the Family is a national resource for research, education and information about the impact of media on children and families. Based in Minneapolis, Minnesota, the National Institute on Media and the Family was created to provide information about media products and their likely impact on children to parents and other adults so they can make informed choices. Home of Kid Wise TV ratings.

TVTurnoff Network

www.tvturnoff.org
Come discuss it, learn more about it, and see how others have turned it off. TVTurnoff Network helps children and adults watch less television and promotes healthier lives and communities.

Parents Television Council

www.parentstv.org
The Parents Television Council (PTC) was established in 1995, offering private sector solutions to restore television to it roots as an independent and socially responsible entertainment medium. This website includes top ten best and worst shows to watch with your family, TV ratings, family guides, articles, and more.

Computer Safety

The Internet, initially the domain of adult users, has rapidly become a place where people of all ages surf for fun and information. Children increasingly have easy access to the Internet through school, the library and home computers. The world of information is at a child's fingertips for school projects, homework, interest areas, hobbies and play. Read on to find out how to protect your child and screen the content that is coming through your computer and into your house.

Did you know...

"In fiscal year 1998, the FBI opened up roughly 700 cases dealing with online pedophilia, most of them for posting child pornography, and about a quarter dealing with online predators trying to get children under 18 to meet with them. By 2000 that figure had quadrupled to 2,856 cases." Source – "The Web's Dark Secret" Newsweek, 3/19/01.

Based on interviews with a nationally representative sample of 1,501 youth ages 10 to 17 who use the Internet regularly, approximately one in five received a sexual solicitation or approach over the Internet in the last year. One in thirty-three received an aggressive sexual solicitation- a solicitor who asked them to meet them somewhere; called them on the telephone; sent them regular mail, money or gifts. One in four had an unwanted exposure to pictures of naked people or people having sex in the last year. Source – "Report Statistical Highlights." From the National Center for Missing and Exploited Children, Crimes Against Children Research Center and Office of Juvenile Justice and Delinquency Prevention. 6/00

The most popular celebrities searched for were Britney Spears, Pamela Anderson, Backstreet Boys, Jennifer Lopez and Eminem. Pokemon was the popular specific toy or game searched. Playboy was the most popular media property. Source – "Alexa Research Finds 'Sex' Popular on the Web..."*Business Wire*. 2/14/2001

According to NetValue, children spent 64.9 percent more time on pornography sites than they did on game sites in September 2000. Over one quarter (27.5%) of children age 17 and under visited an adult web site, which represents 3 million unique underage visitors. Of these minors, 21.2 percent were 14 or younger and 40.2 percent were female. Source – "The NetValue Report on Minors Online..." *Business Wire*. (Taken from study by NetValue, Internet activity measurement service) December 19, 2000.

Pornographers disguise their sites (i.e. stealth sites) with common brand names, including Disney, Barbie, ESPN, etc. to entrap children. They also purchase common websites when they expire before the original user has a chance to renew them.

If you are wondering what you can do to protect your children and combat pornography in you home there are a few simple steps you can take:

Keep track of what your kids are viewing on the Internet. If you are not sure how to pull up a "history" on your computer, it's easy. Simply:

- Click on History (which is on your toolbar at the top). It may just be an icon, so scroll over the icons individually and a name will appear for that icon.
- On the left you'll see a list of the last few days, and under that the names of the sites visited.
- A really clever child (and most are) might delete the history. If the history is cleared, that in itself may be a warning sign that something is wrong.
- For basic protection, you can easily restrict the types of sites the browsers will allow. In Internet Explorer, click on:
- Tools/Internet Options/Content
- The first paragraph is "Content Advisor", click "Settings"
- You'll be asked to enter a password so that only you can change the parameters

- You can then set the level of language, nudity, sex, and violence

There is more help out there through different websites and Internet filters. A site with great links is **www.webroot.com**; it's a site for software to protect businesses and homes. It also has a great section about children. Click on their ChildSafe box, and it will guide you through some great tips and products. Also visit **www.crayon-crawler.com**, which gives you a browser that you can download that acts as a sifter for all sorts of common problems.

Some other sites to check: **www.cybersitter.com**, **www.cyberpatrol.com**, **www.safesurf.com**, and **www.netnanny.com**.

The most important thing is to get to know your kids and your computer! Discuss these topics with them, educate them about the dangers of pornography, and keep your computer in an open place in your home. Don't write yourself off as a parent who does not know much about computers. If you don't know much about how to work your computer, learn. Your children shouldn't expect that they can slide by undetected because their parents are "techno-dummies".

Read on for more helpful information regarding the Internet and computers in your home.

Some tips for parents:

These tips for safeguarding your child's Internet use are from the *U.S. Department of Education: Parents Guide to the Internet.*

Interacting with Others on the Internet:

Just as we tell our children to be wary of strangers they meet, we need to tell them to be wary of strangers on the Internet. Most people behave reasonably and decently online, but some are rude, mean, and even criminal. Teach your children that they should:

- Never give out personal information (including their name, home address, phone number, age, race, family income, school name or location, or friends' names) or use a credit card online without your permission.
- Never share their password, even with friends.
- Never arrange a face-to-face meeting with someone they meet online unless you approve of the meeting and go with them to a public place.
- Never respond to messages that make them feel confused or uncomfortable. They should ignore the sender, end the communication, and tell you or another trusted adult right away.
- Never use bad language or send mean messages online.
- Also, make sure your children know that people they meet online are not always who they say they are and that online information is not necessarily private.

Limiting Children to Appropriate Content on the Internet

Even without trying, your children come across materials on the Internet that are obscene, pornographic, violent, hate-filled, racist, or offensive in other ways. One type of material – child pornography – is illegal. You should report it to the Center for Missing and Exploited Children by calling 1-800-THE LOST (843-5678) or going to www.missingkids.org. While other offensive material is not illegal, there are steps you can take to keep it away from your children and out of your home.

Make sure your children understand what you consider appropriate for them. What kinds of sites are they welcome to visit? What areas are off limits? How much time can they spend, and when? How much money, if any, can they spend? Set out clear, reasonable rules and consequences for breaking them.

Make online exploration a family activity. Put the computer in the living room or family room. This arrangement involves everyone and helps you monitor what your children are doing.

Pay attention to games your older child might download or copy. Some are violent or contain sexual content.

Look into software or online services that filter out offensive materials and sites. Options include stand-alone software that can be installed on your computer, and devices that label or filter content directly on the web. In addition, many Internet Service Providers and commercial online services offer site blocking, restrictions on incoming e-mail, and children's accounts that access specific services. Often, these controls are available at no additional cost. Be aware, however, children are often smart enough to get around these restrictions. Nothing can replace your supervision and involvement.

Find out what the Internet use policy is at your local library and school.

Sources:

Kids Online Project. Outgrowth of the Internet Online Summit: Focus on Children held in Washington D.C., December 1997.

National Center for Missing and Exploited Children, (at www.missingkids.org) *Child Safety on the Information Highway. Consumer Reports*. June, 1997 and September, 1997.

Family Contract for Online Safety

(from **safekids.com**)

Kids' Pledge

1. I will not give out personal information such as my address, telephone number, parents' work address/telephone number, or the name and location of my school without my parents' permission.
2. I will tell my parents right away if I come across any information that makes me feel uncomfortable.
3. I will never agree to get together with someone I "meet" online without first checking with my parents. If my parents agree to the meeting, I will be sure that it is in a public place and bring my mother or father along.
4. I will never send a person my picture or anything else without first checking with my parents.
5. I will not respond to any messages that are mean or in any way make me feel uncomfortable. It is not my fault if I get a message like that. If I do I will tell my parents right away so they can contact the service provider.
6. I will talk with my parents so that we can set up rules for going online. We will decide upon the time of day that I can be online, the length of time I can be online, and appropriate areas for me to visit. I will not access other areas or break these rules without their permission.
7. I will not give out my Internet password to anyone (even my best friends) other than my parents.
8. I will be a good online citizen and not do anything that hurts other people or is against the law.

Child sign here

I will help my child follow this agreement and will allow reasonable use of the Internet as long as these rules and other family rules are followed.

Parent (s) sign here

Helpful Websites

Connect For Kids

www.connectforkids.org

This nonprofit site provides news and information on issues affecting kids and families, over 1,500 helpful links to national and local resources, and two e-mail newsletters.

GetNetwise

www.getnetwise.org

GetNetWise is a public service brought to you by a wide range of Internet industry corporations and public interest organizations. The GetNetWise coalition wants Internet users to be only "one click away" from the resources they need to make informed decisions about their family's use of the Internet.

Yahooligans! Parents Guide

www.yahooligans.com

Search under "Parents Guide". Provides tips and guidelines for safe surfing with your family, monitoring tools, educational information and more.

Kid Friendly Websites

The World Wide Web (WWW) is a wonderful resource for children. It can be compared to a gigantic library containing information on almost every topic imaginable. We scoured the web for the best sites for kids and families. We hope that you find this list fun and helpful.

Online Resources

American Library Association's Great Web Sites for Kids

www.ala.org/greatsites

One of the best resources for kid friendly websites and helpful information. A committee selects sites based on specific criteria:

- Authorship/Sponsorship: Who put up the site?
- Purpose: Every site has a reason for being there – what is it?
- Design and Stability: A great site has personality and strength of character.
- Content: A great site shares meaningful and useful content that educates, informs, and entertains.
- Read more about their criteria and browse through some of their recommended sites.

Berit's Best Sites for Children

www.beritsbest.com
This is a directory of safe sites for children up to the age of 12. Sites are rated and listed by subject.

Fact Monster from Information Please

www.factmonster.com
This is a great site for kids needing help with a report or project. You can search this site by keyword or by subject category.

Virtual Reference Shelf

www.loc.gov//rr/askalib/virtualref.html
Great for reports and general information. Over 30 links from Arts and Music, History, Quotes, Almanacs and more.

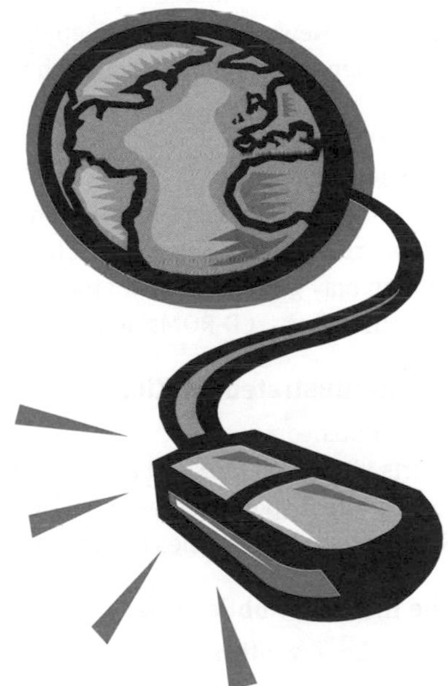

Yahooligans

www.yahooligans.com
Presented by the popular website Yahoo!, Yahooligans! is a web guide for kids. Children can use the search engine to find information or they can click on the many categories geared for kids. There are also parent and teacher guides to help adults utilize this web guide for kids.

Dictionaries

www.dictionary.com

www.onelook.com

www.webster.com (go to the kids section!)

Encyclopedias

www.britannica.com

www.encyclopedia.com

Thesaurus

www.bartleby.com

www.thesaurus.com

Reading

ALA - American Library Association

www.ala.org/alsc

The American Library Association collected and reviewed this list of sites.

Create Your Own Newspaper – CRAYON

www.crayon.net

CRAYON automates the process of constructing a personalized, Web-based newspaper for free! To use this site, simply click on Create Your Free Newspaper, enter your e-mail address, and choose a password.

Scholastic Newszone

www.scholastic.com

Scholastic Newszone is the homepage for all the editions of Scholastic News Online. The homepage is updated daily with the day's news, sports, special events and polls.

Seussvile

www.seussville.com

The Cat in the Hat, Sam-I-Am, Horton Hears a Who!, and the rest of the Seuss characters welcome you to Seussville. Check out Dr. Seuss's playground in cyberspace. You can play games, chat with the Cat in the Hat, win prizes, and find out about new Dr. Seuss books, CD-ROMs and much more.

Sports Illustrated for Kids

www.sikids.com

Sports Illustrated for Kids has interactive activities and games as well as stories on today's latest sports heroes. Check out the day's scores, stats, and standings at the Stat Center. Good articles included from the printed magazine version.

The Internet Public Library: Story Hour

www.ipl.org/youth/storyhour

Offered by the Internet Public Library. Here students can hear and/or read stories by clicking on the picture icon or the site. Some stories offer audio narration with the text.

Time for Kids

www.timeforkids.com

This companion to the Time for Kids magazine connects youth with up to the minute news and current events. The site also includes a dictionary, measurement conversion table, country information and games. Full text articles are available in English and Spanish.

Writing

Kid Authors

www.kidauthors.com

Kid Authors is a creative place for kids to share their stories and poems for other people to read. Stories are posted by genre (mystery, fairy tales, etc.) and writers can fill out an easy online form.

Penpal Box

www.ks-connection.org

Children wishing to write to other children can find a pen pal by going to this website. This site is safe for use and permission from parents is a must.

Stuart Stories

www.stuartstories.com

This site can be used for online reading and writing practice. They can access the site, choose the activities they want, and do a writing activity. Appropriate for children ages 3 to 15.

Telling Tales

www.tellingtales.com

This site has excellent activities to help children with their writing. "Stuff to Do" is the page containing diverse writing exercises. There are story starters, a "Mad Lib" page, files for characters and plots, and skeletons (outlines) that help provide a start for writing ideas.

Language Arts

Ask Jeeves For Kids

www.ajkids.com

Jeeves uses a unique search tool that allows kids to ask questions on almost any subject while providing fast, easy, and safe ways to find answers.

English Zone

www.english-zone.com

This website provides over thirty interactive exercises in grammar, vocabulary, idioms and spelling. The exercises are divided into three levels: easy, intermediate, and advanced. Students are able to click onto the answers and check their work when they are done.

Fun Brain

www.funbrain.com

Find games for any subject. This website can make studying fun for any child! Kids can choose the level of difficulty they wish to play.

Education Place

www.eduplace.com/kids/

This site has all kinds of mind games. One is an online version of MAD LIBS. In Wacky Web Tales, the user is asked to produce words to create a funny story.

Science/Social Studies

Discovery School

school.discovery.com

Explore natural phenomena, go back in time, or examine a variety of exciting themes at the Discovery Channel School Online.

National Geographic For Kids

www.nationalgeographic.com/kids

From the famous National Geographic is a website with articles, games and quizzes for kids. This site provides an accessible menu at every page. Nice photographs and world information available.

NASA Kids

www.nasa.gov

For students K-8. This site has sections on Space and Beyond, Rockets and Airplanes, Projects and Games, and Pioneers and Astronauts. This site is full of child friendly information such as space, space suits, living in space, sundials, weather, the water cycle, careers, and astronomy.

Planet Pals

www.planetpals.com

A website dedicated to preserving the planet. Kids can do searches, read articles, or talk about saving the planet Earth. A wonderful environmental site.

Ranger Rick

www.nwf.org/kids

Offered by the National Wildlife Federation, this website has activities dealing with the endangered animals. It gives ideas for kids in specific age groups.

Sounds of the World's Animals

www.georgetown.edu/cball/animals/animals.html

This site has a simple menu. Choose sounds listed by the animal or by the language. Also included for young readers is *Spelling the Sounds of the World's Animals.*

SpaceKids

www.spacekids.com

Space and science news stories written for young users, a space Q&A section hosted by a team of science teachers, interactive Shockwave games, and a photo gallery. Lots of entertainment for kids of all ages.

StarChild

starchild.gsfc.nasa.gov/docs/StarChild/StarChild.html

This is a learning center for young astronomers put together by a special team at NASA. This site covers everything you'd want to know about the universe and includes many high quality photographic images.

The Wild Ones

www.thewildones.org

This site offers an exciting opportunity for children to preserve endangered species. Each section at this site is designed to improve survival aspects for endangered species.

The Wonderful World of Insects

www.earthlife.net/insects

A glossary is provided. Information on classification of the insect orders is excellent. Kids – follow the link to The Bug Club.

Who is Dr. Universe?

www.wsu.edu/DrUniverse

There isn't a single question you can't ask Dr. Universe! She'll answer your question herself or go to Washington State University's research team for advice. She goes to libraries, field sites, or virtually anywhere to get your question answered.

Math / Money

A+ Math

www.aplusmath.com

This is a helpful site for elementary and middle school students working on their basic skills. Flash cards are generated quickly and are provided for many topics.

Ask Dr. Math

forum.Swarthmore.edu/dr.math

Have a question about a math problem? Ask Dr. Math! Simply submit questions to Dr. Math by filling out his Web form or by sending him an e-mail for help, and you will receive an answer to your question via e-mail.

Bank High School

www.bankhs.com

Bank High School is tuned to the more sophisticated user with Flash 6 a requirement. Learn how to manage money, how banks can be of assistance, how stocks and bonds boost savings, what credit is, how to finance a car, and much more.

Bank Jr.

www.bankjr.com

This web site, powered by Zion's Bank, teaches elementary and grades 6+ all about money, ask the Money Kid and get answers on the web site, learn about the history of money, money basics, money math, money in your life, and more. Take a quiz in each section. Parents should become involved too.

H.I.P. Pocket Change

www.usmint.gov/kids

Want to start a coin collection? Here's the place to start, including a tour of the U.S. Mint, adventures & games. Teachers have lesson plans, a guide and a library for resources.

Figure This

www.figurethis.org

Find challenging math questions for children ranging from Algebra, Geometry, Measurements, Numbers, and Statistics and Probability. Funded by the U.S. Department of Education, and the National Science Foundation.

Kids Bank

www.kidsbank.com

A website specifically designed for children to learn about money and banking.

Math Forum

www.mathforum.org/dr.math

Swarthmore graduate students find answers to your mathematical stumping questions for elementary students to college students.

Young Investor

www.younginvestor.com

Young Investor introduces the fundamentals of money and investing in a colorful way that might grab the attention of the youthful set. Sign up on your first visit and the Young Investor pages tailor their content to your age group.

Government

The White House for Kids

www.whitehousekids.gov

The White House, its history, moments of the Presidency, kids and pets in the White House.

Afterschool.Gov

www.afterschool.gov

Kids and teens now have access to government information appropriate to their age group, from the Federal Government. Useful information such as college opportunities and funding, information on substance abuse, health, math, fun stuff, and lots more.

First Gov For Kids

www.kids.gov

Links to federal kid's sites along with some of the best kid's sites from other organizations all grouped by subject. Explore, learn and have fun.

50 States.com: States and Capitals

www.50states.com

This is an amazing site. It is perfect for elementary school kids, up to high school. It gives you information on state capitals, state birds, governors, congressional representatives, and much much more!

Homework

Ask Dr. Math

forum.Swarthmore.edu/dr.math

Have a question about a math problem? Ask Dr. Math! Simply submit questions to Dr. Math by filling out his Web form or by sending him an e-mail for help, and you will receive an answer to your question via e-mail.

FunBrain

www.funbrain.com

Hundreds of good homework sites are found here.

Merriam-Webster Online

www.m-w.com

An online Webster Dictionary and Thesaurus.

For Tweens

Backyard Jungle

www.backyardjungle.org

Backyard Jungle is a participatory multimedia site where kids learn about ecology and new ways to explore their natural surroundings.

Don't Buy It

www.dontbuyit.org

Don't Buy It challenges kids to question advertising, evaluate media, and become smart consumers.

It's My Life

www.pbskids.org/itsmylife

It's My Life invites kids to share their feelings about the social, emotional, and physical issues that affect them.

The Plastic Fork Diaries

www.plasticforkdiaries.org

Tweens explore their relationship to food: nutrition, athletic performance, cultural significance, and the vanishing family meal.

General Websites

Cyberkids

www.cyberkids.com
The Cyberkids Launchpad provides interesting spots on the Web to explore. Immerse yourself in art, computers, music, science, nature, museums, entertainment, and all kinds of other activities.

4 Kids

www.4kids.org
Find links to safe educational and informative websites. Take the Kids Quest challenge, find answers to technology questions, play games, color books, and interactive musical instruments.

Funology

www.funology.com
Kindergarten-5th grade jokes, games, magic tricks, trivia and recipes.

Haring Kids.com

www.haringkids.com
Interactive activities to inspire a love of learning and art, online books, authorized art shows.

Headbone

www.headbone.com
This site allows kids to do everything from write and edit to design and maintain the pages. There are interactive virtual communities, head to head games, fun columns, hidden messages and more.

Kids Domain

www.kidsdomain.com
Great family resource. Reviews on books, toys, games and movies. Ideas for holiday fun, crafts, travel and more.

Kidlink

www.kidlink.org
Join Kidlink's moderated global dialogs, e-mail, chats, and interactive projects. Available in several languages.

KidsCom

www.kidscom.com
An Educational and Entertaining Electronic Playground for kids ages 4 to 15 that emphasize the creativity of youngsters. In English, German, French and Spanish.

Mama Media

www.mamamedia.com
This website helps children to gain technology fluency and expands their minds thorugh playful learning.

Nick Jr.

www.nickjr.com
This site is great for younger children. Use the Quick Search to find what you are looking for quicker. The Quick Search is organized by: Age-by-Age Activities, Activity Finder, Nick Jr. Shows, and Message Board.

Noggin

www.noggin.com
Lots of activities for kids including Sesame Street games.

PBS Kids

www.pbskids.org
This is the hangout for all of the favorite PBS stars: Arthur, Theodore Tugboat, Mister Rogers and more. Each TV site offers activities, games, and coloring pages.

Planet Oz Kids

www.planetozkids.com
Oban the Knowledge Keeper and his fellow storytellers will take you through the world of myths and legends. This site presents common themes found in stories from various cultures of the world and invites you to learn about the myths and legends of your country and other cultures.

Sesame Workshop

www.sesameworkshop.org
Fun for both parents and kids, find your favorite characters and activities and even an interactive Elmo!

The Case.com for Kids

www.TheCase.com/kids
Who doesn't love a good mystery? At TheCase.com you can create your own mysteries, read scary stories, and try out magic tricks.

World Kids Network

www.worldkids.net
This site is dedicated to the advancement of children's education. It's motto – "Be anyone, do anything, or find almost anything". You can do anything from join clubs, play games, do homework, visit museums, or even be a volunteer for the World Kids Network (WKN).

Chapter 10

At Home Fun

Chapter 10

At Home Fun

The next time your kids are whining for something to do, or you just want to get them away from the TV, try some of these fun and easy at home activities. Kick back and have fun with your kids! These ideas are also great for playgroups.

Play Clay Recipe

Every child loves clay! They love it so much, the store bought stuff seems to disappear fast (sometimes in their tummies). A batch of this moldable mush will keep them busy and building. Store it in airtight containers to make it last for a few weeks. And don't worry if they eat it, it's made from the goodness of your own kitchen!

Ingredients:

- 1 cup all purpose flour
- 1/2 cup salt
- 1/2 teaspoon cream of tartar
- 1 cup water
- 1 teaspoon vegetable oil
- food coloring

Mix the flour, salt, cream of tartar, water, and oil in a saucepan. Cook over medium heat until it holds together (keep mixing or it will stick to the bottom of the pan). When the clay is cool enough to touch, knead it on a floured surface, divide it into smaller balls, and add a different shade of food coloring to each ball.

Foil Figures

Use aluminum foil to mold a masterpiece. Kids can create their own statues, people, or creatures out of aluminum foil. These fun figures can strike any pose your child likes!

What Can I do with Butcher Paper?

What can't you do with white butcher paper? Roll the paper out as far as the eye can see and let your kids loose. They can create an imaginary world full of landscapes, houses, and roadways for their favorite toy figures. Have them trace their feet and hands and turn them into monsters. Have a group of kids create a mural and hang it on your back fence. The ideas are endless.

Crayon Rubbings

Kids can collect simple items from the backyard: leaves, flowers, pine needles, small rocks, bits of wood, or old screen. Lay the items under some lightweight paper and rub gently with a flat crayon until the picture appears. Hint: Tape the paper down when possible for an easier etching!

Paint to Music

Get your kids' bodies and imaginations moving. Grab your paints and set your kids free. Try different moods of music and have them paint what they hear. Is it happy or sad? Fast or slow? Are the lines long or short? Is one song a certain color? Change the music up and see what they produce! Try jazz, blues, salsa or classical music. You might want to take this activity outside to manage the mess! To make a cleaner indoor variation use crayons, markers, or colored pencils on a big sheet of butcher paper.

Blind Fold Drawings

This fun drawing game is a great thing to try with kids and adults. Brainstorm some basic objects with your kids. Write the items or characters down on small pieces of paper and put them in a bowl. Each person can draw a piece of paper out of the bowl, tie up their blindfold, and draw away. Set a timer. When the timer goes off, see if the kids can guess what the others have drawn!

Homemade Mock Chalk

This tough counterpart is great for use on concrete. Mix two parts plaster of paris with one part warm water. Add powdered tempera paint to get the desired color. For each stick, line a toilet paper tube with waxed paper, seal one end with tape, and pour in the mixture. Tap the tube to release bubbles. Let the mixture harden. Voila, this chalk will last for years.

Chalk Painting

Create a watercolor masterpiece on your driveway by drawing with chalk before or during a light rainstorm. Big, basic images work the best! Your child's art will rank up there with Monet when the storm subsides.

Rose-Colored Windows

On a gray day or in the middle of the winter, satisfy your longing for flowers and springtime by trying this fun activity. Use washable paints to create a flower garden on your window. Use paintbrushes and fingers to create stems, leaves, and different flower blossoms. This will add a splash of color and fun to a gray day. (FamilyFun)

Ice Cube Painting

Freeze colored water in ice cube trays; children can paint with the ice cubes. This slippery art project will provide plenty of fun and color any day of the week. Freeze a popsicle stick in each section to provide a little more control for younger children. Coffee filters work well to paint on with this medium because they absorb the water well.

Finger Paint

Ingredients:

- 2 tablespoons sugar
- 1/3 cup cornstarch
- 2 cups cold water
- 1/4 cup clear dishwashing liquid
- food coloring
  (for vibrant colors, use food coloring paste)

Mix the sugar and cornstarch in a small pan, and then slowly add the water. Cook over low heat stirring until the mixture becomes a smooth, almost clear gel (about 5 minutes). When the mixture is cool, stir in the dishwashing liquid. Scoop equal amounts into several containers and stir in the food coloring.

Make Tiny Bubbles

For a slew of miniature bubbles, tape together a bunch of plastic drinking straws. Dip one end in the bubble solution, hold the other about one inch from your mouth (do not put your lips on the straws) and blow. Learn how to blow all kinds of bubbles at www.bubblemania.com. (FamilyFun)

Homemade Bubble Wands

You can use straws and strings to weave together some of the best bubble wands in existence. Here are a few other ideas from FamilyFun Magazine:

Miniature Paper Clip Wand

How to make it: Bend a paper clip into a bubble wand shape.
Dipping container: Cap from a small jar.
What you'll get: A single baby bubble.
Flyswatter Bubblette Wand
How to make it: Grab a clean flyswatter.
Dipping container: Frisbee turned upside down.
What you'll get: Cumulus cloud-like masses of mini bubbles.

Classic Coat Hanger Wand

How to make it: Bend hanger into a circle and handle. Wrap the circle with string.
Dipping Container: Upside down trash can lid.
What you'll get: A lo-o-o-ng bubble!

Giant Hula Wand

How to make it: Dig out your hula-hoop.
Dipping container: Kiddie pool.
What you'll get: Say aloha to the biggest bubbles ever!

Bubble Recipe

Ingredients:

- 3 cups water
- 1 cup dishwashing liquid
- 1/3 cup light corn syrup
- add food coloring for colored bubbles, if desired

Mix all ingredients together and what have you got? Our favorite bubble recipe! Store your bubble blend in a covered container. Great tip: The best time to blow bubbles is when the air is calm and muggy, such as after a rain shower. Bubbles last longer when it's humid.

Here are some other recipes to try out to find the perfect mega-bubble mixture:

Recipe 1

- Dawn Ultra or Joy Ultra - 1 part
- distilled water - 15 parts
- glycerin or white Karo Syrup - 1/4 part

Recipe 2

- Joy - 2/3 cup
- water - one gallon
- glycerin - three tablespoons

Recipe 3

- Regular Dawn or Joy - 1 part
- distilled water - 10 parts
- glycerin or white Karo Syrup - 1/4 parts

Recipe 4

- Ultra Ivory Blue - 1 cup
- water - 12 cups
- glycerin - 1 Tablespoon

Play Four Square

Remember playing four square at recess? You can create this fun game in your driveway in a bounce! Draw a four square court on your driveway with chalk, grab a good ol' red playground ball and let the games begin. See if you can remember all of the variations for your kids (Giants, baby bounce, double bounce, etc.) Or, try having players call out the name of a country, a state, an animal, a movie star, or another category. A player is out if they repeat something that's already been said.

Materials:

- red playground ball
- chalk
- four Players

Play Ball!

Pack a Costume Suitcase

To encourage hours of magic, masquerade, and make-believe, pack old suitcases with dress-ups and disguises. Store the suitcases under your child's bed. We recommend scouring your closets, attic, dollar stores, and local thrift stores for any of the following items:

- Fancy old dresses, scarves and purses
- Hats- top, straw, witch, police, fireman, or cowboy hat, Easter bonnets, baseball caps, chef's toques, football helmet, hockey mask
- Feather boa
- A piece of sheer, velvet, or heavy fabric with a dress clip—an instant cape!
- Shoes of all kinds—cowboy boots, Chinese slippers, high heels
- Bathrobe or a kimono
- Wigs and fake fur for beards and sideburns
- Bandanas
- Costume jewelry and plastic bead necklaces

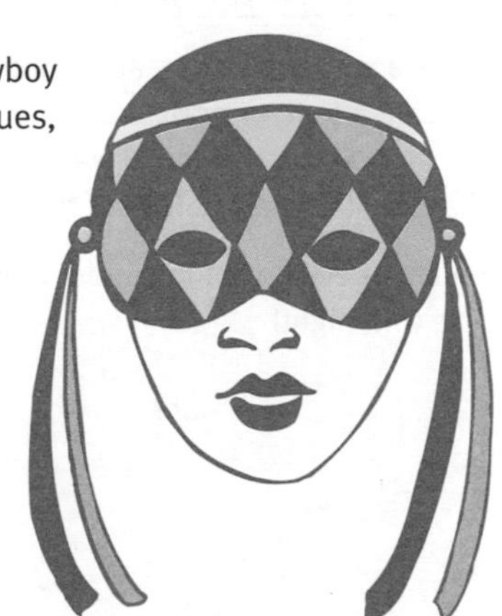

- Eyewear—nonprescription glasses, shades, and goggles
- Lipstick and eye shadow
- A black eye pencil for whiskers and mustaches
- Plastic Fangs
- Wands
- Crown or tiara
- Angel Wings, Devil Horns
- Tutu
- Masks
- Dad's old ties
- Sports jerseys
- Scrubs and a stethoscope
- Old swimsuits, fins, snorkel and mask
- Umbrellas

Act Out Stories from Books

The story line of almost any book can be acted out. Some that work best are nursery rhymes, songs, or simple books. Props are not necessary, but you can bust out your costume suitcase and the kids are set. Have them make animal noises or sing songs. Let them alternate roles or change the ending of the story.

Tailor the Toilet Paper

Buy the cheap stuff when it's on sale. Offer each child a roll and let them wrap away. Play "Wrap the Mummy," or use the toilet paper to "mend wounds," create casts, or head wraps. Let them stuff their clothes with toilet paper and have a rolling race across the lawn. Did you ever think toilet paper could be so fun?

Camp-Out Indoors

Create a wilderness retreat in your own living room. Drape your table in an old sheet to create a tent, or grab a real one of your own. Grab your canteen and some sleeping bags. Roast marshmallows over the stove, make smores, and eat hot dogs. Grab a flashlight and turn off all of the lights. Tell ghost stories!

You might even want to set out a bunch of your favorite stuffed animals to make it an extra *wild* night!

Pet Rocks

Scout around your yard or be on the lookout during a nature hike for rocks that would make great faces. Look for rocks that have face-like features. Stick pebbles, plastic googly eyes, and pom-poms in place with regular glue or a glue gun. Add detail to your rocks with fun fur, sparkles, acrylic paint, yarn, or anything you can find around the house. Be creative!

Become a Master Builder

Cardboard boxes of all shapes and sizes are good starters for any building project. Children can tape them together and paint on them. In no time, ordinary boxes become houses, buildings, fire trucks, or forts. Start by collecting cardboard boxes in various shapes and sizes. Tape the boxes shut with packing tape, or leave them open depending on what the master builder has in mind. Using markers, crayons, or tempura paint your kids can decorate the boxes with windows, columns, drapes and mailboxes. You can even add tissue paper flowers, bushes, or paper flags. If you don't have plain brown boxes, wrap yours with butcher paper or turn them inside out and tape them back together.

Shining Stars

With this handy stargazing device, your kids won't have to wait until nighttime to view their favorite constellations. Instead they can cast their own stellar images on a wall or ceiling in a darkened room.

Materials:

- marker
- large paper cup
- pushpin or thumbtack
- flashlight

Draw a constellation (such as the Northern Cross, or the Big or Little Dipper) on the bottom of a large paper cup. Then use the pushpin to make a small hole in the center of each star. Turn off the lights and hold the cup so that the bottom is pointing toward a wall. Shine the flashlight into the open end of the cup, angling it a bit to diffuse the rays, and enjoy a starry view. (FamilyFun)

Spin Art

Dig out your old record player or go to your local thrift store to find a cheap used one. Poke a hole in the center of a paper plate, set it on the record player as if it were a record. Have your kids hold the tips of one or more markers (crayons or colored pencils work too) on the plate and turn the player on. Repeat on the other side of the paper plate.

Listen to a Rain Stick

Your child can make a rain stick of his own from a cardboard mailing tube and dry rice or beans. Here's how:

Materials:

- 1/2 pound of finishing nails
- hammer
- cardboard mailing tube
- 1-2 cups of small beans or rice
- tape
- acrylic paint
- paintbrushes

Randomly hammer nails into the sides of the cardboard mailing tube. Ideally the nails should be almost as long as the tube is wide. With one end of the tube securely capped (tape if necessary), pour the beans or rice into the cylinder. Then place a hand over its open end and tilt the tube to test the sound. You can pour out some of the filler or add more until you achieve the sound you like. (If you want a slower-sounding fall, hammer in more nails.) Cap the open end and tape. Now decorate the outside of the rain stick with acrylic paint. Once the paint dries completely, tilt the stick, close your eyes, and listen to the rainfall. (FamilyFun)

Wind Bags

Throw your grocery bag to the wind with this kite-flying feat. First, tie together the handles of a plastic shopping bag with the end of a ball of string. Staple a few 2-foot lengths of ribbon to the bottom of the bag for kite tails. Now find a windy spot outdoors and start running. As the bag fills with air, slowly let out the string and the kite should begin to soar and dive. (FamilyFun)

Make Paper Bag Puppets

You can make enough puppets for your own puppet show in a matter of minutes!

Materials:

- colored markers/paint
- plain brown lunch size paper bag
- scrap pieces of fabric
- stapler
- yarn, string, raffia, or fun fur

Draw or paint a face on the paper bag. Add hair from yarn, or clothes from pieces of scrap fabric. Have your kids put on a puppet show together. When you're done, store them up and pull them out another day.

Self Portrait Plates

This activity can work for kids of any age. This mask-making project is a real crowd pleaser. The kids can cut out pictures from magazines and paste them together in a Picasso-like self-portrait. Or they can get extra creative and give their piece two different eyes and two different ears, crazy hair, or wild expressions. Use something sturdy like a paper plate or poster board as the backbone for this project. You will need something that will absorb all of that glue!

Set out magazines, markers, crayons, construction paper, yarn, fun fur, glue sticks, scissors, and other decorating supplies. Use the supplies set out to create hair, eyes, lips, noses, freckles, and other features. These fun masks are great for parties and groups!

Rainbow Stew

Mix 1/3 cup sugar, one cup cornstarch, and four cups of cold water. Cook until thick and divide into three bowls. Add a generous amount of red, blue, and yellow food coloring so that each bowl contains a separate color. In a heavy-duty sealable bag, place about three tablespoons of each color they've requested. Roll the bag to push the air out and then seal and tape closed with a bit of duct tape.

Now knead, squish, and squash, the balls of color into every possible color combination.

Juice Box Boat Races

Turn your empty juice box into a boat in a matter of minutes. All you need is an empty juice box, a couple of extra straws, and some sail décor!

Cut a rectangular sail from the scrap plastic or paper. Let your kids personalize their sails with markers, glitter, stickers, or crayons. Punch a hole at each end and thread the straw through. With the scissors or the tip of a knife, cut a small "X" in the center of the empty juice box, insert the straw, and sail. Float your boat in the wading pool and blow through another straw to send it sailing. Have "yacht races" for popsicle prizes, or have them see what tricks they can maneuver with their little juice boat.

Make a Family Quilt

This project will require a little more time for the parent but will become a treasured keepsake in years to come. Have everyone in the family pick out his or her favorite fabrics and cut them into 8-inch squares. Emphasize that they should choose a fabric that represents their own personality in some way. Create a patchwork quilt out of the colorful scraps that they have selected.

More Great Resources

FamilyFun Boredom Busters
Edited by Deanna F. Cook

Find 365 creative, inventive, and expertly chosen projects that will ensure there is always something fun to do every single day of the year. Features bright, full color photographs.

FamilyFun Crafts
Edited by Deanna F. Cook

The perfect resource for busy families in search of creative and exciting ways to turn free time into fun family time, Disney's FamilyFun Crafts nurture a child's creativity through painting, drawing, paper crafts, kitchen crafts, nature crafts, homemade toys, and much more. Color illustrations.

The Little Hands Big Fun Craft Book
Creative Fun for 2-6 Year Olds
By Judy Press

Make a hearts and flowers necklace, a handprint family tree, a noodle nametag, or a tooth fairy pouch. Over 70 fun arts and crafts projects encourage creativity.

You can find any of these books online and in bookstores. If you're looking for a great deal try www.half.com, or buy "used" from **www.amazon.com**.

In The Garden

As winter ends, we look forward to spring and summer, which bring rebirth in nature. Soon the days will be longer, school will be out, and families will spend more time outside. If you're looking for a fun outdoor activity that allows the whole family to participate, consider a family garden! From selecting your vegetables and flowers, preparing the earth and planting, to finally harvesting, gardening can be a wonderful way to involve your children in a healthy hobby you can also enjoy.

Life Lessons of Gardening

Along with the fun of getting dirty, gardening helps children learn valuable lessons about patience as they wait for vegetables to grow, responsibility as they see how necessary their care is to the garden, and even loss when flowers die at the end of a season. "They learn about nurturing a life and what it takes to keep something alive," says Amy Gifford, an education associate for the National Gardening Association.

The garden can teach us and our children profound lessons about life and the world around us. Here are just a few of the many benefits of gardening with your family:

Science

It teaches them about the lifecycle and the wonder of nature, not to mention earth science and the effects we have on our environment. Kids also get a first hand account into the miracle of life trapped inside a single seed - something to be discovered and cherished.

Life 101

Gardening offers a great opportunity to connect with nature on a deeper level - by touching it, caring for it, and watching it grow. Gardening teaches the rhythms of the seasons and the life cycle. The garden is life's lessons in action- there is no telling or listening - only doing. If they don't water the plants, they'll die. If they don't tend the weeds, they'll take over. Though the lessons seem small, it is the first step towards larger ideas and responsibilities.

Relaxation

Gardening has also been shown to reduce stress - no matter what your age. The quiet, calming effect of gardening can soothe the stressed out or overstimulated child. Even better, the garden appeals to all five of our senses - we can see, touch, smell, hear, and even "taste" our garden. The healing effects of gardening are well documented, and are even being used in programs to help children of abuse and/or broken homes to rebuild their self-esteem.

Family Time

It's also a great time to connect with your kids. Talk together, or work quietly along side each other. You never know - you may rediscover your child in the backyard pumpkin patch. "Dig in" and have fun!

Other benefits of gardening for children include:

- Improvement in fine and gross motor skills
- Improved social skills
- Enhanced self-esteem
- Enhanced sensory perception and creativity

Garden Tips

Gardening can be made easy and fun for children of all abilities by keeping in mind a few things:

- Caring for their own section of the garden can give children a great feeling of accomplishment as they watch their own plants grow and change.
- Let kids have their own spot. If they want to toss 10 seeds in one hole, let them and they will see what happens. Learn from experience.

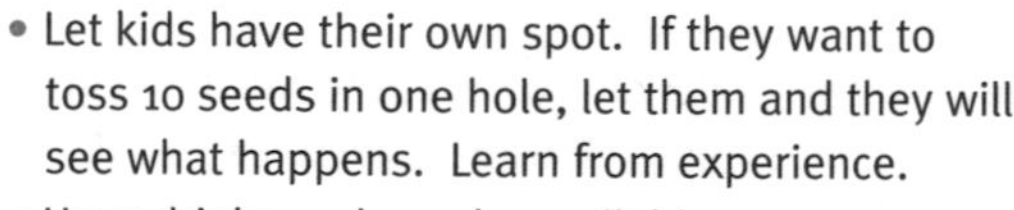

- Have drinks and snacks available.
- Provide small or child-sized tools for better grip.
- Use larger seeds for easier handling; place smaller seeds into a spice jar and sprinkle for easier planting.
- Allow for frequent rest breaks.
- Plant plants that grow quickly and easily.
- Modify the garden using raised beds, containers, or trellises, to make gardening easier for a child with special needs.

Create Your Own Grass Man

Paint a silly face on a medium size terra cotta pot. Place some gravel at the bottom of the pot, fill it with soil, and sprinkle a handful of grass seeds on the surface. Keep it damp and in a light place. In a few weeks, the grassy hair will grow. But if you don't take control, it will grow and grow and grow. Give it a trim and create your own grassy hairstyle.

Magic In A Pot

Place some pebbles at the bottom of a bucket or a 9-inch planting pot. Fill the pot to the brim with potting compost. Sprinkle about 20 seeds on the top, cover them with a bit of compost, and water them. Leave the pot in a warm, light place. After a couple of weeks, seedlings will begin to show. When you have good growth from your seedlings, you can put the pot outside. Place little plastic figures or tiny gnomes among the little plants.

Seed Starter Ideas

Flowers

Fill an empty egg carton with compost. Push one seed into each cup so that it is covered by the soil. Water to make the soil damp. Shoots should appear after about a week or two. When the shoots are strong enough, transfer them into the garden.

Vegetables

Use empty yogurt containers (from a six pack of yogurt). Fill it with compost and plant your vegetable seeds. Tape a picture of what you have planted to the side of the container. When the plant is big enough, transfer it to the garden.

Picture Pots

Give your plants a personality by decorating their pots. Paint bugs, flowers, polka dots, zebra stripes, or create a spooky castle.

To paint pebbles and pots, use acrylic or poster paint. To make sure they are shiny and waterproof, mix the paints with PVA glue. Use one part PVA glue to every two parts paint.

Ping Pong Ball Plant Labels

Plant curious Ping Pong labels all over your garden. Simply make a hole in a Ping Pong ball and stick it on top of a plant cane. Use waterproof pens or markers to decorate them and write the name of the plant.

Grow A Sweet Potato

The perfect indoor gardening project, this sweet potato vine is quick and easy to grow.

Materials:

- Sweet potato that has begun to sprout
- 2 toothpicks
- Glass jar
- Terra-cotta pot and potting soil

Pierce the middle of the sweet potato with toothpicks, one on each side, and suspend over the jar. Fill the jar almost to the top with lukewarm water and set it on a bright windowsill. Be sure that the root end of the potato, called the pointier, faces downward. In 7-14 days, you'll see whiskery rootlets growing under the water. In a week or two, you should see tiny red sprouts at the top, which will soon open into red-veined green leaves. When growth is about 6-8 inches high, transplant the potato into a flowerpot. Fill the pot about a third of the way with soil, put in the tuber and add soil up to the growth. Cover the tuber completely to discourage rotting. Water often to keep the soil lightly moist. (FamilyFun)

Community Gardens

Bellevue Botanical Gardens

12001 Main St, Bellevue

425-451-3755

www.bellevuebotanical.org

Hours: 7:00am-Dusk

Price: Free. Donations are accepted.

Enjoy year-round beauty in the garden and trails.
Spring: Pulmonia, Rhododendrons, Tulips, and Camellias.
Summer: Blue Angel, Chrysanthemum, Hydrangea, Amber Waves, Night Raven, Neon Flash, and Hansa.
Fall: Bright red, yellow, orange, copper, coral leaves mixed with the evergreens.
Winter: Sparkleberry, Beautyberry, Chinese Witch Hazel, Crabapple, Oregon Grape, Rose Hips, Midwinter Fire, and Fuchsia.
Stroll along the tranquil trail of The Lost Meadow with the Western Red Cedar, Douglas Fir, Big Leaf and Vine Maple trees as your guide. Refresh your senses along the Yao Japanese Garden path, the Waterwise Garden, Serene Woodlands, Alpine Rock Garden, and the Botanical Reserve. Please note that dogs are not allowed in the gardens.

Bradner Garden Park

29th Ave S and S Grand, South Seattle

206-684-4075

www.cityofseattle.net/parks/parkspaces/gardens.htm

Hours: Daily from 4:30am to 11:30pm

Price: Free

This new park was built with gardening education in mind. The 1.6-acres is one of the first pesticide free gardens and thus provides a great habitat for butterflies and other animals that would otherwise be driven away.

Kubota Garden
Renton Ave S and 55th Ave S, Seattle
205-684-4584
www.kubota.org
Hours: Daylight
Price: Free

The serene Kubota Garden is a 4.5 acre Japanese style garden hidden in the city offering a welcome escape to busy city life. Designed by Fujitaro Kabuta beginning in the late 1920's, the gardens were continually manicured for six decades becoming the beautiful landscaped which envelopes the garden today. The Seattle Landmarks Preservation Board declared Kubota Garden a National Historic Landmark over 30 years ago, and it is now kept by the Seattle Parks & Recreation. The one mile trail is filled with a wide variety of birds and other wildlife, stone gardens, overlooks, water-falls, stone mountain side with a mini walk into the mountains, springs, ponds, the Fera Fera forest, and 12, 000 year old stones left by the last glacier.

Washington Park Arboretum
2300 Arboretum Drive E, Seattle
206-543-8800
depts.washington.edu/wpa
Hours: 10:00am 4:00pm (Visitors Center)
Exit off Hwy 520 (Buses 11, 43, and 48 run near the Arboretum)

The Washington Park Arboretum hosts 230 acres of spectacular urban green space on the shores of Lake Washington adjacent to The University of Washington. Its 230 acres comprise a dynamic, living museum with collections of oaks, conifers, camel-lias, Japanese maples and hollies that are known internationally as the largest in the country, an extensive network of trails, a Japanese garden, Woodland garden, and Rhododendron glen.. The University of Washington, in association with the Center for Urban Horticulture, manages the Arboretum.

Great Gardening Books

The Garden Book
DK Publishing

Colorful photographs and step-by-step instructions show you how to create over 50 projects from a miniature garden that fits into the palm of your hand to grass people with heads you can groom. Perfect for budding gardeners who want to get growing.

Kid's Gardening
by Kevin Raftery, Kim Gilbert, and Jim M'Guinness

Now young readers will know from whence those carrots came. This full-color extravaganza contains nearly a hundred pages of wipe-clean cardstock, hundreds of illustrations, dozens of growing activities, plus 15 varieties of vegetable, flower and herb seeds.

National Gardening Association Guide to Kids' Gardening
National Gardening Association

This is the official youth gardening guide of the 250,000 member National Gardening Association. It combines more than 70 gardening project ideas with practical how-to advice on starting and maintaining a youth garden. Included with the purchase of each book is a free six-month membership in the National Gardening Association.

Roots, Shoots, Buckets & Boots: Gardening Together With Children

Sunflower Houses: Inspiration from the Garden-A Book for Children and Their Grown-Ups
by Sharon Lovejoy

The pictures and illustrations alone are enough reason to buy these books. The author keeps a young child's attention span in mind and emphasizes the small wonders a garden brings. The projects are not only kid-friendly, but also give a child reason to stick it out from planting to harvest. These books go one step further in skillfully weaving in science, folklore, and practical gardening information.

Helpful Websites

www.kidsgardening.com
The National Gardening Association is a non-profit organization established in 1972 to help people through gardening. This site is one of the best resources we have found. It includes helpful gardening tips, activities, books, and more. It is both an excellent educational and a family resource.

www.raw-connections.com/garden
This is a fun website for kids. It teaches kids about everything from planning a garden, to how to keep a garden healthy.

Chapter 11

Parties and Gatherings

Chapter 11

Parties & Gatherings

Is child is turning another year older, or are you in charge of the next school carnival or family reunion? This is definitely the chapter for you! Most of the businesses listed below are not only great for birthday parties, but are perfect venues for family get-togethers, annual family company parties, sport celebrations, play group outings, cub scout and girl scout parties, school fundraisers or picnics, and so forth. Little did I realize before writing this chapter how many fun and totally creative activities are available for gatherings with children. I hope you have as much fun learning about all of these resources as I have!

Family Entertainers

A Giggleworks Production

253-874-4101

www.giggleworks.net

Price: $175: 1/2 comedic interactive magic show, and ? hour balloon animals.

$325 2 hours: company picnics

$125/$200/hr: Clowns, jugglers, caricature artists, and face painting.

They do parties, picnics, company picnics, grand openings, school events, and more. Activities include magic shows, balloon art, caricatures, face painting, stilt walking, clowns, and juggling.

Animal Crackers (Musical Entertainment for Kids)

206-232-1078

www.nancymusic.com

Price: $110 for a 30 minute program.

With 17 years experience, Mother Goose on guitar does holiday songs including Gung Hay Fat Choy, Ramadan, The Colors of Winter, Eight Days of Light. She also teaches a short guitar course. She's been on stage with Bill Cosby, Burl Ives, Shirley Jones, Lilly Tomlin, and at concerts with Randy Sparks and others. Original CD's available.

Balloons To Go with Sparky The Clown

253-833-3558

Price: $95 for up to 15 children.

A one hour show geared for a variety of ages. Sparky begins with a fun magic trick to introduce himself to the children. Magic presentation lasts 15-20 minutes and includes a magic birthday cake. Guests will not go away empty handed because Sparky finished the party with making specialized balloon animals for everyone.

Bubbles The Clown

206-365-4520

www.bubblestheclownnw.com

Bubbles will bring a piece of the circus to you! She's fun, gives prizes, candy, balloons, games and all the "hoopla" to tickle your fancy.

Bruce Meyers Magician and Comedian

Seattle

360-652-5779

800-430-5779

www.brucemeyersmagic.com

Price: $225 for a 1-hour magic show.

Bruce Meyers starts his show by pulling a live rabbit out of a wizard hat! Later in the show a dove is pulled out of the same hat. The birthday child receives a top hat full of magic tricks, and each guest receives a magic wand.

The magic show ends with a magic birthday cake. Bruce Meyers has over 30 years of experience.

Caricatures Let's Face It

425-486-8478

Price: $125 hour, 2 hour minimum. (approx. 10 caricatures)

Detailed, humorous, full face caricatures are their specialty. Caricatures are drawn on 9x12 white heavy paper and enclosed in a large, sturdy envelope. His experience includes teaching high school art classes for 28 years.

Charles The Clown

206-361-7171

www.charlestheclown.com

Price: $175

Charles is a magician and a clown with 30+ years of experience with over 75 radio and television appearances and was also featured in Parents magazine. He has performed to children around the world, from orphanages in Vietnam to Hollywood. He comes dressed as a regular person, and in a fun, non-threatening way, slowly becomes a clown in front of the group. He brings along his giant dog puppet that "performs" as his partner. He makes balloon sculptures, and ends the show by making a special balloon hat for the birthday child. The entire performance lasts approximately 1 hour.

See ad in back

Charlie The Juggling Clown

425-481-7143

www.charliethejugglingclown.com

Charlie is known internationally and is multi-talented when it comes to entertaining. He combines a unique performance of magic, juggling, plate spinning, trick cartooning, pantomime, audience interaction, and clowning. As a U.S. representative, Charlie traveled to Singapore to perform at the inaugural Clown-Around-The-World Festival. His wife, "Pookie" specializes in appearances as a clown in hospitals and nursing homes.

Clay Martin's Puppet Theater

425-831-2109
800-300-5196

www.leapfrog-entertainment.com

Clay Martin's theater has been is business for over ten years. His programs include the 300 year old story of Punch & Judy, King Arthur, and Robin Hood, and The Hounds of Baskerville. His Victorian Toy Theater is quite unique, where last year he performed the production of Mozart's Opera, Bastien & Bastienne with professional opera singers accompanied by a live string quartet. He also includes a short lecture on the history and construction of puppets and marionette's.

Cricket (The Clown)

425-774-0937
206-356-9221 (cell)

Price: $100.00 an hour

Cricket performs at birthday parties and other special events face painting, sculpting balloon animals, and performing a magic show. Cricket was awarded the prestigious "Golden Bootie Award" several years ago for excellence in children's entertainment.

*Note: Cricket is a non-scary Barbie Princess-type clown.

David's Party Train

253-460-3494

E-Mail: gtrainnut@yahoo.com

Price: $265 for Party Train, $250 Choo Choo Slide

David will bring his party train to your designated location where up to 16 children can safely ride in enclosed cars. Also available for rental is the ever popular Choo-Choo Jump-n-Slide, inflatables, face painting, and twisty animal balloons. Please note that a 25% deposit is required.

Deano The Clown

206-324-5055

www.deanotheclown.com

Deano arrives on a unicycle and begins by memorizing everybody's name. He knows over 600 games, tells stories (member of the Seattle Story Tellers Guild), performs juggling, magic, stilts, kits, face painting, dance, songs, fiddle playing, skits, mime, puppets, ventriloquism, and dare I say...more (He also speaks Swedish, German, French, Russian, and English). He is also experienced performing for children with special needs.

Genii Blue The Clown

425-557-6742

geniiblue.tripod.com

Price: $100 (10-12 kids), $120 (12-15 kids), $140 (15-20 kids).

Genii Blue's motto, "As long as the world doesn't run out of children, I'm happy!". She has been performing as a clown since 1989. Her performances include an age appropriate magic show, face painting, balloon sculpturing, and a character who teaches children about safety named Saf-Tee the Clown. At Christmas time, she becomes Zoe, a performing elf.

Dollie's World

253-474-2050

www.dolliesworld.com

Price: $245 for 1 ? hours.

"Invite a princess to your party!". Dollie comes dressed as a princess, and brings costumes for 10 children, does face painting, magic shows, balloons, juggling, and arts and crafts. She does themed parties including Fairy, Princess, Dragon, Knight, Circus, Create-a-Critter, Little Hero, Glamour Party with make-up and fashion show, Luau, and seasonal.

Li'l Buckaroos

425-844-8787

www.lil-buckaroos.com

Give Buckaroo Bob a call to reserve a few of his Shetland ponies, and miniature horses named Bambi, Simba, Princess, Annie, Aladdin, Rosey, Daisy, Rocky, and Dakota. Buckaroo Bob specializes in pony events for children ages 2-7 (65 lbs. maximum). For safety, children are seat belted to the saddle. Buckaroo Bob is available for birthday parties, picnics, reunions, and school events.

Little Pony Express Pony Rides

206-439-1865

www.seattleponyrides.com

Price: $125/hr for 1 pony, $175/hr for 2 ponies. You choose the location.

They bring 1 or more gentle ponies to your party or event. Ponies are led by experienced handlers who will make your children's experience both safe and fun. Their theme parties include cowboys and sheriffs, Toy Story, Zorro, unicorns, and so on. One pony per 10 children, but 2 ponies are recommended. Yep, clean-up is provided.

Magic For Mid-Sized Multitudes

425-806-8734

www.temagic.com

Price: $150 for a 30-35 minute magic show.

With over 20 years of experience together, Tim and Erien perform an interactive and age appropriate magic show filled with silly tricks and a surprise (real) birthday cake for the birthday child.

Merry Makers

253-572-0172

800-585-1500

www.merrymakers.net

Price: $125+, depending on size of group, hours, travel time, and activities.

Activities include Jumparoos, slides, interactives (Sumo Wrestling), face painting, magic shows, and clowns. Reservations should be made between 1-3 months in advance.

Scooter & Franny The Clowns

206-932-4166

Price: $150/hour, weekends only.

Husband and wife duo perform a comedy magic show, tailored to the age of children. Children participate in "baking" cookies-pink and white circus animal cookies that children get to munch on during the show. They also have an activity in which they blow up a balloon that pops open a box full of candy for the children. The show also includes making balloon animals.

The Dickens Carolers

206-320-7007

(206-861-1099)

www.dickenscarolers.com

Price: $185 1/2 hour minimum, 45 minutes $230, 1 hour $260

For 25 years, The Dicken's Carolers have brought professional traditional and contemporary holiday performances to adoring audiences. A four part harmony quartet, soprano, alto, tenor and bass, come dressed in elegant Victorian wear, complete with velvet dresses, and tailcoats and top hats. Whether your occasion is an intimate setting, or a large gathering, this is a musical treat enjoyed by all.

The Tumble Bus

206-364-5887

Price: $185 for 1 hour

The Tumble Bus comes right to your door or designated location, complete with equipment, padding, etc. located inside the bus. All you need to bring is socks and comfortable clothes. Safety is the top priority. Children will enjoy an hour filled with tumbling instruction and fun.

Reptile Man

360-668-8204

Price: $185/hour, or $125/hour (Son' show).

The Reptile Man brings 15 animals to your party destination, including an alligator your child can pet (and have his/her picture taken with), a choice of snakes including a yellow python, a tortoise, iguana, and lizards. You can also hire his son, who is in college for basically the same show.

Roving Reptile Ranch

425-483-2031

Price: $150+

Children and adults alike will be fascinated with an animated 45 minute presentation of up close and personal contact with 1 dozen different animals and creatures. Experience live interaction with a Madagascar scorpion, hissing cockroaches, a leopard gecko, a monkey tailed skink, an Australian dragon lizard, an iguana, a turtle, a toad, a 4 foot alligator, a 3 foot Savanna monitor, and a choice of 5 non-venomous snakes.

Party Facilities

Arena Sports

www.arenasports.net/

Arena Sports Seattle

4636 E Marginal Way S, Seattle

206-762-8606

Arena Sports Magnuson

7400 Sandpoint Way NE, Seattle

206-985-8990

Arena Sports Redmond

9040 Willows Rd, Redmond

425-885-4881

See ad in back

World Cup or NHL Package

Party Package from $125 - $205.

This package includes 40 minutes in the party room, and 50 minutes on the new arena Field Turf for soccer, football, kickball and ultimate Frisbee (or in-line hockey-Magnusen only)! A Li'l Kickers instructor is available to supervise the activities and host the party. The birthday child receives a T-shirt. Refreshments come in the form of 3 Large (14") Xtra Cheese pizzas with three pitchers of your favorite soft drink to wash it all down.

Party reservations must be paid in full. You may cancel up to 7 days prior to party date, otherwise you will receive a rental credit minus the $25 rescheduling fee.

All That Dance
8507 35th Ave NE, Seattle
206-524-8944
www.all-that-dance.com
Party Package: Varies according to your needs.
A private instructor is provided to lead the kids in dances and art activities.

Big League Connection
15015 NE 90th Street Bldg. 3, Redmond
425-885-2862 (Reservations for group/team event, lesson, party, or batting cages.)
www.bigleagueconnection.com
Party Package: $120 includes 6,800 of field, 1 batting cage, and party room for 1 hour.
"BLC" will work together with you to schedule the event catered to your needs.

Brunswick Majestic Lanes
1222 164th SW, Lynnwood
425-743-4422
www.brunswickbowl.com
Hours: Monday-Thursday 9:00am-12:00pm, Friday-Saturday 9:00am-2:30pm, Sunday 8:00am-12:00pm.
Party Package: $15.99 per person.
This includes balloons, paper products, hot dogs and chips or pizza, a surprise gift for the birthday child, and an extra game pass for all children.

Build-A-Bear Workshop
Alderwood Mall
Bellevue Square
Tacoma Mall
866-232-7386
www.buildabear.com
Price: $10+ per child. Each guest can choose from a wide variety of animals which they get to stuff themselves. Clothes and accessories are available for additional costs.

Cougar Mountain Zoo

19525 SE 54th St, Issaquah

425-391-5508

425-392-6278 (Reservations)

www.cougarmountainzoo.org

Hours: January-November 9:00am-5:00pm

Birthday Package: $96 for up to 10 children. $8 for each additional child.

Optional: $58 Decorated birthday house for 1 hour. $30 Mountain Lion Kiosk 1 hour. Includes Free admission, a guided 1 hour tour, free return visit coupon, feeding and touching of the unique wildlife animals, a special birthday picture on the zoo's birthday throne surrounded by Macaws, and plush zoo toy for the birthday child.

Imagine Children's Museum

3013 Colby Ave, Everett

425-258-1006

www.ImagineCM.org

Birthday Bash: *$95 non-members, $85 members. $5 for additional guests.*

This package accommodates up to 13 children, and includes party invitations, free admission including accompanying adults, 90 minutes use of their party room and birthday throne, and a museum t-shirt for the birthday children.

Caboodle Bash: *$130 non-members, $115 members. $6.50 for additional guests.*

This package accommodates up to 13 children, and includes party invitations, free admission including accompanying adults, 90 minutes use of their party room and birthday throne, cupcake and juice for each child, free next-visit admission coupon for each child, and a museum t-shirt for the birthday children.

Whole Kit'n Kaboodle: *$250 non-members, $220 members. $6.50 for additional guests.*

This package accommodates up to 25 children, and includes party invitations, free admission including accompanying adults, 90 minutes use of two party rooms and 2 birthday thrones, cupcake and juice for each child, free next-visit admission coupon for each child, and a museum t-shirt for the birthday children.

Creatively Yours

Crossroads Mall, Bellevue

425-747-2280

A party at Creatively Yours includes ceramic art pieces for 10-16 people ($12+ per person), a party room, and a host/hostess.

Chuck E. Cheese

Party Information Line
425-778-6566 Lynnwood
425-746-5000 Bellevue
253-813-9000 Kent
www.chuckecheese.com (Receive an extra $5 in tokens for booking party on line)

Basic Party Package:
$10.99/per child. A decorated table for 90 minutes, a host/hostess, the Chuck E Cheese and friends show, a personal visit by Chuck E Cheese, 2 slices of pizza per child, soft drink with free refills, a slice of cake per child, and 20 tokens per child are included.

Super Party Package:
$15.99/per child. The Basic Package plus an additional 12 tokens per child, party bags, 500 point ticket voucher for birthday child, and 100 point ticket voucher for paid party guests.

*At participating Chuck E. Cheese locations, book your party on Monday-Thursday and receive an additional $7 worth of tokens per child, and unlimited table use.

Dance Academy of Bellevue

775 112th NE, Bellevue
425-454-6008
www.danceacademyofbellevue.com
Times Available: Saturdays: 3pm, 5pm, or Sundays: 12, 2, 4 Parties last 90 minutes.
Birthday Bash: *$170 (Dance Academy Students), $190 (Non-Dance Academy Students)*
Price includes non-refundable deposit.
They provide juice, set up, clean-up, and a birthday T-Shirt for the birthday child. Parents provide cake, plates, napkins, forks, favor bags, and decorations (optional).

Family Fun Center
7300 Fun Center Way, Tukwila
425-228-6000
www.fun-center.com
Hours: 10:00am-10:00pm (June-August), 10:00am-9:00pm (September-May)
Rocky's Basic Package: *$7.95 per person.*
This includes the Kidopolis- a huge indoor, soft-ground play area, 3 Frog Hopper rides, and 10 tokens.
Bullwinkle's Backyard Package: *$12.95 per person.*
This includes 1 kids meal, 1 Kidstown wrist band good for 3 hours, and 10 tokens.
Bullwinkle Package: *$17.95 per person.*
This includes 1 round of miniature golf, laser tag, the rock wall, bumper boats, and a choice of Kidopolis or go karts.
Late Night Package (Friday/Saturday 6-9pm): *$22.95 per person.*
This includes unlimited go karts, bumper boats, miniature golf, laser tag, and one other main attraction.

Funtasia Family Fun Park
7212 220th St SW, Edmonds
www.familyfunpark.com
Hours: Monday-Thursday 11:00am-11:00pm, Friday 11:00am-Midnight, Saturday 10:00am-Midnight, Sunday 10:00am-11:00pm.
Party Package #1: *$9.95/person (For children under 42")*
Includes the Fun Fortress Playland pass, a decorated party table for 1 hour, plates and napkins, birthday balloons, one slice of pizza per person, 24 oz. of soda, and ice cream.
Party Package #2: *$15.95/person (For children under 56")*
Includes 18 hole miniature golf, a Fun Fortress Playland pass, 4 attraction tokens, a decorated party table for 1 hour, plates and napkins, birthday balloons, one slice of pizza per person, 24 oz. of soda, and ice cream.
Party Package #3: *$15.95/person*
Includes 18 hole miniature golf, 5 attraction tokens, a decorated party table for 1 hour, plates and napkins, birthday balloons, one slice of pizza per person, 24 oz. of soda, and ice cream.
Party Package #4: *$21.95/person*
Includes 18 hole miniature golf, 7 attraction tokens, 2 batting cages tokens, a decorated party table for 1 hour, plates and napkins, birthday balloons, one slice of pizza per person, 24 oz. of soda, and ice cream.

Glacier Bowling Lanes

9630 Evergreen Way, Everett
425-353-8292
www.glacierlanes.com
Hours: Monday-Friday 7:00am-11:30pm, Saturday & Sunday 6:00am-Midnight
***Package A:** $9/person.*
This includes 2 hours of bowling, ball and shoes, unlimited soft drinks, balloons, cups, plates, and napkins, hot dogs, a group picture, a free game coupon, and a gift for the birthday child.
***Package B:** $8/person.*
This includes 2 hours of bowling, ball and shoes, unlimited soft drinks, balloons, cups, plates, and napkins, a group picture, a free game coupon, and a gift for the birthday child.

Gymboree Play & Music

www.gymboree.com

Lynnwood
3205 Alderwood Mall Blvd Suite G
425-775-4782

Seattle
7400 Sandpoint Way NE Suite 105
206-522-2045

Redmond Town Center
7321-164th Ave NE #1133
425-702-8811

Issaquah
735 NW Gilman Blvd Suite E
425-392-8438

An enthusiastic teacher lead the party with songs, colorful parachutes, tunnels, and bridges. They also decorate for the party and clean up afterwards. This is a perfect activity for children ages 1 to 5 years old.

Kent Valley Ice Centre

6015 240th St, Kent
253-850-2400
www.familynightout.com
Hours: 8:00am - 11:00pm
Bronze Regular: *$107 for 8 people. Additional guests $12.50.*
Includes admission, skate rental, table decorations and paper products, pop, ice cream cup. Private party room: $45. 30 minute lesson: $52
Bronze Deluxe: *$134 for 8 people. Additional guests $15.50*
Includes the Bronze Regular package plus Godfather's Pizza (2 med's) or hot dogs and fries.
Silver Deluxe: *$164 for 8 people. Additional guests $17.*
Includes the Bronze Deluxe package plus 30 minute skate lesson or private party room.
Gold Deluxe: *$194 for 8 people. Additional guests $18.*
Includes Silver Deluxe package with both the 30 minute skate lesson and the private party room.

Lake Forrest Park Swimming Pool

14540 NE Bothell Way, Lake Forrest Park
206-364-7946
Party Package: *$70 for 14 swimmers.*
Spend 1 1/2 ours at their indoor swimming pool with an on duty life guard, games & activities.

Laser Quest

2210 S. 320th, Federal Way
253-946-4500
www.laserquest.com
Birthday Package: *$12/person for children ages 6 and older.*
This package includes 2 games of laser tag in their multi-level maze, and free use of the party room.

Odyssey Maritime Discovery Center

2201 Alaskan Way Pier 66, Seattle
206-374-4000 x 108
www.ody.org
Hours: Tuesday-Saturday 10:00am to 5:00pm, Sunday 12:00pm-5:00pm
This is a hands-on maritime museum, complete with virtual computer films simulating boat, kayak, and other maritime rides.

***Tugboat:** $150/$175.*
This includes two-hour room rental with decorations and paper products, and a choice of theme related invitations. Choose the theme of Pirates, Mermaids, or a Sea theme.
***Ferry Boat:** $200/$225.*
This includes the Tugboat party package plus cake, juice, an activity, a party facilitator, and treat bags.
***Cruise Ship:** $295/$300.*
This includes the Tugboat party package plus cake, juice, two activities, a party facilitator, deluxe treat bags, and a gift for the birthday child.

*Note: All prices are for 15 children and 10 adults. Extra children are $5 each. You can add on pizza for $3 per person to any package.

Pacific Science Center
Seattle Center
206-443-3625
www.pacsci.org
***Package 1:** $155-15 people (non-members), $135-20 people (members)*
Includes the Party Room for 2 hours (you decorate), welcome sign, exhibit passes, party invitations, and a map.
***Package 2:** $285-15 people (non-members), $265-20 people (members)*
Includes all the above plus 40 minute Super Science Show (based on party theme), 20 minute liquid nitrogen ice kingdom demonstration, birthday cake (choose flavor), plates, napkins, forks, party bags, and party decorations for the following themes: Dinosaurs, Astronomy, Butterflies, or Candy.

•Note: Party packages available on Saturdays and Sundays at 10:00am, 12:30pm, 3:00pm.

Pump It Up
11605 NE 116th St, Kirkland
425-820-2297
www.pumpitupparty.com
Experience one of a kind indoor inflatables, including bouncers, 20' slides, climbing walls, a basketball bounce house, and a rock 'em sock 'em colliseum. Be sure to bring your socks!

***Classic Party:** $195, Monday-Thursday, $230 Friday-Sunday. 25 Friends.*
This includes 1 1/2 hours of play time, and 1/2 in the party room, plus party invitations.
***Mini-Classic Party:** $150, Monday-Friday before 3pm. 15 Friends.*
This includes 1 hour of play time, and 1/2 in the party room, plus party invitations.

Extras: *$2.95 per person for pizza and soda, $2.50 per person for goodie bags,* $10 for 12 helium balloons, and $20 for 26 helium balloons.

Remlinger Farms
32610 NE 32nd St, Carnation
425-333-4135
www.remlingerfarms.com
Prices: May - September: $299 for up to 15 guests, $13.75 per additional guest.
October Weekends: $349 for up to 15 guests, $16.75 per additional guest.
October Mondays and Fridays: $299 for up to 15 guests, $13.75 per additional guest.
Birthday Party Packages:
This includes admission for each guest to the Coutry Fair Family Fun Park, decorated Party Corral inside of the Fun Park, your own party hostess to set up, serve, and clean up, pizza and salad for each guest (adult and child), cake and ice cream, beverages, party favors, hats, and ballons.

Samena Swim and Recreation Club
15231 Lake Hills Blvd, Bellevue
425-746-1160
www.samena.com
Dolphin Package: *$175 ($105)*
This includes one hour in the pool, one hour in party room, and a party coordinator who leads games and activities in the pool.
Orca Package: *$220 ($170)*
This includes 15 invitations, cake and candles, punch, golf fish crackers, a balloon bouquet, 15 party bags, orca table setting, and clean up, one hour in the pool, one hour in party room, and a party coordinator who leads games and activities in the pool.

Skate Deck
9700 19th Ave SE, Everett
425-337-0202
425-338-5252 (Party Reservations)
www.everettskatedeck.com
Party Package: *Ranges in price from $48 to $68 (up to 6 people)*
Includes admission & quad skate rental, a reserved table for 45 minutes, ice cream & pop, place settings, and a stuff shop buck for birthday person. All you bring is the cake, and candles.

Extra: Inflatable fun for only $2.50 each, an extra large pizza $15.00, or Hot Dogs for $1.50 each.

Southbridge Seattle Symphony Music Discovery Center
Benaroya Hall
200 University, Seattle: entrance on 2nd & Union
206-336-6600
www.soundbridge.org
Soundbridge is a wonderful place for children to learn, explore, and indulge in music splendor. With daily musical storytelling, instrument exploration, classes, student recitals, lectures, workshops, and the following exhibits: "Meet the Musicians, Conductors and Composers" past and present, Listening Posts, musical skills computer games, Virtual Conducting, and "Science of Sound–Music as a Science".

Birthday Celebration: *$150 (includes annual family membership)*
Spend up to 3 hours at the Music Discovery Center. They will provide 45 minutes of musical storytelling, singing, dancing, and instrument entertainment, tailored to the family/theme. They will provide the table, and a designated area for the part, and assist in set-up & clean-up. Once the "directed entertainment" is finished, children are free to explore the Music Discovery Center.

The Creation Station
19511 64th Ave W, Lynnwood
425-775-7959
www.creationstationinc.com
Hours: Monday-Saturday 10:00am-6:00pm, Sunday 10:00pm-5:00pm (Sept-June).
Price: $4.95 per creator.
Children can choose from over 115 objects to build their one of a kind creations. With materials such as recyclable plastic, foam, wood, fabric, tubes, donated by local businesses and manufacturers, children have the freedom and opportunity to become inventors, artists, and crafters. This is such a unique studio, with something for everyone.

Movie Theaters

Galaxy 12
1 Galaxy Way, Monroe
360-863-8665
Party Package: *13.50/person(Minimum of 6)*
Includes reserved movie seating, a party room, host/hostess, kids meal (popcorn, Icee, & candy), and a behind the scenes projection tour.

Loews Alderwood Mall 16
18733 33rd Ave W, Lynnwood
425-921-2980
Party Package: *$10/person (Minimum of 8)*
Includes a personal pizza, curly fries, ice cream, popcorn, & a movie.

Stanwood Camano Village Cinema 5
6996 265th St NW, Stanwood
360-629-0514
360-629-8305 (Birthday Reservations)
Party Package: *$7/person (minimum of 20)*
Includes a movie, 12 oz drink, and a small popcorn.

Parks

Camp Long
5200 35th Ave SW, Seattle
206-684-7434
www.camplong.org
The Pond Party: *$150 for 15 kids*
Children go out to the Polliwog Pond with nets, water containers, and field microscopes to catch frogs, salamanders, and water insects.
The Nature Scavenger Hunt: *$150 for 15 kids*
Children search in the forest and fields for varieties of natures leaves, make a collage.
Camp Long Rock Climbing: *$200 for 8 kids, $250 for 15 kids (age 8+)*
Take turns repelling down Camp Long's rock glacier. Climbing equipment and instruction is provided, along with some refreshments. Signed waivers from parents are mandatory.

Carkeek Park
950 NW Carkeek Park Rd, Seattle
206-684-0877
www.cityofseattle.net/parks
Hours: 6:00am-10:00pm
Monday-Friday 10:00am-4:00pm (Environmental Learning Center)
Birthday Party Package: *$90 (10 children), $100 (15 children), $120 (20 children).*
This activity is designed for children who love birds, fish, and bugs. The Environmental Education Center will provide a naturalist, theme activities, and decorations. You provide refreshments, utensils, paper products. Be sure to make arrangements three weeks in advance.

Discovery Park

3801 W Government Way, Seattle
206-386-4236
206-386-4273 (Party Reservations)
www.cityofseattle.net/parks
Hours: 4:30am-11:00pm
Party Packages: *Saturdays and Sundays at 9:30am-11:30am or 4:00pm-6:30pm.*
A Batty Birthday: *$250, ages 5+*
Birthday Birds: *$200, ages 4+*
Party Plants: *$250, ages 6+*
Super Silly Slugs: *$200, ages 4+*

Nature-themed parties include a staff lead hike, campfire, crafts, and stories. You provide the refreshments

Party Rental

A Party Jumps Co Too LLC

866-444-JUMP
www.apartyjumpco.com
Rain Proof Party Jumps.

Air Play Party Rentals

800-422-0838
www.airplaypartyrental.com
Kids Bouncers, Quad Bungee Jump, Climbing Wall, Dunk Tanks, Rat Race Obstacle Course, Sabertooth Tiger Slide, Sumo Wrestling, Tents, Tables, & Chairs

Astro Jump

800-823-5867
www.astrojump.com
New 2005 Units: Indoor/Outdoor
Giant Slide, Obstacle Course, Boxing, Huge Jump Selection, Jump, Climb, Slide Combo, Backyard Slides, Kettle Corn & Ice Cream, Indoor Units, BBQ Picnic

Bouncy House Inflatables Inc

877-BOUNCE-1
www.bouncyhouse.com
25 different Inflatables for sale or rental. Free Delivery to most areas, rain or shine.

Party Stores:

Birthday Express
11220 120th Ave NE, Kirkland
425-250-1060
800-424-7843
www.BirthdayExpress.com
Over 100 unique and popular kid's themed birthday party packages, plus piñatas, cake supplies, and party prizes.

Display & Costume
5209 Evergreen Way, Everett
425-353-3364
Hours: Monday-Friday 9:00am-8:00pm, Saturday 9:00am-6:00pm, Sunday 11:00am-5:00pm

Display & Costume
11201 Roosevelt Way NE, Seattle
206-362-4810
www.displaycostume.com
Hours: Monday-Friday 8:30-8:30, Saturday 9:30am-6:00pm, Sunday 11:00am-5:00pm

Dollar & Party Store
22803 44th Ave W, Mountlake Terrace
425-744-1436
Hours: Monday-Friday 9:00am-7:00pm, Saturday 10:00am-7:00pm, Sunday 10:00am-5:00pm.

Party City

Everett
1523 132nd St SE
425-357-9501
Hours: Monday-Friday 9:30am-9:00pm, Saturday 8:30am-9:00pm, Sunday 10:30am-6:00pm.

Everett
8630 Evergreen Way
425-348-9031
Hours: Monday-Friday 9:30am-9:00pm, Saturday 8:30am-9:00pm, Sunday 10:30am-6:00pm.

Lynnwood
18415 33rd Ave W
425-673-2662
Hours: Monday-Friday 9:30am-9:00pm, Saturday 8:30am-9:00pm, Sunday 10:30am-6:00pm.

Marysville
1254 State Ave
360-657-4991
Hours: Monday-Friday 9:30am-9:00pm, Saturday 8:30am-9:00pm, Sunday 10:30am-6:00pm.

Woodinville
18027 Garden Way NE
425-485-9303
Hours: Monday-Friday 9:30am-9:00pm, Saturday 8:30am-9:00pm, Sunday 10:30am-6:00pm.

The Party Store
19720 44th W, Lynnwood
425-776-9111
Hours: Monday-Friday 9:00am-9:00pm, Saturday 9:00am-7:00pm, Sunday 10:00am-6:00pm.

Chapter 12

Seasonal Events

Chapter 12

Seasonal Events

One can't help but think of family traditions when making plans during the four seasons of the year. Between annual family picnics and reunions in the summer, football in the fall, holiday traditions during the winter, or spring break vacations, building positive family memories is a value we all share.

In a world where everything is continually changing, traditions serve as a source of strength and stability. Each in their own way, families bring together their religious and ethnic traditions that bind and sustain family members both in good times and difficult circumstances.

Family traditions have multiple benefits. They provide comfort and security within families, anticipation for upcoming events, and opportunities for distant relatives to meet annually for joyous reunions. Traditions impart a sense of identity, help navigate change, teach values, pass on ethnic and religious heritage, teach practical skills, problem solving, and generate wonderful memories. Whether you attend a festival or event every year as a family, or you have a special tradition in your home, the benefits are unmistakable and the memories are sure to last a lifetime!

Recommended Books on Building Family Traditions

Little Things Long Remembered-Making Your Children Feel Special Every Day
-By Susan Newman

The Book of New Family Traditions-How to Create Rituals for Holidays and Everyday
-By Meg Cox

New Traditions-Redefining Celebrations for Today's Family
-By Susan Abel Lieberman

Mrs. Sharp's Traditions-Reviving Victorian Family Celebrations of Comfort and Joy
-By Sarah Ban Breathnachs

Winter: December-February

Holiday Festivities

King County

Auburn

Santa Parade & Festival: "Glitter & Glee for Santa & Me!"
707 Auburn Way N
253-939-3389
www.auburngoodoldays.com
Date: December 3, 2005
Festive events fill the evening as families celebrate the beginning of the Christmas season. The Santa Parade begins at 4:30pm, followed with the tree lighting at City Hall Plaza, and the Community sing-a-long.
This is a memorable event for all ages.

Bellevue

Bellevue Botanical Garden's "Garden d' Lights" Display
12001 Main St
425-451-3755
www.bellevuebotanical.org
Date: 1st Saturday after Thanksgiving through the 1st of January.
Price: Free. Donations are accepted
This is a spectacular presentation of Rhododendrons, Fuchsia, grapes along grapevines, lilies and much more, made entirely of colored lights. Enjoy live entertainment Monday-Thursday for the first couple of weeks. This is also a good time to donate to the garden, as Goldiwarts the Frog greets your children, while holding a donation box.

Santa's Toyland Parade

Bellevue Square

425-454-8096

www.bellevuesquare.com

It's time for Santa's Arrival at Bellevue Square. Begin the magical holiday season at Bellevue Square, including the annual parade held along Bellevue Way. Always held the day after Thanksgiving, children can see the official arrival of Santa Claus, be dazzled with lights, food, holiday décor, and live entertainment

Bothell

City of Bothell Winterfest

Park at Bothell Landing

9919 NE 180th St

www.ci.bothell.wa.us

Date: December 2nd

Hours: 6:30pm – 7:30pm

Price: Free

Come join the fun with caroling, the annual lighting of the holiday tree, the arrival of Santa, and free hayrides through the park.

Enumclaw

Enumclaw Christmas Parade

Cole Street, 6:00 pm

360-825-7666

Date: 1st Saturday in December

Issaquah

Issaquah's Reindeer Festival at Cougar Mountain Zoo

19525 SE 54th St, Issaquah

425-391-5508

www.cougarmountainzoo.org

Date: December 1st-23rd

Hours: Daily from 10:00am-7:00pm.

Prices: Seniors 62+: $8, Adults 13-61: $9.50, Children 2-12: $6.50, and 2 & under: Free

Sit on Santa's lap daily from 10:30am-1:00pm, and 4:30-7:00pm.

Find Rudolph and friends at the annual Issaquah's Reindeer Festival. Visit Santa in his house, and enjoy an atmosphere of music, lights, and holiday cheer. Children can write a letter to Santa and put it in his special mail box, listen to an Elf read their favorite story, and participate in art projects. Personal cameras are allowed.

Maple Valley

Christmas Creche Exhibit

The Church of Jesus Christ of Latter-day Saints
26800 236th Place SE
425-413-7566
Date: Held the 1st Friday & Saturday in December
Time: 6:00pm-9:00pm
More than 200 nativity scenes from around the world displayed in a festive holiday setting, live musical performances, live nativity and children's activities. Free.

Holiday Lights at the Lodge

Lake Wilderness Park and Beach
Date: December 2nd 2005
Gather around the lodge as the Mayor officially lights up the holidays, and enjoy children's musical performances.

Mercer Island

Community Hanukkah Celebration

Stroum Jewish Community Center
3801 Mercer Way
206-232-7115
Date: 1st Sunday in December
The annual Festival of Lights honors the celebration of Hanukkah. As one of the largest Hannukkah celebrations in Seattle, families are sure to be filled with holiday cheer and children delighted throughout the afternoon festivities. Traditionally held the first Sunday in December, the celebration includes festive music, scrumptious food, decoration splendor, and a variety of arts and crafts.

Snoqualmie

Santa Train at Snoqualmie Valley Railroad

38625 SE King St
www.trainmuseum.org/SantaTrain.asp
Date: First 3 weekends following Thanksgiving (including Thanksgiving weekend).
Hours: 9:00am-3:00pm.
Ticket Sales: 10:15am-5:00pm (Beginning in October).
Online Ticket Sales start in September.
Price: $12 for guests 2 and older, or $11 for advanced ticket sales.

Since 1969, The Santa Train has had the pleasure of taking children up the 20 minute ride from North Bend to Snoqualmie to visit with Santa in the historic Snoqualmie Depot. Santa passes out a small gift for each child, and families enjoy hot cocoa and baked goodies in a restored railway kitchen car. While in the Upper Snoqualmie Valley, this is a good time to visit the local holiday tree farms.

Seattle

Downtown Seattle Holiday Festivities

Thousands of locals make the annual trek to downtown Seattle for holiday shopping, events, and programs. Department stores are filled with holiday grandeur,

Holiday Carousel

The Holiday Carousel, located in Westlake Park, brings smiles and cheers to thousands of children each year. For a small donation, children can go on this classic whimsical ride while parents can take a much needed rest.

Holiday Trolley

Climb aboard the nostalgic Holiday Trolley during your downtown visit. You can catch the street car at Pioneer Square, Pike Place Market, and along 1st Avenue. Children are sure to be enchanted with Santa's elves on board for the ride. The Trolley is free and sure to be a treat.

Kwanzaa Festival

206-587-4935
Date: December
Kwanzaa is the annual African American celebration of the Harvest, with the focus on: **Imani** (Faith), **Kujicahagulia** (Self-Determination), **Kuumba** (Creativity), **Nia** (Purpose), **Ujamaa** (Cooperative Economics), **Ujima** (Collective Work and Responsibility), and **Umoja** (Unity). The festival features live entertainment, African musical instruments demonstrations, crafts, cultural exhibits, educational seminars, and more.

Tree Lighting Celebration & Holiday Parade

Downtwon Seattle
A great beginning to the holiday season is downtown Seattle's annual holiday parade and festivities. Starting at 8:45am on 7th Ave, and ending at Macy's (Bon-Macy's), this parade is filled with continuous entertainment and is one of the largest parades of the year. The culminating event is when Santa makes his traditional entrance, announcing the Christmas season has arrived. At 5:00pm, Westlake Center hosts the annual tree lighting ceremony, concluding with colorful explosive fireworks.

Woodinville

Woodinville Light Festival

Woodinville Community Center, Woodinville City Hall, and Brittany Park Retirement Community
Date: 1st weekend in December
The Woodinville Light Festival is an annual community tradition. Santa Clause is coming to town on Friday, just in time for the Tree Lighting at 7:00pm at City Hall. Free rides are available aboard the Elf Express Lighted Train to each event site. Activities at the Woodinville Community Center and Brittany Park Retirement Community include Santa's Workshop, Santa Photos, Model Train Displays, Holiday Light Displays and Crystal Courtyard and Arts & Crafts.

Yarrow Point

Winter Holiday Caroling

Enjoy the annual Winter Holiday Caroling held during the week preceding Christmas. Meet at Town Hall for refreshments and singing. A horse-drawn sled and bonfire add to the festivities.

Snohomish County

Arlington

Hometown Christmas

360-435-3708

www.arlington-chamber.com

Hometown Christmas begins on the 1st Saturday in December with the arrival of Santa during the Christmas Parade. Following the parade, a Christmas Tree Lighting ceremony is held in Legion Park. Throughout the month of December on weekends, shoppers can climb aboard for a wagon ride down Olympic Ave.

Brier

Brier Park Tree Lighting

Brier Park
2903 228th St SW
www.ci.brier.wa.us/
Date: 1st Saturday in December
Hours: 6:30 p.m. Santa Arrives, tree lighting to follow
Price: Free
Community celebration with arrival of Santa, opportunity for holiday photos with Santa, caroling and musical entertainment, hot chocolate for all and beautiful tree lighting ceremony.

Granite Falls

Christmas Tree Lighting

Jim Holm Park
S Granite Ave
www.granitefallswa.com
Date: First Saturday after Thanksgiving
Get into the holiday spirit at an old fashioned Christmas celebration. Tree lighting will be followed by festivities, games, and refreshments at the Community Center.

Lynnwood

Lynnwood Civic Lights

Lynnwood Recreation Center 19100 44th Ave W
425-771-4030
www.ci.lynnwood.wa.us
Date:
Hours: 6:00pm – 9:00pm
Price: Free but food donation accepted at the door
Park at the Lynnwood Fire Station and come inside for free photos with Santa Claus. Next, visit the Lynnwood Recreation Center for a fun family movie, or continue along the path to the Lynnwood Library where children can jump and slide in a pile of real snow, delivered fresh from the mountains. At the library you will find arts and crafts created just for kids. Live entertainment completes the experience as local schools perform and bring holiday cheer.

Crèche Festival

The Church of Jesus Christ of Latter-day Saints
4001 44th Ave SW
www.christmascreche.com
Date: December 9th & 10th from 5:00pm-9:00pm & 2:00pm-9:00pm
Price: Free
This annual event is filled with hundreds of unique nativities made in countries around the world, including Africa, South America, Europe, Asia, Russia, and the Pacific Islands. Locals add their own creations and collections, including a live nativity. Community musicians perform throughout the event, including school bands, orchestras and choirs. Children can make holiday treasures in the craft room.

Marysville

Merrysville for the Holidays Winter Celebration & Electric Light Parade

Downtown Comeford Park
514 Delta Avenue
360-363-8400
www.ci.marysville.wa.us
Date: December 3rd
Price: Free
Join in the Merrysville holiday cheer during the annual twilight Electric Light Parade, followed with the luminous water tower lighting, and a special visit from Mr. and Mrs. Santa Claus. Filled with live musical concerts, lots of food and holiday treats, this is event is a delightful event for all.

Christmas Tree Farms

Carnation Tree Farm

31523 NE 40th St, Carnation
425-333-4510
www.carnationtreefarm.com
The historic Carnation Tree Farm has been a family tradition for this Norwegian family for over 100 years. Choose a selection of Douglas Fir, Fraser Fir, Grand Fir, Noble Fir and Norway Spruce. Gather in the old barn's gift shop filled with hundreds of ornaments, hand-crafted gifts, wreaths, Cedar garland, mistletoe, holly, and tree stands. Enjoy complimentary hot cider. Be sure to schedule your trip to the tree farm on a Saturday or Sunday when they can visit with Santa and take a Christmas pony ride.

Cedar Falls Farms
15200 Cedar Falls Rd SE
North Bend
888-3216

Crown Tree Farm
13005 424th SE, North Bend
425-888-1506
www.crowntreefarm.pscta.org
Choose from Douglas, Grand, Noble, Shasta, and Turkish fir trees 5-18' tall. Wreaths, swags, holly, boughs for sale. Sip hot cider around a warming fire.

Christmas Creek Tree Farm
15515 468th Ave SE, North Bend
425-488-2099
www.yourchristmastree.com
Take the scenic drive up to North Bend on a weekend in search of your family's Christmas tree. Choices include Grand Firs, Noble-Shasta, Nordman, and Douglas Firs from table top size to 8'9'. On Saturdays and Sundays, visit with Santa is his sleigh, go for a hay ride, and enjoy complimentary hot cider as you warm up around the bon fire. For those who like to shop, visit the quaint Christmas shop at the farm.

Holiday Mountain Trees
Hwy 18 & SE 104th St
3 Miles East of Preston
Snoqualmie
253-838-7979

Keith & Scott Tree Farm on Middle Fork Ranch
43342 SE Mt. Si Rd, North Bend
425-888-1170
Upper Snoqualmie Valley's oldest family tree farm.

McMurtrey's Red-Wood Farm
13925 Redmond-Woodinville Rd NE, Redmond
425-482-6798
www.red-woodfarm.com
A local U-cut tree farm filled with Noble Fir and Fraser Fir trees. Also available for purchase are wreaths, swags, mistletoe and holly. Take the family on a wagon ride and enjoy complimentary hot cocoa and freshly pressed apple cider, and candy canes for the kids.

Mountain Creek Tree Farm
6821 440th Ave SE, Snoqualmie
425-888-1770
Located in a beautiful, peaceful setting near a creek, bring your family to this farm and choose from a plethora of large Douglas, Fraser, Grand, Noble, and Turkish Fir trees. Visit the farm's gift shop filled with handmade craft items.

Papa's Tree Farm
26429 SE 200th
Exit off Hwy 18
Hobart
Choose from a variety of home grown evergreens Fir trees.

Pilchuck Secret Valley Christmas Tree Farm
9533 Mose Rd, Arlington
360-435-9799
Choose your family tree from a large selection of Christmas trees. Afterwards, cozy up to a warm fire and enjoy hot drinks, or shop at the Christmas store.

Redmond Tree Farm
14001 Redmond-Woodinville Rd
425-487-3447
For those who wish to stay close to home, visit this local tree farm. Once you've picked your family's tree, you can go on a hay ride, enjoy free candy canes, and hot drinks.

Trinity Tree Farm
14237 228th Ave SE, Issaquah
425-391-8733
www.trinitytreefarm.com
Douglas Firs, Fraser Firs, Grand Firs, and Noble Firs are available at this U-cut tree farm.
This is a perfect place to take a family Christmas photo. Sit around the bonfire and sip on complimentary hot chocolate, coffee, or cider. Visit the log cabin gift shop.

New Years Celebrations

New Years Eve @ The Space Needle

One of the biggest and most popular events with the induction of the New Year, is held at The Seattle Space Needle. View the dramatic Pyrotechnic effects and fireworks display, also visible from surrounding neighborhoods. Crowds are plentiful, so it's a good idea to reserve a hotel early to view the celebration in a less crowded environment, especially for those with small children, or simply to avoid traffic.

Lunar New Year Celebration/Chinese New Year

Chinatown/International District
401 S Jackson, Seattle Union Station Great Hall
206-382-1197
www.cidbia.org/events.asp
Date: 2006 - February 4th
Hours: 12:00pm-6:00pm
Price: Free Admission

In the midst of the chill of winter, the lunar New Year represents a forerunner of spring. In the first day of the two-week New Year celebration, you'll find sprays of quince branches whose early rosy blossoms represent the first "blush" of renewal.

There is almost no time of year more festive in Chinese communities. 15-20 thousand local visitors celebrate Chinese/Lunar New Year at the International District with cultural dances, the sound of firecrackers and lucky red envelopes containing money given to children at family gatherings. Children will be dazzled with the dragon and lion dancing in the street, and everyone will enjoy the plentiful arts and crafts booths, and food court ($3 fee). Women pick through fruit stands for bright-colored tangerines and order crisp-roasted pigs for family feasts. Shops sell sweet candies and sugar-preserved fruits, to be given as gifts or served at parties.

Tet Festival

Seattle Center
206-706-2658
www.tetinseattle.org

This festival celebrates the Vietnamese Lunar New Year. Enjoy the rich heritage and culture of the Vietnamese, including traditional musical performances. This festival is run 100% by volunteers, so please give them a call to help preserve this annual tradition.

Winter Events

Snohomish

Saturday Night Movies at Harvey Airfield
9900 Airport Way, Snohomish (Hanger 15)
360-568-6034
www.harveyfield.com
Date: Second Saturday of each month November – March
Hours: 7:00pm
Prices: Free
Bring the family for a night of aviation. Aviation movies, appropriate for all ages, are shown in the heated Hanger 15, featuring a large video screen and surround sound. Enjoy free popcorn and soda during the movie.

Spring: March-May

Apple Blossom Festival
Wenatchee
509-662-3616
Date: April: 1 1/2 week celebration
The Apple Capital of the World invites you to join them for the huge celebration marking the beginning of the apple growing season. Activities include a carnival, clowns, and live entertainment.

Basking Robbin's Free Scoop Night
www.baskinrobbins.com
Date: April
Participating Baskin Robbins give a free scoop to patrons on this special night to benefit children's literacy.

Earth Day Celebration

Point Defiance Zoo & Aquarium
Tacoma
253-404-3636
www.pdza.org
Date: Earth Day (usually held in April)
Hours: 9:00am-5:00pm
With the beautiful Puget Sound in the background, Point Defiance Zoo & Aquarium has one of the top zoo's in the country, with 29 acres to see and enjoy. There are many attractions for families to see such as: beluga whales, polar bear cubs, sharks, pachyderms, and many tropical fish. Special events honoring the earth and it's preservation throughout the day.

King County

Arlington

Pioneer Days

Stillaguamish Valley Pioneer Park and Museum
20722 67th Ave NE
360-435-7289
www.stillymuseum.org
Date: May 21st
Hours: 1:00 p.m. – 4:00 p.m.
Prices: Free (if you visit museum admission prices will apply)
Come find out how the pioneers lived and worked back in the good 'ol days. See hands on demonstrations and activities, fun for the whole family.

Bothell

Community Egg Hunt

Westhill Sportsfields 1
9417 88th Ave NE
425-486-7430 x 4422
www.ci.bothell.wa.us
Date: Saturday before Easter Sunday
Hours: 10:30 a.m.
Price: Free
A traditional Easter Egg Hunt for children through 6th grade. Please bring a can of food to donate to Bothell's Hopelink Food Bank.

Arbor Day Celebration
Brickyard Road Park
16800 Brickyard Road NE
425-486-7430
www.ci.bothell.wa.us
Date: Arbor Day
Hours: Varies so please call
Price: Free
The City of Bothell Park invites you to celebrate Arbor Day by volunteering to help with landscaping projects. Bring your gloves and hand tools, and all other landscape materials are provided, concluding with refreshments.

May Day Mini Fair
Center Courtyard at Country Village
720 238th Street SE
425-368-2294
www.countryvillagebothell.com
Date: Last Saturday in April
Hours: 10:00am – 6:00pm
Price: Free
Celebrate the May Day weekend with a May Day Mini Fair at the Country Village Shops in Bothell. There will be crafters and artists, live music, and activities for children.

2006 Earth Day Events including Arbor Day
Woodmoor Elementary School
Date: Saturday, mid April
The City's Arbor Day Celebration has several ways families can make this day special. Volunteer to help in a restoration project, or head over to the Spring Garden Fair at to purchase a rain barrel, and talk with City Tree Board members about tree preservation and care.

Seattle

Cherry Blossom & Japanese Cultural Festival
Seattle Center
206-723-2003
Date: April
A 3 day celebration of the Japanese culture held at the Center House in the Seattle Center. This is a community event for all cultures to enjoy, and began almost 30 years ago when the late Prime Minister of Japan, who had spent time in Seattle as a student, gave the gift of one thousand cherry trees to celebrate the U.S. Bicentennial in 1976.

During the festival you will have the privilege of being entertained by professional Japanese puppeteers and their exquisite puppets, elegant Japanese dancers and more

Rain Dance
Seattle's Waterfront
Date: Spring
The Waterfront's annual featuring a taste of the neighborhood. Guests are treated to the finest in Waterfront dining, live entertainment, and fabulous prizes. Rain Dance has grown to one of the largest free fine dining and entertainment events in Seattle. A variety of sponsorship opportunities are available including event sponsorship, food and beverage sponsorships, and product giveaways.

Seattle International Children's Festival
Seattle
206-684-7346
www.seattleinternational.org
Date: Mid-May
Cost: Visit on Family Day, and 2 children are free with each paying adult.
Ages 3 and up
Bring the family and enjoy unique and creative performances from cultures and performers around the world. Performers vary from year to year. Recent countries represented include Germany, Spain, Mexico, Turkey, Asia, Native America, Vietnam, Republic of Congo, Kora, Pan-Asia, Africa and France, and the USA. Activities during the festival include Hula Hoops, making and flying your own kite over the fountains, clay stations, creating your own hat and marching in a parade, putting together traditional instruments, fishing for gifts, an inflatable planetarium, and art projects.

Seattle Cheese Festival
Pike Place Market
www.seattlecheesefestival.com
Date: May
Cheese enthusiasts can spend the weekend walking along Pike Place Market and sample dozens of cheese, including the freshest goat cheese straight from Bainbridge to award winning blue from Ireland. Cheese experts are on hand to answer questions. While parents stroll, children can go on a scavenger hunt with a delicious treat awaiting them.

Woodinville

All Fools Day Parade

Downtown Woodinville
Park and Ride on 175th to 132nd Ave NE
Date: Held the last Saturday in March (or April 1st if on a Saturday).
Time: 11:00am
This is a silly, delightful parade filled with children, clowns, music, animals, drill teams, floats and fun. Awards are given out to "The Most Foolish" parade participants.

Snohomish County

Brier

Easter Egg Hunt

Brier Park
2903 228th St SW
www.ci.brier.wa.us
Date: Saturday before Easter
Time: 10:00am
Price: Free
Children up to 10 years of age can participate in a traditional Easter Egg Hunt. You might want to bring your camera for when the Easter Bunny makes a special visit.

Edmonds

Annual Model Railroad Show

Francis Anderson Center
700 Main St
425-483-3322
www.edmondswas.com
Date: March 6th
Hours: 11:00am – 4:00pm
Price: Free Admission
For the little ones who adore trains, this is a wonderful annual family event featuring hundreds of model railroad displays. Witness the incredible talent and hard work of the members of the Western Model Railroad Association.

Edmonds Easter Egg Hunt

Edmonds City Park
Third Ave and Howell
425-771-0230
www.edmondswa.com
Date: The Saturday before Easter
Hours: 10:00am
Price: Free
The annual traditional Easter egg hunt for the whole family to enjoy. Groups are divided by age group, and the event concludes with a visit from the Easter bunny.

Edmonds Scandinavian Festival Day

Masonic Center – Edmonds Lodge Sons of Norway
515 Dayton St
425-712-9788
www.edmondswa.com
Date: May 7th (Changes annually so call for exact day)
Hours: Pancake Breakfast 7:00am – 1:00pm, Festivities 8:00am – 3:00pm.
Prices: Free Admission, breakfast $5.00 per person
This event is held annually to help raise money for local scholarships. The day begins with a scrumptious pancake breakfast, and includes an exhibition of Norwegian folk costumes, and traditional music and games.

Hand On Farm

15308 52nd Ave W
425-743-3694
Date: April- for School/Play Groups only. You must make reservations.
Price: $2.50 per person. Pumpkins $2+ each.
Gather together friends and family, and call for a springtime tour of the interactive and tactile petting animal farm. Spring is especially fun with all the new animal babies abounding throughout the farm. Children will get to hold baby chicks, pet pygmy goats, feed calves from a bottle, and see the adorable piglets playing in the mud. The tour will last 30-45 minutes.

Puget Sound Bird Fest

Downtown Edmonds, Edmonds Marsh, and Edmonds Waterfront
425-771-0227
www.edmondswa.com
Date: Second Saturday in May (Migratory Bird Day)
Hours: 8:00am – 10:00am: Bird walks along the beach and marsh
10:00am – 4:00pm: Birding authors, children's activities, education workshops.
Price: Free

This fest is a celebration of birds and nature. Their mission is "to increase awareness of species of birds that spend all or part of their lives in the Puget Sound region...especially the environs of Edmonds". Observe birds in their native habitats, and learn how to preserve birds and other wildlife in your area. Specified bird viewing stations are set up for spectators, and families will enjoy the several workshops, children's activities, informational exhibits, and birding/nature walks.

Spring Beach Clean – Up

Olympic Beach
Dayton St & Admiral Way
425-771-0227
www.ci.edmonds.wa.us
Date: April 23rd (can change so call first to confirm)
Hours: 10:00am – 12:00pm
Price: Free

Wear your gloves and boots, the clean up bags will be provided. Help keep our beaches clean and afterwards you will be treated to a Shoreline Exploration at low tide.

Twilight Trailwalk

Yost Park
96th St and Bowdoin
425-771-0227
www.ci.edmonds.wa.us
Date: Earth Day Week
Hours: 7:00pm – 8:30pm
Price: Free

Did you know that the evening is filled with birds and animals who become active at nighttime? You're invited to take a walk on the Shell Creek Trail with Discovery Program Ranger-Naturalists, and learn about some of the wildlife that inhabit the Yost Park forest and wetlands. The evening concludes with hot chocolate and storytelling. All ages are welcome. Meet in the shelter above the pool.

The Edmonds Jazz Connection

Daytime Venues: Edmonds Conference Center – 201 4th Ave N,
Edmonds Theater – 415 Main Street, and Masonic Lodge – 515 Dayton Street.
Evening Venue: Edmonds Woodway High School – 7600 212th St SW
206-835-8363
www.jazzconnection.org
Date: Saturday of Memorial Day Weekend
Hours: Daytime Programs 10:00am – 5:00pm, Gala Evening Event 7:00pm -10:00pm
Prices: Daytime Programs (yes all three locations) free of charge.

The Gala Evening Event: reserved seating $35.00, general admission $25.00.
For those who simply love good jazz. This event is more than a "festival." The Edmonds Jazz Connection brings together students, professional musicians, and the arts community. During the preceding week, professional Jazz musicians visit classrooms to work one on one with the students. On Saturday, school Jazz groups perform to filled auditoriums. Sit back and enjoy the Gala Evening charity performance spotlighting national Jazz professionals. Proceeds benefit the Burned Children Recovery Foundation. Donations are gratefully accepted.

Everett

Arbor Day Ceremony

Langus Riverfront Park
400 Smith Island Road
425-257-8369
425-257-8582
www.everettwa.org
Date: Arbor Day – Mid April
Hours: 10:30am
Price: Free
Celebrate Arbor Day and participate in a tree planting project.

Family Fun Fair

Forest Park
802 Mukilteo Blvd
425-257-8369
www.everettwa.org
Date: Saturday in mid April
Hours: 11:00am – 3:00pm
Price: Free
This is a great opportunity for families to learn about the resources in the area, including the library, local schools, DSHS, dentistry, Girl Scouts, Boys and Girls club, etc. Each provider has an informational booth with activities for children.

Fishing Kids Cast For Kids Fishing Event at Silver Lake

Silver Lake
11405 Silver Lake Rd
425-257-8355
www.everettwa.org
Date: Mid May
Hours: 8:00am – 3:00pm
Price: $5.00 Registration Fee
This event is a great opportunity for introducing fishing. Children ages 5 to 14 years,

are guided by expert fishers in learning how to fish. Registered participants receive a t-shirt, with a fishing pole and tackle provided. Register early, as this event sells out quickly.

Flowerize Downtown

Hewitt and Colby

425-257-8300

www.everettwa.org

Date: May 13th

Hours: 8:00am – 9:30am

Prices: Free

Bring your gardening gloves and tools and help beautify downtown Everett with planting a beautiful array of flowers in beds and containers. Free refreshments provided.

Lynnwood

Annual Egg Scramble and Canned Food Drive

Lynnwood Athletic Complex

3001 184th Street SW

www.ci.lynnwood.wa.us

Date: Saturday before Easter

Hours: Bunny Arrives on the Fire Truck at 10:00am

Hunt Times: Ages 3-4 years 10:10 a.m., 1-2 years 10:20am, special needs up to age 10 years 10:20am, 5-7 years 10:40am, 8-10 years 10:50am

Price: Free, but a can of food donation appreciated.

Annual traditional Easter egg scramble for all ages 1 – 10 years including children with special needs.

Lynnwood Annual April Pools Day

Lynnwood Recreation Center

425-771-4030

www.ci.lynnwood.wa.us

Date: Changes yearly so please call

Hours: 1:00pm – 5:00pm

Price: Free

Water Safety event for youth ages 7 – 12 years and their families. 3:30 – 5;00 p.m. open swim included for all participants. Prizes and snacks also provided.

Multicultural Fair

Cedar Valley Community School
19200 56th Ave W
425-670-8984
www.ci.lynnwood.wa.us
Date: April 24th – subject to change
Hours: 12:00pm – 4:00pm
Price: Free Admission

A fun-filled family event celebrating the richness of the diverse city community with storytellers, dancers and musicians, arts and crafts, ethnic food samples, free books and a lot of audience participation.

Granite Falls

Easter Egg Hunt

Eagle Park
North Alder Avenue and Galena Street
360-691-5244
www.granitefallswa.com
Date: Saturday before Easter
Hours: TBA
Price: Free

A traditional Easter egg hunt, games, and contests for the whole family.

Snohomish

Bull Riders Challenge

Evergreen State Fairgrounds
360-568-2355
Date: Weekend in April
Time 8:00am-10:00pm

Bring the family to a real Rodeo! Brave Cowboys rope and ride throughout the day, and EquiFriends, a charity program for those who are disabled, offers horseback rides during the two day event.

Honoring Their Memory (Civil War Ceremony & Re-enactment)

GAR Cemetery
360-568-2526
www.cityofsnohomish.com
Date: April 9th
Hours: Begins at 1:00pm
Price: Free

A North/South battlefield re-enactment begins at 2:00pm. A special ceremony commemorating soldiers/sailors/marines of both sides of the conflict who resettled in the Puget Sound begins at. 4:00pm at the "Guardian of the West" monument.

Snohomish Easter Parade and Festival

1st Street (between Union Ave. & Ave. D.)
360-568-2526
www.cityofsnohomish.com
Date: March 26th
Hours: 11:00am
Price: Free
Meet the Easter Bunny at the annual Easter parade. Other activities include an Easter Bonnet Contest (no age limit and pets are welcome), and an Easter Egg Hunt (children 8 and younger). For those who participate in the contest, you can sign up that morning at 9:30am. Contestants are invited to ride on the Chamber Float in the parade.

Mt. Vernon's Tulip Festival

Mt. Vernon
Take exits 221-236
360-428-5959
www.tulipfestival.org
This is worth the trip to Mt. Vernon to view the breathtaking fields of rainbow colored tulips and daffodils. Be sure to pick up a map at local businesses. There are two tulip farms you can visit, including Tulip Town, and Roozen Gaarde. Each has unique features and activities for families, and freshly picked tulips for sale with shipping available to anywhere in the U.S. Art shows, Alpaca farms, and several other events are located throughout town.

Tulip Town
15002 Bradshaw Rd
360-424-8152
www.tuliptown.com
Hours: Open daily in April 9:00am-6:00pm
Cost: $4 for ages16+

Roozen Gaarde
15687 Beaver Marsh
800-732-3266
360-424-8531
www.tulips.com
Hours: Open daily in April 9:00am-7:00pm

Summer: June-August

*Note: All summer concerts listed are FREE!

King County

Auburn

Auburn Good Ol' Days

707 Auburn Way N, Auburn
253-939-3389
www.auburngoodoldays.com
Dates: August 11, 12, 13 2006
Hours: Friday-Sunday 9:00am-6:00pm, Saturday 9:00am-10:00pm.
Price: Free Admission
Participants will enjoy art shows, parade, model trains and airplanes, a juried floral exhibit, merry-go-round and other fun rides, classic car & truck show, the Auburn Hoop Classic, the Honey Bucket Brigade, live entertainment, a 5K Run, and lots of good food.

Fourth of July Festival In the Park

Les Grove Park
11th & Auburn Way
253-931-3043
www.ci.auburn.wa.us
Date: 4th of July
Time: 11:00am-4:00pm
Begin the day with the children's parade, followed with rides, arts and crafts, live entertainment. There is plenty of food

Kids' Summer Sounds

Les Grove Park
11th and Auburn Way S
Date: Wednesdays July-August
Time: 12:00pm
Features musicians, magicians, and juggling shows.

Sundown at Game Farm Park

Len Chapman Amphitheater
3030 R St SE
Date: Friday nights: July-August
Time: 7:00pm
Features jazz, pop, blues, Latin rhythms, fiddling, and rock-n-roll.

Bellevue

Bellevue Art Museum Fair

510 Bellevue Way NE
425-519-0770
www.bellevuearts.org
Date: Last weekend in July
On display are upscale arts and crafts including pottery, glass, and paintings by local artists. Several food vendors will accompany the fair.

Bellevue Family 4th

Bellevue Downtown Park
10201 NE Fourth St
425-452-4106
www.bellevuedowntown.com
Date: 4th of July
Time: 6:00pm-11:00pm
An evening performance by the Bellevue Philharmonic tops the event, along with family activities.

Bellevue Festival of The Arts

1916 Pike Place, Seattle
206-363-2048
www.bellevuefest.org
Date: July 28-30, 2006
The Bellevue Festival of the Arts offers a superb array of finely crafted items including jewelry, photography, textiles, glass, fine art, woodworking, sculpture, ceramics and pottery.

6th Street Arts & Crafts Fair and Taste of Bellevue

Downtown Bellevue
The 6th Street Arts & Crafts Fair features over 120 artists from across the nation, showcasing original artwork, jewelry, home décor, paintings, woodworking, sculpture and more as part of downtown Bellevue's arts festival.

Live At Lunch-Summer Concert Series
Throughout downtown Bellevue
425-453-1223
www.bellevuelive.com/liveatlunch/liveatlunchschedule.htm
Date: Tuesdays and Thursdays from 12:00pm-1:30pm. Check the website for the current schedule and location.

Bothell

Father's Day Car Show
Country Village
720 238th St SE
425-483-2250
www.countryvillagebothell.com
Date: June –Father's Day
Hours: 12:00pm – 3:00pm
Price: Free
Bring Dad out for a fun afternoon, along with your vintage vehicle if you have one. Dad's can enter a drawing for a $50.00 gift certificate, along with other prizes.

Freedom Festival
Bothell Landing Park
425-486-7430
www.ci.bothell.wa.us
Date: 4th of July
Time: Begins at 11:30am
Free Parking @ Bellevue Square after 6:00pm
The festival begins with a children's parade at 11:30am, followed with the Grand Parade at noon. The parade route stretches along Main St to Bothell-Everett Hwy. After the parade, walk (or bike) over to the park too see the re-enactment of the Battle of Concord set along the bridge and river. Children and adults alike treasure this reminder of how America earned its freedom. Old fashioned living quarters and tools are on display, including hand-on activities, along with inflatables and tasty treats.

Greater Bothell Arts and Crafts Fair
UW Bothell/Cascadia Campus
18115 Campus Way NE
www.BothellFair.org
Date: August
Hours: 10:00am – 6:00pm
Price: Free

Every August, Bothell's downtown is filled with art, music, and fun. Local artists display their fine art, quality crafts, along with scrumptious food, Ikebana flower arranging, and free arts and crafts for children. You can also take the family on a train ride, through a maze, bounce on an inflatable, or climb the rock wall.

National Night Out Against Crime

Bothell Police Department
18410 101st Ave NE
Tuesday August 2
6:00pm-9:00pm

RiverFest

Downtown Bothell
Main Street & 185th St
425-486-7430
www.ci.bothell.wa.us
Date: August
Hours: Tires and Tunes Car Show 10:00am – 4:00pm, Concert 1:00pm – 3:00pm
City Show and Tell 11:00am – 2:00pm, Children's Activities 1:00am – 3:00pm,
Price: Free Admission
Come celebrate Bothell's heritage and the Sammamish River. Family activities include inflatable amusement rides, the hobby expo, live musical concerts, the unique City Show and Tell and much more.

Summer Concerts

Park at Bothell Landing Amphitheater
9919 NE 180th St
Date: Friday Evenings: July-August
Time: 6:30pm-8:00pm

Burien

Summer Concerts

Lake Burien School Park
SW 148th Street and 16th Avenue SW
Date: Thursdays
Time: 6:30pm-8:00pm
The perfect way to relax and enjoy a summer evening!
In case of inclement weather it will be moved to the Burien Community Center Auditorium, 425 SW 144th.

Carnation

Camlann Medieval Faire

Camlann Medieval Village
10320 Kelly Rd NE
425-788-8624
www.camlann.org
Date: Weekends in August
Hours: 11:30am-6:00pm
Come to Camlann's annual Medieval Fair and go back in time...to the year 1376 in Chauncer, Englad when knights, jostling, archery and tournaments ruled the day. Visit the Medieval village, craft demonstrations, minstrels (live entertainment) including storytelling, vintage meals. You can even rent period clothing to really feel you are back in time.

Duvall

SummerStage 2005

McCormick Park
Rain site: Cherry Valley Elementary School at 26701 NE Cherry Valley Rd
Date: Wednesdays July - August
Time: 6:30pm- 8:30pm
A variety of musical and stage performers for families.

Enumclaw

Gateway Concert Band

Goodwill Park
Downtown Enumclaw
Date: August
Time: 7:00pm
Bring a lawn chair or a blanket and enjoy a traditional pops concert in the park.

Scottish Highland Games

King County Fairgrounds
45224 284th Ave SE, Enumclaw
206-296-8892
Date: Last weekend in July
Cost: $9-$12
Scottish dancing, piping and drumming, pipe bands and athletic events, food, Celtic Arts Showcase vendors, pubs, entertainment, Scottish farm animals and dogs.

Fall City

Music In The Mountains

Central Ski Area Plaza
Snoqualmie Pass
Date: Saturday July –August
Time: 2:00pm

Shakespeare in the Park

Snoqualmie Falls Forest Theater
www.fallcityarts.com
Date: Friday July
Time: 7:30pm
Come and delight your senses at the annual Shakespeare in the Park. Bring your family, friends, a blanket and a picnic and enjoy. This event is FREE!

Federal Way

Red, White & Blues Festival

Celebration Park
1095 S 324th
www.cityoffederalway.com
Date: July 4th
Time: Begins at 4:00pm
Bring the family and your appetite for an evening of fun. Activities for children include inflatables and sports clinics, along with live musical entertainment, and art displays. Fireworks begin shortly after 10:00pm.

Outdoor Concert Series

Steel Lake Park
253-835-6900
Date: Wednesday evenings July-August
Time: 7:00pm
Grab a friend, and bring the family to enjoy live music.

Issaquah

Concerts On The Green

Issaquah Community Center
Date: June- August
Time: 7:00pm- 8:30pm
Picnicking begins at 6:00 PM with concession items available. Please leave your pets at home.

Shakespeare in the Park
Issaquah Community Center Green Lawn
Date: Thursday-Saturday early July
Time: 7:00pm

Skate Park Demo Day
In front of Issaquah Community Center
Date: August
Time: 1:00pm - 4:00pm
Participants under the age of 18 will be required to have a participant waiver form signed by a parent or guardian. Helmets will be required for all participants. Skateboards and Inline Skates only.

Kenmore

Kenmore Summer Concerts
St. Edwards State Park
Date: Thursday nights July- August
Time: 6:30pm - 8:00pm
Purchase a hot meal from Bastyr, or bring a picnic and sit back to enjoy great music in a beautiful environment.

National Night Out
Kenmore City Hall
6700 NE 181 St.
425-486-2784 (Questions)
206-205-7652 (Questions)
Date: August (dates vary)
Time: 6:00pm - 9:00pm
America will celebrate the Annual National Night Out against crime (NNO). This is an evening when communities join forces to promote police-community partnerships, crime prevention, drug and violence prevention, safety, and neighborhood unity. The evening is dedicated to building a safer neighborhoods.

Police officers and Fire fighters will be barbecuing hamburgers and hotdogs Police vehicles and fire fighting vehicles will be on display for all to view and check out. There will also be information available for the following:

- Block watches
- House checks
- Personal safety
- Fingerprinting and ID cards for kids
- Bicycle registration cards
- Home fire prevention

Teen Activity Night

Inglemoor High School

206-205-7652 (Questions)

Date: Saturdays in mid-July through August

Time: 7:00pm -10:00pm

The Kenmore Police sponsors and chaperones four summer dances for teens. Music will be provided by a disc jockey from Action Entertainment. Everyone in attendance will have a chance to win one of many door prizes, which include tickets to Mariner baseball games, Wildwaves water park and movie passes, just to mention a few. Pizza and soda will be provided. Best of all its FREE!!!!

Kent

Canterbury Arts Festival

Mill Creek Canyon Earthworks Park

742 E Titus St

www.ci.kent.wa.us/arts

Date: August 19th & 20th, 2006

Hours: 10:00am-6:00pm

Cost: $2 Button = 2 days of activities!

This is one of the biggest and best arts festivals in Puget Sound. Usually held on a weekend, families come to enjoy two days of culture, music, fine art, theater, dance, crafts, food booths, and several workshops for young children to adults. Workshops include classes in Irish dance, beginning harp, country dancing, magic, and juggling. They have dedicated a Family Stage with live music performances, juggling acts, and puppet shows especially geared towards children. Also special for children are several hands-on activities where children can make leather treasure maps, do crafts, create a unique hats, refrigerator poetry, a Lego playing table, and much more.

Cornucopia Days-Festival of the Valley

Lake Meridian, Kent

253-852-LION

www.kcdays.com

Date: July: Thursday-Sunday

This is the largest family festival in South King County. Enjoy 4 days filled with over 600 vendors stretched over 18 blocks, and several events to choose from including a carnival, bluegrass music festival, skateboard and inline skate races, bike races, a fun run, soccer tournament, a parade, and the infamous Dragon Boat Races held on Lake Meridian.

Fourth of July Splash

Lake Meridian Park
14800 SE 272nd St
www.ci.kent.wa.us/
Date: 4th of July
Time: Begins at 12:00pm
Old fashioned fun and games and live entertainment await families and friends. Professtional stage entertainers throughout the day, along with a pie eating contest, a classic car who, and hands on activities for children. The highlight of the event begins at 9:00pm as the Rainier Symphony performs and choreographs with one of the largest fireworks display in South King County. Free Park and Ride service is available at the following locations: Horizon Elementary, Kentwood High School, Kent Fire Station #75, Covington Library, and Metro Park & Ride.

Kent Kids Arts Day

Kent Commons
525 Fourth Ave N, Kent
253-856-5050
www.ci.kent.wa.us/arts
Date: March 4, 2006
Time: 10:00am-4:00pm
Cost: $5 for Adults & Children, 2 and under Free
Experience a day of creating art masterpieces, including African Wrap dolls, sewing bean bags on antique sewing machines, bean mosaics, Japanese Ink paintings, collage buttons, Vietnamese dragon puppets, hats, and more. Local entertainers perform throughout the day, and several activities abound with face painting, planting a little garden, puppet theater, and an indoor/outdoor play area.

Summer Concerts at the following parks:

253-856-5050
artscommission@ci.kent.wa.us

Playground Performances

West Fenwick Park
3824 Reith Rd.
Date: Thursdays: July to August
Time: 12:00pm

Picnic Performances
Mill Creek Canyon Earthworks Park
742 East Titus
Date: Wednesdays: July to August
Time: 12:00pm

Take Out Tuesdays Performances
Kent Kherson Peace Park
2nd Ave. S and Gowe St.
Date: Tuesdays: July to August
Time: 12:00pm

Lake Meridian Park Performances
14800 SE 272nd St.
Date: Thursdays: July to August
Time: 7:00pm- 8:30pm
Date: Tuesday-Thursday July- August
Time: 12:00pm- 1:00pm and 7:00pm- 8:30pm

Kirkland

Centennial 4th of July Celebration
Marina Park & Juanita Beach
www.kirklandrotary.com
Date: 4th of July
Time: 9:00am
Beginning at 9:00am, children can participate in art activities, followed with the Children's Parade at 11:00am. For $5 each, you can purchase a rubber duck for the 1:00pm Duck Dash.

Kirkland Summer Performing Arts Series
Marina Park
425-413-8800 x 202
Date: Tuesdays &Thursdays July - August
Time: 7:00pm
Date: Wednesdays July - August
Time: 10:00am

Lakewood

American Lake Park
9600 Veterans Dr SW
Date: Tuesday evenings: July-August
Time: 6:30pm-8:30pm

<u>Maple Valley</u>

Kid's Festival

Lake Wilderness Park and Beach
425-413-8800 x 202
Date: July 29th, 2006
Activities include a children's concert, inflatables, hands-on arts, and crafts, sandcastle building concert, side walk chalk art show, train rides, face painting, model plane building, carousel, clowns, jugglers, and water games.

Music in the Park

Lake Wilderness Park and Beach
425-413-8800 x 202
www.ci.maple-valley.wa.us/parks/parks.htm
Date: Thursdays in July –August
Time: 6:30pm- 8:30pm

<u>Mercer Island</u>

Fun Mobile

Pioneer Park
SE 68th and Island Crest Way
Date: Mondays in August
Time: 10:30am-12:00pm
The Fun Mobile moves across the Island all summer long popping into camps, beaches, and parks. The Fun Mobile is chalk full of games, arts and crafts, snacks. It's fun and it's FREE!

Mostly Music in the Park

Mercerdale Park
77th Ave. SE and SE 32nd St.
Date: Sundays July & August, and Thursdays in August.
Time: 7:00pm-9:00pm
The annual Arts Council's summer family concert series invite you to pack a picnic dinner or get take-out from a local eatery and come to enjoy an evening of entertainment.

Newcastle

Concerts In The Park

Lake Boren Park
SE 84th Ave- just off Coal Creek Parkway SE
425-649-4444
Date: Wednesdays July -August
Time: 6:30pm-8:00pm
This is a wonderful environment for the whole family. All concerts are free of charge, so bring your lawn chairs, blankets, and join us for the show. Bring a picnic or enjoy Papa Murphy's freshly baked pizza that will be served during each concert.

Newcastle Days

Lake Boren Park
SE 84th Ave- off Coal Creek Parkway SE
206-818-3992
Date: Mid September
Newcastle Days 2 day festival is geared for family fun. Sit back and enjoy live concerts while eating delicious food, or play games and take the kids on a pony ride. Saturday morning Newcastle Days hosts a large car show with some of the finest show cars in the state. Be sure to stick around Saturday night for the spectacular choreographed fireworks over Lake Boren Park.

Movies In The Park

Lake Boren Park
SE 84th Ave- just off Coal Creek Parkway SE
Date: Fridays in August
Time: Dusk
Bring the family for Moonlight Movies at Lake Boren Park as the park is turned into a giant cinema. Come join us as we transform. Great fun for the entire family.

Normandy Park

Music In The Park

Marvista Park
SW 200th St and 4th Ave SW
Date: Sundays July-August
Time: 5:00pm-6:30pm

North Bend

Festival at Mt. Si (formerly Alpine Days)

Si View Community Center
400 SE Orchard Dr
Date: mid August
A summer tradition in the Valley for over 30 years, the Festival at Mount Si celebrates North Bend's community spirit by preserving the past, celebrating the present and embracing the future

Snoqualmie Railroad Days

Downtown
Date: early August
Come see the parade which includes a helicopter dropping (small) prizes. There are also arts & crafts, food, live music, bike ride, classic car show, children's entertainment & games, a train, scooter, and helicopter rides!

Trails Fest

Rattlesnake Lake
206-625-1367
www.wta.org.
Date: Saturday in mid July
Time: 9:00am – 4:00pm
Price: Free Admission
Trails Fest is a hands-on event for all ages, providing families and other adventurers with a fun and safe environment to explore the outdoors. The 1hour hike to Rattlesnake Lake is 4 miles roundtrip, with a 1,175 gain in elevation.

Pacific

Pacific Days

Pacific City Park
253-833-2856
www.cityofpacific.com
Date: Mid July
A festival including a grand parade, children's parade, karaoke contest, Police K-9 demonstration, Fire Department demonstration, dancing, and musical performances.

White River Bluegrass Festival
253-833-2856
www.cityofpacific.com
Date: June
An all day and evening event filled with "jammin' musical performances by local and national bluegrass artists. This festival has a nice personal setting where the performers and the spectators mingle. Bring your blanket, lawn chairs, a picnic, or choose from a variety of food vendors, and get ready to sit back and relax!

Redmond

Arts In The Parks
425-556-2392 (Information)
Date: July & August.
Be sure to call for annual dates, locations, and performance information.
Throughout the months of July and August, families can be filled with cultural glee as performers dance to Cuban and Scandinavian music dressed in bright colorful costumes.
Live concerts continue to please the crowd throughout the summer, and you won't want to miss the annual Shakespeare in the Park performance.

Renton

Cinema on the Piazza
South 3rd St between Burnett Ave S and Logan Ave S
425-226-4560
Date: Saturdays July - August
Time: Dusk

Freddie's Fabulous Fourth of July
Gene Coulon Beach Park
425-430-6500
Date: 4th of July
Time: 12:00pm
Park and ride the shuttle over to the park for a full day of festivities. Activities include inflatables and face painting available for children, along with live entertainment, a car show, and the culminating firework finale overlooking Lake Washington beginning just after 10:00pm.

Kidd Valley Family Concert Series
Coulon Park
1201 Lake Wash. Blvd
Date: Wednesdays June- August
Time: 7:00pm

Ikea Renton River Days
Liberty Park
1055 South Grady Way
Date: July

Play Day in the Park
Highlands Neighborhood Center, Kennydale Park, Kiwanis Park, Philip Arnold Park, Teasdale Park, and Tiffany Park
Date: Wednesdays July - August
Time: 12:00pm- 2:00pm
Join the community for a fun filled afternoon of games, crafts and incredible inflatables!

Picnic Pizzazz Kids Entertainment Series
425-430-6700
Kiwanis Park
815 Union Ave. NE
Date: Thursdays July - August
Time: 12:00pm
Entertainment is free and concessions will be available for a nominal fee. For more information, call.

Summer Fest at Renton Park Building and Playgrounds
Highlands Neighborhood Center, Kennydale Park, Kiwanis Park, Philip Arnold Park, Teasdale Park, and Tiffany Park
Date: June - August
Time: 11:00am- 3:00pm
Listen to loads of giggles as children ages 6 to 11 participate in a plethora of special activities, creative crafts, games and events. A free drop-in program will be hosted.

Sammamish

Kids First
Pine Lake Park
228th Ave SE at SE 24th St
Date: Tuesdays July & August
Time: 12:00pm-1:00pm

National Night Out
Neighborhoods throughout the City of Sammamish
425-836-5674
Date: Tuesday in early August
Time: 7:00pm- 10:00pm

Summer Nights in the Park
Pine Lake Park
228th Ave SE at SE 24th St
Date: Thursdays July - August
Time: 6:30pm-8:00pm

Shakespeare in the Park
Pine Lake Park
228th Ave SE at SE 24th St
Date: Saturday in mid July
Time: 6:30pm

SeaTac

Music In The Park
Angle Lake Park
19408 International Blvd
206-973-4680
Date: Sundays July - August
Time: 5:00pm-6:30pm
Pack a picnic basket and bring a blanket or lawn chair. Inclement weather will move the concerts SeaTac City Hall, 4800 S. 188th St.

International Festival
Angle Lake Park
19408 International Blvd.
Date: June

Shakespeare In The Park
Angle Lake Park
19408 International Blvd.
Date: Friday mid July
Time: 7:00pm

Tree Lighting Ceremony
SeaTac City Hall
4800 S 188th St
Date: Thursday December 1
Time: 6:30pm
Celebrate the beginning of the holiday season with your friends and community. Enjoy live entertainment and refreshments along with special friends and surprises.

Seattle

Arab Festival
Seattle Center
Date: August
Music, film, dance, exhibits, food, coffee tent, lectures, and children's activities. Saturday night dance party from the diversity of the Arab world.

Art In The Garden
P-Patch Community Gardens-Ballard
25th Avenue NW and NW 85th Street
Date: Last Saturday in July
Take a stroll in the The Ballard P-Patch, a non-profit community garden. On this special day, you'll see more than fresh produce as more than 30 local artists display their artwork in this beautiful setting, along with music, poetry, refreshments, and a silent auction. Children also get to take part with special activities just for them. The gardens are handicap accessible and include a children's garden.

Ballard SeafoodFest
Market Street and Ballard Ave
206-784-9705
Feast upon the freshest array of seafood while enjoying live entertainment and activities for the whole family.

Bite of Seattle
If you consider yourself a food connoisseur, this is the place to be. With dozens of local restaurant booths and food products, you can listen to live musical entertainment while you munch on a plethora of tastes.

Bumbershoot Festival
Seattle Center
Date: Labor Day Weekend
Treat yourself to visual splendor as thousands of artists display their original and eclectic artwork, along with live entertainment and lots of good food.

Caribbean Festival

Bring a blanket and your appetite the annual Caribbean Festival at the Myrtle Edwards Park. Listen to a variety of African and Caribbean music and cuisine.
Downtown Seattle Out to Lunch Concert Series
Westlake Park, Harbor Steps, Occidental Park and numerous Downtown office buildings.
More than 60 live jazz and classical performances throughout the summer, all held during lunchtime.

Fourth of July-Ivars

Myrtle Edwards Park
Broad St
206-587-6500
Date: 4th of July
Time: 12:00pm-11:00pm
Children will be enthralled with all the activities available, including face painting, clowns, magicians, inflatables, and live musical entertainment. The spectacular firework show begins at 10:00pm along the Waterfront.

WaMu Family 4th

Gasworks Park
2101 N Northlake Way
www.familyfourth.org
Date: 4th of July
Time: 12:00pm
Daytime activities include the kite making, legos, kiddie cars, bubble fun, and more. Overlooking Lake Union the thrilling firework show begins, at approximately 10:00pm.

Italian Festival

Celebrate the Italian culture through art, food and live entertainment. Children can participate in the infamous and traditional grape stomp, and the pizza toss event.

Lake City Summer Festival

Lake City Community Center
12531 28th Ave NE
206-362-4378
Date: August
Auto show, salmon bake and parades.

Magnolia Summer Festival
Magnolia Village
32nd Ave W and W McGraw St
Date: August
Community festival featuring a kids parade, art show and more.

Pista sa Nayon
Seward Park
5902 Lake Washington Blvd S
206-684-4075
Date: July
A Filipino American community festival celebrating heritage and traditions through music, dance and live entertainment.

Summer Family Concerts
Magnuson Park
7400 Sand Point Way NE
206-684-7026
Date: August
Time: 7:00pm

Tuesday Lunchtime Music Series
Hamlin Park
16006 15th Ave NE
Richmond Beach Saltwater Park
2021 NW 190th St
Date: Tuesdays August
Time: 12:00pm-1:00pm

Wednesday Concerts in the Parks
Richmond Beach Community Park
2201 NW 197th St
Date: Wednesdays August
Time: 7:00pm-8:30pm

Seafair
Date: July-August
A five week celebration throughout the community ending with the culmination of the hydroboat races. All across the Puget Sound, you're sure to find local parades, festivals, and pirates.

SeaFair-Seattle

www.seafair.com/x75.asp

Date for 2006: July 10th to August 6th

This event is the largest annual festival in Seattle. SeaFair activities include the Milk Carton Derby on Green Lake, Pirates landing on Alki Beach, a marathon, a ? marathon, a triathlon, Torchlight 5K & 8K run just before the Torchlight Parade, SEAFAIR fleet arrival, Hydroplane racing on Washington Lake, and Air Show featuring the famous US Navy Blue Angels. There is also live music, arts & crafts booths, and lots of yummy food.

Seafair Torchlight Parade

Downtown Seattle

Date: July

One of Seattle's largest parades with more than 100 partipants including Seafair Pirates and clowns, drill teams, bands, floats, Miss Seafair and motorcycle drill teams; special seating area for handicapped and wheelchair guests available by reservation, space limited, call **206-728-0123**.

Seattle Music Fest

Alki Beach

Date: Mid August

Summer Stop Family Beach Festival

Downtown's one and only summertime beach festival is an annual hit attracting thousands of people to the Retail Core for a day of fun in the sun. Downtown's Pine Street transforms into an urban beach with colossal sand castles, beach volleyball, live music stages and many other great activities for kids and families. Sponsorship opportunities range from title and presenting to sponsoring a SummerStop music stage, volleyball court, etc.

TibetFest

Seattle Center

Date: August

Free Event

This festival is a great opportunity for families to join in the traditional festivities of the Tibetan culture. Listen to age old stories as told with song, dance, and colorful costumes. Special activities geared towards children are available.

Shoreline

Celebrate Shoreline Anniversary Events

Connie King Skate Park at Paramount School Park
Ridgecrest Elementary School
Richmond Beach Saltwater Park
206-418-3383
Date: August

Celebrate Shoreline Teen Event

Paramount School Park
Connie King Skate Park
15300 8th Ave NE
206-418-3383
Date: Friday in August
Time: 12:00pm-8:00pm
Just when summer seems to grow tired, Shoreline spices it up with a skateboard competition, followed by a live band concert! Teens will enjoy great prizes, delicious food, music, giveaways, local bands, and tough competition, all for free.

Skykomish

Show n Shine

Date: Mid August (Saturday)
Time: 10:00am-4:00pm
"Shine" up your antique model T, carriage, or Hot Rod and "show" it off at the annual Skykomish Show N Shine (registration required). Or...you can simply stop by and see the huge selection of unique and old fashioned vehicles.

Snoqualmie

Snoqualmie Railroad Days

Railroad Ave
425-888-0021
hey-diane@hotmail.com
Date: Early August
Various Times
Come see the parade which includes a helicopter dropping (small) prizes. There are also arts & crafts, food, live music, bike ride, classic car show, children's entertainment & games, a train, scooter, and helicopter rides!

Tukwila

Music in the Park

Cascade View Community Park
14211 37th Ave S
Date: Wednesdays July - August
Time: 6:30pm-7:30pm

National Night Out Against Crime

Various Neighborhoods
206-242-8084 (Neighborhood Sign Up)
206-242-8410 (Crime Prevention Office)
Date: Tuesday August
Time: After 4:30pm
The purpose of NNO is to bring the community – neighbors, public safety workers and your elected officials – together in a united effort to prevent crime. You are responsible for organizing the NNO party in your neighborhood (i.e.potlulck, pizza, ice cream). Be sure to sign up and the city officials will come to your neighborhood for Q&A. Turn on outside lights and spend a fun evening outdoors meeting new neighbors or getting reacquainted with old ones. Tukwila officials include members of the Police and Fire Departments, City Council, City administration, Police Explorers, Traffic Volunteers and the Community Policing Citizen Advisory Board. A number of these City representatives will visit every listed NNO gathering.

Tukwila Car Show

S 144th & Hwy 99
Date: Saturday in August
Time: 10:00am-2:00pm
Spend the afternoon viewing a unique collection of refurbished and classic vehicles.

Woodinville

Sammamish Valley Fourth of July Fireworks Celebration

J.B. Instant Lawn
NE 145th St (State Route 202)
Time: 6:00pm to 11:00pm
The cities of Woodinville and Redmond join together in celebrating the Fourth of July. Enjoy an evening filled with live entertainment, games and the "best" fireworks show west of the Sammamish! Free shuttle service to and from event site. Fireworks blast off at 10:30pm.

Woodinville Summer Concert Series

DeYoung Park
13680 NE 175th St
Date: Thursdays July - August
Time: 12:00pm- 1:15pm
If inclement weather arises, performances will be held at the Woodinville Community Center.

"VIVA Woodinville!"

Woodinville Community Center 11:00am to 4:00pm.
City Hall 12:00pm to 3:00 pm.
Join in the celebration of the City of Woodinville's anniversary of its incorporation. Enjoy Latino dance and music performances, arts and crafts, a community art show, and a slice of a "birthday" cake.

Yarrow Point

Fourth of July

www.yarrowhunts.com
Yarrow Point and Hunts Point host the annual Independence Day celebration. Families will enjoy a traditional parade of classic cars, homemade floats, decorated bikes and trikes. Other activities include music, food, games for children, and more. The culminating event of the evening is the awesome firework show overlooking Cozy Cove.

Snohomish County

Arlington

Arlington Festival Street Fair with Art in the Park

Haller Park, Olympic Avenue & Memorial Park
360-403-0149
www.arlington-chamber.com
Date: July 8th – 10th
Olympic Ave is filled with over 100 crafters and vendors, and has activities and entertainment for kids and families. Sponsored by the Greater Arlington Chamber of Commerce, this event attracts visitors from all around, and includes a round-trip shuttle bus from the Street Fair to the Fly In.

Arlington EAA Fly - In

Arlington Airport
4700 188th St NE
360-435-5857
www.nweaa.org
Date: July 5th – 9th
Hours: Wednesday – Saturday 8:00am – 6:00pm, Sunday 8:00am – 2:00pm
Kids activity tent open daily from 9:00am – 3:00pm.
Prices: Non-member daily $15.00 and $40.00 weekly
*Wednesday is free for all kids accompanied by an adult.

If you're ready for a thrilling air show, the Northwest Experimental Aircraft Association Fly-In is filled with experimental aircraft enthusiasts, and is the 3rd largest exhibition of its kind in the United States. Enjoy daily air shows, exhibits, workshops, plus activities for kids.

Pioneer Picnic

Stillaguamish Valley Pioneer Park and Museum
20722 67th Ave NE
360-435-7289
www.stillymuseum.org
Date: August 21st
Hours: 10:00am
Prices: Free
Since 1912, the Stillaguamish Valley Pioneers have been gathering together to reminisce and share the experience of heritage in the valley with newcomers.

Rusty Relics Car Show

Stillaguamish Valley Pioneer Park
20722 67th Ave NE
425-337-3882
Date: Mid July
Established in 1972, this car show attracts a wide variety of classic cars to the Stillaguamish Valley Pioneer Park.

Show N' Shine Car Show

Olympic Avenue
360-435-3611
360-435-2777
www.arlington-chamber.com
Date: June 4th (or 1st Saturday of June)
Hours: 9:00am – 5:00pm
Price: Free
This annual car show fills Olympic Ave with vehicles of all vintages, to the delight of car enthusiasts.

Stillaguamish Festival of the River

River Meadow County Park
20416 Jordan Rd
360-435-2755 x 22
Date: August 13th – 14th
Hours: Saturday 10:00am – 8:00pm, Sunday 10:00am – 7:00pm
Price: Free
Native American Pow Wow, tribal salmon bake, music, arts and crafts, storytellers, children's activities, wildlife displays, logging show, & environmental education displays.

Brier

SeaScare

Downtown Brier
425-778-4389
206-498-7426
www.ci.brier.wa.us/seascare/index.html
Date: August 10th
Hours: 7:00pm
Price: Free
This is a fun hometown event that brings the sea creatures of Brier and the community together for an evening of delight. The Porch Light Parade begins at 7:00pm, along with the carnival. After the parade there is an outdoor movie in the Serendipity parking lot, so be sure to bring your lawn chairs and blankets.

Edmonds

An Edmonds Kind of 4th

Downtown Edmonds

www.edmondswa.com/Events/4th/index.html

Date: 4th of July

Time: 11:30am

The Children's Parade begins the days festivities at 11:30am. The community joins in the celebration with a loading and firing demonstration, and the Fire Department Waterball competition, both held at City Park, and live entertainment at Civic Stadium. The firework show begins at 10:00pm at the Civic Center.

Annual Children's Carnival

Frances Anderson Center Playfield

700 Main St

425-771-0230

www.edmondswa.com

Date: July 29th

Hours: 5:30pm - 8:00pm

Price: Free Admission

A carnival dedicated to children, complete with games, inflatable play rooms, contests, food and fun for the whole family to enjoy.

Family Concerts

Frances Anderson Center Amphitheater

700 Main St

425-771-0228

www.ci.edmonds.wa.us

Date: Thursdays

Time: 11:30am-12:30pm

American Sign Language is available.

Concerts in the Park

Edmonds City Park

3rd and Pine

Date: Sunday afternoons: July – August

Time: 3:00pm – 4:00pm

Taste of Edmonds
Civic Center Playfield
Bell St & 7th Ave
www.edmondswa.com/Events/Taste/index.html
Date: Mid August
Time: Friday – Saturday 11:00am – 10:00pm, Sunday 11:00am – 7:00pm
Price: $3.00 per person, Free for children age 12 and under
Bring your appetite and your family for a day filled with delicious food and fun. Live musical performances accompany this event..

The Edmonds Art Festival
Francis Anderson Center
700 Main Street
425-771-6412
www.edmondsartfestival.com
Date: Father's Day Weekend
Hours: Friday and Saturday 10:00am – 9:00pm, Sunday 10:00am – 6:00pm
Prices: Free
One of the Pacific Northwest's oldest and largest arts festivals, we offer a rich array of visual and performing arts and art events in a stunning natural setting. The Festival truly has something for everyone, with performing arts, seminars, classes, children's activities, musicians, and storytellers. A striking limited-edition Festival poster and a poster created by a junior artist will be specially produced to commemorate the event.

Waterfront Festival
Edmonds Marina
www.edmondswaterfrontfestival.com
Date: June
Hours: Friday 11:00am – 10:00pm, Saturday 10:00am – 10:00pm, Sunday 11:00am – 7:00pm
Price: Free Admission
Family boat building contests, kit boats, live entertainment, kids inflatable arcade, free trout fishing for kids, food booths, free shuttles and a beer and wine garden with live entertainment for adults.

Wenatchee Youth Circus
Civic Center Playfield
6th and Bell St
425-771-0230
www.ci.edmonds.wa.us
Date: July
Hours: Tuesday 7:00pm, Wednesday 1:00pm and 7:00pm.
This is a spectacular circus act performed strictly by people (no animals).

Everett

Animal Farm
Forest Park
802 Mukilteo Blvd
425-257-8300
www.everettwa.org
Date: Daily June 4th – August 21st
Hours: 10:00am – 4:00pm
Young and old are welcomed to a little barnyard in the city. With a wide variety of animals including rabbits, ducks, pigs, goats, ponies, and llamas. You can wonder freely among the farm animals or participate in the many education programs offered. Twenty minute group tours for preschool and grade school classes can be scheduled.

Free pony rides for children 2 years and older from 2:00 p.m. – 3:00 p.m. daily. For safety there is a weight limit of 70 lbs. and all rides are subject to weather conditions and availability of staff and ponies.

Biringer Farm "Pig Out On The Farm" Fest
Hwy 529, Everett
425-259-0255
www.biringerfarm.com
Date: Mid July
Time: 9:00am to 4:00pm
Price: Free Admission.
Feast upon their "Bodacious Barbeque": Roast pig on a spit, and treat yourself to fresh strawberry shortcake. Activities include free fishing, a kite show, giant strawberry ride, hog calling contest, strawberry shortcake eating contest, train ride, slides and animals.

Children's Concerts Series

Legion Park
Alverson and West Marine View Drive
Date: Tuesdays in July – August
Time: 12:00pm – 1:00pm
A series of free outdoor performances for children.

Cinema Under the Stars

Thorton A Sullivan Park at Silver Lake
425-257-8380
www.everettwa.org
Dates: Friday evenings July – August
Hours: Movies begin at dusk
Price: Free Admission ($1.00 donation appreciated)
Family movies shown outdoors for all to enjoy.

ComCast Waterfront Series Concerts

Port Gardner Landing
1600 West Marine View Drive
Date: Thursday evening: July – August
Time: 6:30pm – 8:30pm

Dahlia Show

Floral Hall in Forest Park
802 Mukilteo Blvd
www.everettwa.org
Date: August
Hours: Saturday 1:00pm – 6:00pm, Sunday 10:00am – 4:30pm
Price: Free Admission
Enjoy The Annual Beautiful Array Of Colorful Dahlias By Award-Winning Enthusiasts. Sponsored By The Snohomish County Dahlia Society.

Everett 4th of July Festival

Everett Waterfront
www.everettwa.org/parks
Date: 4th of July
Time: Begins at 8:30am
Start the day off right with the Yankee Doodle Dash at 8:30am. At 11:00am, the Old Fashioned Fourth of July Parade begins (25th & Colby). The Everett Symphony serenades the evening firework show over the Puget Sound. The Everett Aquasox baseball stadium also has activities throughout the day, concluding with thrilling firework presentation.

Family Series Concerts

Forest Park
802 Mukilteo Blvd.
Date: Sunday afternoons: July – August
Time: 1:30 p.m. – 3:00 p.m.

Jetty Island Days

10th St Boat Launch and Marine Park
425-257-8304 (Reservations for groups of 12+)
425-257-8305
425-257-7308
www.everettwa.org
www.everettwa.org/parks/recreation/jetty/jettyinfo.htm
Date: July 5th – Labor Day
Hours: Wednesday through Saturday 10:00am – 5:50pm, Sunday 11:00pm – 5:50pm.
Ferry departs every 30-45 minutes.
Take a free 5-minute passenger ferry to Jetty Island to beautiful salt water park. Daily tours, nature walks are available, along with scheduled Environmental Discoveries, special group tours, Campfire programs, children's crafts, Interpretive Hut and puppet show. Opening day is filled with treasure hunts and special events.

Music on the Plaza (Light Rock Series)

Snohomish County Courthouse Plaza
3000 Rockefeller Avenue
Date: Wednesdays
Time: 11:30am – 1:00pm

Nubian Jam

Forest Park
802 Mukilteo Blvd
425-303-1800
www.everettwa.org
Date: July 30th
Hours: 11:00am – 8:00pm
Price: Free
Forest Park Will Come Alive With The Music, Dance, Food And Arts Of The Annual Nubian Jam Community Festival From Contact Snohomish County Black Heritage Committee.

Sorticulture Garden Art Show

Evergreen Arboreteum and Gardens in Legion Park
Alverson Blvd
425-257-6309
www.everettwa.org
Date: Mid June Hours: Friday 4:00pm – 9:00pm, Saturday 10:00am – 6:00pm
Price: Free
This Garden Art Show Provides Everything You Can Think Of From Mosaics To Trellises; From Whimsical To Classical, Thrift Area, Kids Craft Booth And Planting Booths, Demonstrations, And How-To's.

Lake Stevens

Lake Stevens AquaFest

Main Street
425-3977-2344
Dates: July-last weekend
Hours: Saturday 10: 00am – 9:00pm and Sunday 10:00am – 5:00pm
Price: Free
A community festival parades, arts and crafts, food booths, carnival, car show, live entertainment, fireworks and sporting events.

Lynnwood

4th of July Celebration

Lynnwood Athletics Complex (Lynnwood High School)
3001 184th St SW
425-775-1971
Date: 4th of July
Time: Evening
An evening of live musical entertainment accompanies plentiful activities for children including inflatables. The fantastic firework show begins at approximately 10:00pm.

Wonderstage

Lyndale Park Amphitheater
18927 72nd Ave W
Date: Wednesdays at 12:00pm
Late June-August
Free performances and concerts for children

Shakespeare in the Park

Lynndale Park Amphitheater,
18927 72nd Ave W
425-771-4030
Dates: Thursday evenings July – August
Hours: 7:00pm
Price: Free

A series of free outdoor performances in a wooded setting reminiscent to Shakespeare's theater in the round.

Marysville

Annual Homegrown Festival

3rd & State St
360-659-4997
360-629-9695
Date: August 12th – 13th
Hours: 10:00am – 7:00pm
Price: Free Admission

Downtown Marysville will be a marketplace showcasing local produce, artisans, musicians and artistes.

Marysville Sounds of Summer Concert Series

360-363-8400

Music Under the Stars

Lions Centennial Pavillion in Jennings Memorial Park
6915 Armar Road
Date: Friday evenings July 15th – August 19th
Time: 7:00pm – 9:00pm

Music Under the Noon Shadow of the Watertower

Sunrise Rotary Gazebo in Comeford Park
514 Delta Ave
Date: Wednesdays at Noon: July 13th – August 17th
Time: 12:00pm – 1:30pm

Marysville Strawberry Festival

316 Cedar Ave, Marysville
360-659-7664
www.marysfest.com
Date: June 9th-18th , 2006
The festival begins with a Golf Tournament, the Salmon Ceremony, and Tribal parade. Festivities throughout the week include a Fashion show, the infamous Trike Race, Carnival along with a talent show. Friday marks the opening of the market along with open strawberry fields and live entertainment. Saturday begins with the Berry Run, and concludes with a Kiddie Parade at 6:00pm and the Grand Parade at 8:00pm.

Mill Creek

Children's Concert Series

Library Park
15429 Bothell-Everett Highway
Date: Wednesdays in August
Time: 12:00pm – 1:00 p.m.

Mill Creek Festival

Mill Creek Blvd
Date: Saturday in Mid July
Time: 4:30pm – 6:00pm
Outdoor live entertainment.

Music and BBQ at the Market

15605 Main St
425-357-3240
www.central-market.com
Date: Friday and Saturdays in July and August
Hours: Friday 4:00pm – 8:00pm, Saturday 12:00pm – 6:-00pm
Live Music and BBQ's for all in the Mill Creek Town Center.

Monroe

Antique Tractor Show and Threshing Bee and Sky Valley Stock Show

Frohning Farm
19524 Tualco Loop Rd
360-568-1289
www.skyvalleyantiquetractor.com
www.monroehistoricalsociety.org
Date: Mid August
Hours: 9:00am – 5:00pm
Price: Adults $5.00, children 12 and under free, seniors 62 and over free on Friday. Daily Pancake Breakfast at 10:00 a.m. $4.00 per person.
A display of vintage agricultural equipment in operation, tractor events, and various children's activities.

Evergreen State Fairgrounds

14405 179th Ave SE
360-805-6700
425-388-3200 (24 Hour Event Line)
www.evergreenfair.org
Date: 2006 – August 24th to September 4th
Time: Weekdays: 10:00am to 10:00pm – Weekends: 10:00 to 11:00pm
Prices: Adults: $8.00 Children $4.00 (6 to 15), Seniors: $6:00 (62 to 89) over 90 is free.
Group rates: Family special: 2 adults 4 children (or seniors) $20.00
The Evergreen State Fair is filled with fun family activities, including rides, a petting farm, auto races, a carnival, live entertainment, lots of food, horse shows, circus, and a farmers market.

Monroe Fair Days Parade

Main St
360-794-5488
www.chamber-monroe.org
Date: August 27th
Hours: 11:00am
Huge Parade to kick off Evergreen State Fair

Mountlake Terrace

Tour De Terrace

Mountlake Terrace, Lynnwood
425-776-7331
www.tourdeterrace.org
Date: July 28-30, 2006
Includes Parade, 5K Run Car Show, Pancake Breakfast

Mukilteo

Lighthouse Park Festival

609 Front Street
425-353-5516
Date: Friday August
Time: 5:00pm – 9:00pm
5K/10K race, fishing derby, and community parade.

Snohomish

Annual Corn Roast and Fly-In

Location: Harvey Field
9900 Airport Way
360-568-1541
www.harveyfield.com
Date: August 27th
Hours: 12:00pm – 4:00pm
Activities include; hot buttered corn, antique airplane rides, spot landing and flour-bombing, skydiving exhibition, aviation education/kid activities, aircraft static displays, food and ice-cream vendors, antique car show, dunk tank Snohomish (Snohomish County Fire Fighters)

Freedom Fest

Stocker Farms
10622 Airport Way
360-657-7613
800-965-4673
www.freedomfest.org
Prices: $9.00 - $38.00, ages 5 and under: Free
Group rates: Family pass: $55.00 (must be immediate family and be present at gate)
Date: August
Christian Music Festival. Includes concerts with over 30 artists, children's activities and stage, water zone, rock wall, motorcycle stunt jumpers, inflatable, camping, teaching, and sports.

Kla Ha Ya Days Festival & Parade

Downtown (1st Street) Snohomish
SR 9 and Marsh Rd. Snohomish
360-568-7076
www.klahayadays.com
Date: July
Hours: 10:00am – 10:00pm (Concert Begins at 7:00pm)
Price: $15.00 per car, children under 6 free
The Kla Ha Ya Days Parade begins at 11:00am. Events include: pizza Olympics, Bed Races, Frog Jumping Contest, Swing Dance, Salmon BBQ, and a great collection of silly contests for all to enter. Hot air balloons fill the night sky with a warm glow along with the live entertainment of "Jamie's Rock & Roll Legends" and "The Bobbers". There is plenty of grass seating for the whole family to have a first class view of all the activities, including the festivals firework finale. This is a family-fun summer event you won't want to miss!

5K River Run and Kids Dash (Just before the start of the Parade)

8k run is through the streets of Snohomish out and back along the river. 1 mile run/walk flat course through downtown Snohomish with the Kid's Beat the Parade dash immediately following the last runner. Awards for 1st thru 3rd overall and by division. Random prize drawing for all participants. Kid's Dash not timed as all are winners and all will get prizes.

Kla Ha Ya Days Street Fair and Arts & Crafts Festival

Downtown Snohomish –Union Street
360-568-7076
www.klahayadays.com
Dozens of restaurants and antique shops await Kla Ha Ya Days participants as you stroll along the street fair filled with arts and crafts booths.

Stanwood

Stanwood Camano Fair

Stillaquamish Fairgrounds
6431 Pioneer Hwy
360-629-4121
www.stanwoodcamanofair.com
Date: August 4,5,6 2006
Admission: Adults: $7.00, Children (5 to 12) and Seniors: $5.00, 5 and under Free
Special: 3 day pass: $14.00 per person

Time: 9:00am to midnight Friday & Saturday, 9:00am to 6:00pm Sunday
See animals, carnival, live entertainment, kids games, parade, food, etc. It is the largest community fair in the state.

Woodway

Community Fair
Downtown Woodway
206-542-4443
www.townofwoodway.com
Date: August 27th
Hours: 10:00am – 2:00pm
Price: Free Admission
Please come and enjoy a great lunch, community information booths, live entertainment, children's activities and bike parade, and a perfect opportunity to get to know your neighbors.

Out of Town Festivals & Special Events:

Puyallup Fairgrounds
110 9th Ave SW, Puyallup
253-845-1771
253-841-5045 (24 Hour Hotline)
www.thefair.com
Dates: Puyallup Fair: September 8-24, 2006
Puyallup Spring Fair: April 20-23, 2006
Enjoy animal shows, car shows, antiques & collectibles, home and garden Shows, sports & recreation, seasonal & holiday events, arts & crafts

Silverdale Whaling Days
Skagit County Fairgrounds, Waterfront Park
Date: Mid August
A family summer celebration featuring arts and crafts, food, parade, run and duck race.

Ethnic Fest
501 S. I St, Tacoma
253-305-1000
Date: Last weekend in July
The Ethnic Fest is true to it's name as they celebrate the diverse cultures from around the world. There are plenty of arts and crafts, food booths, and live entertainment, including the ever popular Tacoma Idol.

Renaissance Fantasy Faire
Minter Creek Ranch
10215 State Road 302, Gig Harbor
253-851-4114
Date: Weekends in August
Step back into 16th-century Scotland with the sporting events of jousting and equestrian events, and sword fighting. The Faire is filled with live entertainment, children's activities, and arts and crafts demonstrations..

Farmer's Markets

Bothell Farmer's Market
Country Village – 23718 Bothell Everett Highway
425-486-7430
Hours: Fridays- May through October.
Enjoy this Country Village tradition with cut flowers, local honey, nuts, seasonal fruits, veggies, and many beautiful hand-crafted items.

Edmonds Summer Market
5th Ave North and Bell Street
425-774-0900
425-775-5650
Hours: Saturday from 9:00am – 3:00pm.
Sponsored by Edmonds Historical Museum features fresh produce, flowers and handicrafts.

Maltby Farm Fresh Produce
19523 Broadway Ave, Snohomish
360-668-0174
Hours: Monday-Saturday 10:00am to 6:00, Sunday 10:00am to 5:00pm.
Family owned, grow most of produce, have an organic section.

Renton Farmers Market
The Piazza
South 3rd St between Logan and Burnett Avenues
Date: Tuesdays June 7- September 20
Hours: 3:00pm-7:00pm

Tukwila International Farmers Market
14300 Tukwila International Blvd
206-407-3428
market@ci.tukwila.wa.us
Date: Wednesdays July - August
Hours: 3:00pm-7:00pm

Farms

King County

Mountain View Berry Farm
7617 E Lowl-Lamr Rd, Snohomish
360-668-3391
Hours: 9:00am-6:00pm during July.
U-Pick and already picked blueberries for sale.

Remlinger Farms
32610 NE 32nd St, Carnation
425-333-4135
U-Pick and ready picked berries. Strawberries in June, and raspberries in July.

Schuh Farms
9828 SR 532
360-629-6455
Date: April-October, plus ? prices on produce during the first weekend in November.
Hours: 9:00am-7:00pm
This is a fresh farmer's market filled with a huge variety of produce.

Whitehorse Meadows Blueberry Farm
38302 NE State Road 530 NE, Arlington
360-436-1951
Hours: Thursday –Sunday 10:00am-dusk
Open for business in July, when blueberries are ripe for picking. You can pick the berries yourself, or buy them already picked fresh from the farm. It is recommended to wear long sleeves if you are going to pick the berries yourself.

South 47 Farm
15410 NE 124th, Redmond
425-869-9777
www.farmllc.com
Summer Hours: Thursday-Saturday 10:00am-5:30pm
Come visit this is organic produce and flower farm. With both U-Pick and just picked fresh fruits and vegetables available for sale. They grow raspberries, marionberries, snow, snap, and English peas, 5 varieties of lettuce, Walla Walla onions, cucumbers, bell peppers, Swiss chard, garlic, Pak choi, Napa cabbage, lavender, herbs, flowers, and more. Farming plots are also available to the community. Reserve them early as they sell out fast.

Snohomish County

Biringer Farm
Hwy 529, Everett
425-259-0255
www.biringerfarm.com
Hours: Subject to weather
Dates:
Strawberries: Mid-June/July
Raspberries: End June/July
Tayberries: End June/July
Pumpkins: End September/October
Call for updated information about the farm.

Biringer's Berry Barns:
Marysville: Fourth & State
Everett: 6200 at Shop & Save
Lynnwood 5026 196th SW at Wight's Nursery
Shoreline: 18005 Aurora Ave N at Highland Ice Arena
Seattle: Northwest Market St. at Sunset

Due's Berry Farms
14003 Smokey Pt Blvd, Marysville
360-659-3875
Hours:Depends on weather- call ahead of time.
U-Pick strawberry farm, open from June until July, depending on season, weather, etc. Call ahead of time for current updates.

Free Movie Showings: PG & G Ratings

Cinema 17
1101 Supermall Way, Auburn
253-735-6721
Time: Tuesdays, Wednesdays @ 10:00am

Alderwood Cinemas-Stadium 7
3501-184th SW, Lynnwood
425-776-3535
Time: Tuesdays, Wednesdays @10:00am

Cineplex Odeon
17640 138th Pl NE, Woodinville
425-398-1400
Time: Saturday 10

Crossroads Cinemas
1200 156th NE, Bellevue
425-562-7230
Time: Tuesdays, Wednesdays @ 10:00am

Loews Alderwood Mall 16
18733 33rd Ave W, Lynnwood
425-921-2980
Time: Wednesdays @ 11:00am

Regal Alderwood Stadium 7
3501 184th St SW, Lynnwood
425-776-3535
Time: Tuesdays, Wednesdays @ 10:00am

Regal Everett 9
830 SE Everett Mall Way, Everett
425-290-5596
Time: Tuesdays, Wednesdays @10:00am

Regal Mountlake 9
6009 SW 244th St, Mountlake Terrace
425-744-1112
Time: Tuesdays, Wednesdays @ 10:00am

Regal Marysville 14
9811 State Ave, Marysville
360-659-1009
Time: Tuesdays, Wednesdays @ 10:00am

Renton Village Cinema
25 S Grady Way, Renton
425-228-7241
www.amctheatres.com
Time: Wednesdays @ 10:30am

Fall: September-November

King County

Arlington

Airport Appreciation Day
Arlington Airport
360-435-5857
360-403-3470
www.arlington-chamber.com
Date: Mid September
Hours: 9:00am – 2:00pm
Price: Free for kids
Take a ride in the friendly skies! The Airport offers free flights for all kids ages 7 to 18.

Battlefield Farm Pumpkin Patch
24030 SR 9 NE (just off Hwy 9)
360-435-2556
October Hours: 9:00am-6:00pm
Ride the coach pulled by an antique tractor and search for the perfect pumpkin.

Hometown Halloween
Downtown Arlington
360-435-5757
www.arlington-chamber.com
Date: October
Hours: TBA
Festival that includes trick or treating, a pumpkin decorating contest, costume contests, a parade of scarecrows, and the great "Pumpkin Roll" down 1st Street Hill.

Bothell

Fall Car Show
Country Village
23718 Bothell Everett Highway
425-483-2250
www.countryvillagebothell.com
Date: September
Hours: 12:00pm – 4:00pm
Price: Free Admission
Enter a car or come just for the fun of it! Live music, food and more. Admission free. $10.00 fee to enter a car, prizes & dash plaques.

La Fiesta Viva!
Country Village
23718 Bothell Everett Highway
www.FiestaViva.org
Date: Mid September
Hours: 10:00am – 6:00pm
Price: Free
This event honors and celebrates Independence and the cultures of Mexico, Guatemala, Central and South America. Activities include train rides, face painting, children's crafts, cultural exhibits, homemade Mexican food, dancing, music, and more.

Annual Harvest Festival and Pumpkin Painting Contest
Country Village
23718 Bothell Everett Highway
425-483-2250
www.countryvillagebothell.com
Date: October

Safe Halloween

Country Village and Main Street

www.ci.bothell.wa.us

Date: October 31st – Halloween

Hours: 5:00pm – 7:00pm

Price: Free

Children under 13 are invited to trick-or-treat at the Country Village shops and in downtown Bothell. Activities include face painting and a fish pond with prizes.

Carnation

Remlinger Farms

32610 NE 32nd St

425-333-4135

www.remlingerfarms.com

Date: October 1st –31st

Hours: Weekends 10:00am-5:00pm

Prices: Adults & Children $12, Children under 1 Free

Fall Harvest Festival, plus Country Fair Family Fun Park, especially designed for children ages 10 and under. Activities include a 4-H animal barnyard, pony trail ride, Tolt River steam train ride, hay maze, hay jump, climbing wall, canoe ride, antique car ride, farm theater, swing carousel, mini rollercoaster, mini Ferris wheel, play area, and a real vintage fire truck and school bus that children can play in. Remlinger Farms is wheelchair and stroller accessible. Also located on the farm's grounds is a full-service bakery, restaurant, ice cream parlor, and picnic areas.

Federal Way

Wild Waves & Enchanted Village: Fright Fest

36201 Enchanted Pkwy S

253-661-8000

www.sixflags.com

Date: October 1st-30th. Weekends only.

You're sure to be frightened as you skimmer through a haunted house, stroll along the Street of Screams, and thrill your heart with "spooktakular" Enchanted Village rides.

Issaquah

Cougar Mountain Zoo

19525 SE 54th St
425-391-5508
www.cougarmountainzoo.org
Date: October 30th 10:00am-4:30pm
Prices: Seniors 62+: $7, Adults 13-61: $8.50, Children 2-12: $6, and 2 & under: Free
Go on an adventure hunt and receive a goody bag, watch wild animals feed on special pumpkin treats, play guessing games with a chance to win a prize. Come in a costume and receive a complimentary return visit coupon.

First established in 1972 for the purpose of educating and preserving endangered animals, the zoo has influenced a greater appreciation and awareness, and educated the public about the earth's wildlife community. Visitors receive rare close encounters with Reindeer, Antelope, Lemurs, Birds, Macaws, and other wildlife.

Issaquah Salmon Days

155 NW Gilman Blvd
425-392-0661
www.salmondays.org
Date: October 1st and 2nd (always held the first Saturday and Sunday in October)
Time: 10:00am to 6:00pm
Price: Free admission
Almost 300 arts and crafts booths, over 50 food vendors, and best of all... a salmon barbecue accompanied with live music. Travelocity picked this festival as one of top 10 "local secrets, and big finds".

Kent

Kent Halloween Party

Kent Commons
525 Fourth Ave N
253-856-5050
Date: October 29th 2005, and October 28th 2006
Time: 3:00pm-6:00pm
Price: $3/person, 2 and under Free
Kids have the option of wearing their costume to Kent's annual Halloween Party. Professional artists and entertainers will accompany your family, along with carnival games, including the ol' favorite fishing for treats, face painting, and hands-on art projects. This is a fun, safe activity and is recommended for children preschool age through 5th grade.

Redmond

South 47 Farm

15410 NE 124th
425-869-9777
www.farmllc.com
Date: July-October
Hours: Fridays, 10:30am-11:30am
Price: $5 per child
Bring your mom to the farm for a special Mommy & ME program on Friday mornings for a hayride, a pick of child-sized portion seasonal crops, and activities.

Snohomish County

Edmonds

Hand On Farm

15308 52nd Ave W
425-743-3694
Date: Weekends in October
Hours: 10:00am-5:00pm. School/Play Groups available weekdays.
Price: $2.50 per person. Pumpkins $2+ each.
A tour guide will lead you through the tactile farm, where children can feed and pet friendly animals, including pygmy goats, pigs, cows, roosters, a turkey, and much more. Explore the vegetable garden as you take the Hidden Bear Trail to Stamp Maze and Pumkinland. The tour will last 30-45 minutes.

Hot Autumn Nites Car Show and Festival

Downtown Edmonds
425-776-6711
www.edmondswa.com/Events/Carshow/index.html
Date: Saturday in mid September
Hours: Car Show 9:00am – 5:00pm, Outdoor 50's street dance 6:00pm – 10:00pm
Price: Free Admission
Over 400 shined and polished cars and trucks, muscle cars, and vintage classics compete at the festival. A fresh Farmer's Market awaits guests along with a Chili and salsa Cook-off. All are bound to have fun at the outdoor 50's dance.

Edmonds Halloween Downtown

Downtown Edmonds
425-776-6711
www.edmondswa.com/Events/Halloween/

Date: October 31st

Hours: 5:00pm – 7:00pm
Price: Free
You're invited to go Trick or Treating in downtown Edmonds for a safe and fun way to spend Halloween. Pets are welcome to accompany families.

Moonlight Beach Adventures

Marina Beach
425-771-0227
Date: September 10th
Hours: 7:00pm – 9:00pm
Fun night with stories, songs and touch tanks.

Watershed Fun Fair

Yost Park
9535 Bowdoin Way
425-771-0227
www.ci.edmonds.wa.us/Discovery_Programs
Date: Mid September
Hours: 11:00am – 4:00pm
Price: Free
Come to this annual family event for all ages. Guided walks, nature crafts, and face-painting, as well as informational exhibits and demonstrations. Bring a picnic lunch, and enjoy the park trails and playground.

Everett

Biringer Farm Pumpkin Country

Hwy 529
425-259-0255
www.biringerfarm.com
Date: Throughout the month of October.
Cut pumpkins off the vine, visit the "Not So Scary" Boo Barn, take a journey through the corn maze, wood teepee, pumpkin village, and miner's cabin. Wear a costume and get a treat!

Goblin Splash

Forest Park Swim Center

425-257-8300

www.everettwa.org

Date: October

Hours: 7:00pm – 8:30pm

Price: One Canned Food Donation

Just bring a can of food, and you are welcome to swim the night away. Staff dress up in fun (not scary) Halloween costumes and provide safe Halloween activities and games.

Haunted Forest: Halloween Fun at Forest Park

Forest Park

425-953-4043 (Call to verify times and prices)

www.everettwa.org

Date: October 20th – 24th & 27th – 31st

Hours: 6:00pm – 10:00pm

Prices: $7.00 per person, $1.00 off with canned food donation

Come visit the "scariest forest in all of Snohomish County".

Mutt Strut

425-257-8300

Date: Mid September

Dog Walk and Pet Showcase with fun categories for all dogs and their owners. Participants must register for the event, and receive a T-shirt, dog's bandana, and goodies. There will be dog vendors, demonstrations, and activities. The location and date change annually, so be sure to call each September for further information. The proceeds are given to the Everett Animal Shelter and Everett's Off Leash Parks.

Monroe

Baylor Farm Pumpkin Patch

28511 Ben Howard Rd

360-793-0822

October Hours: 10:00am-4:00pm

Wagon rides, gourds, Indian corn and stalks, and pumpkins are plentiful atht eh farm. Pumpkins are $.10/lb.

Mukilteo

Lighthouse Festival

Rosehill Community Center
304 Lincoln Ave
425-353-5516
www.mukilteofestival.org/
Date: September 9th – 11th
Hours: Parade times and events pending announcement.
Children's Activities: Saturday 1:00pm – 5:00pm, Sunday 12:00pm – 5:00pm.
Fireworks Saturday Dusk – 8:00pm
Price: Free Admission
Fun filled days of parades, fun run, artist booths, juried art show, children's activities, free entertainment, food and much, much more.

Snohomish

Charlie's Organic Gardens

15001 Old Snohomish Monroe Rd
425-238-2287
October Hours: 9:00am-7:00pm
Hay rides and a variety of organically grown pumpkins.

Hagen Vegetables

8203 Marsch Rd
360-568-4120
Hours: Saturday 9:00am-6:00pm, Sunday 10:00am-6:30pm
Free hay rides on weekends. A variety of pumpkins for sale, along with delicious fresh hot buttered corn!

The Farm
7301 Rivershore Rd
425-334-4124
www.thefarm1.com
Date: September-October 31st. Weekends
Hours: 10:00am-6:00pm.Make reservations for weekday appointments.
U-Pick flowers, pumpkins, and corn. This is a farm filled with activities for toddlers to adults. For $5 a child (adults free), tour the hay maze in the barn and slide into a barrel of hay, then visit the petting animal farm. Next is an adorable skit of the real 3 little pigs, then onto the wagon for a ride out to the pumpkin patches. Children can pick their favorite pumpkin, and end the event under the pavilion for an ice cream treat. For $5 per person, or $20 per family, older children and families will enjoy the corn maze shaped as Washington State. This maze includes lookout bridges and several exits.

Stocker Farms
10622 Airport Way (near Harvey Airfield)
360-568-7391
October Hours: 9:00am-7:00pm, Sunday 10:30am-6:00pm
Acres of pumpkins and fall decorations available for sale.

Stanwood

Pioneer Produce Pumpkin Patch
SR 532
360-639-3580
October Hours: 11:00am-6:00pm
U-pick pumpkins fresh from the vine, and hay rides throughout the farm.

Shuh Farms
9829 Hwy 523
360-639-6455
Hours: 9:00am-7:00pm
Pumpkins, corn, apples, squash, corn stalks, hay bales, and straw bales for sale.

Events Offered Throughout The Year

Edmonds

Third Thursday Art Walk

Downtown

425-776-3778

www.edmondswa.com/Events/ArtWalk/index.html

Date: Third Thursday evening of each month

Hours: 5:00pm – 8:00pm

Prices: Free

Enjoy a relaxing stroll downtown while you shop and discover the work of local artists.

Everett

Labyrinth Walks

Wiggums Hollow Park

2808 10th Street

425-257-8300

www.everettwa.org

Date: Monthly, contact for exact dates and times

Hour: varies

Price: Free

Walk the winding path of the labyrinth and meet new friends, celebrate diversity through the artwork in the park and learn new things about each other every month. Some months feature refreshments and hot cider, others prompt you to bring along a sack lunch. Please remember to dress appropriately for the northwest weather.

Granite Falls

American Legion Breakfasts

301 S. Granite Ave

Date: 1st Saturday of each month

Each month a breakfast is sponsored by American Legion Post & Auxiliary #125.

Lynnwood

Trolley Tours

Heritage Park
19921 Poplar Way
425-744-6478
www.ci.lynnwood.wa.us
Dates: First and Third Saturdays and Wednesday in June, July & August, First and Third Saturdays in September, and First Saturday in October – May.
Hours: 12:00pm – 3:00pm
Tour guides will entertain riders with stories of the trolly's history.

Library Gallery

Lynnwood Library
19200 44th Avenue
425-744-6459
www.ci.lynnwood.wa.us
Dates: June – October (actual dates depend on artist showing)
The Lynnwood Library Gallery showcases local and regional artists on both the amateur and professional level.

Fantastic Fridays (Music Concert Series)

Edmonds Community College – Triton Union Building
20200 68th Ave W
425-771-4030
www.ci.lynnwood.wa.us
Date: Friday Evenings September – May (call for upcoming schedule)
Hours: 7:30pm
Prices: Free but a suggested donation is Adults $3.00 and Children $2.00
Features a wide variety of Family Friendly free music performances.

Shoreline

Shoreline Historical Museum "Hands-on Days"

749 N 175th St
206-542-7111
Dates: 4th Saturday of each month.
Time: 11:00am-3:00pm
Museum hours: Tuesday-Saturday: 11:00am-3:00pm
Drop in for fun, free history-related projects for children ages 4-12.

Chapter 13

Volunteer Opportunities

Chapter 13

Volunteer Opportunities

A great way to build values in your family is to volunteer together. Read on to find valuable information about volunteering along the Puget Sound.

Did you know:

- Youth who volunteer are more likely to do well in school, graduate, vote, and be philanthropic –UCLA 1991
- Young people who volunteer just one hour or more a week are 50% less likely to abuse drugs and engage in at-risk behavior –America's Promise 2001
- 89% of households give to charities each year
- 44% of American adults volunteer
- 83.9 million American adults volunteer every year. That's a value of over 9 million full-time employees at a value of $239 billion!

A new study shows that people who begin volunteering as students are:

- Twice as likely to volunteer as adults.
- More likely to give generously to charitable causes.
- More likely to teach their own children to volunteer.

Courtesy of **www.independentsector.org**

What To Expect When Volunteering

Volunteering is different for every person. No two people will have the same experience. There are a few things that will be similar, especially when you first start. Here is a short list of what you should know and what you might expect.

- Be prepared to work.
- Be prepared to wai.t
- Be prepared to fill out forms.
- Wear reasonable clothes.
- Remember you only get out what you put in.

The Rights of a volunteer

- Volunteerism itself is a basic right
- Volunteers have a right to know what is expected of them.
- Volunteers have the right to good training.
- Volunteers have the right to be treated with respect.
- Volunteers have a right to set goals for themselves.
- Volunteers have a right to feel good about their service.

Volunteer Opportunities

There are several resources available for volunteering that are too numerous to list in this chapter, but are listed in other chapters. Look in Chapter 3: Community Resources. Call your local community center for opportunities to volunteer. Chapter 17: Health and Childcare is filled with hospital information. Call your nearest hospital for a list of volunteer positions. Watch for holiday volunteer opportunities, especially during the months of November and December. Another option that is always in need of volunteers is your local elementary school. Reading to children is always needed and appreciated. Find out the requirements for each school, and your services will be greatly appreciated.

Food drives, toy drives, clothes/coat drives, and school supply drives are an easy, yet fulfilling way to give to others in need. Local department stores during specific times throughout the year, collect these items and are a safe venue for knowing your donated items will be received by those they are stating to help.

Volunteer Centers

Family Volunteer List:

Serving together as a family is possible! Check out these opportunities to enrich your time together as a family through volunteering.

Volunteer Match

This is an excellent website for gathering volunteer information specifically for you and your family. You simply enter your zip code, highlight your interest(s) base, and you will see a list of local organizations and special events that are in need of volunteer help. It includes appropriate ages and specific information for each match. Possible points of interest include animals, art, the homeless, religion, senior citizens, sports and much more.

The Points of Light Foundation

Located in Washington D.C., this is foundation works with the Volunteer Center National Network. The two work together to help troubled communities solve problems. Their services reach 170 million people in diverse communities, with 360 volunteer centers and 2.5 million volunteers. They have a partnership with over 79,000 other organizations, including the Family Strengthening and Neighborhood Transformation, Kids Care Club, 50+ Volunteering Initiative, AmeriCorps*VISTA Strengthening Communities Initiative, and Disaster Preparedness & Volunteers. This is a great opportunities for families to serve.

Seattle Works

2123 E Union St
206-324-0808
www.seattleworks.org
Seattle Works strives to bring together young adults in their 20's and 30's to serve their community. There are several avenues in which to volunteer. Search their monthly calendar online to find the right fit for you, and/or your family. You may also sign up to receive e-mails filled with opportunities and activities for service.

United Way of King County

107 Cherry St
206-461-3655
The United Way is well known for helping the homeless, but did you know they also strive to help prepare children for school, and provide nutritional meals for children in need during the summer? To find out when and how you may serve, including youth, visit their website for specific information, including a calendar of upcoming events.

United Way of Snohomish County

917 134th St SW Suite B1, Everett

425-921-3400

The United Way is well known for helping the homeless, but did you know they also strive to help prepare children for school, and provide nutritional meals for children in need during the summer? To find out when and how you may serve, including youth, visit their website for specific information, including a calendar of upcoming events.

Volunteers of America

6559 35th Ave NE

206-523-3565

Volunteers of America is a nationwide, spiritually based organization built to provide services for people and their communities. There services range from helping abused children to the serving the homeless.

Washington State Parks Volunteer Program

360-902-8583

Helping hands are needed everywhere. Both short-term and long-term help is available for families, schools, couples, service organizations. This website lists, which opportunities are available, making it easy to decide where your interest lie. You can fill out a volunteer application online.

Washington State 4-H Program

Snohomish County

425-357-6044

King County

206-205-3100

Find information for volunteering in gardening, 4-H youth, environment, nutrition, agriculture, child development, and clothing and textiles. Each club offers different levels of community service to fit individual and family lifestyles. They also have a program specific for youth called the Teen Ambassador Program.

Volunteering with Animals

Forest Park

802 Mukilteo Blvd, Everett

425-258-6911

Opportunities for volunteering at Forest Park are limited to weekends and the summer. Youth can assist in giving pony rides to children, and caring for the animals in petting farm.

The Humane Society

13212 SE Eastgate Way, Bellevue

425-641-0080

www.seattlehumane.org

The Humane Society formed HTC, The Humane Teen Club, for 13-15 year olds. This program provides an opportunity to volunteer while learning the benefits of animal companionship and animal welfare during monthly classes and independent service project and research paper service projects. Youth must apply for this program. It is a 10 month commitment. Visit their website to download or print the application form. Once the program requirements are completed, teens may apply for further select volunteer opportunities at The Humane Society.

Hours: 1st Saturday 10-12

Progressive Animal Welfare Society: PAWS

5305 44th Ave, Lynnwood

425-787-2500

Shelter Hours: Tuesday/Wednesday 12:00pm – 6:00pm, Thursday/Friday 12:00pm - 7pm, Saturday/Sunday 11:00am – 5:00pm.

Volunteer positions include dog walking, cat room attendant, foster care program, PAWS walk, and more.

Volunteering with Children

Big Brothers Big Sisters
1600 S Graham St, Seattle
King & Pierce Counties
206-763-9060
www.bigsandlittles.org
For teens 16+, you may apply to volunteer 1 hour weekly. Activities include spending time with assigned Little Brother or Little Sister reading, playing games, and arts and crafts on the campus of the child's school, during the school year. Financial donations are also accepted.

Boys and Girls Club
107 Cherry St #200, Seattle
King County
206-461-3890
www.positiveplace.org
Beginning at age 14, youth may volunteer as a tutor, sports volunteer (referee games), a help counselor, monitor children, and more.

Volunteering at Museums

Kids Quest Children's Museum
155 108th NE, Bellevue
425-637-8100
www.kidsquestmuseum.com
Hours: Tuesday-Saturday 10:00am-5:00pm, Friday extended hours open until 8:00pm, Sunday 12:00pm-5:00pm
They have a youth volunteer program, including training youth how to volunteer.

The Children's Museum Center

305 Harrison St, Seattle Center
206-441-1768
206-448-0910
tcm@thechildrensmuseum.org
www.kidsquestmuseum.com
Hours: Monday-Friday 10:00am-5:00pm, Saturday and Sunday 10:00am-6:00pm.
Most volunteer opportunities exist Monday-Friday 10 am - 5 pm, Saturday and Sunday 10 am - 6 pm.
Volunteers must be 16 or older. Positions include floor monitor, service in the museum shop, storyteller, birthday party & school greeter, service in the artist studio, and more.
Each volunteer receives free admission and free guest passes to the museum, a letter of reference (if requested), on-going training, invitations to exhibit openings and special events, and a copy of The Gazette newsletter.

Center For Wooden Boats, The

1010 Valley, Seattle
206-382-2628
www.cwb.org
Hours: Open daily from 7:00am-10:00pm.
Winter Hours: 10:00am-5:00pm.
Prices: Free
Located south of Lake Union, this hands-on maritime history museum offers programs for children and families on Wednesdays. To volunteer, you must be 14 or older. There are a variety of positions available, each with it's own responsibilities. You must go through a general volunteer orientation. Volunteers receive training in maritime skills (sailing, and construction), one free hour of boat time for every three hours of volunteer time, flexible hours for students, develop new skills, and invitations to volunteer parties and special events.

Naval Undersea Museum

#1 Garnett Way-Keyport
360-396-5547
This is a technology museum appropriate for children ages 8 and older. The exhibit tells of the day-to-day life of the Trident Family. Their mission is to "preserve and collect naval undersea history for the benefit of the US Navy as well as the people of the United States". Those who wish to volunteer receive their job responsibilities during their orientation and training.

Museum of Flight
9404 E Marginal Way, South Seattle
206-764-5720
206-768-7126 (Volunteer Coordinator)
www.museumofflight.org
High School Students can sign up for the MAP, the Museum Apprenticeship Program. For more volunteer information, visit .
Positions include Air Force One / Concorde Host, Computer Power User, Database and Scheduling, Data Entry, Docents, Education Collection Crew.

Experience Music Project-EMP
325 Fifth Ave North (Seattle Center) Seattle
206-367-5483
877-367-5483
www.emplive.com
Volunteer positions at the EMP include visitor services volunteer, program support volunteer, and group volunteering. You may apply online. Those who are 14 or 15 need to e-mail the EMP first, before applying for a volunteer position

Cultural Volunteering

Chinese Information and Service Center
409 Maynard Ave S, Seattle
206-624-5633
www.cisc-seattle.org
There is not an age limit for volunteering. Positions include administration team, community technology center, teaching assistant, lab monitor, and ESL / Naturalization Program. Responsibilities for volunteers are given at orientation and training.

El Centro de la Raza
2524 16th Ave S, Seattle
206-329-9442
Positions for service include senior program activities, ESL class tutors, citizenship class tutors, kitchen assistants, senior activities volunteer, food bank volunteer.

Japanese American Citizens League
316 Maynard Ave S, Seattle
206-622-4098
www.jaclseattle.org
Volunteers at this league serve by filling positions as a member.

Jewish Family Service

1601 16th Ave, Seattle

206-461-3240

Students 12 and older, and those younger who are accompanied by an adult, may volunteer to serve in the following positions at the food bank, as a companion for seniors, big pals, just to name a few. More opportunities online.

Jewish Federation of Greater Seattle

2031 3rd Ave, Seattle

206-443-5400

Those ages 16 or older may apply as a volunteer. Positions include study buddy and JFS Big Pal Program. To find out more, send an e-mail to to request more volunteer information.

Korean Community Counseling Center

23830 Hwy 99 204A, Edmonds

206-784-5691

Positions for volunteers include teaching computer literacy for elders, service in their youth program, and office work.

Seattle Indian Center

611 12th Ave S, Seattle

206-329-8700

Volunteer positions are given during the application process. It usually involves serving in the community as needed.

Society of African Americans USA

1218 E Cherry St, Seattle

206-860-0531

Currently in transit. Call for more information.

United Indians of All Tribes Foundation

Daybreak Star Art & Cultural Center, Discovery Park

206-285-4425

www.unitedindians.com

There are several positions one can serve including with the noted children's preschool Head Start, the homeless youth home, and the cultural program for the gallery store.

Urban League of Metropolitan Seattle
105 14th Ave, Seattle
206-461-3792
www.urbanleague.org
Positions include general office work (data entry, stuffing envelopes, compiling packets), graphic design (for marketing purposes), helping with special events (phone calls, greeting guests, set up, break down), manning Urban League tables at various events, light maintenance/ clean up (painting), and tutoring. These are just a few of the opportunities. If you wan to know more there, is a printable page on their website to fill out, and they will send you a current list.

Shakespeare in the Park
Snoqualmie Falls Forest Theater
425-222-6004
425-880-6364
Date: Friday July
Time: 7:30pm
Come and delight your senses once again for the annual Shakespeare in the Park. This is a free event for the community, and therefore many volunteers are needed to fulfill the production. For more information about Fall City Arts volunteer opportunities, please give them a call.

Disability Assistance

Catholic Community Services
100 23rd Ave S, Seattle
206-325-5162
www.ccsww.org
For those who would like to volunteer, type in your county, and a see a list of information pertaining to your county. Some examples include becoming a summer book buddy, child care volunteer, children\'s program volunteer, and chore services volunteer.

Community Services for the Blind and Partially Sighted
9709 3rd Ave NE, Seattle
206-525-5556
www.csbps.com
There are several opportunities to volunteer. All volunteers are well trained. Call to find out how you can lend your services for their current needs.

Deaf-Blind Service Center
2366 Eastlake Ave E, Seattle
206-323-9178

Little Bits Therapeutic Riding Club
19802 NE 148th, Woodinville
425-882-1554
Little Bit Therapeutic Riding Center is a non-profit organization which gives children with disabilities, ages 2 Ω and older, an opportunity to focus on their abilities as they go horseback riding in a beautiful, peaceful environment.

Group/Party projects are available throughout the year without training or orientation needed. All other volunteer positions require a 2 hour/week commitment, with training and orientation provided by Little Bits. Responsibilities include grooming, tacking, leading, side walking, mounting, and dismounting.

Easter Seal Society of Washington
521 2nd Ave W, Seattle
800-678-5708
www.seals.org

Food Distribution

Beacon Avenue Food Bank
6230 Beacon Ave S, Seattle
206-722-5105

Bothell Food Bank
18220 96th Ave NE, Bothell
425-485-6521

Des Moines Area Food Bank
22225 9th Ave S, Des Moines
206-87 8-2660

Downtown Food Bank
1531 Western Ave, Seattle
206-626-6462

Edmonds Food Bank
828 Casper St, Edmonds
425-778-5833

Federal Way Food Bank
1200 S 336th St, Federal Way
253-838-6810

Food Lifeline
1702 NE 150th St, Shoreline
800-404-7543
www.foodlifeline.org

Highline Food Bank
18300 4th Ave S, Seattle
206-433-9900

Issaquah Food Bank
179 1st Ave SE, Issaquah
425-392-4123

Kent Community Service Center Food Bank
525 N 4th, Kent
253-856-5180

Kirkland Multi-Service Center
302 1st St, Kirkland
425-889-7880

Lynnwood Food Bank
5326 176th St SW, Lynnwood
425-745-1635

Northwest Harvest
711 Cherry St
206-625-0755
www.northwestharvest.org

Redmond Food Bank
16225 NE 87th St, Redmond
425-882-0241

University District Food Bank
4731 15th Ave NE, Seattle
206-523-7060
You can help by sorting donations, distributing food, and as a farmer's market helper.

West Seattle Food Bank
3518 SW Genesee St, Seattle
206-932-9023
Donations collection hours are: Monday through Friday 9:00am-3:00pm, and open until 7:00pm on Wednesdays. You may also make an appointment to deliver donations.
Volunteer positions include working the Farmer's Market on Sundays from June to October, home deliveries, and data entry.

Homeless Services

Family Service
615 2nd Ave, Seattle

Union Gospel Mission
206-723-0767

Helping Hands

American Red Cross
1900 25th Ave S, Seattle
206-323-2345
Most volunteers at the American Red Cross are expected to have a six month commitment, with many positions requiring training.

Habitat for Humanity
306 Westlake Ave N, Seattle
206-292-5240
For those 15 years or older, service begins with orientation, and proceeds to the building site where you will be given an assignment in building a home for a needy family. Monetary donations are always accepted.

Salvation Army
Everett: **425-259-8129**
Federal Way: **253-946-1346**
Seattle Temple: **206-783-1225**
Seattle White Center: **206-767-3150**
Help is needed for the holiday season, food bank, to help tutor children, and to help the homeless. Volunteers need to be 16 years of age or older.

Seattle Goodwill
1400 S Lane St, Seattle
206-329-1000
Positions for volunteering include tutoring in math, ESOL, and reading/writing; computer lab assistant, reader and book recorder just to name a few.

Literacy

King County Library System
960 Newport Way NW, Issaquah
425-369-3200
www.kcls.org
Positions vary with each library. Visit the King County Library website to search for volunteer information at the library you choose to serve.

Literacy Action Center
8016 Greenwood Ave N, Seattle
206-782-2050
Volunteers are asked sign a commitment for 6 months to 1 year, with a minimum of 1 hour per week.

Literacy Council of Seattle
811 5th Ave, Seattle
206-233-9720
www.literacyseattle.org

Washington Literacy
220 Nickerson St, Seattle

Volunteering with Seniors

Central Area Senior Center
500 30th Ave S, Seattle
206-726-4926
There is not an age requirement for those who would like to volunteer. Responsibilities including helping with special events, and food preparation.

Federal Way Senior Center
4016 S 352nd, Auburn
253-838-3604

Greenwood Senior Center
525 N 85th St, Seattle
206-297-0875
Families and youth are invited to help cook lunch, help with speial events, garden, and more.

Highline Senior Center
1210 SW 136th St, Burien
206-297-0876

Issaquah Valley Senior Center
105 2nd Ave NE, Issaquah
425-392-2381
Volunteers at any age can help with special events, activities, and more.

Lynnwood Senior Center
5800 198th St SW, Lynnwood
425-670-6401
Volunteer positions include community service, clean up, helping with projects, helping with art classes and more.

Northshore Senior Center
10201 E Riverside Dr, Bothell
425-487-2441
Volunteers at any age can serve the center by helping with the mail, helping in the kitchen, social services, and more.

Northwest Senior Activity Center
5429 32nd Ave NW, Seattle
206-932-4044

Senior Services of Seattle/King County
1601 2nd Ave
206-448-5757
www.seniorservices.org
Positions include African American Outreach, Congregate Meals, Meals on Wheels, Senior Rights Assistance, Volunteer Transportation, Senior Shuttles, Nutrition Transportation, Senior Wellness Project, Senior Centers, and Adult Day Health Centers. Responsibilities vary with each job.

Shoreline Senior Activity Center
18560 1st Ave NE, Shoreline
206-365-1536
Help with front desk, gift shop, kitchen, or entertainment center.

Southeast Seattle Senior Center
4655 S Holly St, Seattle
206-722-0317
Serve as a receptionist, cashier, or help with bingo.

Youth

Central Area youth Association
119 23rd Ave, Seattle
206-322-6640
www.seattle-caya.org
Volunteering with the tutoring program requires a 2 hour per week commitment. Patience and a positive attitude is a must, along with knowledge about math, art, and/or language.

Central Youth and Family Services
1901 Martin Luther King Jr. Way S, Seattle
206-322-7676
Help with grounds keeping.

University District Youth Center
4516 15th Ave NE, Seattle
206-526-2992

Sport Venues

Volunteer positions at sports venues are few and can be difficult to find. Minor leagues and college teams tend to offer the most opportunities.

Seattle SuperSonics: Basketball
Key Arena @ Seattle Center
www.supersonics.com

Seattle Storm: Basketball
Key Arena

Seattle Mariner's: Baseball
Safeco Field
www.seattle.mariners.mlb.com

Everett Aquasocks: Baseball
www.aquasocks.com
425-258-3673

Seattle Seahawks: Football
206-827-9777
www.seahawks.com

Everett Hawks: Indoor Football
Everett Events Center
www.everetthawks.com

Seattle Sounders: Soccer
League:
Seahawk Stadium
800-796-KICK
www.seattlesounders.net

Seattle Thunderbirds: Hockey
Key Arena
206-448-PUCK
www.seattle-thunderbirds.com
Volunteers must work in 2-4 hour shifts as Thunder-Mission Patrol. Responsibilities include hanging up schedules, and running the puck shoot booth.

Everett Silvertips: Hockey
Everett Events Center
425-252-5100
www.everettsilvertips.com

University of Washington Huskies

206-543-2200

www.gohuskies.collegesports.com

Volunteer positions vary. The following sports venues are possibilities.

Men's Spectator Sports:

Baseball, Basketball, Crew, Cross Country, Football, Golf, Soccer, Swimming, Tennis, and Track

Women's Spectator Sports:

Basketball, Crew, Cross Country, Golf, Gymnastics, Soccer, Softball, Swimming, Tennis, Track, and Volleyball.

Chapter 14

Memories and Keepsakes

Chapter 14

Memories & Keepsakes

Now that you have been given plenty of ideas on how to make memories with your family, here are some resources to help you preserve these precious memories! We have included a list of scrapbook stores and some of their most popular classes to get you organized and preserving those stacks of pictures. I've even included someone who will make your scrapbook for you! What more could you ask for?

Scrapbook Supplies

Keepsakes By Kelli –Custom Memory Albums

www.kbk-custommemoryalbums.com
If your photographs are in piles, drawers or boxes and you can't imagine trying to fit them all into a scrapbook, you might want to contact Kelli. Using your pictures and memorabilia she will create a contemporary, customized album that you will be proud to display and share for generations to come! Visit her website for pricing and details.

King County

Scrapbook Galaxy @ Ballard Camera
1836 NW Market, Ballard
206-783-1121
www.ballardcamera.com
Hours: Monday-Saturday 9:30am to 6:00pm.
Weekend demonstrations (check website for dates), selection of scrapbooking paper, embossing materials and tools, rubber stamps, paper punches, stickers, photo corners, and more.

Bumble Bee
Located in North Bend
206-683-3394
www.shopbumblebee.com
K-I Memories-modern design, good quality paper and embellishments, coordinated in packs of themes and colors. This is strictly an online store.

Creating A Good Book
9501 State Ave Suite J, Marysville
360-653-5934
www.creatingagoodbook.com
Hours: Monday-Saturday 9:30-8:30, Sunday 12:00pm-5:00pm.
Scrapbooking supplies, paper, punches, embellishments, ribbons, and a large selection of paper.
Classes: Beginners, cards, Croppin' The Night Away, die cut club, paper bag books, etc.

Impress Rubber Stamps-Bellevue
2588 Bellevue Square Mall
425-453-2748
www.impressrubberstamps.com
Hours: Monday-Saturday 9:30am-9:30pm, Sunday 11:00am-7:00pm.
Rubber stamps, 8x11 & 12x12 paper, punches, embellishments for scrapbooks and cards, instructional books, and free demonstrations.
Classes: Stampers Morning & Stampers Night-a free bi-monthly class held on Tuesday mornings, and Wednesday nights plus 10% off same day purchases, Take Ten: basic cards, water colors, wedding, water color sparkle, color pencil class and more.

Impress Rubber Stamps-Tukwila
120 Andover Park E
206-901-9101
www.impressrubberstamps.com
Hours: Monday-Friday 9:30am-9:00pm, Saturday 9:30-5:30, Sunday 11:00am-5:00pm.
Rubber stamps, 8x11 & 12x12 paper, punches, embellishments for scrapbooks and cards, instructional books, and free demonstrations.

Impress Rubber Stamps-Westlake Center
400 Pine St #310, Seattle
206-621-1878
www.impressrubberstamps.com
Hours: Monday-Saturday 9:30am-9:00pm, Sunday 11:00am-6:00pm.
Rubber stamps, 8x11 & 12x12 paper, punches, embellishments for scrapbooks and cards, instructional books, and free demonstrations.
No Classes Available

Impress Rubber Stamps-University Village
2621 NE Village Lane, Seattle
206-526-5818
www.impressrubberstamps.com
Hours: Monday-Saturday 9:30am-9:00pm, Sunday 11:00am-6:00pm.
Rubber stamps, 8x11 & 12x12 paper, punches, embellishments for scrapbooks and cards, instructional books, and free demonstrations.
Classes: Stampers Morning & Stampers Night-a free bi-monthly class held on Tuesday mornings, and Wednesday nights plus 10% off same day purchases, Take Ten: basic cards, water colors, wedding, water color sparkle, color pencil class and more.

InkogNEATo
253-854-6203
www.inkogneato.com
Online scrapbooking and rubber stamps supply. They also carry one-of-a kind memory book kits. View these unique styles online.

Inspired Memories

163 Aurora Ave N, Shoreline

206-542-7737

www.inspiredmemories-wa.com

Hours: Monday- Friday 10:00am-8:00pm, Saturday 10:00am-7:00pm, Sunday 11:00am-5:00pm.

Paper, stickers, albums, adhesives, tools, stamps, and embellishments.

Classes: All levels of scrapbooking, card making, stamping, Scrappin' the Night Away, Little Books for Everyone, kids card classes.

Inspired Memories

21104 International Blvd, SeaTac

206-824-2286

www.inspiredmemories-wa.com

Hours: Monday-Friday 10:00am-8:00pm, Saturday 10:00am-7:00pm, Sunday 11:00am-5:00pm.

Paper, stickers, albums, adhesives, tools, stamps, and embellishments.

Classes: All levels of scrapbooking, card making, stamping, Scrappin' the Night Away, Little Books for Everyone, kids card classes.

The Mad Scrapper

1590 NW Gillman Blvd, Issaquah

425-427-8871

www.madscrapper.com

Hours: Monday-Friday 10:00am-8:00pm, Saturday 10:00am-6:00pm, Sunday 11:00am-5:00pm.

Acid -free stickers, 12 x12 paper, metal embellishments, albums, cardstock, ribbons, and rubber stamps.

Classes: Beginning to advanced, including classes created just special for kids.

Make An Impression

1175 NW Gillman Blvd Suite B 8, Issaquah

425-557-9247

www.makeanimpression.net

Hours: Monday-Thursday 10:00am-6:00pm, Friday 10:00am-8:00pm, Saturday 10:00am-6:00pm, Sunday 11:00am-5:00pm.

Rubber Stamps, embellishments, brass templates for embossing, paper, cardstock, stickers.

Classes: Memory boxes, journals, floral collage, rubber stamping basics, stenciling, and more. Students receive a same day 10% discount on regular priced items.

Monkey Love Rubber Stamps

23 Queen Anne Ave N, Seattle
206-283-7897
Hours: Tuesday-Friday 11:00am-7:00pm, Saturday & Sunday 12:00pm-5:00pm.
Brass templates, ink, embellishments, large selection of paper, punches, markers, buttons, ribbon, and of course, rubber stamps.
Classes: Free make and take classes, mini photo albums, sparkling water, accordion books, cards, seasonal items.

Paper Tree

Bellevue Square
425-451-8035
www.papertreenw.com
Hours: Monday-Saturday 9:30-9:30, Sunday 11:00am-7:00pm.
Complete range of custom invitations and announcements for every occasion. Personal and business stationery, unique gifts, specialty cards, gift wrap and more.

Papyrus

5 locations
www.papyrusonline.com
They carry a scrapbooking line called, "Doojigees", and also fine stationary, frames, and box cards. They do custom printing for announcements and invitations.

Papyrus-Bellevue
124 Bellevue Square
425-455-2422
Hours: Monday-Saturday 9:30am-9:30pm, Sunday 11:00am-7:00pm.

Papyrus
1210 4th Ave, Seattle
206-464-1505
Hours: Monday-Friday 9:00am-6:00pm, Saturday 10:00am-5:00pm.

Papyrus-Pacific Place
600 Pine St 3rd Floor #340, Seattle
206-382-9172
Hours: Monday-Saturday 9:00am-9:00pm, Sunday 11:00-6:00pm.

Papyrus-Northgate Mall
401 NE Northgate Way, Suite #563, Seattle
206-363-8055
Hours: Monday-Saturday 10:00am-9:00pm, Sunday 11:00am-7:00pm.

Papyrus-University Village

2621 NE University Village St #Q621, Seattle

206-523-0055

Hours: Monday-Saturday 9:30am-9:00pm, Sunday 10:00am-7:00pm.

Precious Memories

13317 NE 175th St, Woodinville

425-488-3911

www.preciousmemoriesscrapbooking.com

Hours: Monday -Friday 10:00am-8:00pm, Saturday 10:00am-6:00pm, Sunday 12:00pm-5:00pm.

This store makes scrapbooking easy with pre-made packets. You'll find a collection of packets for holidays, seasons, special occasions, nature, and more.

Rubber Soul

Redmond Towne Center

425-882-3333

www.rubbersoul.com

Hours: Monday-Saturday 10:00am-9:00pm, Saturday 11:00am-7:00pm.

Vintage stationary, ribbons, card sets, rubber stamps, Make And Take(free), and creations for children, scrapbook and journal art, and more.

Classes: Water colors, white on white, basics, holiday, seasonal, calligraphy, children's card making, and much more.

Scrapbook Nook

26129 104th Ave SE, Kent

253-859-9040

www.scrapbooknook.info/

Hours: Monday- Friday 10:00am-9:00pm, Saturday 10:00am-6:00pm.

Die cuts, instant letters, stickers, scrapbooking tools, paper, and more.

Classes: Basics, Moonlighters, Accordion Flip Book, Razzle Dazzle Bazzill, and more.

Scrapbook Storey

2156 S 314th, Federal Way

253-529-1500

Hours: Monday- Saturday 10:00am-6:00pm, Sunday 10:00am-5:00pm.

Scrapbooking items including stickers, embellishments, 12 x 12 paper, albums, etc.

Classes: Seasonal themes, monochromatic, Disney, wedding, scrapbooking with accessories, baby themes, moonlight classes meet bi-monthly Friday nights and includes 10% off same day purchase plus door prizes. Free Super Scrapper card. Spend $50, receive $5 purchase.

The Bee's Knees Scrapbook

15100 SE 38th S, Bellevue

425-614-2518

www.thebeeskneesscrapbooks.com

Hours: Monday-Friday 10:00am-7:00pm, Saturday 10:00am-5:00pm, Sunday 11:00am-4:00pm

Classes: Delightfully Disney, Braggin' About Baby, fabric paper, mini books, seasonal themes, and basics.

The Polka Dot Stop

909 SW 152nd St, Burien

206-242-9892

www.thepolkadotstop.com

Hours: Tuesday- Friday 11:00am-6:00pm, Saturday 10:00am-5:00pm, Sunday 12:00pm-4:00pm

Stamps, 12 x 12 paper, albums, ribbon, stickers, punches, inks, cards, pens, etc. Sign up for the frequent shopping list: Spend $150, receive $20 in free merchandise.

Classes: Paper Iris folding, basic stamp and scrapbooking, punch, cookbook, etc.

Unique Creations Scrap & Stamp

18111 East Valley Hwy, Kent

425-257-3707

Hours: Monday-Saturday 10:00am-6:00pm, Sunday 12:00pm-4:00pm

Classes: In fall, winter & spring

Snohomish County

Fun Stamps

18920 28th Ave W, Lynnwood

425-670-6759

www.funstamps.net

Hours: Monday & Wednesday 10:00am-8:00pm. Tuesday, Thursday, Friday, & Saturday 10:00am-6:00pm, Sunday 12:00pm-5:00pm

You'll find a large collected of stamps, plus tags, stamping, kits, punches, eyelets, brushes, watercolor tools, and more.

Classes: Basic stamping, Bold & Beautiful Textures, holiday, pencils, watercolor, plus.

Lasting Memories
3333 184th St SW Suite X (near Mervyn's) Lynnwood
425-670-3721
www.lasting-memories.com
Hours: Monday-Friday 9:30am-8:00pm, Saturday 9:30am-6:00pm
Come in every Tuesday come in for a free Make 'n Take page, plus weekly internet specials, over 400 die cuts, color copies, stickers, ribbon, and a huge selection of 8 x 11 and 12 x12 paper.
Classes: Girls Night Out, Moonlight Madness, Delightfully Disney, Getting Started, Beyond Basics, and much more.

Papyrus-Alderwood Mall
3000 184th St SW Suite #562, Lynnwood
425-771-5830
www.papyrusonline.com
Hours: Monday-Saturday 10:00am-9:30pm, Sunday 11:00am-7:00pm
They carry a scrapbooking line called, "Doojigees", and also fine stationary, frames, box cards, and do custom printing for announcements and invitations.

Scrapbook Zone
9621 NW Mickelberry Rd, Silverdale
360-692-5707
www.scrapbookzonewa.com
Hours: Monday-Friday 10:00am-7:00pm, Saturday 10:00am-6:00pm, Sunday 12:00pm-4:00pm
Stamps, 12 x 12 paper, albums, ribbon, stickers, punches, inks, cards, pens, etc.
Classes: Super crops, chalk and ink, holiday, color blocking,

Stampin' In The Rain
Country Village
23718 7th Ave SE, Bothell
425-408-9050
www.stampin-in-the-rain.com
Hours: Tuesday-Saturday 11:00am-6:00pm, Sunday 11:00am-5:00pm
Classes: Glitz Spritz & Moon Shadow Mist, Flag Tag books, calligraphy, Sparkling Water, all occasion cards, thank you cards, photo album, and more.

Stamper's Ink

11419 19th Ave St SE Suite 103, Everett

425-316-3545

Hours: Monday-Thursday 10:00am-8:00pm, Friday and Saturday 10:00am-6:00p, Sunday 12:00pm-5:00pm

Classes: Twinkle H2o, dry embossing, scrapbooking pages (2), cards, and more. Students receive 10% off same day purchase.

The Paper Zone

9423 Evergreen Way, Everett

425-355-7703

www.paperzone.com

Hours: Monday-Friday 8:00am-7:00pm, Saturday 10:00am-6:00pm. Sunday 11:00am-6:00pm.

Great Photographers

Bella Photography

Redmond

425-836-4080

bellaphotography@hotmall.com

www.bellaphotographynw.com

Hours: By appointment

Specialty: infants, toddlers, children, siblings.

See ad in back

Christine's Baby Photography

P.O. Box 77328, Seattle

206-352-9485

www.beautifulbabyphotos.com
Hours: By appointment only.

Specialty: Baby portraits: Birth to toddlers.

Folk Photography

10315 Wallingford Ave N, Seattle

206-313-7610

www.folkphotography.com

Hours: By appointment.

Specialty: Children's portraits.

JC Penny Co
Northgate Mall
401 NE Northgate Way Suite 475, Seattle
206-364-2232
www.jcpenny.com
Hours: Monday-Friday 10:00am-7:00pm, Saturday 10:00am-6:00pm, Sunday 10:00am-5:00pm.
Specialty: Children's photography.

Jennifer Loomis Photography
Seattle
206-329-4772
www.jenniferloomis.com
Hours: By appointment only.
Specialty: Award winning art photographer specializing in pregnancy, newborns, & families.

Photazz
1014 Bellevue Square, Bellevue
425-635-0200
www.photoazz.com
Hours: Monday-Saturday 10:00am-6:30pm, Sunday 11:00am-5:30pm.
Specialty: Babies & children. $99 Special Baby Plan: Birth to 9 years (pictures every 3 months).

Teddi Yaeger Photography
206-856-7960
www.teddiyaeger.com
Specialty: Babies, and pregnancy.

Tonya Davis Photography
31 NE 69th St, Seattle
206-619-5221
www.tonyadavisphotgraphy.com
Hours: Call for appointment.
Specialty: Children & families.

Yuen Lui Studio
900 Virginia St, Seattle
206-622-0338
www.yuenluistudio.com
Hours: Tuesday-Saturday 9:00am-5:30pm.
Specialty: Children, babies & families.

Yuen Lui Studio
924 Northeast 63rd St, Seattle
206-523-5707
www.yuenluistudio.com
Hours: Tuesday-Thursday 9:00am-8:00pm, Wednesday-Friday 9:00am-5:30pm.
Specialty: Children, babies, & families.

Yuen Lui Studio
10855 NE 8th St, Bellevue
425-453-1606
www.yuenluistudio.com
Hours: Monday-Wednesday, Friday-Saturday 9:00am-6:00pm, Tuesday 9:00am-8:00pm, Sunday 10:00am-5:00pm.
Cost: Moderate, ask about the special Heritage Plan.

Snohomish County

Acclaimed Photography – Kerri Kirshner

Bothell

425-481-6555

www.acclaimedphoto.com

Hours: By appointment.

Cost: Moderate.

Specialty: Photographs children, babies, & maternity.

Brian Thompson Photography

360-568-1167

Snohomish

www.brian-photo.com

Specialty: Children, families, events.

Chapters Photography

23716 8th Ave SE, Bothell

425-415-1267

Hours: Monday-Thursday 10:00am-4:30pm, Friday-Saturday 10:00am-6:00pm.

Specialty: Babies, children, families.

Fowler Portraits

23003 97th Ave W, Edmonds

425-776-4426

www.FowlerPortraits.com

Hours: By appointment: Tuesday-Friday 9:00am-5:00pm, Saturday 10:00am-1:00pm.

Specialty: Experienced children's photographer, also family portraits.

JC Penney Co

Alderwood Mall, Lynnwood

425-771-2107

www.jcpenneyportraits.com

Hours: Monday-Friday 10:00am-7:00pm, Saturday 10:00am-6:00pm, Sunday 11:00am-5:00pm.

Specialty: Children & families.

Kiddie Kandids @ Babies R Us
19500 Alderwood Mall 544, Lynnwood
425-967-0060
www.kiddiekandids.com
Hours: Monday-Saturday 9:30am-8:00pm, Sunday 11:00am-6:00pm.
Specialty: Newborn and toddler portraits. Customers can add specialty borders and custom text to portraits, or purchase products like mugs, mouse pads, totes, holiday ornaments, etc. Their studios are fully-digital, so you can take your portraits home the same day.
See ad in back

LJ Peters Photography
901 1st St, Snohomish
360-568-8126
800-555-8126
www.ljpetersphotography.com
Hours: Monday-Friday 10:00am-5:30pm
Specialty: Families, children, and digital imaging.

Spectrum Photography
20828 53rd Ave W, Lynnwood
206-227-9487
www.spectrum-photo.net
Hours: Monday-Friday 10:00am-5:30pm - by appointment.
Specialty: Specializes in baby and child photography.

Target Stores
9601 Market Place, Lake Stevens
425-397-9862
www.target.com
Hours: Monday-Friday 10:00am-7:00pm, Saturday-Sunday 10:00am-4:00pm.
Specialty: Children.

Yuen Lui Studios
18411 Alderwood Mall Parkway, Lynnwood
425-771-3423
www.yuenluistudio.com
Hours: Monday-Friday 9:00am-5:50pm, Sunday 10:00am-5:00pm. Extended Fall hours.
Specialty: Babies, children and families.

Wal-Mart Portrait Studios
1400 164th SW, Lynnwood
425-741-8748
Hours: Sunday-Friday 10:00am-7:00pm, Saturday 9:00am-8:00pm.
Specialty: Children's portraits.

Wal-Mart Portrait Studios
8924 Quilceda Blvd, Marysville
360-657-4393
Hours: Tuesday-Saturday 10:00am-7:00pm, Sunday-Monday 10:00am-4:00pm. Call for an appointment.
Specialty: Children's portraits.

Chapter 15

Feeding and Clothing the Crew

Chapter 15

Feeding & Clothing the Crew

Like everyone else, I've tried to figure out how to save money on groceries. Here are some great ideas, and even better…people to help.

Feeding The Crew

Did you know...

- Children who eat 3+ meals per week together as a family have healthier diets.
- Families who eat together are less likely to smoke, abuse alcohol, receive top grades in school, and have a better self image

Money Saving Grocery Tips

Just about everyone would like to save money on groceries. It's one our highest monthly expenses. Here are some great ideas, and even better...people to help.

Pick the Right Store

Even though stores are becoming increasingly diversified in what they sell, each has a core strength. Quickly learn the core strengths of the stores near you. Basic grocery stores, for example, are excellent at providing product and price selection, frequent shoppers programs, and double coupon days. However, their bulk store counterparts have their own niche of offering good pricing on high-volume, name brand non-perishables. National drugstore chains and superstores are best for health and beauty products.

Know Before You Go

Never make a trip to the store without making a list and checking your inventory. This act alone will save you time and money. It's also a good idea to quickly assemble any coupons you plan to use.

Eat First

Statistics show you spend about 17% more when shopping while hungry. Grocery stores have learned over the years about the subtle influences of smells and locations. This can include the aroma of freshly baked bread, the site of a perfectly seasoned, slow-turning chicken, or maybe the intrigue of new munchies, strategically placed on the end-cap of an isle. We've all fallen for them. Everything looks good when our stomachs are crying out for food. If you're shopping with your children, be sure their little stomachs are also full.

Be Ad Savvy

Check out the ads each week. They often come in the Sunday paper, or during the week in the mail. I have personally bookmarked the website of my favorite grocery stores where they list the local ads online. This is less messy and paper free. You may have already figured out that stores will often mark a few of its products down low to attract you to their store, in hopes of recouping the cost as you stay and complete your shopping list at their store. This often works since most people prefer one-stop shopping. The key is to watch for the best buys, and plan to pick up those items on the way to somewhere else (dropping the kids off at school, on the way to work, etc.)

Coupons and Rebates

It takes work to save money on groceries, but coupons and rebates are worth the time. The best way to use them is to first, find them, and then plan your menus for the week based on what you find. If you don't find a use for a particular coupon, toss it. Also, be aware that many items listed in the weekly circulars are not that good of a deal-the best are usually on the first page or two.

Store Brands – Try it, You May Like it!

Generic is a thing of the past. Besides the social stigma, most of the stuff tasted pretty bad. Grocery marketers found that this lead to, at best, a reluctant customer base. Thankfullyy, generic has evolved into store brands. These give you a more interesting label and much better taste. While not all are as perfect- each requires some experimenting-many are worthy of our kitchen shelves. The biggest difference is in the price, where you will routinely notice 25%-50% savings off the name-brand products.

Fight Against Impulse Buying

As was stated before, never go into a store without a plan. Even if you are only picking up a few things, put them on a list, plus a dollar figure you plan on paying. Another important consideration is time. Where possible, give yourself plenty of time to quickly scan and compare prices. However, don't give yourself so much time you end up wandering the isles.

Comparison Shopping

Once or twice a year, take a few hours to visit stores and compare prices. Remember to compare apples to apples so that your assessment is accurate. Be sure to compare the base price, not the sale price. One helpful thing to look for in comparison shopping with a store is to look at the unit price. This will show you what the product costs per ounce or pound and allows you to quickly compare two competing products or brands. Another consideration is the expiration or "use by" date found on most perishable products (ie. milk, eggs, cottage cheese). Be sure the sale item isn't marked down because it's expiring in two days (unless you plan to consume it that quickly).

Beware of Gimmicks

Buying 10 bottles of catsup for $10 isn't the same value as 10 boxes of cereal for $10. Both sound like a deal, but they are never equal and some aren't even much of a deal at all. It's also important to understand the store's rules on buying multiple items .The sale may cleverly advertise buy 10 for $10, but it usually doesn't mean you have to buy that quantity to get that deal. Check with the store's customer service first, but it's usually possible to buy three for #3 or seven for $7.

The Moment of Purchase

Stores offer hundreds of thousands of individual items for sale and their prices change daily. Because of human error, it is very common for a price to not get changes accurately in the store's computer system. Be sure to watch the scanning items for these mistakes, and try to quickly review the receipt before you leave the store, or if you're shopping with little ones, after you're back in the car. Once you leave the parking lot, it's usually not worth it to come back and dispute your bill.

Control the Experience

It isn't always possible to shop alone, but we have all seen it, maybe even been there ourselves: A mother with small children enters the store, the pleading and begging start almost immediately. Before long, mom has either left in frustration with only half the shopping done or the kids have persuaded her to buy $20 worth of items not on her list. On the other hand, it's good for children to learn good grocery store behavior and shopping techniques. Try taking one child at a time (maybe two) so you can both manage and control the experience, and teach good shopping behavior.

Other Great Ideas

Try Mealsharing

If you have some good friends in the neighborhood or close by, this idea might work out perfectly for you and your family. It may sound a bit different, but I know of several families who have tried and loved this idea.

Here's how it works: Each family takes a turn cooking for the other two families one night per week. The catering family shops, prepares and delivers the meal for a total of twelve people or family members. Busy schedules are taken into account, so the catering schedule often changes on a weekly basis. The menus are all agreed upon in advance with likes, dislikes, and food allergies accounted for. The meals can be well balanced with a salad, bread, and an entire entrée.

Groups who have tried this agreed that the additional cooking one night per week was worth the two nights off. They were also encouraged by spending less than average on groceries each week. It actually costs less for the three day period, even though they spent more on their assigned nights because buying in larger quantities often means lower prices.

Cook For A Month In Advance

The main idea: Cooking a month's worth of meals and side dishes during one eight-hour session and then storing them in the freezer. You can end up spending less than $150 a month on family dinners. You can also do a small cooking session for breakfast foods like waffles and muffins.

Choose your recipes in accordance with the weekly or monthly supermarket circulars, then plan your once-a-month cooking around what is on sale. Let's say you're going to make several chicken recipes with boneless chicken breast, it helps to buy chicken on sale at $1.99/lb instead of $3.99/lb.

Before a marathon cooking session on Friday or Saturday, you would do as much preparation as possible. This includes chopping and grating vegetables, and browning ground bee.

If you're just starting out, the idea of cooking a month's worth of food can be overwhelming. Try a mini-session to prepare food for the next week or two. Instead of making one tray of lasagna, make three, and freeze two. When you take your cooking to the monthly level, try taking 15 recipes and doubling them so you'll only be eating the same meal twice. If you need some ideas for frozen meals, take a look in your grocer's freezer to see what prepared meals freeze well.

Good Books for Freezer Cooking

Freezer Cooking Manual from 30 Day Gourmet: A month of Meals Made Easy

Frozen Assets: How to Cook for a Day and Eat for a Month

Cookin' Freezer Meals

www.dvo.com/freezer_recipes.html
Pay $14.95 and download 100 perfect freezer meal recipes.

Local Meal Preparation Kitchens

Dinner's Ready
Locations throughout the Puget Sound
425-493-0780
www.dinnersready.com

Month of Meals
18005 NE 68th St, Redmond
425-867-1516
www.monthofmeals.com

Other Resources

The Grocery Game

www.thegrocerygame.com
Save a bundle on groceries each week playing the Grocery Game. The concept is simple, and "Teri" does all of the work. Each week, print "Teri's List"' off of the Grocery Game website. Teri finds the sales, coupons, and secret sales of the major stores in your area.

Teri recommends stockpiling. Because grocery stores want you to shop weekly, you may get a few bargains, but you are forced to buy things that are high priced because you need them that week. Teri's Shopping List is designed each week to stock your shelves the cheapest way possible. After you stick with the list for a few weeks, you will begin to see how much you have and how little you have spent, with very little effort. Soon your personal "Need" list gets shorter and shorter as you begin to sop from your own stockpile.

Teri also recommends saving coupons for when the deals are HOT! Redeem them during the week they are already on special.

Websites to Visit

The concept is the same for all of these websites. They provide printable coupons for big name brands and services. Browse around for products that you routinely buy and snag a coupon.

www.coolsavings.com

www.couponcart.com

www.eversave.com

Clothing The Crew-Specialty Shops

Have you ever wondered why everyone else has really unique things that you just can't seem to find in stores? It's because they shop in some of our locally owned stores. Take an afternoon and browse through some of these great hidden treasures. You'll also find the information for well known stores needed for the majority of baby and mother needs, and baby proofing businesses to keep your little one safe.

King County

Babies R Us
17500 Sounth Center Pkwy, Tukwila
206-575-1819
Hours: Daily, 9:30am-9:30pm

Baby Depot At Burlington Coat Factory
1101 Supermall Way, Auburn
253-735-9964
Hours: Monday-Saturday 10:00am-9:00pm, Sunday 11:00am-6:00pm.

Birth & Beyond
317 NW Gilman Blvd, Issaquah
425-392-6665
Hours: Monday-Friday 10:00am-6:00pm, Saturday and Sunday 11:00am-5:00pm

Birth & Beyond
2610 E Madison, Seattle
206-324-4831
Hours: Monday-Friday 10:00am-6:00pm, Saturday and Sunday 11:00am-5:00pm.

Go To Your Room
13000 Bellevue-Redmond Rd, Bellevue
425-453-2990
Hours: Monday-Saturday 10:00am-6:00pm, Sunday 12:00am-5:00pm.
See ad in back

Carter's Childrenswear
1101 Supermall Way, Auburn
253-804-3155
Hours: Monday-Saturday 10:00am-9:00pm, Sunday 11:00am-6:00pm.

Clover
5335 Ballard Ave NW, Seattle
206-782-0715
www.clovertoys.com
Hours: Monday-Saturday 10:00am-6:00pm, Sunday 10:00am-5:00pm.
Items: Classic toys and games, handcrafted toys, art supplies, science kits, natural fiber bedding and clothing

Country Kids Boutique
1540 Cole, Enumclaw
360-825-4066
Hours: Monday-Sunday 10:00am-8:00pm.
Items: Bedding, clothes, stuffed animals, and blankets.

Fancy Frocks & Fairy Tales
Country Villlage
23718 7th Ave SE Suite C, Bothell
425-483-1191
www.fancy-frocks.com
Hours: Monday-Saturday 10:00am-6:00pm, Sunday 11:00am-5:00pm.

Flora And Henri Outlet
705 Broadway E, Seattle
206-323-2942
Hours: Monday-Friday: 9:00am-5:00pm

Flora And Henri
717 Pine, Seattle
206-749-9698
Hours: Monday-Saturday10:00am-6:00pm, Sunday 12:00am-5:00pm

Gymboree
2 Locations
Pacific Place
206-287-1991
Hours: Monday-Saturday: 10:00am-8pm, Sunday: 11:00am-6:00pm
(Summer Only) Monday-Saturday: 9:30am-9:00pm, Sunday: 11:00am-6:00pm

Southcenter Mall
206-246-8997
Hours: Monday-Saturday: 10:00am-9:30pm. Sunday:11:00am-7:00pm

Hanna Anderson Retail Store
2681 University Village Ct NE, Seattle
206-729-1099
Hours: Monday-Saturday: 9:30am-9:00pm, Sunday: 11:00am-6:00pm

KidsGear
1420 5th, Seattle
206-624-0756
Hours: Monday-Sunday 10:00am-6:00pm

Lamb's Ears
820 102nd NE, Bellevue
425-688-1080
Hours: Monday-Saturday 10:00am-6:00pm

Limited Too
3 Locations
Bellevue Square
425-455-4945
Hours: Monday-Saturday 9:30am-9:30pm, Sunday 11:00am-7:00pm.

Southcenter Mall, Tukwila
206-242-1508
Hours: Monday- Saturday 10:00am-9:30pm, Sunday 11:00am-6:00pm.

Redmond Towne Square
425-558-7571
Hours: Monday-Saturday10:00am-9:00pm, Sunday 11:00am-6:00pm.

Oh Baby
1504 Cole St, Enumclaw
360-825-9565
Hours: Monday-Friday 10:00am-5:30pm, Saturday 10:00am-4:00pm.

Oilily
133 Bellevue Square
425-688-0663
Hours: Monday-Saturday: 9:30am-9:30pm, Sunday: 11:00am-7:00pm.

Once Upon A Child
26121 104th SE, Kent
253-850-7585
Hours: Monday-Friday 10:00am-7:00pm, Saturday 10:00am-6:00pm, Sunday 12:00pm-5:00pm.

OshKosh B'Gosh
17953 Gardert Way NE, Woodinville
425-483-1997
Hours: Monday-Saturday 10:00am-9:00pm, Sunday 11:00am-6:00pm.

OshKosh B'Gosh Factory Outlet
4092 Factoria Square mall SE, Bellevue
425-957-7217
Hours: Monday-Saturday 10:00am-9:00pm, Sunday 11:00am-6:00pm.

Rave Girl
832 Southcenter Mall, Tukwila
206-244-9099
Hours: Monday-Saturday 10:00am-9:30pm, Sunday: 11:00am-7:00pm

Rising Stars
7404 Greenwood N, Seattle
206-781-0138
Hours: Monday-Saturday 10:00am-6:00pm, Sunday 10:00am-4:00pm.
Features locally made clothing & toys.

Sweet Pea's
4822 Ranier S, Seattle
206-722-1031
Hours: Tuesday, Thursday, Friday 10:00am-5:30pm, Wednesday 10:00am-7:00pm, Saturday 10:30am-5:00pm.
See ad in back

Talbot's Kids
207 Bellevue Square
425-450-3375
Hours: Monday-Saturday 9:30am-9:30pm, Sunday 11:00am-7:00pm.

The Children's Shop
4114 E Madison, Seattle
206-328-7121
Hours: Monday-Friday 10:00am-6:00pm, Saturday 10:00am-5:00pm.
See ad in back

Snohomish County

Babies R Us The Baby Superstore
19500 Alderwood Mall Pkwy, Lynnwood
425-672-3220
Hours: 9:30am-9:30pm

Burlington Coat Factory
24111 Hwy 99, Edmonds
425-776-2221
Hours: Monday-Saturday 10:00am-9:00pm, Sunday 11:00am-6:00pm.

Gap Kids & Baby Gap
3000-184th SW, Lynnwood
425-776-8214
Hours: Monday-Saturday 10:00am-9:30pm, Sunday 11:00am-7:00pm.

Go To Your Room
13000 Bel-Red Rd, Bellevue
425-453-2990
Hours: Monday-Saturday 10:00am-6:00pm, Sunday 12:00am-5:00pm.
See ad in back

Gymboree Store
Alderwood Mall, Lynnwood
425-771-4558
Hours: Monday-Saturday 10:00am-9:30pm, Sunday 11:00am-7:00pm.

Hanna Andersson Outlet
13620 NE 175th St, Woodinville
425-485-7998
Hours: Monday-Saturday 10:00am-6:00pm, Sunday 11:00am-5:00pm.

Just Babies
11524 Mukilteo Speedway Suite 104, Mukilteo
425-315-8888
Hours: Wednesday-Saturday 10:00am-5:00pm.

Kinder Britches
422 Main ST, Edmonds
425-778-7600
Hours: Monday-Friday 10:00am-6:00pm, Saturday 10:00am-5:30pm, Sunday 12:00am-4:00pm.

Merry Go Round
1014 116th Avenue, Bellevue
425-454-1610
Hours: Monday-Saturday 10:00am-6:00pm, Sunday 12:00am-5:00pm.

The Children's Attic
9019 Evergreen Way, Everett
425-355-0169
Hours: Tuesday –Saturday 11:30am- 5:00pm.

Resale Children's Clothing & Furniture

King County

A Child's Closet
5025 25th NE, Seattle
206-985-4402
www.achildscloset.com
Hours: Monday-Saturday 10:00am-6:00pm, Sunday: 12:00pm-4:00pm.
Resale Items: Children's clothing, shoes, toys, baby gear, saucers, and high chairs.
New: Raingear, RobEez baby shoes, baby joggers, name brand clothing.

Again & A Gain
4832 California Ave SW, Seattle
206-933-2060
Hours: Monday-Saturday: 10:00am-6:00pm.
Resale Items: Children clothes, maternity clothes, books, strollers, cribs, shoes, toys, and games

Bootyland
1321 E Pine, Seattle
206-328-0636
Hours: Monday 12:00pm-3:00pm, Tuesday-Saturday 11:00am-5:30pm, Sunday 12:00pm-5:00pm.
Resale Items: Children's clothes, shoes, maternity clothing, new handmade vintage clothing, diaper covers, and organic slings.
Walk-In Consignment: Tuesday-Friday, and Sunday 1:00pm-3:00pm.

The Basement Exchange
15705 NE Main St, Duvall
425-788-5170
Hours: Tuesday-Saturday 10:00am-6:00pm.
Resale Items: Children's clothing.

Heaven Sent Children's Resale
1200 24th, Federal Way
253-946-2229
Hours: Monday-Friday 10:00am-6:00pm, Saturday 10:00am-5:00pm, Sunday 12:00pm-5:00pm
Resale Items: Children's clothes, maternity clothes toys, books, furniture, swings, high chairs.

Kids By Gosh
26834 Maple Valley Hwy Suite 1, Maple Valley
425-432-9336
Hours: Monday-Friday 10:00am-7:00pm, Saturday 10:00am-6:00pm, Sunday 10:00am-6:00pm.
Resale Items: Children's clothing, accessories, and toys.

Kids On 45th
1720 N 45th, Seattle
206-633-5437
Hours: Monday-Saturday 10:00am-6:00pm, Sunday: 11:00am-5:00pm
Resale Items: Children's clothing (sizes 0-10), strollers, high chairs, big toys.

Kym's Kiddy Corner
11721 15th NE, Seattle
206-361-5974
www.kymskiddycorner.com
Hours: Monday-Saturday: 10:00am-5:30pm
New and Used Items: Furniture, toys, clothes (sizes 0-10), shoes, strollers, etc.
See ad in back

Labels
7212 Greenwood N, Seattle
206-781-1194
Hours: Tuesday-Saturday: 10:00am-6:00pm, Thursday: 10:00am-8:00pm, Sunday 12:00pm-5:00pm.
Resale Items: Children's contemporary clothing.

Ladybugs & Babybugs
262 S 3rd St, Buckley
360-829-2220
Hours: Monday, Tuesday, Thursday, and Friday 10:00am-5:30pm, Wednesday 10:00am-6:30pm, Saturday 10:00am-4:00pm.
Resale Items: Children's clothes, maternity clothes, nursing clothes, toys, strollers, high chairs, infant swings, and furniture.

Me 'N Mom's Consignment Boutique
2821-B NW Marker St, Ballard
206-781-9449
Hours: Monday-Friday: 9:30am-6:00pm, Saturday-Sunday: 10:30am-5:00pm
Items: Quality new & used furniture and clothing for mothers and children.

Saturday's Child Consignment
18012 Bothell-Everett Hwy, Bothell
425-486-6716
Hours: Monday-Saturday: 10:00am-5:00pm, Sunday: 12:00am-4:00pm.
Resale Items: Children's clothing, maternity clothes, toys, strollers, shoes, books, and games.

Sweet Cheeks Consignment
13635 First Ave S, Burien
206-241-0540
Hours: Monday-Saturday:10:00am-5:00pm.
Resale Items: Children's clothing, furniture, toys, and books.

The Pregnant Pause
2709 E Madison St, Seattle
206-726-8555
Hours: Monday: 12:30pm-3:30pm, Tuesday-Saturday: 10:00am-5:00pm.
Resale Items: Children's clothing, toys, strollers, high chairs, changing tables, maternity clothing, and nursing clothing.
Plus: Hand-sewn quilts, and knitted baby items

Tree House For Kids
15742 Redmond Way, Redmond
425-885-1145
Hours: Monday-Wednesday: 9:00am-6:00pm, Thursday: 9:00am-8:00pm, Friday 9:00am-6:00pm, Saturday: 10:00am-5:00pm, Sunday: 1:00pm-5:00pm.
Resale Items: Children's clothes (sizes 0-14) and accessories, shoes, toys, strollers, car seats, books, and costumes.
New: Children's clothing, RobEez, dance clothes, dance shoes, raincoats, and umbrellas.

Snohomish County

A Children's Warehouse

10809 Mukilteo Speedway, Mukilteo
425-349-1919
Hours: Tuesday-Thursday: 10:00am-5:30pm, Friday: 10:00am-4:00pm, Saturday: 11:00am-5:00pm.
Resale Items: Children's clothes, furniture, toys, and maternity clothes.

City Kids Quality Consignment

9726 Edmonds Way, Edmonds
425-775-7627
Hours: Monday-Friday 10:00am-5:00pm, Saturday 11:00am-5:00pm.
Resale Items: Children's clothes, maternity clothes, furniture, strollers, swings, toys.

Just For Kids

7510 Beverly Blvd, Everett
425-347-5002
Hours: Monday-Saturday 9:00am-9:00pm, Sunday 10:00am-6:00pm.
Resale Items: Children's Clothing (up to size 16), maternity, bouncers, bassinets, strollers, etc.

Kids Exchange

1339 State Ave, Marysville
360-659-6040
Hours: Monday-Saturday 10:00am-4:00pm.
Resale Items: Children's Clothing, toys, equipment.

Saturday's Child

18012 Bothell-Everett Hwy, Bothell
425-486-6716
Hours: Monday-Saturday 10:00am-5:00pm, Sunday 12:00am-4:00pm.
Resale Items: Children's clothing, maternity clothes, toys, strollers, shoes, books, and games.

Children's Furniture

King County

Babies R Us
17500 Sounth Center Pkwy, Tukwila
206-575-1819
Hours: 9:30am-9:30pm.

Baby Depot At Burlington Coat Factory
1101 Supermall Way, Auburn
253-735-9964
Hours: Monday-Saturday 10:00am-9:00pm, Sunday 11:00am-6:00pm.

Bellini Children's Designer Furniture
10635 NE 8th St, Bellevue
425-644-8288
Hours: Monday-Saturday 10:00am-6:00pm, Sunday 12:00pm-5:00pm.

Continental's Kids Rooms
2111 1st Ave, Seattle
206-441-1822
Hours: Monday, and Friday 9:30am-7:00pm, Tuesday, Wednesday, and Thursday 9:30am-6:00pm. Saturday 9:00am-5:30pm, Sunday 12:00pm-4:30pm.

Go To Your Room
13000 Bellevue-Redmond Rd, Bellevue
425-453-2990
Hours: Monday-Saturday 10:00am-6:00pm, Sunday 12:00am-5:00pm.
See ad in back

***KC's Woodshop**
206-244-5451
www.kcwoodshop.com
Hours:
Handcrafted bunk beds.

***Merry Go Round**
11111 NE 8th, Bellevue
425-454-1610
www.merrygoroundkids.com
Hours: Monday-Saturday 10:00am-6:00pm, Sunday 12:00am-5:00pm.

***Merry Go Round**
1014 116th Ave NE, Bellevue
Hours: Monday-Saturday 10:00am-6:00pm, Sunday 12:00am-5:00pm.

Pottery Barn Kids
302 Bellevue Square, Bellevue
425-451-2966
Hours: Monday-Saturday 9:30am-9:30pm, Sunday 11:00am-7:00pm.

The Land Of Nod
University Village
2660 NE 49th, Seattle
206-527-9900
Hours: Monday-Friday 10:00am-9:00pm, Saturday 10:00am-7:00pm, Sunday 11:00am-6:00pm.

The Tin Horse
1815 N 45th, Seattle
206-547-9966
Hours: Monday-Friday 10:00am-8:00pm, Saturday 10:00am-6:00pm, Sunday 12:00am-5:00pm.

Snohomish County

Babies R Us The Baby Superstore
19500 Alderwood Mall Pkwy, Lynnwood
425-672-3220
Hours: 9:30am-9:30pm

Burlington Coat Factory
24111 Hwy 99, Edmonds
425-776-2221
Hours: Monday-Saturday 10:00am-9:00pm, Sunday 11:00am-6:00pm.

Baby-Proofing

One Safe Home
253-735-4709

Safety For Toddlers
425-487-3460
www.safety4toddlers.com

Maternity Clothes

Birth And Baby
www.birthandbaby.com

Designer Maternity Factory A
10676 NE 8th, Bellevue
425-451-1945
Hours: Monday-Thursday 10:00am-7:30pm, Friday and Saturday 10:00am-6:00pm.

Mimi's Maternity
Bellevue Square
425-452-6094
Hours: Monday-Saturday 9:30am-9:30pm, Sunday 11:00am-7:00pm.

Mimi's Maternity
Westlake Center, Seattle
206-624-9494
Hours: Monday-Saturday 9:30am-9:00pm, Sunday 11:00am-6:00pm.

Motherhood Maternity
Bellevue Square
425-454-1355
Hours: Monday-Saturday 9:30am-9:30pm, Sunday 11:00am-7:00pm.

Motherhood Maternity
442 Southcenter Mall, Tukwila
206-246-7111
Hours: Monday-Saturday 10:00am-9:30pm, Sunday 10:30am-7:30pm.

Motherhood Maternity Outlet
Supermall of The Great Northwest, Auburn
253-833-9025
Hours: Monday-Saturday 10:00am-9:00pm, Sunday 11:00am-6:00pm.

Village Maternity (& Breastfeeding Supply)
2635 NE University Village Mall
206-523-5167
www.villagematernity.com
Hours: Monday-Saturday 9:30am-9:00pm, Sunday 11:00am-6:00pm.

Chapter 16

Health and Childcare

Chapter 16

Health & Childcare

Because finding all of the health resources available can be a maze of confusion, this chapter combines them into one place. Read on to find state health resources, immunization information, and more.

Pediatrician Guide

How to Select A Pediatrician

Most parents and children develop close and lasting relationships with their pediatrician. If you select a pediatrician who matches your personality and needs, working together to keep your child healthy will prove to be an enjoyable experience.

Your pediatrician will become much more than a person who cares for your child when he or she is sick. Your pediatrician will be a friend who offers reassurance, advice and guidance throughout your child's years of growth and development.

Things to Consider

Before beginning the selection process, parents should think about what things are most important to them when choosing a pediatrician.

- Would you feel more comfortable dealing with an older doctor or a younger doctor?
- Would you prefer a male or female physician?
- Is it important for the doctor's office to be close to your home or work?
- Does your health insurance plan limit your choice of physicians?

When you've determined your preferences, there are several sources you can use to find the names of specific doctors. Your obstetrician, friends and relatives may all have suggestions and recommendations or, you may use a hospital's physician referral service. These services can find a pediatrician in your insurance plan and provide you with information about the doctor's training, board certification, office hours, and more.

Schedule an interview to meet the pediatrician you are considering. This introductory visit will help you determine whether you feel comfortable asking the doctor questions and whether his or her answers make sense to you. Many pediatricians will schedule an interview with you at no charge.

What Should You Ask the Office Staff?

It is not uncommon for parents to talk with a pediatrician's office staff as often as they talk to the doctor. You'll want to feel comfortable with your pediatrician's staff and ask them some important questions about the practice.

Here are a few suggestions:

- How many patients are usually seen in an hour?
- How long do patients usually wait to see the doctor?
- What are the office hours?
- Are there designated phone hours to speak to the doctor?
- Will I be able to speak with a nurse to seek routine information?
- Will my child have a primary physician, or do several doctors share patient care responsibilities?

Is someone available to handle emergencies during evening or weekend hours?

What Should You Ask the Doctor?

Mothers and fathers have hundreds of questions about their child's health and development. Be assured that pediatricians are accustomed to answering lots of questions and most delight in sharing their knowledge and experience to help children start healthy lives.

When you talk with the doctor, don't be shy about asking questions. Pediatricians understand how important a child's health is to parents.

Here are possible questions to ask when interviewing a doctor:

Is the physician certified by the American Board of Pediatrics or other specialty-board?

- Where did the doctor attend medical school and receive postgraduate training?
- When hospitalization is necessary, does the pediatrician admit patients to a hospital specializing in pediatric care?
- What other members of the staff assist the doctor in caring for patients? What are their roles and qualifications?
- What are the doctor's views on issues like breastfeeding and bottle-feeding? Opinions vary among pediatricians, so it may be helpful to have a pediatrician who shares your same feelings.
- What are the doctor's views on well-baby care and early childhood development? Answers to these types of questions may tell you whether your philosophy of child-raising corresponds to the pediatrician's.

Editorial provided by pediatric nurses from the St. Louis Children's Hospital Answer Line for BJC Health System.

Physicians & Surgeons Referral & Information

The following is a list of the best local resources for the right physician or surgeon for you and your family.

Academy of Eye Physicians & Surgeons of Washington
206-441-9762

Children's Hospital & Regional Medical Center
206-987-2500
866-987-2500
www.seattlechildrens.org

Everett Clinic
425-339-5432

King County Medical Society
206-621-9393
www.kcmsociety.org

Evergreen Hospital Medical Center
12040 NE 128th St, Kirkland
425-899-3000 (Physician Referral)
425-899-3000 (Health Line)

Head Injury Hotline
206-329-1371

KidCare CHAP
300 Elliott Ave W, Seattle
206-284-0331

King County Medical Society
200 Broadway
206-621-9393
www.kcmsociety.org
In operation since 1888, with over 4,200 Physician and Surgeon Members.

Northwest Hospital Medical Information and physician Referral

Seattle
206-633-4636
www.nwhospital.org

Overlake Hospital Medical Center
1034 116th Ave NE, Bellevue
425-688-5211
www.overlakehospital.org
24 Hour Physician Referral

PacMed Clinics
888-472-2633
www.pacmed.org

Stevens Hospital
21601 76th Ave W, Edmonds
425-640-4066
425-774-2229 (Birth Center)
www.stevenshealthcare.org

Swedish Medical Center
800-793-3474
www.swedish.org

UW Physicians
800-489-3627
www.uwphysicians.org

Valley Medical Center
425-656-4636
www.valleymed.org
Free Physician Referral Service
500 doctors, 75 specialties

Valley General Hospital
14701 179th Ave SE, Monroe
360-794-1411
www.valleygeneral.com

Virginia Mason Medical Center
888-862-2737
www.virginiamason.org

Washington State Medical Association
2033 6th, Seattle
206-862-6490

Washington Association of Naturopathic Physicians
206-547-2130

Washington Osteopathic Medical Association
206-937-5358

Immunizations

The following information was obtained by the Washington State Department of Health, and the National Center for Disease Control.

Childhood Immunizations are Important!

- Childhood immunizations are a safe and effective way to keep children from getting sick.
- In the last 50 years, vaccines have helped to nearly wipe out measles, diphtheria and polio.
- Vaccines strengthen the immune system by helping the body to recognize and fight the viruses and bacteria that cause disease.
- Eating right, clean drinking water and sanitation also help stop disease, but even in the cleanest of places, the viruses and bacteria that cause disease and death still exist.
- Vaccine side effects are very rare. A child's risk of having a health problem from an immunization is much less than their risk of suffering from the disease itself.
- Vaccines not only protect the child who receives the immunization; they also protect every one of us from these terrible diseases. The more children who have been vaccinated, the greater the protection for children and adults who haven't received all their vaccinations.

- The best way to protect our children and society is to vaccinate children ages 2 years and younger.
- There are national databases that watch out for potential problems with vaccines. Government vaccine surveillance systems are in place to identify potential issues with vaccines.
- As science progresses, new vaccines are discovered that will help with other childhood diseases.

Immunization Facts

- Children should have 80 percent of their immunizations by age two.
- Infants are often more vulnerable to disease than older children and adults because their immune systems cannot easily fight off bacteria or viruses. Often, the effects of disease are more serious in infants than in older children.
- Many vaccine-preventable diseases have no cure or treatment.
- A disease may not currently be present in a community, but disease outbreaks can and do occur in communities that are not protected.
- Ten serious childhood diseases are preventable. Among unimmunized populations of the world, 600,000 children die each year from pertussis (whooping cough). In 1995, King County had its highest level of pertussis cases - 251- in 30 years.
- 55,000 cases of measles and 130 deaths were reported during the 1989-1991 measles epidemic in the U.S. Nearly half the deaths were of children under age two who had not been immunized. The biggest cause of the epidemic was failure to vaccinate children against measles on time-between 12 and 18 months of age.
- Immunizations save money. Vaccine-preventable diseases cost 16 times more in medical related expenses than the vaccine that prevents the disease. The nationwide 1989-1991 measles outbreak caused 44,000 days of hospitalization resulting in $100 million in direct medical costs. This does not include direct costs to families, such as lost days of work, school and child care

Immunization Guidelines

The following information was obtained by Washinton State Department of Health and the National Center for Disease Control.

State Vaccine Requirements for Washington School Entrance (Grades K-12)

DTP,DtaP, DT, Td: 5 doses of any combination unless 4th dose was given on or after 4th birthday.
Students 7 years or older: 3 doses of any combination.
One does of Td required 10 years after last dose.

Polio (IPV): 4 doses unless the 3rd dose was on or after 4th birthday.

Measles, Mumps, Rubella (MMR): 2 doses of a measles-containing vaccine with the 1st dose on or after the 1st birthday. 2nd dose by age 5 or entry into kindergarten

Hepatitis B: 3 doses

Varicella: 1 dose on or after 1st birthday.
2 doses if vaccine given at 13 years or older.

Hepatitis A: 2 doses on or after 2nd birthday for grades K-3 only.

More Information...

Anyone can download or request a free copy of the "Parents guide to Childhood Immunizations." This is a 94-page booklet introducing parents to 12 childhood diseases and the vaccines that can protect children from them.

Visit: **www.cdc.gov/nip/publications/Parents-Guide**

Order a free booklet from the National Immunization Program on the same link.

This printed bound version is available in English and Spanish and features children's drawings.

Immunization Links & Resources

American Academy of Pediatrics (AAP)

www.aap.org
The mission of AAP is to attain optimal physical, mental, and social health well being for infants, children, adolescents and young adults.

American Medical Association (AMA)

www.ama-assn.org
The AMA disseminates up-to-date information of health and medical practice, medical ethics and education to physicians and to the public.

Bill and Melinda Gates Children's Vaccine Program (Gates CVP)

www.childrensvaccine.org
Gates CVP was established to promote equal access to lifesaving vaccines worldwide. This site provides information on advocacy issues, clinical issues, service delivery, immunization financing, safe injections, other related organizations, etc.

Every Child By Two (ECBT)

www.ecbt.org

The goals of ECBT are to raise awareness of the critical need for timely immunization and to foster putting in place a systematic way to immunize all of America's children by the age of two.

Immunization Action Coalition (IAC)

www.immunize.org

This website has abundant useful information about immunization, immunization resources and their newsletter Needle Tips.

ImmTrac

1-866-624-0180

ImmTrac is a statewide immunization registry that electronically keeps track of your child's immunization record. This helps providers to see what immunizations your child has had and which immunizations are needed. ImmTrac can also print out shot records for your child's daycare or school and notify you when shots are due. Your child's information is only available to doctors, childcare centers and schools. Please call their toll-free number to find out how to register your child for ImmTrac.

National Immunization Program (NIP)

www.cdc.gov/nip

This is a comprehensive website that provides immunization information to the public and health professionals, including training, education materials, promotions, statistics, vaccine safety and disease surveillance.

National Network for Immunization Immunization (NNII)

www.immunizationinfo.org

Great information on vaccines and the diseases they prevent.

Health Organizations & Services

Washington Children's Health Insurance Program (CHIP)

P.O. Box 45536 Olympia, Wa 98504-5536
1-877-KIDS-NOW (1-877-543-7669)
fortress.wa.gov/dshs/maa/CHIP/Index.html
The Children's Health Insurance Program (CHIP) is a national health insurance plan for children. Children qualify for CHIP based on family income and the number of members in the family. CHIP covers well-child exams, immunizations, health care provider services, prescriptions, hearing and vision exams, dental service and mental health services. Applications for CHIP are accepted during Open Enrollment. Call to find out dates for enrollment or visit their website.

Medicaid

800-562-6188
800-562-3022
www.cms.hhs.gov/medicaid/state.asp?state=WA
www.adsa.dshs.wa.gov (DSHS)
www.cms.hhs.gov/medicaid/ (National)

What is Medicaid?

The Washington Medicaid program pays medical bills for people...

- who qualify for a category of Medicaid
- who have low income or cannot afford the cost of healthcare
- who have resources (assets) under the federal limit for the category of Medicaid

WIC

1-800-942-3678
WIC is a special nutrition program that helps women, infants, and children. WIC provides nutritious food, nutrition education and counseling; breastfeeding support and counseling for pregnant and breastfeeding women. Eligibility is determined by income level, as well as, medical and nutritional need. Call their main number to find a WIC office near you or to obtain information about the program.

Public Health Assistance

Health services for uninsured, low-income individuals and families. Clients served: 1 through 18 years, 60 years and over, and pregnant women with medical coupons

Public Health Clinic Locations:

Alder Square Public Health Center
1404 Central Ave S Suites 101 & 112, Kent
206-296-4500
Hours: Monday-Friday 7:30am-5:30pm

Auburn Public Health Center
20 Auburn Ave SE, Auburn
206-296-8400
253-833-8400 (Local)
Hours: Monday-Thursday 7:30am-5:40pm, Friday 7:30am-5:00pm.

Auburn Medical Arts Building
126 Auburn Avenue Suite 400, Auburn
206-296-8400
253-833-8400

Columbia Public Health Center
4400 37th Ave S, Seattle
206-296-4650
Hours: Monday and Thursday 7:30am-8:00pm, Tuesday and Wednesday 7:30am-6:00pm, Friday 7:30am-5:00pm.

Delridge Community Center
4501 Delridge Way SW,
Seattle 206-296-4533
Hours: Wednesdays only, 8:00am- 5:00pm

Downtown Public Health Center
2124 - 4th Ave, Seattle
206-296-4755
Hours: Monday-Friday 8:00am-5:00pm

Eastgate Public Health Center
14350 SE Eastgate Way, Bellevue
206-296-4920
800-244-4512
Hours: Monday-Friday 8:00am-5:00pm

Enumclaw WIC
1417 Battersby Avenue, Enumclaw
360-825-3146

Federal Way Public Health Center
33431 13th Place S, Federal Way
253-838-4557 (Federal Way)
206-296-8410 (Seattle)
Hours: Monday-Friday 7:30am-5:30pm

Kent Teen Clinic
613 West Gowe, Kent
206-296-7450
Hours: Monday-Friday 8:30am- 5:30pm.

Lynnwood Medical & Dental Clinic
4111-194th St SW, Lynnwood
425-775-2589

North Public Health Center
10501 Meridian Ave N, Seattle
206-296-4765 (general information)
206-296-4990 (appointments)
Hours: Monday 7:30am-6:30pm, Tuesday and Thursday 7:30am-8:30pm, Wednesday and Friday 7:30-5:00pm.

Northshore Public Health Center
10808 NE 145th St, Bothell
206-296-9787
Hours: Monday 8:00am-7:00pm,
Tuesday-Friday 8:00am-5:00pm

Springwood Public Health Center
13111 SE 274th St, Kent
206- 296-4930
Hours: Monday-Friday
8:00am-5:00pm

Health District Snohomish
3020 Rucker Ave # 308,
Everett
425-339-5200

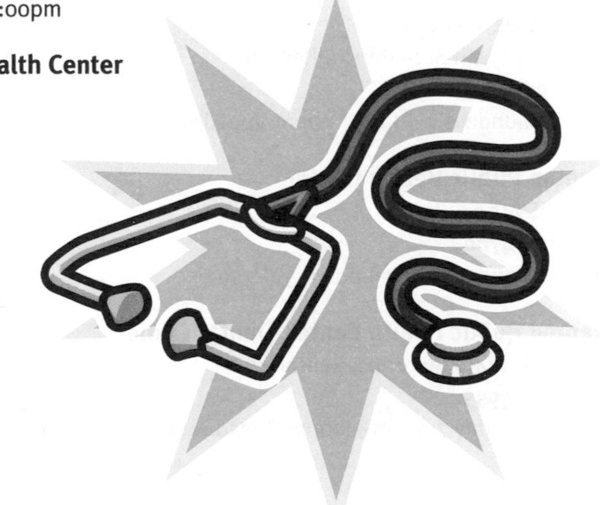

Dental Assistance

Dental services for uninsured, low-income individuals and families. Clients served: 1 through 18 years, 60 years and over, and pregnant women with medical coupons.

Public Dental Health Clinic Locations:

Columbia Public Health Center, Dental Clinic
4400 37th Ave S, Seattle
206-296-4625
Hours: Monday, Tuesday, Thursday and Friday 8:00am-6:30pm, Wednesday 8:00am-5:00pm.

Downtown Public Health Center, Dental Clinic
2124 4th Ave, Seattle
206-205-0577
Hours: Monday-Friday 8:00am-5:00pm

Eastgate Public Health Center, Dental Clinic
14350 SE Eastgate Way, Bellevue
206-296-9726
Hours: Monday-Friday 8:00am-6:00pm

North Public Health Center, Dental Clinic
12359 Lake City Way NE, Seattle
206-205-8580
Hours: Monday-Wednesday and Friday 7:45am-5:00pm, Thursday 7:45am-6:00pm.

Renton Dental Clinic
10700 SE 174th St Suite 101, Renton
206-296-4955
Hours: Mondays 7:30am-7:00pm, Tuesday-Friday 7:30am-5:00pm

Renton Public Health Center
3001 NE 4th St, Renton
206-296-4700
Hours: Monday-Friday 8:00am-5:00pm

Renton Public Health Center, Dental Clinic
10700 SE 174th Suite 101, Renton
206-296-4955
Hours: Monday 7:00am-7:00pm, Tuesday-Friday 7:00am-5:00pm.

White Center Public Health Center

10821 8th Ave SW, Seattle

206-296-4646

Hours: Monday 7:00am-7:00pm, Tuesday 7:00am-7:30pm, Wednesday-Friday 7:00am-5:00pm.

University of Washington-School of Dentistry

Seattle

206-685-9014 (Adult emergencies)

206-616-6996 (Adult new patient and non-emergency)

206-543-3525 (Child clients)

Lynnwood Medical & Dental Clinic

4111-194th St SW, Lynnwood

425-775-2589

Community Health Dental Centers

Adult Emergencies & Children 1-19

Everett

425-258-1892

Hours: Monday – Friday 7:15am – 5:30pm.

Lynnwood

425-741-1134

Hours: Monday-Friday 7:30-5:30

Health Education Resources

American Cancer Society-Puget Sound Metro Market

728 134th St SW Suite 101, Everett

425-741-8949

www.cancer.org

Information for employees, at work sites throughout the community, about support and assistance for cancer patients and their families.

American Heart Association
King County - Greater Snohomish County
710 2nd Ave Suite 900, Seattle
206-632-6881
www.americanheart.org
Age-appropriate education for school-age children to teach them the importance of taking care of their hearts by eating healthy foods, exercising daily, and being tobacco-free.

Nutrition, education, and weight management programs specifically targeting how to make healthier food choices, the importance of exercise, and how to reduce fat intake.

First Aid/CPR

The following organizations provide first aid training:

Advantage CPR & First Aid Training
Maple Vally
425-432-7614

American Red Cross
2530 Lombard Ave, Everett
425-252-4103
www.snohomishcountyredcross.org

America Red Cross
1900 25th Ave S, Seattle
206-726-3534
www.seattleredcross.org

CPR & First Aid Training Center
Seattle
206-622-2408

CPR Training Center
Mountlake Terrace
425-775-4836

I Know CPR
7601 76th Pl NE, Marysville
360-651-7502

Chapter 17

Pregnancy & Infant Resources

Chapter 17

Pregnancy & Infant Resources

One of the most special and life changing events in life is the birth of your child. There are many resources, books, and support to help smooth this transition. May you find the educational and medical resources, and support you need.

Community Education & Awareness Programs

Childbirth Education

Auburn Regional Medical Center
Plaza One 202 Division, Auburn
253-333-2522
www.armcuhs.com/p97.html
Childbirth Classes: child birthing, mom's class, for new mom's 13-20 class, and post-partum.

Big Belly Services
222 10th Ave. East, Seattle
206-725-7758
www.bigbellyservice.com
The Big Belly Services is a place for childbirth education, and doula services in Seattle area. Their focus is on natural childbirth.
Classes: Homebirths & un-medicated births, postpartum, art & "right brain"techniques, early pregnancies, and after birth.

Bradley Classes with Various Instructors

www.bradleybirth.com/info-request.asp
Classes: Teaches strength through nutrition, also healthy pregnancies. They focus on husband-coached childbirth, and discourages medical interventions.

Evergreen Hospital Medical Center

12040 NE 128th St, Kirkland (Classes also offered in Sammamish)
425-899-3000
www.evergreenhealthcare.com
Childbirth Classes: Childbirth preparation, birthing for the first time, Christian class, teens class, postpartum classes, labor and birth refresher course, hypno-birthing, and one day seminars.

Gracewinds Parinatal Services

1421 NW 70th St., Seattle
206-781-9871
866-781-9871
www.gracewindsperinatal.com
Email: gracewinds@comcast.net
Childbirth Classes: Prenatal yoga, postpartum conditioning, siblings class, infant massage, infant CPR, and new mom groups.
Services: Lactation consultation, breast pump rental, massage, labor and postpartum Doulas, chiropractic and acupuncture, nutrition counseling, and perinatal counseling.

Great Starts Birth and Family Education

2517 Eastlake Ave E Suite 102, Seattle
206-789-0883
www.greatstarts.org
Classes: Pregnancy, Childbirth, the Newborn, Guide to Having a Baby, & Step-by-Step Illustrated Guide to Pregnancy & Childbirth. Most classes available in both English and Spanish.
Other: Breastfeeding counseling service (by phone or in-home), parenting consultation, parenting groups, book groups, and educational events for families.

Highline Medical Center
16251 Sylvester Rd.SW, Burien
206-439-5576
www.highlinemedicalcenter.org
Childbirth Classes: Birthing with deep relaxation, childbirth preparation, childbirth refresher course, pregnancy aquatics, and preparation for breastfeeding.

Kyndal May, Confident Birthing, Birth & Bodywork
14220 NE 21st St., Bellevue
206-663-6767
www.birthandbodywork.com
Email: kyndal@birthandbodywork.com
Offers educational classes in: Confident birthing and are passionate about creating community to support new families for new and expectant parents, to connect and support each other.

Northwest Hospital & Medical Center
1550 N. 115th St, Seattle
206-364-0500
206-368-1168 (Child Birth Class Info)
www.nwhospital.org
Childbirth Classes: Childbirth & newborn, childbirth refresher class, early pregnancy, baby massage, baby safety classes, and family classes for dads, siblings, & grandparents.

Overlake Hospital Medical Center
1035 116th Ave.NE, Bellevue (also classes in Issaquah)
425-688-5900
425-688-5259 (Class Information)
www.overlakehospital.org
Childbirth Classes: Preparation for childbirth & newborn care, childbirth refresher, early pregnancy, expecting multiples, & conscious fathering classes.

Providence Medical Center
1001 N.Broadway, Everett
425-304-6000 (Class Information)
www.providence.org
Childbirth Classes: Fast track seminars in Spanish, birthing, pre-term birth for mom's at risk, Boot Camp for Dads, childbirth refresher courses, & Kangaroo Kapers for sibings.

Swedish Medical Center
747 Broadway, Seattle
For Classes: 206-215-3338
www.swedish.org
Childbirth Classes: Child birthing, childbirth refresher course, newborn care, prenatal seminars, private childbirth class (in your home), prenatal parenting, infant CPR & safety classes, prenatal parenting, and breastfeeding.

Birthing Centers & Services

This information is strictly informational. It is the parent's responsibility for further research and interviewing to find out which birthing center is acceptable for your needs.

King County

AquaDoula Potable Birthing Spas
425-348-6729
800-275-6144

Best Beginnings Family Health & Birth Center
19514 64th Ave W, Lynnwood
425-771-9000

Cascade Midwives & Birth Center
2808 Colby Ave, Everett
425-348-0565

Charlotte Geddis LM-Special Delivery
Arlington
360-435-3927

Community Birth & Family Center
2200 24th Ave E, Seattle
206-720-0511

Eastside Birth Center PS
14700 NE 8th Suite 115, Bellevue
425-746-5566

Evergreen Hospital
12040 NE 128th St, Kirkland
425-899-1000
425-899-3000 (Evergreen Health Line)

Northwest Hospital Childbirth Center
1550 N 115th, Seattle
206-364-0500
www.northwestbabies.org
Childbirth Education: 206-789-0883
Physician Referral: 206-633-4636

Overlake Hospital Childbirth Center
1035 116th Ave NE, Bellevue
425-688-5326
www.overlakehospital.org
Childbirth Classes: 425-688-5259

Puget Sound Midwives & Birth Center
425-823-1919
www.birthcenter.com
Home or Birth Center Birth

Seattle Birth Center
1705 E Madison
206-328-7929
www.seattlebirthcenter.com
Home or Birth Center Birth
Water Birth Available

Stevens Hospital Birth Center
21601 76th Ave W, Edmonds
425-774-2229

Valley General Hospital
14701 179th Ave SE, Monroe
360-794-1488
www.valleygeneral.com

Snohomish

Aquadoula
425-348-6729

Cascade Midwives & Birth Center
2808 Colby Ave, Everett
425-348-0565

Charlotte Geddis LM-Special Delivery
Arlington
360-435-3927

Northwest Hospital Childbirth Center
1550 N 115th, Seattle
206-364-0500

Puget Sound Midwives & Birth Center
13128 Totem Lake Blvd NE Suite 101, Kirkland
425-823-1919
www.birthcenter.com

Stevens Hospital Birth Center
21601 76th Ave W, Edmonds
425-774-2229

Valley General Hospital
14701 179th Ave SE, Monroe
360-794-1488
www.valleygeneral.com

Breastfeeding Resources/Lactation Services

Birth & Baby
www.birthandbaby.com

Providence Everett Medical Center
425-304-6160

Valley General Hospital
14701 179th Ave SE, Monroe
360-794-7497

Post Partum Depression Support Groups

Pacific Mothers Support, Inc
1407 132nd Ave NE Suite #10, Bellevue
425-462-0577
800-578-2260

Family Resources
21029 W Richmond Rd, Bothell
425-485-3295

Le Leche League
206-522-1336

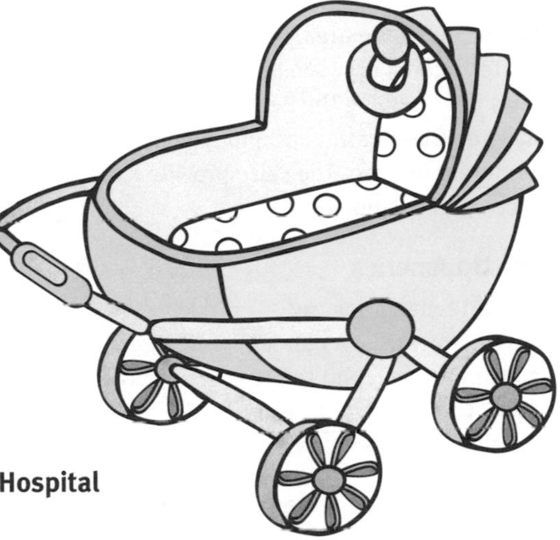

University of Washington Medical Center –Lactation Services
1959 NE Pacific Ave, Seattle
206-598-4628

Women's Clinic At Overlake Hospital
Bellevue
1051 116th Ave NE Suite 200
425-688-5389

Issaquah
6520 226th Pl SE Suite 130
425-688-5787

Diaper Service

Baby Diaper Service
6559 5th Place S, Seattle
206-634-2229
www.seattlediaper.com

Pure and Natural Diaper Service Inc
206-767-1807

Sunflower Diaper Service
206-782-4199

Parenting Resources

Best Sitters Babysitting Service

206-682-2556

425-455-5533

www.bestsittersinc.com

If you are new to the area, or are simply looking for a screened and experienced babysitter, age 25 or older, this is the service for you. This is a local family business, who has been serving the Seattle area since 1969. Each babysitter has had a Washington State Patrol background check. Be sure to call early if you have a babysitter preference. They also provide housekeeping services, hostess helpers, and adult companionship services.

Buckle Up America

www.buckleupamerica.org

Buckle Up America is a national campaign with a mission to "increase the proper use of safety belts and child safety seats-changes that will save lives and prevent injuries". Their website lists current safety belt and child restraint use statistics, information and headlines.

Children's Hospital & Regional Medical Center

4800 Sand Point Way NE, Seattle

206-987-2000

866-987-2000

www.seattlechildrens.org

Ranked one of the top hospitals in America by U.S. News and World Report, Children's Hospital offers services specifically designed for children and their families. Above and beyond medical services, Children's Hospital also include parenting classes, infant and child CPR classes, classes for children with special needs and their siblings, events, support groups, Pathways: A parent lecture series, and Child Health Advice Online.

The Child Health Advice list specific body areas, including head, mouth, chest, skin, etc. Go to the area of concern, click on possible health concerns, and read about the explanation of that specific health problem, including the causes(s), when to call a doctor, and home care information. This is extremely useful, and easy to understand.

Child & Family WebGuide

www.childandfamily.info

This website, sponsored by Tufts University, is a directory that provides information and links to hundreds of sites on parenting advice and information related to child development. Topics are available for specific ages, which ranges include children who are 0-2, 2-6, 6-13, and 13-19. Topics include family, parenting, education, learning, child development, health, mental health, resources, and recreation, and new medical sites. A favorite link is Ask An Expert, where you can directly ask your question and receive a prompt response, or read already asked questions. Experts fall into the following categories: Education Expert, Family Expert, Health Expert, and Child Development Expert.

Children's Resource Line

206-987-2500
206-987-2400 (24 Hour Children's Health Topics)
888-741-2400 (24 Hour Children's Health Topics)

www.seattlechildrens.org

Sponsored by Children's Hospital, services include free, confidential nurse consultation for help with your child's health, and finding a doctor

Community Birth & Family Center

2200 24th Ave E, Seattle
206-720-0511

www.communitybirth.org

Post-partum depression support groups, mothers group,

Family Help Line

206-233-0139
800-932-HOPE

This is a free parent information line with tops for parents and family resources throughout Washington State.

Postpartum Support International of Washington (Depression After Delivery)

206-283-9278

www.ppmdsupport.com

Offers emotional support to postpartum mothers and their families. Speak with a volunteer mother who experienced postpartum mood disorder and recovered.

March of Dimes

www.modimes.org
The mission of the March of Dimes is to improve the health of babies by preventing birth defects and infant mortality.

Find information on birth defects, newborn screening, premature babies, weight gain during pregnancy, and most anything you'd like to know about babies. They have an amazing pregnancy and newborn health education center on their website.

March of Dimes sponsors many local events to raise awareness and money for research and programs to prevent premature babies.

MOMS Club International

www.momsclub.org
This is support group for stay-at-home moms. They offer activities for moms and their kids, including playgroups, park outings, mom's night out, field trips, and much more. MOMS Club chapters are in the following cities: Bothell/Kenmore, Duvall, Kent, Marysville, Mill Creek, Redmond, Renton, Seattle North, Seattle Northeast, Seattle Northwest, and Silverdale. Visit www.momsclub.org , and click on Chapter Links, to find more information on local chapters in your area.

North Seattle Family Center

3200 NE 125th St Suite 2, Seattle
206-364-7930

www.chawa.org
This center is dedicated to families and provides family activities, tutoring, WIC, food banks, parenting classes, CPR training, PEPS (Program for Early Parents Support), and more.

North Seattle Postpartum Doula Services

206-784-5676 686-5115

www.seattlepostpartum.com
"Soften the transition into parenting" with professionally trained postpartum Doulas, who come to your home for postpartum care, including overnight care.

Services include mother care and nursing support, feeding techniques, birth recovery and massage, assistance in newborn care, care of other children in the family, and household support (meal preparation, laundry, light housekeeping, household management, infant massage instruction, etc.). New Parent Groups are also available.

PEPS (Program for Early Parent Support)
206-547-8570

www.pepsgroup.org

PEPS hold weekly confidential parent groups run by trained PEPS leaders. Parents share their concerns, issues, joys, and make crafts, learn songs and stories to be shared with their children. PEPS hopes that these meetings will help prevent abuse and neglect in families, and promote confident parents who together will reach their highest potential. The following PEPS groups are available: Newborn Program: birth to 4 months, Infant/Toddler Program: birth – 3 years, Teen Parent Program: birth– 3 years, and PEPS in Espanol: birth – 3years. Scholarships are available.

SIDS Foundation of Washington
4649 Sunnyside Ave. N Suite 348, Seattle

206-548-9290

www.sidsofwa.org

execdirector@sidsofwa.org

The SIDS Foundation of Washington is dedicated to educating the public about SIDS, and provides information and emotional support for bereaved families. Their extensive research is geared towards eliminating this tragic "medical phenomenon". Visit their website to find information about upcoming events.

Tender Loving Care-Childcare for Mildly Ill Children
1201 Terry Ave, Seattle

206-583-6521

www.vmmc.org/tlc

Tender Loving Care-Childcare for mildly ill children is for working parents who are unable to take time off work. They take care of children, ages 1-12, with most common childhood illnesses. A registered nurse on-site to monitor your child's symptoms. This was originally set up for Virginia Mason employees, and has grown to include the community. Call to make reservations quickly, before spots get filled, and be sure to list your child's symptoms to sure your child will be accepted.9289

Great Books

For Moms:

Pregnancy Childbirth and the Newborn - The Complete Guide
By Penny Simkin, Janet Whalley, Ann Keppler

The Girldfriends Guide to Pregnancy
By Cikci Lovine

The Mother of All Pregnancy Books: The ultimate Guide to Conception, Birth and Everything in Between
By Ann Douglas

What To Expect When You're Expecting
By Heidi E. Murkoff

Your Pregnancy Week by Week
By Glade B. Curtis, Judith Shuler

Hot Mama- How to Have a Babe and Be a Babe
By Karen Salmansohg

For Dads:

The Expectant Father – Facts, Tips and Advice for Dads To Be
By Armin A. Brott

My Boys Can Swim! The official Guys Guide to Pregnancy
By Ian Davis

Websites

Pregnancy and Infants:

www.babycenter.com
Sign up for a weekly email about the stages and development of your pregnancy. You'll also find great articles and comment boards.

www.drspock.com
Helpful information on all of the stages of raising your child.

www.johnsonbaby.com
Parent learning center with great articles.

Breastfeeding:

www.aap.org/family/brstguid.htm
www.breastfeedingonline.com
www.hmhb.org
www.lalecheleague.org
www.lamaze.org
www.4women.gov

Chapter 18

Special Needs & Disabilities

Chapter 18

Special Needs & Disabilities

Having a child with special needs or disabilities require parents to have additional resources at hand. The American Academy of Pediatrics research on early child development has shown that a child's environment and what a child experiences during their first few years of life significantly influences the development of their brain structure. By accessing specialized services for your child, and utilizing the opportunities that are available and by law, are his right to obtain, you will enhance and improve their abilities for the rest of their life.

I am grateful to report, there is so much information available at our fingertips, there's too much to squeeze into one chapter. My hope is to provide parents, grandparents, friends, and care givers of children with special needs, a quick reference guide. May you find the source for the tools, information, resources, programs and services you need to bless the lives of these truly special children.

Did you know...

- The U.S. Maternal and Children Health Bureau (MCHB) found that 20% of all households have children with special care needs.
- The National Survey of Children with Special Needs, as reported in *Pediatrics*, 1998, found that children with special needs "are at increased risk for chronic physical, developmental, behavioral, or emotional conditions...also require health and related services beyond that required by children generally."

Local Oraganization & Resources

Children's Hospital & Regional Medical Center
4800 Sand Point Way NE, Seattle
206-987-2000
866-987-2000
www.seattlechildrens.org
Ranked one of the top hospitals in America by U.S. News and World Report, Children's Hospital offers services specifically designed for children and their families. Above and beyond medical services, Children's Hospital also include parenting classes, infant and child CPR classes, classes for children with special needs and their siblings, events, support groups, Pathways: A parent lecture series, and Child Health Advice Online.

The Child Health Advice list specific body areas, including head, mouth, chest, skin, etc. Go to the area of concern, click on possible health concerns, and read about the explanation of that specific health problem, including the causes(s), when to call a doctor, and home care information. This is extremely useful, and easy to understand.

Center for Human Disabilities & Development (CHDD)

University of Washington
chdd@u.washington.edu
depts.washington.edu/chdd
206-543-7781
The CHDD is one of the largest and most comprehensive centers for children with special needs. More than 600 faculty and staff, plus doctoral and post-doctoral students, are available to provide services for children with developmental disabilities, their families, and friends. They focus on two major programs which serve to strengthen and support each other.

Research:The Mental Retardation & Developmental Disabilities Research Center

Clinical Services, Training, and Community Outreach

Clinics include: Autism, Genetics, Child Development, Congenital Hypothyroidism, developmental Pediatric Consultation, Feeding, FAS, High Risk Infant, Neurogenetics, Pediatric Audiology, and PKU.

Answers for Special Kids (ASK)
300 Elliott Ave W Suite 300
Seattle, Wa
800-322-2588

Child Care Resources

www.childcare.org

This is a non-profit organization in King County who offer their services in six different languages. Services are dedicated to children with special needs and their families and child care providers, including community information, child care information and referrals for parents.

Child Care has three locations:

Seattle/North King County
1225 S Weller Suite 300, Seattle
206-329-1011
206-329-5544 (Referral Line)
Hours: Monday-Friday 8:30-5:00

East King County
16315 NE 87th St Bldg B, Redmond
425-865-9450 (Referral Line)
425-865-9033 (Provider Line)
Hours: Monday, Tuesday 9:00-4:30

South King County
841 N Central Ave Suite 126, Kent
253-852-1908
253-852-3080 (Referral Line)
253-852-2566 (Provider Line)
Hours: Wednesday, Thursday 8:30-4:30

Easter Seals of Washington

www.wa.easterseals.com

Easter Seals of Washington's mission is to "creates solutions that change the lives of children and adults with disabilities or other special needs and their families". This mission is accomplished with the help of several programs, including assistive technology which gives the tools, technology assessment, and training for people with disabilities. Camp *Stand by Me* provides a safe environment which focuses giving opportunities to participate in activities such as swim, ride horses, sing, and eating s'mores. Child care supports families by providing the highest quality childcare and education for children.

EDLAW, Inc

1310 Minor Ave #207,
Seattle, Wa 98101
www.edlaw.net

Infant Toddler Early Intervention Program
P.O. Box 45201
Olympia, Wa 98504
360-902-8488
800-322-7864
www.wa.gov/dshs/iteip/iteip.html

Seattle Human Service Department-Child Care Referral
www.cityofseattle.net/humanservices/fys/ChildCare/InfoAndReferral.htm
You will find child care information and referrals for children with special needs who are the age of birth to 14 years. The referral service is free for families with low to moderate incomes in King County.

Seattle Public Schools-Special Needs
www.seattleschools.org/area/speced/seaac.htm
This is the Seattle Public School's website for children and adolescents with special needs. You will find information on meetings, classes, the annual resource fair, contact information, monthly newsletters, and much more.

The Center for Children with Special Needs
www.cshcn.org
The Center for Children with Special Needs is a program at The Children's Hospital and Regional Medical Center in Seattle, Washington. The Center focus on improving care for children with special needs through education research, and evaluation, it also list news, events, programs, resources, and center activities, and provide links to camps for special needs children, health information, building on family strengths program, parent support program, Families as Teachers program (an awesome doctor-family role-reversal program), reports, and facts sheets, and so much more, all sponsored by CSHCN and The Children's Hospital and Regional Medical Center.

The Father's Network
www.fathersnetwork.org/707.html
As the name suggests, this website was organized by fathers with the desire to provide current information and resources to support families and those involved in the lives of children with special needs. This is a national program, and this website is the site for the Washington State chapter.

The Northwest Americans with Disabilities Act and Information Technical Center (Northwest ADA & IT Center)

www.theinitiative.ws/ada.html

The Northwest Americans with Disabilities Act and Information Technical Center (Northwest ADA & IT Center) provides training, education, and technical assistance relating to the Americans with Disabilities Act. You will find monthly reports, statistics, and information for public awareness and outreach.

Washington State Department of Social and Health Services

Aging and Disability Services Administration

800-422-3263

www.aasa.dshs.wa.gov

Washington State Special Needs Statistics and Data

www.mchb.hrsa.gov/chsch/state-data/wa.htm

Washington State statistics on issues related to health care for children with special needs.

Public Schools Districts: King & Snohomish Counties

By law, every school district must include or refer to a birth to three early intervention program for children with special needs. The following is the information for the birth to three programs in each school district.

Auburn School District

253-931-4900

www.auburn.wednet.edu

Bellevue School District

425-456-4000

www.bsd405.org

Edmonds School District

425-670-7000

www.edmonds.wednet.edu

Everett School District

425-385-4000

www.everett.k12.wa.us/everett

Federal Way Public Schools

253-945-2000

www.fwps.org

Issaquah School District
425-837-7000
www.issaquah.wednet.edu

Kent School District
253-373-7000
www.kent.k12.wa.us

Lake Washington School District
425-702-3200
www.lkwash.wednet.edu

Lake Stevens School District
425-335-1500 (or 7500)
www.lkstevens.wednet.edu

Marysville School District
360-653-7058
www.mslv.k12.wa.us

Mercer Island School District
206-236-3310
www.misd.k12.wa.us

Monroe School District
360-794-7777
www.monroe.wednet.edu

Mukilteo School District
425-356-1274
www.mukilteo.wednet.edu

Northshore School District
425-489-6000
www.nsd.org

Seattle Public Schools
206-252-0207
www.seattleschools.org

Snohomish School District
360-563-7300
www.sno.wednet.edu

Snoqualmie Valley School District
425-831-8000
www.snoqualmie.k12.wa.us

Stanwood Camano School District
360-629-1200
www.stanwood.wednet.edu

National Organizations

Applied Research Center

www.arc.org

www.arcofkingcounty.org/guide/support/organizations/king
Arc serves as a resource guide for children and adults with developmental disabilities and their families. It is devoted to promoting and improving supports and services. The association also fosters research and education with issues concerning developmental disabilities.

National Institute of Mental Health (NIMH)

Public Information and Communications Branch
6001 Executive Blvd Room 8184, MSC 9663
Bethesda, MD 20892
866-615-6464

The National Dissemination Center for Children with Disabilities (NICHCY)

www.nichcy.org/stateshe/wa.htm

NICHCY
P.O. Box 1492
Washington, DC 20013
800-695-0285
E-mail: nichcy@aed.org
The National Dissemination Center for Children with Disabilities provides the information to the state-level offices in Washington State for the departments listed below. They can put you in touch with resources in your community and provide you with information and assistance about disability issues in Washington State

Wrights Law

www.wrightslaw.com

If you want to information about the laws your child is entitled to, this is an excellent resource. This website is filled with updated information about special education law(s), how to be an advocate for children with disabilities, and mounds of articles, newsletters, and resources on a plethora of topics. You will find access to bookstores, services, products, and law libraries. They have references to other websites, and a schedule of the Wrightslaw training and seminars. They even have a section for "new parents" who might be feeling overwhelmed and need more answers and guidance.

Disability-Specific Organizations

ADD/ADHD

Attention Deficit Information Network, Inc.
58 Prince St
Needham, MA 15234
412-341-1515
www.addinfonetwork.com
Attention Deficit Disorder Association (ADDA)
P.O. Box 543
Pottstown, PA 19464
484-945-2101
mail@add.org
www.add.org

Children and Adults with Attention-Deficit/Hyperactivity Disorder (CHADD)
8181 Professional Place, Suite 150
Landover, MD 20785
301-306-7070
800-233-4050 (Voice mail to request information packet)
www.chadd.org

Aphasia

National Aphasia Association
4156 Library Rd
Pittsburgh, PA 15234
412-341-1515
www.aphasia.org

Autism Spectrum Disorders

Autism Society of America
7910 Woodmont Ave Suite 300
Bethesda, MD 20814
800-3-AUTISM
www.autism-society.org

FEAT of Washington
17171 Bothell Way NE PMB #207, Seattle
206-763-3373
www.featwa.org

Blind/Visual Impairments

American Council of the Blind
1155 15th St NW Suite 1004
Washington, DC 20005
800-424-8666
www.acb.org

American Foundation for the Blind - West
111 Pine St Suite 725
San Francisco, CA 94111
415-392-4845
sanfran@afb.net
www.afb.org

Community Services for the Blind & Partially Sighted
9709 Third Ave NE, Suite 100
Seattle, WA 98115-2027
206-525-5556
www.csbps.com
www.sightconnection.com (Adaptive Aids Store)

Brain Injury

Brain Injury Association of Washington
800 Jefferson St, Suite 600
Seattle, WA 98104
206-388-0900
800-523-5438 (in Washington)
biawa@biawa.org
www.biawa.org

Head Injury Support Group
St. Peter Hospital
413 Lilly Road N.E.
Olympia, WA 98506

National Brain Injury Association of America
8201 Greensboro Dr Suite 611
Mclean, VA 22102
800-444-6443
www.biausa.org

Cerebral Palsy

United Cerebral Palsy Association
1660 L St NW Suite 700
Washington, DC 20036
800-872-7197
www.ucp.org

Developmental Disabilities/Mental Retardation

PROVAIL
3670 Stoneway N
Seattle, WA 98103
206-363-7303
206-440-2206
www.provail.org

The Arc of Washington State
2600 Martin Way E, Suite D
Olympia, WA 98506
360-357-3279
888-754-8798 (in Washington)
info@arcwa.org
www.arcwa.org

Down Syndrome

National Down Syndrome Congress
1370 Center Dr Suite 102
Atlanta, GA 30338
800-232-6372
www.ndsccenter.org

National Down Syndrome Society
666 Broadway 8th Floor
New York, NY 10012
800-221-4602
www.ndss.org

Dyslexia

The International Dyslexia Association
The Chester Bldg Suite 382
8600 LaSalle Rd
Baltimore MD 21286
410-296-0232
www.interdys.org

Epilepsy

Epilepsy Foundations of America
4351 Garden City Dr
Landover, MD 20785
800-332-1000
www.epilepsyfoundation.org

Epilepsy Foundation of Washington
3800 Aurora Ave Nh
Suite 370
Seattle, WA 98103
206-547-4551
800-752-3509
mail@epilepsywa.org
www.epilepsywa.org

Fragile X

National Fragile X Foundation
San Francisco, CA 94119
800-688-8765
www.fragilex.org

Learning Disabilities

Council for Exceptional Children, Division for Learning Disabilities
1110 N Glebe Rd
Arlington, VA 22201
888-CEC-SPED
www.cec.sped.org

Learning Disabilities Association of America
4156 Liberty Rd
Pittsburgh, PA 15234
412-341-1515
www.idaamerica.org

Learning Disabilities Association of Washington
16225 NE 87th St, Suite B-4
Redmond, WA 98052-3537
425-882-0792
800-536-2343 (Information and referral, in WA)
425-882-0820 (Business Line)
www.ldawa.org

National Center for Learning Disabilities
381 Park Ave S Suite 1401
New York, NY 10016
212-545-7510
www.ncld.org

Speech and Hearing

National Association of the Deaf
814 Thayer Ave
Silver Spring, MD 20910
301-587-1788
www.nad.org

Signing Exact English Center for the Advancement of Deaf Children
P.O. Box 1181
Los Alamitos, CA 90720
562-430-1467
www.seecenter.org

Washington Speech-Language-Hearing Association
2150 N. 107th St, Suite 204
Seattle, WA 98133-9009
206-367-8704
office@wslha.org
www.wslha.org

Spina Bifida

Spina Bifida Association of America
4590 MacArther Blvd NW Suite 250
Washington, DC 20007
800-621-3141
www.sbaa.org

Washington State Department Oraganizations

State Department of Education: Special Education

Client Assistance Program
Client Assistance Program
2531 Rainier Ave S
Seattle, WA 98144
206-721-5999
800-544-2121 (Washington)
888-721-6072
CAPSeattle@att.net

Councils on Developmental Disabilities
Developmental Disabilities Council
2600 Martin Way E, Suite F
P.O. Box 48314
Olympia, WA 98504-8314
360-586-3558
800-634-4473
EdH@cted.wa.gov
www.ddc.wa.gov

Programs for Children with Disabilities: Ages 3 through 5
Early Childhood Services
Special Education Learning Improvement
Office of Superintendent of Public Instruction
P.O. Box 47200
Olympia, WA 98504-7200
360-725-6078
kwalker@ospi.wednet.edu
www.k12.wa.us

Programs for Children and Youth who are Blind or Visually Impaired
Department of Services for the Blind
402 Legion Way, Suite 100
P.O. Box 40933
Olympia, WA 98504-0933
360-586-6981
800-552-7103
bilpalmer@dsb.wa.gov
www.dsb.wa.gov

Programs for Children and Youth who are Deaf-Blind
Washington State Services for Children with Deaf-Blindness
400 S.W. 152nd St
Burien, WA 98166-2209
206-439-6937
800-572-7000 (Washington)
wsds@psesd.org
www.wsdsonline.org

Programs for Children and Youth who are Deaf or Hard of Hearing
Office of Deaf and Hard of Hearing Services
P.O. Box 45300
Olympia, WA 98504-5300
360-902-8000
800-422-7930
rafferic@dshs.wa.gov
odhh.dshs.wa.gov

Programs for Children with Special Health Care Needs
Children with Special Health Care Needs
Community and Family Health
Department of Health
P.O. Box 47880
Olympia, WA 98504-7880
360-236-3573
maria.nardella@doh.wa.gov

Programs for Infants and Toddlers with Disabilities: Ages Birth through 3
Infant Toddler Early Intervention Program
Division of Developmental Disabilities
Department of Social and Health Services
P.O. Box 45201
Olympia, WA 98504-5201
360-725-3500
loercsk@dshs.wa.gov
www1.dshs.wa.gov/iteip

Protection and Advocacy Agency
Washington Protection and Advocacy System
315 Fifth Ave S, Suite 850
Seattle, WA 98104
206-324-1521
800-562-2702
wpas@wpas-rights.org
www.wpas-rights.org

Regional ADA & IT Technical Assistance Center
Northwest ADA & IT Center
Oregon Health & Science University-CDRC
P.O. Box 574
Portland, OR 97207-0574
503-494-4001
503-418-0296
800-949-4232
nwada@ohsu.edu
www.nwada.org

Special Education Learning Improvement
State Improvement Grant
Office of the Superintendent of Public Instruction
P.O. Box 47200
Olympia, WA 98504-7200
360-725-6088
kbartlett@ospi.wednet.edu
www.k12.wa.us/curriculumInstruct/SpecialEdLearning/default.aspx

Special Education Operations
Office of Superintendent of Public Instruction
P.O. Box 47200
Olympia, WA 98504-7200
360-725-6075
speced@ospi.wednet.edu
www.k12.wa.us/specialed

State CHIP Program
(health care for low-income uninsured children)
The CHIP Program
Washington State Department of Social and Health Services
877-543-7669
fortress.wa.gov/dshs/maa/CHIP/Index.html

State Coordinator for NCLB (No Child Left Behind)
Office of Superintendent of Public Instruction
P.O. Box 47200
Olympia, WA 98504-7200
360-725-6000
www.k12.wa.us

State Developmental Disabilities Program
Division of Developmental Disabilities
Department of Social and Health Services
P.O. Box 45310
Olympia, WA 98504-5310
360-902-8484
www1.dshs.wa.gov/ddd

State Mental Health Agency
Mental Health Division
Department of Social and Health Services
P.O. Box 45320
Olympia, WA 98504-5320
360-902-0790

Telecommunications Relay Services for Individuals who are Deaf, Hard of Hearing, or with Speech Impairments
800-833-6384
800-833-6388
800-833-6385 (Tele-Braille)
877-833-6341 (Speech to Speech)

Organizations Especially for Parents

Community Parent Resource Center

Pierce, North King County vicinity

Parent to Parent Power
1118 S. 142nd St, Suite B-253
Tacoma, WA 98444
253-531-2022
253-531-0246
yvone_link@yahoo.com
support@p2ppower.org
www.p2ppower.org

Parent Training and Information Center (PTI)

Parents Are Vital in Education (PAVE)
6316 S. 12th St, Suite B
Tacoma, WA 98465
253-565-2266
800-572-7368
wapave9@washingtonpave.com
www.washingtonpave.org

Parent-To-Parent
Washington State P2P Programs
State Coordinating Office
2600 Martin Way E, Suite D
Olympia, WA 98506
425-641-7504
800-821-5927
statep2p@earthlink.net
www.arcwa.org

Partners in Policymaking
Washington Developmental Disabilities Council
2600 Martin Way E, Suite F
Olympia, WA 98504
360-586-3566
donnap@cted.wa.gov

Parent Teacher Association (PTA)
Washington State PTA
2003 65th Ave W
Tacoma, WA 98466-6215
253-565-2153
800-562-3804 (in Washington only)
wapta@wastatepta.org
www.wastatepta.org

Other Parent Organizations

Specialized Training of Military Parents (STOMP)
PAVE
6316 S 12th St, Suite B
Tacoma, WA 98465
253-565-2266
800-572-7368
stomp@washingtonpave.com
www.washingtonpave.org

Other Disability Organizations

Easter Seals Washington
521 Second Ave W
Seattle, WA 98119
206-281-5700
800-678-5708
esw@seals.org
www.seals.org

The FAS (Fetal Alcohol Syndrome) Family Resource Institute
P.O. Box 2525
Lynwood, WA 98036
253-531-2878
800-999-3429
vicfas@hotmail.com
www.fetalalcoholsyndrome.org

Washington PAVE
Infant/Toddler Early Intervention Program
6316 S. 12th Street
Tacoma, WA 98465
360-701-7012
800-572-7368
253-565-2266
weecare@olywa.net
www.washingtonpave.org

Summit Assistance Dogs
5458 W. Shore Road
Anacortes, WA 98221
360-293-5609
info@summitdogs.org
www.summitdogs.org

VSA arts of Washington
305 Harrison St, Suite 303
Seattle, WA 98109
206-443-1843
info@vsaaw.org
www.vsaaw.org

Washington State Fathers Network
Kindering Center
16120 NE 8th St
Bellevue, WA 98008-3937
425-747-4004, X. 4286
cmorris@fathersnetwork.org
www.fathersnetwork.org

Independent Living

Statewide Independent Living Council (SILC)
Independent Living Research Utilization Project
The Institute for Rehabilitation and Research
2323 South Sheppard, Suite 1000
Houston, TX 77019
ilru@ilru.org
www.ilru.org
Call for local contact information

Sports Programs

Lake Sammamish Water Ski Club
www.lswsc.org
Formed in 1959, this water ski club is youth and family oriented. They are the oldest and largest water-ski club west of the Mississippi. They have a special waterskiing program for the blind.

Life Enrichment Foundation
www.lifeenrichmentfoundation.org
Life Enrichment Foundation is a local philanthropy that supports recreational activities for people with disabilities in King County.

The Cascade Ridge Racers
www.cascaderidgeracers.com
The Cascade Ridge Racers is an organization which provides people with varying mental and physical disabilities, ages 13-65, with "healthful winter exercise fun...while building confidence and self esteem". Participants head up to the mountains, usually on a Sunday, and learn how to ski. Instructors and coaches are certified by both the Professional Ski Instructors of America (PSIA-NW), and Washington State Special Olympics (WSSO).

Little Bits Therapeutic Riding Club

19802 NE 148th, Woodinville
425-882-1554
www.littlebit.org
Little Bit Therapeutic Riding Center is a non-profit organization which gives children with disabilities, ages 2 ? and older, an opportunity to focus on their abilities as they go horseback riding in a beautiful, peaceful environment.

Programs include Sports Riding, Hippoetherapy (horse is used as a therapy tool), Developmental Model (with physical therapist), Developmental Vaulting, and a Multiple Sclerosis Riding Group.

Ski for All Foundation

1621 114th Ave SE Suite 132
Bellevue, WA 98004
425-462-0978
www.skiforall.org

Special Olympics of Washington

www.sowa.org
The Special Olympics of Washington provide training and competitions in the following seasonal sports:

- Winter: Alpine skiing, cross country skiing, figure skating, speed skating, and basketball
- Spring: Athletics, aquatics, cycling, soccer, and weight lifting.
- Summer: Golf and softball
- Fall: Bowling

Certified volunteer coaches instruct the athletes at local, regional, and state levels.

Washington State TOPSoccer

Washington State Youth Soccer Association

500 336th St Suite 100
Federal Way, WA 98003
253-4-SOCCER
www.wsysa.com

Publications

Exceptional Parent Magazine
555 Kinderkamack Rd
Oradell, NJ 07649
201-634-6550
www.eparent.com

The Complete IEP Guide: How to Advocate for Your Special Ed Child.
By Lawrence M. Siegal, Director of the National Deaf Education Project

Special Needs Project (SNP)
www.specialneeds.com
This is the website for the Special Needs Project (SNP) bookstore. Their website is dedicated to the wide range of issues for children with physical and/or mental disability. This includes books and information about inclusion, and awareness, and what they believe is the most extensive collection of books about Autism and other related conditions.

Resources For Children With Specials Needs

Finding a Specific Camp
find.acacamps.org/finding_a_camp.php

The Center for Children with Special Needs
www.cshcn.org/resources/campcalendar.cfm?intro=yes#attention
Children's Hospital and Regional Medical Center
Seattle, WA
206-987-5325
www.cshcn.org

American Camp Associations
http://find.acacamps.org/finding_special_needs.php

Discover Camp
www.ncaonline.org/discover/resources.html

Children's Hospital
www.cshcn.org/

Easter Seals of Washington
wa.easterseals.com

Overlake Hospital Camps
425-688-5432
www.overlakehospital.org

Pacific Science Center
206-443-2925
www.pacsci.org

Seattle Mama's Website
www.seattlemamas.com
I've included 35 pages of my favorite camps
listed by specific special need (i.e. autism, diabetes, HIV/Aids).

City Specific Camps:

Bellevue Parks & Community Services Specialized Recreation
425-452-7686

City of Seattle Department of Parks and Recreation Summer Program
206-684-4950

Everett Parks & Recreation Department
425-257-8300

Kent Parks, Recreation and Community Services
253-856-5030
www.ci.kent.wa.us

Pierce County Parks & Recreation
253-798-4753

Chapter 19

Parenting Resources

Chapter 19

Parenting Resources

There are many resources in our community for parenting. Listed below are some specific resources for families. As you may have already noticed, Chapter 18 has numerous resources for children with special needs, and Chapter 17 has several resources specifically for pregnant moms, new mothers, and their infants. These two chapters work together as great companion chapters to this chapter.

Love & Logic
800-338-4065
www.loveandlogic.com
If you're looking for easy to use techniques that will help you raise responsible kids who are fun to be around, you may want to attend Becoming a Love and Logic Parent classes. You will learn the specific "how-to's", not just theoretical concepts. Independent facilitators around the country present "Becoming a Love and Logic Parent" classes.
Call for a list of facilitators in your area

What is Love and Logic?

The Love and Logic Process:

- Shared control: Gain control by giving away the control you don't need.
- Shared thinking and decision-making: Provide opportunities for the child to do the greatest amount of thinking and decision-making.
- Equal shares of empathy with consequences: An absence of anger causes a child to think and learn from his/her mistakes.
- Maintain the child's self-concept: Increased self-concept leads to improved behavior and improved achievement.

The Rules of Love and Logic

Rule #1

- Adults take care of themselves by providing limits in a loving way.
- Adults avoid anger, threats, warnings or lectures.
- Adults use enforceable statements.
- Children are offered choices within limits.
- Limits are maintained with compassion, understanding or empathy.

Rule #2

- Childhood misbehavior is treated as an opportunity for gaining wisdom.
- In a loving way, the adult holds the child accountable for solving his/her problems in a way that does not make a problem for others.
- Children are offered choices with limits.
- Adults use enforceable statements.
- Adults provide delayed/extended consequences.
- The adult's empathy is "locked in" before consequences are delivered.

National PTA

www.pta.org

The PTA has developed a new program called How to Help Your Child Succeed. Here are the key points of the program:

- 10 Ways to Foster Your Child's Success
- Talk with your child. Talking early and often with your children helps them trust you as a source of information and guidance.
- Set high but realistic expectations. Paying attention to your children's strengths, while acknowledging where they need assistance can help children develop realistic self-expectations.
- Build your child's self-esteem and confidence. Encourage your children to make choices even if it means making mistakes. This how children learn and grow.
- Keep you child healthy. Promote your children's physical, emotional, and social health.
- Support learning at home. Show that education is important to you and that you value learning.
- Communicate with your child's school. Communicate on a regular basis with the school to stay informed and involved.
- Encourage exploration and discovery. By encouraging your children to develop their interests and seek opportunities to try new things you help them make the most of the world around them.

- Help your child develop good relationships. All children want to fit in and belong. Helping your children develop friendships that affirm them will go a long way to helping them build solid relationships as adults.
- Keep your child safe. Teach your children safety procedures and how to avoid dangerous situations.
- Participate in community service. Children's positive energy and talents can be acknowledged beyond the classroom when used to serve or help others.

How to Help Your Child Succeed, a part of National PTA's Building Successful Partnerships program, is available as a two-part workshop in which participants learn more about the 10 ways and how to put them into practice. To find out how to bring a workshop to your community and or more information on this program, contact your Local PTA, or visit the How to Help Your Child Succeed area on the National PTA website: **www.pta.org**

Changes Parent Support Network

800-212-6842

www.changesparent.org

This is an excellent online resource, providing hundreds of links to informational websites on any type of change a parent, child, or family may face. From changes in your name or address, to birth, career, child development, cultural changes, and so forth.

Children's Home Society of Washington

206-364-7930

www.chs-wa.org

Founded in 1896, this organization introduced adoption to the state of Washington. They offer adoption and family support services, as they have done for over 100 years, and have also become a leading provider for residential and group care for troubled children. You will also find online resources at their website.

Family Help Line

1305 4th Ave Suite 310, Seattle

800-932-4673

www.parenttrust.org/families/helpline.asp

The Family Help Line offers parent information, referrals to community services and support. A family coach will listen to your concerns, offer strategies to help you better manage your family, refer you to parenting classes geared towards your needs, and will send child development information to you home.

Parent Trust For Washington Children

206-233-0156

Potty Training

The following websites offer tips, articles, and information for potty training.

www.pottytrainingtips.com

www.pottytrainingsolutions.com

www.keepkidshealthy.com

Program For Early Parent Support (Peps)

4649 Sunnyside N, Seattle

206-547-8570

PEPS hold weekly confidential parent groups run by trained PEPS leaders. Parents share their concerns, issues, joys, and make crafts, learn songs and stories to be shared with their children. PEPS hopes that these meetings will help prevent abuse and neglect in families, and promote confident parents who together will reach their highest potential. The following PEPS groups are available: Newborn Program: birth to 4 months, Infant/Toddler Program: birth – 3 years, Teen Parent Program: birth– 3 years, and PEPS in Espanol: birth – 3years. Scholarships are available.

Queen Anne Relationship Therapy

1811 Queen Anne Ave N Suite #204

206-283-3374

Talaris Research Institute

Seattle

206-529-6898

www.talaris.org

Tough Love Parent Support Group

206-621-0312

The Washington Traffic Safety Commission

Adoption Resources

Americans Adopting Orphans

www.orphans.com

206-524-5437

A Seattle-based, licensed, non-profit adoption agency specializing in adoption of orphans.

Children's Home Society of Washington

206-364-7930

www.chs-wa.org

Founded in 1896, this organization introduced adoption to the state of Washington. They offer adoption and family support services, as they have done for over 100 years, and have also become a leading provider for residential and group care for troubled children. You will also find online resources at their website.

FindLaw

www.lawyers.findlaw.com

This website provides a directory of local private adoption attorneys. Simply type in your Zip code and state, click on "Practice Area", then scroll down to "Family Law" and select "adoption", then "search."

Ujima Community Services

www.ococujima.org/pages/806369/index.htm

206-760-3456

A Seattle non-profit licensed adoption agency specializing in placement of African-American children with African-American adoptive parents.

Washington Adoption Directory

www.childwelfare.com/Washington_Adoption_listings.htm

In Accordance with the National Adoption Information Clearinghouse, they provide the list of state and local public agencies, private adoption agencies, adoptive family support groups and biological parent or child search support groups, along with their contact information.

Baby Center

www.babycenter.com/refcap/baby/adoption/1374194.html

This website links you to an excellent article entitled, "Forming A Healthy Attachment With Your Adopted Child," by Dr. JoAnne Solchany of the University of Washington-Infant Mental Health Department.

Grief & Loss Support Groups

Community Home Health Hospice

1035 11th Ave, Longview
360-414-5419
800-378-8510

www.chhh.org

Price: This is a free service, but donations are welcome.

They offer support groups for bereaved children - ages 6-12, but they will take younger children if needed.

Summer Camp: This is a three day camp, Friday through Sunday, and is specifically for children suffering with grief or loss.

Compassionate Friends

2 locations:
446 SW 156th St, Burien
25810 15th Ave SE, Covington
206-241-1139
206-241-5650

www.widowedinformation.org

The "Wings" program is for children suffering in grief, loss and pain. This is a support group serviced by Allie Franklin, and a volunteer staff. Allie is trained, licensed and experienced with bereaved children. This program is for children ages 4 to 18 years.

Program: support groups, plus many varied activities such as arts, crafts and games.

Price: No charge, but a $5 donation would be welcome

Classes:
Burien: Meet 2nd & 4th Mondays, 7:00pm to 8:15pm
Covington: Meet 1st & 3rd Tuesdays, 7:00pm to 8:15pm.

Early Head Start National Resource Center (EHS NRC)

202-638-1144 x 642

Operated by ZERO TO THREE (**www.zerotothree.org**), the EHS NRC serves to promote "the building of new knowledge and the sharing of information" by:

Linking and actively engaging the Early Head Start and the Head Start community through opportunities in coordination with the Head Start Bureau's On-line Learning Center, to share resources and learn from one another in a variety of venues;

Creating, collecting, and disseminating information relevant to comprehensive early childhood programs that is timely, accessible, and easy to use; and

Providing professional development opportunities for the Early Head Start and Head Start community through face-to-face meetings and state-of-the-art distance learning experiences.

Grief Works

Auburn
253-333-9420
800-850-9420
www.griefworks.org
Co-founded by Mel Erikson, Grief Works offers bereavement support for children and teens through private grief counseling for ages 5 to 18 years old. They also counsel families called, "Family Huddles". If there is a death in a family, they will go to the home to offer their services. They will not turn away those who cannot pay.
Price: individual: $10.00/hour
Support Groups: $20.00
Donations accepted

Rise & Shine

417 23rd Ave S, Seattle
206-628-8949
www.risenshine.org
This non-profit service focuses on children with HIV and Aids, or children who have parents with HIV & Aids, for ages 8 to 13 years. With a staff who have degrees in social service, and 120 volunteers, Rise and Shine offer support groups, Magic Circle, psycho-therapy, mentor programs (similar to Big Brothers & Big Sister organization), and several kids activities. There is a Garden of Hope for those who have lost a loved one, and can plant a tree in their memory. A summer camp is also available for children 6-18 years old.

Teardrops

806 20th Ave, Seattle
206-227-6294
www.empowerinstituteclc.org
www.counselingseattle.org
Teardrops is a bereavement source for children 8 to 12 years old. The director, Paige Tangncy, has a MA degree in educational psychology, is a certified psychologist.

Group Sessions:
1st session: Meet with parents & caregivers on how to support grieving child.
2nd session: Meet with grieving child, offers counseling, art and games.

Group Meetings: Weekly Saturday afternoons for 8 weeks, $20.00 per session, $5.00 for screening.

The Safe Crossings Foundation (formerly McMullin - Robertson Foundation)
6548 41st Ave NE, Seattle
206-652-4723
www.safecrossingsfoundation.org
This non-profit organization was formed when two lawyers passed away from cancer within a short time of each other, leaving behind their grieving families. Realizing their children needed bereavement counseling, and not having any resources in King County to turn to, the McMullin-2-19 year olds. They offer free services which include one-on-one counseling with children, families, and parents, telephone support to parents, other concerned adults, teachers, and counselors regarding to children's grief, written information and referrals to community services, general education to audiences regarding children's grief, consultation to parents, educators, counselors, and health care professionals. They have a Hospice program, do home visits, and provide bereavement support groups.

Camp Erin-Grief Camp for Children, sponsored by Jamie Moyer of the Seattle Mariners, allows up to 40 grieving children, ages 5-17 to attend. It is held on week-ends, usually in August.

Multi-Generational Resources

Aarp Grandparent Information Center
800-424-3410
www.aarp.org/grandparents

The Brookdale Foundation Group
RAPP: Relatives As Parents Program
212-308-7355
www.brookdalefoundation.org

Child Welfare League of America
202-638-2952
www.cwla.org

Children's Defense Fund
202-628-8787
www.childrensdefense.org

Generations United
202-638-1263
www.gu.org

Grand Parent Again
www.grandparentagain.org

Grands Place
860-763-5789
www.grandsplace.com

National Committee of Grandparents for Children's Rights
866-624-9900
www.grandparentsforchildren.org

Public Benefits

Financial Assistance
877-980-9131
w.wws2.wa.gov/dshs/onlinecso/

Food Stamps
877-980-9131
www.wws2.wa.gov/dshs/onlinecso/

Harborview injury Prevention & Research Center

Healthy Kids Now
(To apply for health insurance for children in low-income families)
877-543-7669

The Seattle-King County Department of Public Health
206-731-2557
Offers grandparents and other kind re-parenting, weekly support groups, counseling, crisis intervention, and outreach programs.

Washington Traffic & Safety Commission
360-
www.wtsc.wa.gov

Great Parenting Books

This is a list of favorite parenting books and resources compiled by hundreds of mama's like yourself. The top picks include:

Caring for Your Baby and Young Child: Birth to Age 5
By American Academy of Pediatrics

Bring Up Boys: Practical Advice and Encouragement for Those Shaping the Next Generation of Men
By James C Dobson

Children's First Steps
By A Lynn Scoresby, Ph.D

Finding the Path: A Novel for Parents of Teenagers
By Jeffrey P. Kaplan, Abby Lederman

Girls Will Be Girls: Raising Confident and Courageous Daughters
By JoAnn Deak, Teresa Barker

Healthy Sleep Habits, Happy Child
By Marc Weissbluth

How To Talk So Kids Will Listen and Listen So Kids Will Talk
By Adele Faber, Elaine Mazlish

The Happiest Toddler on the Block: The New Way to Stop the Daily Battle of Wills and Raise a Secure and Well-Behaved One-to Four-Year-Old
By Harvey Karp, Paula Spencer

Making The "Terrible" Twos Terrific
By John Rosemond

Parenting With Love & Logic: Teaching Children Responsibility
By Foster W. Cline, Jim Fay

Parenting Teens With Love & Logic: Preparing Adolescents for Responsible Adulthood
By Foster W. Cline, Jim Fay

Positive Discipline
By Jane Nelsen

Physical Activities for Improving Children's Learning and Behavior
By Billye Ann Cheatum & Allison A. Hammond

Playful Parenting
By Lawrence J. Cohen

Raising Boys: Why Boys Are Different-And How to Help Them Become Happy and Well-Balanced Men
By Steve Biddulph

Raising Confident Boys: 100 Tips for Parents and Teachers
By Elizabeth Hartley-Brewer

Raising Confident Girls: 100 Tips for Parents and Teachers
By Elizabeth Hartley-Brewer

Raising Your Spirited Child: A Guide for Parents Whose Child is More Intense, Sensitivem Perceptive, Persistent, Energetic
By Mary Sheedy Kurcinka

Setting Limitswith Your Strong-Willed Child: Eliminating Conflict by Establishing Clear, Firm, and Respectful Boundaries
By Robert J. MacKenzie Ed.D

Siblings Without Rivalry-How To Help Your Children Live Together So You Can Live Too
By Adele Faber, Elaine Mazlish

Starting Smart-Creating Intelligent Kids
By A. Lynn Scoresby

Toddlers and Pre-Schoolers: Love and Logic Parenting for Early Childhood
By Jim Fay, Foster Cline

Helpful Websites

The following websites contain great information for parents and caregivers.

www.aap.org
www.babycenter.com
www.family.com
www.fatherhood.com
www.iamyourchild.org
www.parentcenter.com
www.parentingteenstoday.com
www.parentnetassociaton.org
www.parentsoup.com
www.parenting.com
www.zerotothree.org

Chapter 20

Teens

Chapter 20

Teens

Are you wondering how to advise teens concerning the ins and outs of dating? After reading this chapter, your children might come to think of you as the most resourceful person in town when you recommend unique and creative solutions to their dating dilemmas.

Also available are excellent resources for the more serious and difficult issues that teens may face. The recommended books are available online.

Communicating With Your Teen

As teens enter into high school, they become increasingly independent, spending much more of their time outside of their home. Communication is very important and you might have to work at it.

Here are a few tips to help:

- Always make time to hear about their activities, make sure you are actively interested and listening.
- Remember to talk to your teen, not at them.
- Prompt more developed conversation, don't accept just yes or no answers.
- Use "stolen" moments during car trips or standing in line to talk to your teen.
- Find activities that your family will enjoy together such as sporting and school events or outdoor activities that will give you something to discuss together.

Dating and Dances

Dating for Under a Dollar: 301 Ideas

by Blair and Tristan Tolman

This book is for teenagers, young adults, youth leaders, or anyone looking for creative dates that don't cost a lot of money. No more evenings of "What do we do now?" This fun and easy to read book gives hundreds of ideas that can make a real difference. Those who use these fun and original ideas won't ever be able to go back to dinner and a movie. You will be given:

- 43 activities for large group dates
- 107 group dates
- 21 holiday dates
- 53 single dates

The Dance Book: 555 Ways to Ask, Answer and Plan for Dances

by Blair and Tristan Tolman

This book provides hundreds of creative ideas including: 218 ways to ask someone to a dance, 179 ways to say "Yes", 55 ways to say "No", 19 dinner ideas, 16 day dates or after dance activities, 10 steps for planning a dance and 68 dance theme ideas.

Some great ideas from this book include:

Aluminum Foil- With the parent's permission, decorate your potential date's room with aluminum foil. Lay it on top of her bed, wrap it around her things, and tape it onto her door. Stick a poster on her door that says "Don't FOIL me now! ALUMIN-ate my life and go to the dance with me!"

Fish- Fill her bathtub with water and put three live goldfish in it. Hang a poster over the tub which says: "If fishes were wishes, you'd have three. Would one of them be to go to the dance with me?"

Telephone Book- Obtain a telephone book and search through it to locate your first and last names. (Although you may not be listed in the book, you will probably find two separate people with either your first or last name.) Highlight your first name and your last name with a yellow highlighter. Leave a note on her car which asks her to the dance but doesn't say who it's from. Leave another note in her mailbox, one on her porch, and another on her bedroom door. Finally, leave the telephone book on her bed with a note which tells her that the mysterious note writer's name is highlighted inside the telephone book with a yellow highlighter. She must look through it to determine your identity.

To Answer YES to a Dance:

Christmas Lights- One evening when he is at home, arrange a string of Christmas lights on his front lawn so that is spells, "YES!" Plug in the lights, ring the doorbell and hide. (Make sure that you don't leave the home until he has seen the lights)

Marbles- Put a bunch of marbles in between the mattress and the fitted sheet of his bed. Include a message with them that reads, "Yes! I'm sure we'll have a MARBLE-ous time!"

To Answer NO to a dance:

Band-Aids Adhesive Strips- Stick a bunch of band-aids all over a large piece of poster board. On the poster, write, "I wish this was an "OUCHless" answer but I'm HURT to say that I can't go to the dance with you!"

Chapstick Lip Balm- Purchase a tube of chapstick and give it to him with the following poem:
I hope you're not CHAPPED
But I have to say "No"
But STICK around please,
And next time we'll go!

Mummy- Follow these instructions to make a mummy: first, make a dummy by stuffing some old clothing with straw or newspaper. Then completely wrap the dummy in toilet paper or strips of an old sheet. Pin a note to the mummy that says, "I'm sorry I can's go this time....I'm all WRAPPED UP!" Leave the mummy on his front doorstep.

Other Ideas from Seattle Mama To Ask to a Dance:

Pop the Question- Leave helium balloons tied to the porch of your potential date's house. Before you fill the balloons with helium, fill them with confetti. In one of the balloons, place a piece of paper with your name on it mixed in with the confetti. Leave a note that reads "I'd POP if you'd go to the dance with me!"

Piñata- On small pieces of paper write each word, will, you, go, to, the, dance, with, me and than put your name on another piece of paper. Fill the piñata with candy and all of the separate pieces of paper. Hang the piñata on a basketball hoop or somewhere in her yard and leave a small bat or piece of wood so she can break the piñata. Leave a note that asks her to bust the piñata for "breaking" news.

Star Gazing- With permission from your dates parents, place glow in the dark stars spelling out your name on the ceiling of your potential dates bedroom. Leave a sign on their bed that reads: It is written in the STARS for you to go to the dance with me. When they go to bed that night, they will find out who asked them to the dance by staring up at their ceiling.

Kiss the Ground- Place Hershey's Kisses all over his/her bedroom floor with a note that reads "I'd kiss the ground you walk on if you'd go to the dance with me!" Replace one of the kisses flags with a strip of paper that has your name written on it.

Date Ideas

Take a look at the Places To Go and Things To Do, Calendar of Events, or The Great Outdoors chapters for lots of activities and events. Some other cheap date ideas include:

- Have a pool party
- Check out the local museums
- Have a picnic in the park
- Go ice-blocking
- Have a scavenger hunt
- Play games at night like "kick the can" or "Ghosts in the Graveyard"
- Host your own murder mystery game
- Have a barbeque
- Play Frisbee golf
- Go ice skating
- Have a water fight
- Make a gingerbread house
- Fly a kite
- Go to a college football game
- Play board games
- Go to a spring training game
- Make cookies and take them to a friend or neighbor
- Go hit golf balls at the driving range
- Take a hike
- Visit the zoo
- Do some star gazing
- Have a progressive dinner with friends
- Carve a pumpkin
- Go to a playground
- BE CREATIVE!

A Parent's Role in Dating

Be a Model for Healthy Relationships

How is your relationship with your spouse? Do you respect each other and model a strong friendship? Your relationship and behavior speaks far louder than anyone's words. Show your kids how you compromise, give and expect respect, care for, laugh with, and love each other. In turn they will seek out healthy respectful friendships and relationships.

Talk About Boundaries

This can be a tough topic, but it is one that you should all get comfortable with. At the appropriate time discuss sex and the surrounding issues. Make your teenager consider their standards and goals so that they have predetermined what their choices will be before they are in the thick of the situation. Encourage them to come to you with any questions. Instead of lecturing, discuss the topic openly so they will listen to your opinion, yet at the same time feel that they are making their own decisions.

Stay Involved

Know the who, what, when, where's and why's of your child's life. Make it a point to be around when your teenager, their friends, and their dates are in your home. Invite them to spend time in your home often when you are there. Make your home a safe and involved place.

Help Them Understand the Difference Between Dating and Physical Affection

Dating is getting to know and understand someone and building a relationship with him or her. Dating does not mean that there are implied physical advances. Too often, a youth's understanding of a dating relationship is attached to the physical expectations instead of the deepened friendship.

Educate Them About Signs of Abusive Relationships

Your teen should know that being manipulated, verbally put down, pushed or slapped, or being isolated from other relationships are all signs of an abusive relationship.

Teen Dating and Violence

One recent national survey found that 1 in 11 high school students said they had been hit, slapped, or physically hurt on purpose by their boyfriend or girlfriend in the past year. Reports state that 1 in 11 students also had been forced to have sexual intercourse when they did not want to.

(Center for Disease Control and Prevention. Youth risk behavior surveillance-United States, 1999. In: CDC Surveillance Summaries, June 9,2000. MMWR 2000;49(No. SS-5), p.8)

Typically the following behaviors are signs of a potentially abusive relationship:

- Extreme jealousy
- Exhibit controlling behavior
- Unpredictable mood swings
- Alcohol and drug use
- Explosive temper
- Isolates you from friends and family in need for more attention for himself/herself
- Shows hypersensitivity and uses force during an argument
- Blames others for his/her problems and feelings
- Threatens to hurt or kill him/herself if the partner threatens to break up
- You are sometimes afraid of your partner
- You are often apologizing to friends and family for your partner's behavior

Teach your teenager that if they are in a dating relationship that in any way feels uncomfortable, awkward, tense or even frightening, they need to trust their feelings and get out of it. It could become, or may already be, abusive.

Remind them that they always have the right to say no. No boyfriend or girlfriend has the right to tell them what they can or should do, what they can or should wear, or what kind of friends they should have.

To learn more about dating violence and how to help, call the National Youth Violence Prevention Center 866-723-3968 or visit their website www.safeyouth.org.

Crisis Hot Lines

Childhelp USA

800-4-A-CHILD (800-422-4453)

www.childhelpusa.org

The National hotline for the prevention and treatment of child abuse. They offer counselors over the phone who listen and refer you to local services.

Crisis Clinic of King County

206-461-3222

206-461-4922 (Teen Line)

EMPACT
480-784-1500
www.empact-spc.com
If you are considering suicide please call this number first! Trained counselors are there to help!

HopeLine Suicide Hotline
800-SUICIDE (800-784-2433)
www.hopeline.com
This website offers support and help to put a stop to depression and suicide.

Washington Suicide and Crisis Hotline
800-784-2433
800-273-8255

Swedish Medical Center
www.swedish.org/16988.cfm
Information on suicide prevention, including myths, and warning signs.

National Child Abuse Hotline
800-422-4453

National Runaway Switchboard
800-621-4000
24 Hour Hotline providing crisis intervention, information, and referrals.

The Nine Line
800-999-9999
www.covenanthouseny.org
This is a 24 hour hotline for youth and their parents providing intervention, abuse, and referrals.

Rape Recovery Hotline
800-656-HOPE

Community Resources for/about Teens

not MY kid, Inc.
www.notmykid.org
Not MY kid is dedicated to raising awareness about the most prevalent youth and adolescent mental and behavioral health issues including suicide, drug abuse, eating disorders and depression. This is a resourceful site for dealing with teens in crisis.

Parent Teen Guide, LLC

www.parentteenguide.com
Provides free booklets which provide tips for parents with a teen that is struggling in his/her family, home or school.

Domestic and Dating Violence

Domestic Violence Information Line
800-897-LINK

Department of Social and Health Services (DSHS)
866-ENDHARM

www1.dshs.wa.gov/
Report abuse allegations.

not MY kid, Inc.
www.notmykid.org

National Domestic Violence/Abuse Hotline
800-787-SAFE (7233)

www.ndvh.org
The National Domestic Violence Hotline (NDVH) serves as the only center in the nation that provides information regarding 5,000 local and nationwide shelters and service providers available for victims, friends and family who often call for life saving help. The Hotline operates 24 hours a day in over 150 languages with a TTY line available for the hearing impaired.

Rape and Incest Hotline
800-656-HOPE (4673)

www.rainnorg
The Rape, Abuse & Incest National Network (RAINN) is the nation's largest anti-sexual assault organization. RAINN operates the National Sexual Assault Hotline and carries out programs to prevent sexual assault, help victims and ensure that rapists are brought to justice. On the website you will find statistics, counseling resources, prevention tips, new and more.

Drug Abuse Information & Treatment

A Accredited Addiction Treatment Of First Step To Recovery
800-720-6647

Alpha Center For Treatment
10614 Beardslee Blvd, Bothell
425-483-4664
360-384-7187

Center For Counseling & Health Resources Inc
425-771-5166

Conquest Center Inc
PO Box 667, Edmonds
425-742-6481

Division of Alcohol and Substance Abuse (DASA)
206-722-3700 (24 Hour Alcohol and Drug Help Line)
800-562-1240 (24 Hour Alcohol and Drug Help Line)
www1.dshs.wa.gov/dasa
The DASA offers counseling and referral services for alcohol and substance abuse treatment and prevention. Their goals are to:

Turn those who abuse alcohol and drugs into productive and self-supporting citizens Promote safer communities and family stability, reduce crime, health care, welfare, and other social costs associated with alcohol and drug abuse

Improve the academic performance of the children of Washington state.

Avert the onset of addiction.

Evergreen Manor
www.evergreenmanor.org

Hazelden Foundation
800-257-7800

Lakeside-Milam Recovery Centers
Inpatient & Outpatient Programs
Adolescent Residential
12845 Ambaum Blvd. SW, Burien
206-241-0890

Everett Outpatient
111 SE Everett mall Way # A-101
425-267-9573

Edmonds Outpatient
7935 Lake Ballinger Way
425-670-3664

Kirkland Outpatient
10422 NE 37th Circle Suite #B
425-822-5095

Bellevue
425-452-8343

Seattle Outpatient
2815 Eastlake Ave E #100
206-341-9373

Motivations
17311-135th Ave NE Suite C400, Woodinville
425-481-2112

Northwest Alternatives
Youth/Adult Outpatient Treatment

Lynnwood
4230 198th St SW #100
425-774-4333

Everett
3331 Broadway Suite 1003
425-258-1515

Marysville
1227 2nd St
360-651-2366

Olalla Recovery Centers
Alchohol Information and Treatment
12851 SE Lala Cove Lane, Olalla
253-857-6201
800-882-6201
800-833-6388
www.olalla.org

Providence Everett Medical Center
Pacific Campus
425-258-7390

Residence XII For Women
Kirkland
800-776-5944
www.residencexii.com

Ryther Child Center
2400 NE 95th, Seattle
206-525-5050

Schick Shadel Hospital
24 Hour Admission
425-252-2225

www.schick-shadel.com

Therapeutic Health Services
Outpatient Drug/Opiate Treatment
9930 Evergreen Way Suite Z150, Everett
425-347-5152

Valley General Hospital Alcohol/Drug Recovery Center
14701 179th Ave SE, Monroe
360-794-1405

Washington State Alcohol/Drug Clearing House (WSADC)
6535 - 5th Place South, Seattle
206-725-9696 (Seattle)
800-662-9111
clearinghouse@adhl.org
www.clearinghouse.adhl.org
Hours: Monday-Friday 8:00am-5:00pm
The WSADC provides information to the people of Washington State on issues relating to alcohol, tobacco and other drugs. They host video lending library of over six hundred educational videos, hundreds of different free publications, fact sheets, brochures, pamphlets, posters, and educational materials covering alcohol, tobacco and other drug issues.

List of Resources:
- Addiction/Chemical Dependency
- AIDS/HIV/STD's
- Alcohol/Alcoholism
- ASAM Manuals
- Children of Alcoholics

- Co-dependency
- College
- Community
- Diverse Populations
- DUI/Drinking and Driving
- Drug-Exposed Children/FAS/FAE
- Drug-Free Workplace
- Just For Kids
- Just For Teens
- Media
- Older Adults
- Other Drugs
- Parenting
- Pregnancy
- Prevention Science
- Recovery
- Spanish Language
  (other languages too!)
- State/National Reports
- TIPS/TAPS
- Tobacco/Nicotine
- Treatment
- Treatment Professionals
- Violence Prevention
- WAC/WIG

Women's Issues

Washington State Department of Social and Health Services (DSHS)

360-902-7801

360-725-3431: Division of Developmental Disabilities

They provide information and resources available in 8 languages for the following:

- Adoption
- Alcohol/Drugs
- Basic Food
- Basic Health
- Budget
- Child Abuse
- Child Care
- Child Safety
- Child Support

- Child Welfare
- Deaf Services
- Disabilities
- Domestic Violence
- Facing The Future
- Food Stamps
- Foster Parenting
- Infants/Toddlers
- Juvenile Rehabilitation
- Medicaid, Mental Health, Newborn Child
- Prevention Tips
- Sex Offenders
- Victim Services
- Vocational Rehabilitation
- Youth Mentoring

Plus...

Find Answers to these Often Asked Questions Asked:

- How can I report child abuse?
- How can I report domestic violence?
- How can I get drug and alcohol treatment?
- How do I get child support for my children?
- How do I get help to buy food?
- How do I get money to help pay for my bills?
- How do I get information on what help I can get?
- How do I apply for food, cash, or medical benefits?
- How do I apply for help with child care bills?
- How do I adopt a child?
- How do I found out if day care is licensed?
- How do I get assistance for my disabled child?

DSHS has a new website targeting Autism awareness:
www1.dshs.wa.gov/ddd/autism.shtml

Drug Detection & Testing

The Drug Prevention Specialists Inc
21705 Hwy 99, Mountlake Terrace
425-775-1095

Driving

Driving Skills For Life
888-987-8765
www.drivingskillsforlife.com
Ford has given you this great resource for teens and parents. It has teen tips, parent tips, statistics and many links with important information about driving an automobile.

National Teen Safety Driving Council
480-474-8153
How's my teen driving? This is an ongoing program that enables parents to monitor their teenage drivers even when they are not with them for $29.95 annually per vehicle.

Road Ready Teens
www.roadreadyteens.org
Road Ready Teens provides parents of teenagers learning to drive — or those who've just begun to drive — with tips and tools to ease their teens into driving. With Road Ready Teens, teenagers are able to first gain critical experience and driving maturity before they face higher risk situations.

Eating Disorder Information & Treatment

Center For Counseling And Health Resources, Inc.
425-771-5166
www.aplaceofhope.com
This center specializes in the mental and emotional issues of eating disorders, depression, and addiction.

Eating Disorders-Facts for Teens

www.familydoctor.org
A network filled with health facts and informational links to specific health related topics.

Eating Disorder Referral and Information Center

www.edreferral.com/
An excellent data base covering the whole gamut of eating disorders, including building a positive body image. This site provides information and treatment resources for all types of eating disorders.

Family Resources NW

1814 105th St Se, Everett
425-316-3645

National Eating Disorders Association

www.nationaleatingdisorders.org
Education, research, support for individuals and their families. They also provide a referral list for treatment.

Gang & Violence Prevention

Mothers Against Gang Wars

home.inreach.com/gangbang/magw.htm
Mothers Against Gang Wars is dedicated to ending gang violence and the destruction of youth.

National Youth Violence Prevention Resource Center

866-SAFEYOUTH
866-723-3968
www.safeyouth.org
Topics, publications, and Q&A e-mail to a professional on preventative issues concerning violence, including gangs fact sheet, aggressive behavior, abuse, bullying, exposure to violence, hate crimes, and more.

Seattle Team For Youth (STFY)

www.ci.seattle.wa.us/humanservices/fys/Youth/STFY-MOP.htm

The STFY joined forces with the City of Seattle Human Services Department, Seattle Police and 12 community-based agencies to provide free support services for gang-involved and at-risk youth. Its mission is to "divert youth from criminal involvement and to increase their connection with school and educational activities". They work with Seattle youth who have problems relating to gangs, substance abuse, the criminal justice system, homelessness, truancy, or physical or sexual abuse.

Grief Support for Teens

Hospice Net

www.hospicenet.org/html/teenager.html

Helping teenagers cope with grief.

Helpful Teen Websites and Organizations

TeenCentral.Net

www.teencentral.net

This is a website for teens by teens who offer help for teen problems.

Teen Lifeline

602-248-TEEN (8336)

Provides safe, confidential and crucial crisis service where teens help teens make healthy decisions together.

Teen Link

www.teenlink.umn.edu

Teen-Link was developed as a means for educators and other professionals, parents, teachers, youth and anyone working with adolescents or interested in adolescent development to obtain quick access to a variety of resources, both academic and practical, addressing teen issues.

Missing Person Services

Operation Lookout National Center For Missing Youth

425-771-7335

Skill Development or Employment

Job Corps

800-426-5627

jobcorps.doleta.gov/

Sponsored by the U.S. Department of Education, Job Corps offers no-cost education and vocational training for young people ages 16-24. Students learn a trade, earn a high school diploma or GED, and get help finding a good job. Students will receive a monthly allowance, and will continue the allowance for up to 1 year after graduation from the program. Applicants must be a U.S. Citizen or legal resident, and meet income requirements.

GrooveJob.Com

www.groovejob.com/browse/jobs/in/WA/Washington

A list of part time jobs, and jobs for teens in Washington State.

High School Hub

www.highschoolhub.org

Free online academic resource for high school students. It features subject guides for English, math social studies, science and more.

The Teenagers Guide to the Real World Online

www.bygpub.com/books/tg2rw/resumes.htm

this is an online resource for the book *The Teenager's Guide to the Real World* by Marshall Brain. The online resources are offered as a free supplement to the book. Interviewing and resume writing are two of the services offered.

Teen Pregnancy

One Young Parent

www.oneyoungparent.com

Teen site created to encourage, support and inspire teen parents so that they may raise healthier and happier children and be happy themselves. It does not glamorize teen sex, pregnancy or parenting; it simply supports those who are pregnant.

LDS Family Services

Washington Seattle Agency

220 South Third Place, Renton

425-228-0074

They provide counseling and adoption services for pregnant teens.

The National Campaign to Prevent Teen Pregnancy

www.teenpregnancy.org
Its mission is to improve the well-being of children, youth and families by reducing teen pregnancy.

Teen Pregnancy

202-478-8500

www.teenpregnancy.org
The national campaign to prevent teen pregnancy.

Washington Aids Hotline

800-272-2437
800-242-2437 (24 Hour National Hotline)

www.thebody.com/hotlines.html
Washington State test site referrals, counseling, basic information and prevention, literature, clinical trials information referrals.

Preparing and Paying for College

Federal Student Aid

www.studentaid.ed.gov
Information on how to help your child prepare for education beyond high school, including academic and financial information pertaining to college.

Runaways

Over 1.5 million children had a runaway or throwaway episode in 1999. runaway cases occur when a child of 14 years or less leaves home without permission for at least one night. For older children, a runaway is defined as a child who stays out for at least two nights. Throwaway episodes occur when a parent or other household adult tells a child to leave the house without arranging alternative care and prevents the child from returning home.

Runaway/throwaway findings:
- Two-thirds of children are between 15 and 17 years old
- The male-female ratio is equal
- More than half returned home in the same week
- 99% return home
- 21% are physically or sexually abused at home

Why children run away from home:
- 42% have family problems

- 14% because of peer pressure
- 5% because of drug or alcohol abuse
- 4% because of physical abuse

Taken from Child Find, Inc. www.childfindofamerica.org

Child Find, Inc.
800-I-AM-LOST (800-426-5678)

www.childfindofamerica.org
Call this number if you have run away from home and you want to contact your family.

National Center for Missing and Exploited Children
800-THE-LOST (800-843-5678)

www.ncmec.org
The National Center for Missing & Exploited Children's (NCMEC) mission is to help prevent child abduction and sexual exploitation; help find missing children; and assist victims of child abduction and sexual exploitation, their families and the professionals who serve them.

National Runaway Switchboard
800-RUNAWAY (800-786-2929)

www.nrscrisisline.org
To keep America's runaway and at-risk youth safe and off the streets.

Team H.O.P.E.
866-305-HOPE (4673)

www.teamhope.org
Network for families with missing children. Offering hope, guidance, friendship, understanding, coping skills, emotional support and resources.

Substance Abuse

Al-Anon /Alateen
480-969-6144

www.al-anon.alateen.org
Support for family and friends of an alcoholic. Find a list of local meetings on their website.

Drug Test Your Teen

www.drugtestyourteen.com
Website offering at home drug test products to buy. Informative site about drugs and your kids.

Narcotics Anonymous

480-897-4636
Information and support if you have a drug abuse problem. Free and confidential.

Support for Teens With Divorced Families

Bonus Families

www.bonusfamilies.com
Forum for teens to talk to other teens and find solutions to problems they have had with a divorce or separation in their lives.

Chapter 21

Family Vacation Guide

Chapter 21

Family Vacation Guide

Whether you want to plan a family vacation for a day or a week, the great northwest has so much to offer. We have a variety of recreation and unique getaways right in our backyard. You can really "get away" without going far.

49 Degree North Mountain Resort

3311 Flowery Trail Road
Chewelah, Washington
509-935-6649
www.ski49n.com

Voted one of the regions best family resorts, "49" offers great fun and adventure for all ages including wide-open well-groomed runs, moguls, desert dried powder, and hundreds of acres of skiing located in the Colville National Forest. Chewelah Peak Summit offers views of natural wonders such as the Kettle Range. There are Lodge facilities in the base area.

Flying Horseshoe Ranch

3190 Red Bridge Rd
Cle Elum, Washington
509-674-2366
www.flyinghorseshoeranch.com

A fun place for family vacations and reunions. You can lodge in six different places including a log cabin and tepee. There are horseback rides with two wranglers to "show you the ropes". They will help you saddle the horse and teach you how to ride before your 2 to 2 1/2 hour journey through the beautiful country side. Afterwards, you can relax in a hot tub, or go swimming. There are two cook houses, so you can take your own food, or have the "Mama" of the ranch, cook up a delicious meal ($15/person). Open from early spring until late fall, 7 days a week.

Icicle Junction Family Fun Center

Leavenworth, Washington
565 Highway 2
509-548-2400
800-558-2438
www.icicleinn.com
Spend a whole day with the family for activities at the wild & wet bumper boats, batting cages, air hockey, video games, the climbing pinnacle, junction cinema, and a train ride around the park that travels over ponds, with Koi fish to feed! Amenities include a game room, pool rooms, video games and snack bar. Also enjoy the quaint little Bavarian style town nestled amid the beautiful mountains, with its unique shops and restaurants.

Lake Chelan

360-856-5700 x 310
www.nps.gov/lach
Part of the North Cascades National Park, Lake Chelan has 62,000 acres, and is one American's largest lakes. It is surrounded by wilderness and tall mountain peaks. It offers boating, fishing, lakeshore camping, bird watching, hiking & nature walks, wildlife viewing, horseback riding through the beautiful trails, and snow skiing in the winter. Visit the Golden West Visitors Center where you can find information on the many interesting features of this very scenic recreational area..

Lake Roosevelt National Recreation Area

Grand Coulee, Washington
509-738-6266
www.nps.gov/laro
Named after President Franklin D. Roosevelt, Lake Roosevelt offers visitor the opportunity to fish, swim, camp, and canoe. History buffs will want to visit historic Fort Spokane and the St. Paul Mission.

Olympic National Park

Port Angeles, Washington
360-565-3130
www.nps.gov/olym
The three distinct ecosystems including the glacier-capped mountains, the unusually beautiful and rare old-growth rain forest, and more than 60 miles of breathtaking Pacific Coast, make this park one of the most sought-after vacation spots. Take a leisurely ride or bring your hiking shoes and backpack into the forests to enjoy the wildlife and nature at its best.

Mount St. Helens National Volcanic Monument

42218 NE Yale Bridge Rd
Amboy, Washington
360-247-3900
www.ff.fed.us/gpnf
This is a chance for families to see a live volcano. Drive to Windy Ridge, only 4 miles northeast of the crater, for the spectacular view of Spirit Lake. From here you can see the evidence of the volcano's influence, and how the land has re-vegetated, along with the return of wildlife. Be sure to stop at the visitor's center at Silver Lake, 5 miles east of Interstate Highway 5. Mountain climbing to the summit of the volcano has been allowed since year 1986, but with all the recent activity, you will need to acquire current information before you make plans. There are overnight camping spots.

Mount Rainier National Park

Ashford, Washington
360-569-2211
www.nps.gov/mora
Mount Rainier is an active volcano with 35 miles of snow and ice. Families can hike, climb to the summit, snowshoe, cross-country skiing, camping by snow-fed rivers, enjoy wildflowers in the spring & summer, or just go to enjoy the spectacular view. Nearly two million people visit Mount Rainier each year. Most roads open in late May to early October.

North Cascades National Park
Marblemount, Washington
360-856-5700
www.nps.gov/noca
See and enjoy some of the most beautiful scenery in America. Cascading waterfalls, beautiful forests, over 300 glaciers, and jagged mountain peaks fill in the 505,000 acres. Wonderful family activities include: horseback riding, camping, hiking, mountain climbing, fishing, wildlife and bird watching, and boating. Facilities include small boat rentals, horse rentals, hiking trails, professional guides, climbing and backpack services.
Camping areas are available.

"Sea View" Houseboat on Lake Union
206-439-7677
www.seattlebedandbreakfast.com
Price: $175/night (based on 2 night stay), or $210/night (1 night only), plus $10 each additional person.
The cozy Sea View boasts a breathtaking view of downtown Seattle aboard the lower and top decks. A kayak or dingy is provided for guests and a self serve continental breakfast and snacks are included. Guests receive the Seattle Entertainment Coupon Book to save on nearby restaurants and activities.

Whidbey & Camano Islands
888-747-7777
These islands are filled with beaches, golf courses, tons of great shopping, beautiful parks, and historic areas.

Orcas Island
Hop aboard the ferry from Anacortes to Orcas Island for a day, or a week of family activities in hiking, biking, whale watching, golfing, museums, shopping, and great food. Obstruction Pass Park, Mt. Constitution in Moran State Park boasts a 360 degree view stretching to Victoria, B.C.

Orcas Island Vacation Home
650-856-2525
E-mail: melinda_mcgee@hotmail.com
This quaint secluded home located along the shore offers a sweeping view of the Rosario Strait, the Cypress, Sinclair, and Blakely Islands, the Peapod Rocks, and the Cascade Mountains. Guests are sometimes greeted with a bald eagle landing nearby, salmon dancing across the water, or the occasional pod of orcas on parade just off the shore.

Rosario Resort & Spa
1400 Rosario Road. Eastsound
360-376-2222
800-562-8820
http://rosario.rockresorts.com/
This historic resort and marina was first built as an estate belonging to Robert Moran (of Moran State Park). The resort features 54 rooms, the Moran museum, music room and pipe organ, gift shops, lounge, veranda and restaurants. Rosario describes the resorts decorated with "teakwood floors, rich mahogany paneling, original furnishings and Tiffany accents contribute to its elegant ambience". Perched on the hillside next to the gardens and the Cascade Bay, you'll find the guest rooms and suites. A luxurious full service spa is also available.

RV Parks on Orcas Island:

Doe Bay
360-376-2291

Moran State Park
360-376-2326

West Beach Resort
360-376-2240
888-937-8224

Ocean Shores

Enjoy 6000 acres of peninsula along Washington's central Pacific coast, known for Washington's most beautiful and family friendly beaches.

Aaron & Abby's Vacation Beach Rental
360-417-0998
Up to 14 guests can stay at this beach rental which boasts a gorgeous ocean view, Airbath, spa sauna, 42" plasma TV with surround sound, games, movies, play station, and a hot tub.

The Gibson's Bed & Breakfast
125 Taholah Street SE, Ocean Shores
360-289-7960
360-580-9199 (Cell Phone)
Guests are invited to bring their own G-Scale trains (or use the B & B's) to the Garden Railroad, or bring your kayak to launch at their private boat dock for a spectacular ride along the shores. Spend the evening watching a move in the full 6.2 digital Art Deco Home Movie Theater and enjoy ice cream from the 1920 style Soda Fountain. Breakfast is served in the Tea Room near a gas burning fireplace.

The Polynesian
615 Ocean Shores Boulevard NW, Ocean Shores
360-289-3361
Located on the ocean side along the beach, their two bedroom suite sleeps up to 8 people and features a private deck and DVD. Amenities include an indoor pool and sauna, arcade, pool table, a park out back, an on-site restaurant with available room service, and a continental breakfast, park out back. 5 minute through the dunes to the beach.

Silver Waves Bed & Breakfast
982 Point Brown Avenue SE, Ocean Shores
360-289-2490
888-257-0894

RV Parks @ Ocean Shores
Echoes of the Seat Motel & RV
360-289-3358

Ocean Shores Marina & RV Park
360-289-3459

Ocean City State Park/Pacific Beach State Park
360-289-3553

(Campsites also available)

Long Beach

Long Beach hosts 28 miles of the longest natural beach in the United States, with thriving 1,000 year old Western Red Cedars along Willapa Bay. Choose from a plethora of outdoor activities including canoeing, horseback riding, hiking, biking, scenic areas, amusements, lighthouses, military forts, museums, spas, shopping, and great food.

Boreas Inn
607 N Boulevard
360-642-8069
888-642-8069
Voted the "Best Breakfast in the Northwest" in 2005 by Arrington's Inn Traveler, this quiet, peaceful, and serene oceanfront mini resort features breathtaking views, a gourmet breakfast, and a cedar and glass Gazebo with a 32-jet therapeutic spa available to all guests.

Chautauqua Lodge
304 N 14th St
360-642-4401
800-869-8401
www.ocean-front-hotel.com
An oceanfront suite awaits guests at the lodge. Amenities include an indoor heated pool, 2 hot tubs, a game room, on-site restaurant, with kitchenettes and fireplaces available upon request. This lodge is handicap accessible. Pets are welcome.

The Breakers
360-642-4414
800-219-9833
www.breakerslongbeach.com
Stay at the literal spot marking the end of the Lewis and Clark trail. Amenities include an indoor heated pool, 24 acres of beachfront lawn and dunes, sand volleyball, horseshoeing, a large playground, barbeques, picnic tables, and kite flying.

Coeur d'Alene, Idaho

Coeur d'Alene Golf Resort

www.cdaresort.com/golf/index.php

www.cdaresort.com/spa/index.php

The resort overlooks the beautiful Lake Coeur d'Alene, adjacent to the #2 nationally ranked golf course (second only to Pebble Beach). This golf course was described by Chip Beck of the PGA Tour as "one of the finest he has ever seen, lauding it as a course playable for families, yet challenging enough to test the pros". An overnight stay at the resort includes 2 free adult passes to the Silverwood Theme Park.

Cottage By The Lake

406-581-9851

www.cottageby-the-lake.net

Located in a quaint community near the lake, the elegant 3 bedroom cottage features a fully stocked gourmet kitchen, laundry facilities, a living room fireplace, and a lushly landscaped fenced yard with a Coy fish pond and grill. They offer best discount passes for Silverwood Theme Park and Boulder Beach Water Park. Pets are negotiable.

Silverwood Theme Park

www.silverwoodthemepark.com

208-683-3400

(15 miles north of Coeur d'Alene)

Prices: Ages 7-64: $30 -1 day $48 -2 days, Ages 3-7, and 65+: $19 -1 day $28 -2 days.

Dates: Open May-October (1st week)

Welcome to the biggest theme park in the great Northwest. This park has it all...from thrilling rides to kid-friendly rides, magic shows, ice performances, and a huge water park with a lazy river, wave pool, and a tree house just for kids.

Black Rhino Tours

www.blackrhinotours.com

208-765-8687

Price: $89/person

Take the 3 hour Bicentennial tour in a Hum Jeep through the Bitterroot Mountains. Travel deep into the Coeur d'Alene National Forest, and climb to 4,600 feet above sea level. View breathtaking view of the Wolf Lodge Valley, then onto Fernan Lake where you'll enjoy a delicious hot meal. You'll want to bring your camera up close encounters with Elk and other wildlife.

Kayak

www.kayakcoeurdalene.com

208-676-1533

Enjoy a 3 hour kayaking tour of Lake Coeur d'Alene, known for some of the best lake kayaking in the country. Families and children are encouraged to. This is a great activity for birding, as Osprey, Bald Eagles, and the Great Blue Heron are often spotted.

Rider Ranch

www.riderranch.com

208-667-3373

Saddle up for horseback riding or a horse drawn hay ride with gentle, friendly horses. Smell the fresh pine and wild flowers on this "true", 3rd generation 1,000 acre cattle and horse ranch, located in the timberland mountains a short distance from the city. You can choose between a day ride concluding with refreshments, or an evening ride concluding with a dinner.

River Odysseys

www.rowinc.com

800-451-6034

Whether you want to go on a 1 day or up to 6 day trip, with over 20 years experience, guides will take you on this thrilling, one of a kind adventure. Families with children ages 5 and older are eligible, with special designated Family Focus trips.

Canada

Stanley Park

Vancouver, B.C.

Bring your bikes, or rent bikes at a shop just outside the park, and tour the breathtakingly beautiful sites surrounding the park. Bike riding provides visitors an experience you just can't get driving in a car, plus allows for a one day tour. There are plenty of stopping points along the path, including several beaches, an outdoor sprinkler park, a large swimming pool overlooking the lake, and a few lunch spots. Be sure to grab a map at the ticket and information booth near the entrance of the park.

The Stanley Park Aquarium is a must see for all visitors. Here you will have the opportunity for a rare and close up view of the Beluga whales. This alone is worth the visit. The aquarium is filled with sea life and has scheduled animal acts throughout the day.

The Butchart Gardens

Victoria, BC

866-652-4422

www.butchartgardens.com

Fifty five acres of beautiful gardens offer a spectacular feast for the eyes from the many paths and four main gardens. For more than 100 years, these colorful gardens have continued to delight people from all over the world. Families can enjoy the many fountains, waterfalls, breath-taking view of the Sunken Gardens, the Japanese Gardens, and Rose Garden. There is also a gift shop, dining room, and restaurant. On Saturday nights there are fireworks. You'll definitely want to bring your camera.

Whistler Ski Resort Area

Whistler, B.C.

877-932-0606

Between the Whistler and Blackcomb Mountains, there are 8,100 acres of ski able, and ride able terrain. Located just 4-5 hours from Seattle, Whistler offers some of the best skiing in the Northwest. There is plenty of room for an endless variety of entertainment for the whole family. 25 hotels dot the resort which makes it a great place for family reunions. Ask about the special kid's programs.

Wintertime activities:

Snowmobiling, sleigh riding, dog sledding, Bald Eagle Festival (in December when salmon are running), helicopter-tours, snowshoeing, and cross country skiing.

Summertime activities:

White water rafting, bike tours, jet-skiing , fishing, water sports, horseback riding, golf, bear watching, boating & swimming in the many lakes in area plus many more outdoor activities the whole family can enjoy.

Chapter 22

Just for Mamas and Papas

Chapter 22

Just for Mamas & Papas

If you are in need of a romantic overnight getaway, or a spa to relax in for the afternoon… this chapter is for you! Everyone, especially parents, need to take the opportunity to relax and unwind every now and again. After you enjoy some pampering at one of these establishments, you will come home to the kids feeling refreshed, renewed, and rejuvenated.

Bed & Breakfast:

King County

Heart & Soul Houseboat on Lake Union
206-439-7677
www.seattlebedandbreakfast.com
Price: $215/night (based on 2 night stay) or $250/night (1 night only).
You're sleepless in Seattle dream can come true with your own stay on an elegant houseboat. A kayak or dingy is provided for guests, and the top deck boasts a sweeping view of downtown Seattle. A self serve continental breakfast is included.

Mildred's Bed & Breakfast

206-364-5900

www.mildredsbnb.com

Price: $90 to $165/night

Go back into time with this 1860 Victorian home on Capital Hill. Choose from four elegantly decorated rooms including the Lace Room and Rose Room. A quiet and peaceful spot located in the heart of Seattle, sits across from Volunteer Park, the Asian Art Museum, flower conservatory, and the historic brick water tower you can climb for a spectacular view. A supreme breakfast is served in the morning.

A Cascade View Bed & Breakfast

Bellevue

425-883-7078

www.acascadeview.com

Price: $100-$125/night (2 night minimum stay)

Nestled in the quiet and wooded hills of Bellevue with a view of the beautiful Cascade Mountains. Wake up to a scrumptious homemade breakfast with the freshest eggs delivered from their own hens, then take a stroll along the gorgeous rose garden.

A Cottage Creek Inn Bed & Breakfast

12525 Avondale Road NE, Redmond

425-881-5606

www.cottagecreekinn.com

Price: $89 to $125/night

A romantic and secluded English Tudor Bed and Breakfast situated on 3.5 acres of woodland garden area. Close to nature trails, flower gardens, wildlife, and a goldfish pond. Cottage Creek flows through the front where Salmon run in the fall. You can even enjoy an onsite massage. A full breakfast is included.

Amaranth Inn

1451 S Main, Seattle

206-325-4100

www.amaranthinn.com

Price: $75 to $165/night

A 1906 Seattle Craftsman home located less than a mile of downtown Seattle. Elegant guestrooms with gas fireplaces and jetted tubs await guests in a quiet and peaceful setting. Arise in the morning and feast upon an elegant gourmet breakfast!

Artist Studio Loft B&B

16529 91st Ave SW, Vashon Island
206-463-2583
www.asl-bnb.com
Price: $95 to $160/night
Come relax in this luxurious setting filled with gorgeous gardens and nature trails. Sit by the pond where swallows, songbirds, dragon flies, blue heron, and king fisher are often spotted. 3 lovely beaches are located nearby, along with art galleries, and lightly traveled roads perfect for bike riding. Unwind in the evening soaking in the hot tub at the gazebo.

Bacon Mansion

959 Broadway E, Seattle
206-329-1864
www.baconmansion.com
Price: $82 to $179/night
Located in the Historical Harvard-Belmont Landmark District, this 1909 classical Edwardian Style Tudor Mansion boasts 9,000 square feet divided into 4 levels, 3,000 crystal chandeliers, marble fireplaces, and library. Capital Hill and downtown Seattle located near to the Bacon Mansion.

Snohomish County

A Rivers Edge Country Cottage

P.O.Box 614 , Goldbar
360-793-0392
www.ariversedge.com
Price: $85
This cottage boasts a charming, serene view of Mount Index and is the perfect spot for hiking, fishing, kayaking, whitewater rafting, skiing, rock climbing and just relaxing by the beautiful Skyhomish River. After the fun, you can relax and unwind in the hot tub. A full breakfast features homemade blueberry muffins.

Camano Blossom Bed & Breakfast
1462 Larkspur Lane, Camano Island
360-629-6784
www.camanoblossombandb.com
Price: $128/night
This is a perfect place to celebrate an anniversary. Warm hospitality greets guests in this quiet and beautiful setting near nature and birding trails, and the beautiful Camano Island State Park. A homemade breakfast and afternoon snacks are included, with authentic Asian dinner cuisine optional.

Camano Island Waterfront Inn
1054 West Camano Dr, Camano Island
360-387-0783
www.camanoislandinn.com
Price: $120 to $225/night
Ranked in the top 5 B & B's in US by Travel and Leisure Magazine! Located along the waterfront, each room has a private deck with a beautiful view of the Puget Sound, and the Olympic Mountains. Choose between breakfast in the elegant dining room, or breakfast in bed.

Conger's Cedar Inn
5732 Robe Menzel Road, Granite Falls
360-691-3830
www.congerscedarinn.com
Price: $89-$135/night
Voted the "best B & B in Snohomish & Island Counties" by the Herald. Located in the charming town of Granite Falls on 5 acres of woods with a breathtaking view of Mount Pilchuck, and close to the Ice Caves hiking trail, and golf courses.

Country Man Bed & Breakfast
119 Cedar Ave, Snohomish
360-568-9622
www.countrymanbandb.com
Price: $85/night (continental breakfast), $95/night (full breakfast)
An 1896 Queen Anne Victorian B & B located in historic Snohomish with elegant rooms featuring a cozy fireplace and jacuzzi. Antique shopping is 1 block away!

Inn At Barnum Point

464 Barnum Rd, Camano Island
360-387-2256
800-910-2256
www.innatbarnumpoint.com
Price: $100-$199/night
Featured in Sunset magazine in 2002, this serene beachfront B & B home hosts a spectacular view of Salt Water Bay and the Cascade Mountains from each room. Expect to see wild life and beauty in the one hundred year old orchard, launch a canoe or kayak (rentals nearby) from their beach, bring your bikes or rent tandem bikes for the nearby trails at the Camano Island State Park. A boat launch for larger boats is nearby.

McNab-Hogland House

917 Webster St, Mukilteo
425-742-7639
www.hoglandhouse.com
Price: $105-115/night
A romantic escape to a historical turn-of-the-century B & B, located on the bluff in Old Mukilteo. The McNab-Hogland house features five acres of wooded trails heading to the beach, and window views of Whidbey Island and the Puget Sound.

Pillows & Platters

502 Ave C, Snohomish
360-862-8944
www.pillowsandplatters.com
Price: $90/night
Built in 1892, this B & B brings guests a romantic and relaxing atmosphere just a few blocks away from world famous Antique Capitol of the Pacific. A tasty multi-choice breakfast menu is included.

Spirit Ridge Inn

146 Spirit Ridge Lane, Camano Island
360-387-7800
www.spiritridgeinn.com
Price: $100 to $180/night
Located high on the northern ridge of Camano Island, this cabin B & B features a panoramic view of Cascade Mountains and overlooks the Puget Sound. Spend the evening stargazing by the cozy campfire. Handicap Accessible.

Spring Bay Inn-Orcas Island

www.springbayinn.com

Price: $220 to $260/night

A secluded waterfront retreat tranquilly placed amidst 57 acres of hiking trails, wetlands, and forest. Guests can take advantage of the morning guided kayak tour (included) filled with wildlife and sea life. Beginners are welcome, and all equipment, binoculars included, are provided. A healthy, hearty brunch awaits guests in a family style setting.

Whispering Trees Farm Bed & Breakfast

19801 NE 155th Pl, Woodinville

425-788-2315

www.whisperingtrees.com

Price: $125 to $135

True to its name, this quiet and peaceful end-of-the-road setting is surrounded with tall fir trees, gardens, parks and nature trails. Guests can take advantage of the private decks, soothe in the outdoor covered hot tubs.

Wild Lily Ranch

51311 SE 185th Pl SE, Sultan

360-793-2103

www.wildlilly.com

Price: $105/night

Two small log-style cabins feature a potbelly stove and a small refrigerator. Nature enthusiasts will fill refreshed in this peaceful and quiet getaway with nearby snow-capped mountains, streams, and woods. Spend the day among the numerous hiking trails, fishing, rafting, and horseback riding.

Just For Mama!

Beauty & Day Spas

King County

Ageless-The Center For Rejuvenation
601 N 34th St Suite C, Seattle
206-467-1000
www.agelessinseattle.com
Medical Services: cosmetic procedures and surgeries including Botox, Sculptra, Restylane, Lipodissolve, Collagen, chemical peels, and laser treatment.

Services: fillers, facials, biotoning, Oxygen Therapy (helps cellular regeneration), microdermabrasion, epicuren intensive lift, and Rosacea Reduction Facial.

Body Harmony Massage & Spa
206-632-9632
www.bodyharmonyspa.com
Services: Swedish myofascial treatment, hot stone relaxation, foot reflexology, microdermabrasion, deep facial cleansing, Collagen 90II, facial toning, hydrolift facial, herbal wraps, and Dead Sea Mud wrap.

Calluna Day Spa Hypnotherapy & Holistic Retreat
7920 S 120th St, Seattle
206-772-7205
www.callunadayspa.com
Services: therapeutic European facials, herbal wraps, massage by fireplace, candlelight luncheons, warm stone aromassage, seaweed pedicures, meditation, nutrition, body toning, and wellness and lifestyle classes.

Carlin Salon & Day Spa
2138 California Ave SE, Seattle
206-932-5988
www.carlinsalondayspa.com
Services: scalp treatments, foot reflexology, specialized facial treatments, aromatherapy, moisturizing seaweed gel body wraps, hydrotherm massages, moor mud cellulite reduction.

Gene Juarez Salon & Spa

www.genejuarez.com

Services: body and skin care, therapeutic massages, manicures, pedicures, facials, exfoliation, and a full service salon.

Downtown Seattle **206-326-6000**
Bellevue Galleria **425-455-5511**
Redmond Towne Center **425-882-9000**
Northgate Mall **206-365-6000**
Alderwood Mall **425-744-6000**
Southcenter Mall **206-431-8888**
South Hill Mall **425-748-1400**

Habitude Salon & Day Spa

Locks: **206-782-2898**
Fremont: **206-633-1339**

www.habitude.com

Services: revitalizing scalp treatments, cosmetic for eyes and skin, hand and foot treatment, hot rocks sauna and spa, manicure, hydrating salt glow, massages, facials, and a full service specialty salon.

London House Salon & Spa

13028 1sr Ave S, Burien
206-248-6451

www.londhousesalon.com

Services: facials, glycolic peels, microdermabrasion, lymphobiology, aloe body wraps, lash tint, waxing, manicure, pedicure, hair care, tanning.

Olympus Spa

8615 S Tacoma Way, Lakewood
425-697-3000

www.olympusspa.com

Services: body scrub, body massage, skin care, foot massage, body wrap, Tea Ceremony, body moisturizing, paraffin treatment, manicure, and pedicure

Robert Leonard Salon & Spa
2033 6th Ave Suite 151, Seattle
206-441-9900
www.robertleonard.net
Services: skin & body treatments, massage therapy, waxing, lash & brow tints, nail treatment, hair styling & makeup.

Ronna Lane Day Spa
Country Village, Bothell
425-485-4323
www.ronnalane.com
Services: body and facial treatments, massage therapy, hand and foot treatments, waxing, and makeup application and instruction.

Spa Scotta
2648 NE 49th St, Seattle
206-522-5800
www.spascotta.com
Services: skin care and nail therapy, massage and body treatments, waxing, facials, and hand and foot therapy.

Snohomish County

Afterglow Health Spa
613 5th Ave S, Edmonds
425-778-1234
Services: herbal facials, acupuncture, therapeutic and pregnancy massages, and hand and foot treatments.

Complete Elegance Salon & Spa
101 E Main Suite105, Monroe
360-863-9786
Services: full service salon, massage, mineral detoxing body wrap, mineral make-up, hair extensions, and body waxing.

Kathleen's Day Spa
22021 Old Owen Rd, Monroe
360-794-3395
Services: healing holistic approach for body treatments and massages, reflexology, facials, manicures and pedicures.

Le Visage Wellness Center & Spa

4430 106th St SW, Mukilteo
425-493-6868
www.levisagewellness.com
Services: Naturopathic medicine, cranial sacral therapy, Chinese herbal medicine, acupuncture, nutrition and counseling, facial and skin care, body treatments, make-up artistry, and body massage.

Mill Creek Medical Spa

15130 Main St, Suite 210, Mill Creek
425-316-8200
www.millcreekmedspa.com
Services: Botox, Restylane, Blu-U, photo facial/laser facial, microdermabrasion, oxygen facials, chemical/iglycolic peels, vein therapy, rosacea and more.

Mirage Salon & Spa

1521 5th, Marysville
360-657-0441
Services: body treatments including exfoliation, hot shower scrubs, herbal muddy mummy wraps, Swedish massages, deep tissue massages, clinical massages, pregnancy massages, Lomi-Lomi massages, and polarity massages, facials, hair removal, pedicures- reflexology, and manicures.

Mountain Retreat Day Spa

106 S Granite Ave, Granite Falls
360-691-1555
Services: body massages, Swedish relaxation massage, specialize in pain relief, European spa facials, seaweed body wraps, hand treatments, tinting, waxing, and body salt glow, facial foliation, and European facials.
Tinting services - lash and brow.

Olympus Spa

3815 196th St SW Suite 160, Lynnwood
425-697-3000
www.olympusspa.com
Services: body scrub, body massage, skin care, foot massage, body wrap, Tea Ceremony body moisturizing, paraffin treatment, manicure, and pedicure

Ronna Lane Day Spa
Country Village, Bothell
425-485-4323
www.ronnalane.com
Services: body and facial treatments, hand and foot treatments, waxing, massage therapy, and makeup application and instruction.

Shear Perfection Salon & Day Spa
2122 19th St, Everett
425-252-0344
www.myshearperfectionsalon.com
Services: private setting, massage and hydrotherapy, facials, detoxing body wraps, body waxing, mud wraps, and a full service salon.

The Spa & Salon At Hawthorn
16710 Smokey Point Blvd, Arlington
360-657-0507
www.hawthorninn.net
Services: 24 hour massages, hair and skin care, facials, manicure and pedicures, waxing, showers and body wraps.

Team Fitness Spa & Massage (Lake Stevens Day Spa)
1109 Frontier Circle E, Everett
425-397-6855
www.lakestevensdayspa.com
Located inside Team Fitness Gym. Day Spa. Have an experienced team of hair designers, message therapists, skin care professionals, nail artists and make-up artists.
Messages include: Swedish massage, pregnancy for mother-to-be, special massage for the sports-active woman, reflexology, back, neck & shoulder, hot river stone massage, and manual lymphatic drainage massage.
Body treatments include: body wraps, body polish, facial toning, microdermabrasion, aromatherapy facials, oxygen, and thermal mineral facials.
Also have many healing types of foot care.

The Spa... For The Woman Who Cares
10137 Main St, Bothell
425-482-9273
www.thespaforthewoman.com
Services: private setting, specialty skin and body treatments from head to toe including basic skin care, stress relief, spa treatments, hand and feet care, and rejuvenation treatment, holistic nutritional counseling, and therapeutic massage treatments.

The Upper Room Day Spa

3609 W Mukilteo Blvd, Everett
425-267-0147
www.theupperroomdayspa.com
Services: therapeutic body massage, cleansing facials, nail grooming, and luxurious pedicure and foot massage.

Great Websites:

Washington State University

parenting.wsu.edu
Information on strengthening families

www.mariageandfamilies.byu.edu

A peer reviewed publication dedicated to strengthening families.

Prepare-Enrich

www.lifeinnovations.com
Life innovations serve to build strong relationships and marriages.

Pairs

www.pairs.com
"Skills for successful relationships"

Stepfamily Association of America

www.saafamilies.org
Educational information and resources for step families.

www.stepfamily.org

Information on single parenting, co-parenting after divorce,

www.marriagetools.com

An online magazine devoted to developing and maintaining healthy couple relationships.

www.DivorceBusting.com

Dr. Weiner-Davis is a therapist who specializes in helping couples make their relationship better.

www.utahmarriage.org

Online marriage class, and helpful marriage tips.

Chapter 23

Emergency Phone Numbers

Chapter 23

Emergency Phone Numbers

Emergency Phone Numbers

Child Abuse:
Dial 9-1-1

Coast Guard
206-217-6000

Crisis Clinic (24 Hours)
206-461-3222
800-244-5767

FBI
206-622-0460

Forest Fire Reports Only
800-562-6010

US Marshals Service (24 Hours)
206-553-5500

Washington State Patrol
Dial 9-1-1

Police: Non-Emergency Numbers

King County

Burien (24 Hours)
206-296-3311

Des Moines (24 Hours)
206-878-3301

Federal Way (24 Hours)
253-661-4600

Lake Forest Park (24 Hours)
206-364-8216

Mercer Island (24 Hours)
206-236-3500

Normandy Park (24 Hours)
206-248-7600

Port of Seattle(24 Hours)
206-431-3490

SeaTac (24 Hours)
206-973-4900

Emergency Phone Numbers

Seattle (24 Hours)
206-625-5011

Sheriff, King County (24 Hours)
206-296-3311

Shoreline (24 Hours)
206-296-3311

Tukwila (24 Hours)
206-433-1808

Unincorporated King County Police (24 Hours)
206-296-3311

University of Washington
(24 Hours)
206-543-9331

Washington State Patrol (24 Hours)
425-649-4370

Police: Non-Emergency Numbers:

Snohomish County

Arlington – 360-403-3400

Bothell – 425-486-1254

Brier – 425-775-8400

Edmonds – 425-771-0200

Everett – 425-257-8400

Granite Falls _ 360-891-6611

Lake Stevens – 425-334-9537

Lynnwood – 425-744-6900

Marysville – 360-651-5055

Mill Creek – 425-337-1115

Monroe – 360-794-6300

Mukilteo – 425-353-8222

Snohomish – (24 hours) 360-568-0888

Stanwood – 360-629-4555

Sultan – 360-793-1051

Woodway – 425-775-4545

Fire Non-Emergency Numbers

King County Fire District

Burien
206-242-2040

Shoreline
206-546-5716

Kenmore, Lake Forest Park
425-486-2784

Bryn Mawr, Lakeridge, Skyway
206-772-1430

Briarwood, East Renton
425-255-5151

Des Moines
206-878-2210

Federal way
253-839-6234

Mercer Island
206-236-3600

North Highline
206-243-0330

Port of Seattle
206-433-5327

SeaTac
206-973-4500

Seattle
206-386-1400

Shoreline
206-546-5716

Tukwila
206-575-4404

Hospitals

Children's Hospital & Regional Medical Center
206-987-2500
866-987-2500

Evergreen Hospital Medical Center
12040 NE 128th St, Kirkland
425-899-3000 Health Line

Northwest Hospital Medical Information and physician Referral
1550 N 115th St, Seattle
206-364-0500

Overlake Hospital Medical Center
1034 116th Ave NE, Bellevue
425-688-5000
www.overlakehospital.org

Stevens Hospital
21601 76th Ave W, Edmonds
425-640-4066

Swedish Medical Center
800-793-3474

Valley General Hospital
14701 179th Ave SE, Monroe
360-794-1411

Virginia Mason Medical Center
888-862-2737

Emergency Preparedness

The Washington State Department of Health recommends the following guidelines for preparing your household for emergencies.
After a disaster, you and your family should be prepared to be on your own for at least three days. Emergency response teams will be very busy and may not be able to provide immediate care to all who need it. Here is what you can do to protect yourself.

Before disaster strikes

Choose a place for your family to meet after a disaster.

Choose a person outside the immediate area for family members to contact in case you get separated. This person should live far enough away so he or she won't be involved in the same emergency.

Know how to contact your children at their school or daycare, and how to pick them up after a disaster. Let the school know if someone else is authorized to pick them up. Keep your child's emergency release card up to date.

Put together an emergency supply kit for your home and workplace. If your child's school or daycare stores personal emergency kits, make one for your child to keep there.

Know where the nearest fire and police stations are.

Learn your community's warning signals, what they sound like and what you should do when you hear them.

Learn first aid and CPR. Have a first aid kit, a first aid manual and extra medicine for family members.

Learn how to shut off your water, gas and electricity. Know where to find shut-off valves and switches.

Keep a small amount of cash available. If the power is out, ATM machines won't work.

If you have family members who don't speak English, prepare emergency cards in English with their names, addresses and information about medications or allergies. Make sure they can find their cards at all times. Conduct earthquake and fire drills every six months.

Make copies of your vital records and store them in a safe deposit box in another city or state. Store the originals safely. Keep photos and videotapes of your home and valuables in your safe deposit box.

Make sure family members know all the possible ways to get out of your home. Keep all exits clear.

Make sure all family members agree on an emergency plan. Give emergency information to babysitters or other caregivers.

During an emergency or disaster
Keep calm and take time to think. Give assistance where needed.

Listen to your radio or television for official information and instructions.

Use the telephone for emergency calls only.

If you are ordered to evacuate, take your emergency kit and follow official directions to a safe place or temporary shelter

After the emergency or disaster is over
Use caution in entering damaged buildings and homes.

Stay away from damaged electrical wires and wet appliances.

Check food and water supplies for contamination.

Notify your relatives that you are safe, but don't tie up phone lines. They may be needed for emergency calls.

If government disaster assistance is available, the news media will announce where to go to apply.

72 Hour Kits:
I recommend supplying several 72 hour kits... one for the office, one for each car, and one to keep at home. Be sure to update your 72 hour kit every 6 months. The Whatcom County Emergency Management recommends the following list of essentials needed for 3 days. You may add to this list. Pack the following items into an easy to carry backpack.

- Three gallons of water per person.
- Non-perishable food for three days. Ideally, these foods will be lightweight and high in energy. If you pack canned foods, remember a can opener!
- Prescription and non-prescription medications. Include a spare set of glasses.
- Battery powered portable radio. This may be your only source of information during a disaster.
- First aid kit.
- Personal hygiene items.
- Clothing and bedding, including socks, a space saver blanket, etc.
- Special items such as baby needs or contact lens supplies, etc.
- Personal comfort items. Books, games, personal electronics, etc.

A

B

C

N

O

P

R

S

Advertiser Index

Find Anything
"MAMA"
Browse Titles Like:
"Confessions of a Slacker Mom"
"The Mommy Brain"
"How She Really Does it"
and more!
*see back for discounts
www.mamabooks.com

Mamabooks.com
30% off
coupon code: 30%

Mamabooks.com
FREE SHIPPING
*continental US only
Coupon Code: 014

NOW ONLINE!
The Seattle Mama's Handbook
A Reference Guide for Mothers in Seattle
visit us on the web at:
www.seattlemamas.com
The Seattle Mama's Handbook

Buy one
get one
free
Coupon Code: Get One

50% off
Your Next Copy
Coupon Code: 50HB

20% off
Any Product in
our online store!
Coupon Code: OSHB

Free Shipping
on your next order.
Coupon Code: FSHB

Hockey
Figure Skating
Birthday Parties
Castle Ice Cafe offers a wide variety of food & decorations to make YOUR birthday party a truly memorable event, then continue the fun at the Castle Arcade and ice arenas.
(425) 254-8750
Castle ice
at Briarwood
12620 164th Avenue SE • Renton, WA 98059

She'll use the same sense of rhythm to dribble through the defense.
Research proves that early integration of music into your child's daily routine means improving her ability to think, reason, create, and express. With Kindermusik, the world's most respected name in musical learning for newborns to age 7, you and your child will participate together in every step of the learning process.
Music skills to academic skills to life skills.
Kindermusik
Classes filling fast. Enroll today.
Studio 3 Music
Analiisa Reichlin, Director • 425-385-3636
Woodinville • Redmond • Monroe
www.studio3music.com
Free Class Coupon on the Back. Join Us Anytime!

SUPPORT YOUR
LOCAL MAMA

SUPPORT YOUR LOCAL MAMA
Free Shipping (Continental US)
COUPON CODE: SHIP
www.supportyourlocalmama.com

kym@kymskiddycorner.com
Kym's Kiddy Corner
Largest selection in the north end of new & nearly new baby & children's furniture, equipment, toys & clothing.
Now buying equipment, toys & furniture. Receive money the same day!
206-361-5974
11721 15th AVE NE Seattle (near Northgate)

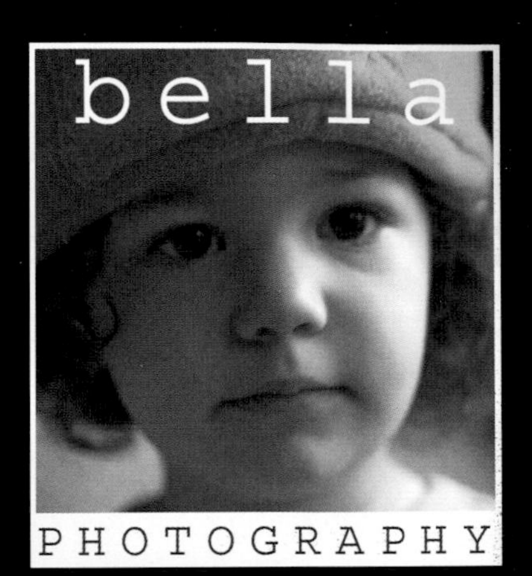

Bella Photography specializes in elegant and artistic portraits of pregnancy, babies, children and families.

black and white
color
sepia
hand tint

Tammy DiDomenico, Photographer

425-836-4080

Portfolio, proofs and pricing can be viewed online at www.BellaPhotographyNW.com

See, Touch & Explore
the WONDERS of the underwater world
SEATTLE AQUARIUM
• Award-winning exhibits filled with colorful sealife
• Touch-pools with seastars, urchins & more
• Themed birthday parties
• Family programs
Contact: 206.386.4300
www.seattleaquarium.org

Crown Cutz
Experts with Children as well as Individuals with Special Needs
Mom & Dad can have their hair done while their children play, alleviating the necessity of childcare!
Featuring:
Fun Furniture, Movies
Video Games, Toyz & Treatz
PARENT'S NIGHT OUT
Parents, enjoy an evening out while your kids enjoy an evening with us!
• Games, crafts and other fun organized events
• Call for details and to RSVP!
12309 15th Ave N.E, Seattle
206-363-TRIM (8746)

Applause Studio
MILL CREEK
Theme Birthday Parties!
Dress-up, Hip Hop, & Circus
It's All Good!!
Applause Studio of Performing Arts
is an ideal place to learn to dance, sing, act and perform. We have classes for all ages and all abilities. You will have fun while our experienced teachers assist you in reaching your true potential!
Art & Cartooning
Website: applausestudio.org
Phone: 425-482-2075

Dahn YOGA
& Healing
stretch your body,
expand your mind.
Experience more than yoga!
Meditation
Energy Healing
Brain Respiration
Stress Management
Holistic Health Workshop
Kids' Classes
Please call to make an appointment for a Private Introductory Session...
www.dahnyoga.com

The Original
CHILDREN'S
SHOP
In Madison Park
206-328-7121
10% off any purchase
with this ad

www.crybabycomforts.com
Crybaby Comforts
Featuring:
Bumbo Baby Sitters
Your baby can't sit-up on their own?
No problem! The Bumbo Baby Sitter is here!

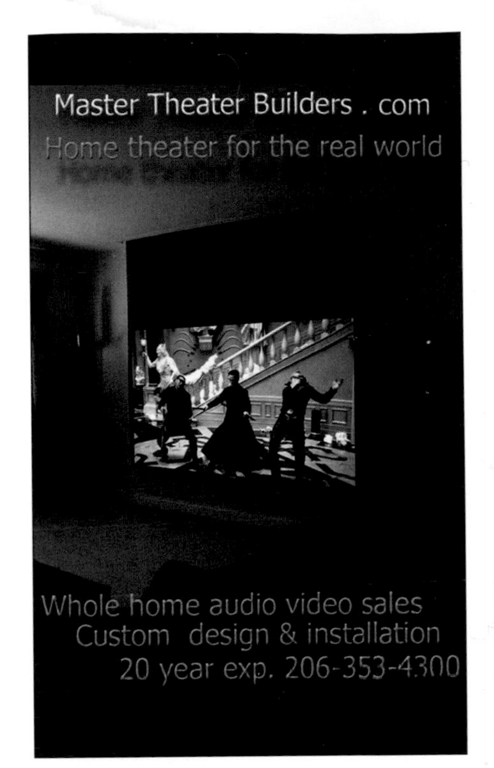
Master Theater Builders . com
Home theater for the real world
Whole home audio video sales
Custom design & installation
20 year exp. 206-353-4300

Nationally acclaimed, Award Winning!
Charles The Clown
Charles The Magician
Seattle's most experienced children's entertainer.
"BEST BET"-Seattle Times
Hilarious Become-a-clown shows for younger children, magic shows and workshops for older kids,
206-361-7171
www.charlestheclown.com

Emergency Numbers for Kids

Emergency Dial

9 1 1

Emergency # to call: ______________________________

Mom's Work #: ______________________________

Mom's Cell Phone #: ______________________________

Dad's Work #: ______________________________

Dad's Cell Phone #: ______________________________

Friend's #: ______________________________

Neighbor's #: ______________________________

My Address: ______________________________

My Home Phone #: ______________________________

Seattle Poison Control Center
1-800-222-1212

Other Important Numbers

Have We Missed Anything?

Do you know of a great family activity, resource or family oriented business? Have any great "Mama" secrets you'd like to share? Send us your information and we may include it in next year's edition!

Seattle Mamas, LLC
P.O. Box 14155 Mill Creek WA 98082
julianne@seattlemama.com
www.seattlemamas.com

To purchase additional copies of The Seattle Mama's Handbook please visit out website: www.seattlemamas.com

The Seattle Mama's Handbook makes a great gift for any family!